A Brief History of Formal Education in British Somaliland Protectorate (1884–1960)

by Dr Abdullahi Deria

LOST COIN

A Brief History of Formal Education in British Somaliland Protectorate (1884–1960)

© Dr Abdullahi Deria, 2022

Published for Dr Deria by Lost Coin Books, London.
Typesetting and Design by Lost Coin
lostcoinbooks@gmail.com
Edited by Mary Davis marydavisediting@gmail.com

LOST C●IN

All rights reserved. Except as may be permitted by the Copyright Act, no part of this publication may be reproduced in any form or by any means without prior permission from the author.

ISBN: 978-1-7399376-6-9

Front cover illustration: The Office Block (front view) of Sheikh School, built in 1945 [222]

Dedication

This book is dedicated first to the memory of my beloved late father who had the foresight to realize the value of education and send me to Sheikh School at a time when the education introduced by the protectorate government was not yet wholeheartedly welcomed by the people of Somaliland Protectorate. Secondly, I dedicate this book to the memory of my multinational teachers at Sheikh School who transformed the illiterate nomad boy that I was into a literate one.

Left: the author; **right**: the author's late father
[May the mercy of God be upon his soul]

Lest we forget! Here are the five Somali educators who, on their own initiative, launched formal education in Somaliland Protectorate in 1942. **Top** (left to right): Mohamoud Ahmed Ali, Yusuf Haji Adan, Mohamed Shire, **bottom** (left to right): Abdisalam Hassan Mursal, Yusuf Ismail Samater. The people of Somaliland owe them a great deal. **We will remember them!**

Contents

Section 1: The author 7

Section 2: Introduction 19

Section 3: Selected historical events
3.1   Beginnings of the British government involvement in Somaliland 29
3.2   The British occupation of the Somaliland Coast 34
3.3   Ethiopia's historical designs on Somaliland territory 39
3.4   The rise and fall of the Dervishes 49
3.5   Attempt at introducing stock taxation/murder of Mr Gibb 73
3.6   The protectorate government in the doldrums 78
3.7   Joint Anglo-Ethiopian Boundary Commission 82
3.8   Legalized injustice in Somaliland Protectorate 91
3.9   Italian occupation of Ethiopia, 1936–1941 98
3.10 Italian occupation of Somaliland Protectorate 1940–1941 102
3.11 British re-occupation of Somaliland/military government established 105
3.12 Civil government replaced the military government 116
3.13 The Anglo-Ethiopian Agreement of 1954 120
3.14 Ill-conceived independence offered to Somaliland 128

Section 4: Formal education
4.1   Small Schools at Coastal Settlements (a) and (b) 142
4.2   The Genesis of British education for British colonial Africa 148
4.3   Attempts at introducing elementary education 155
4.4   Ban of Christian Missions from Somaliland Protectorate 178
4.5   The vexed issue of written Somali 180
4.6   Reviving formal education during WW II 182
4.7   Bell's report of 1944 on formal education programme 191
4.8   Early stages of the educational programme 199
4.9   The civil government built on the 1944 educational programme 239
4.10 Published annual expenditures on the Protectorate, 1900–1960 327
4.11 Epilogue 331

Appendix: Keeping clanism at bay 339
References 355
Map 368

Section 1: The author

I seize this opportunity to put on record my varied life history, which falls into five distinct phases: as a nomad, as a student, as a national civil servant, as an international civil servant and, lastly, as a retiree.

I was born and brought up in a nomadic setting. At about nine years old, as was expected of any nomad boy, I was put in charge of a few milch-camels with their calves. One day, as fate would have it, I slept under a shady tree and lost the camels. The hungry hyena, always on the prowl for a prey, killed one of the young ones. In the eyes of the Somali, the camel is a precious commodity. As I feared, I was chastised for my negligence. I took a decision on the spur of the moment and ran away to Burao town, about 40 miles away, thus spectacularly ending my nomadic life – although not completely. That might have been early 1944 or thereabouts.

Sheikh School

It can be safely assumed that hardly any Somali in my age group who was born in Somaliland Protectorate can claim to have an original birth certificate. In my case, when my late father took me to the District Commissioner's Office in Burao town in (August?)1944 to be enrolled for the Boarding Elementary School at Sheikh town, he informed the Enrolling Committee that I was 10 years old. Hence, my father fixed the year for me and I later supplied the rest of my date and place of birth as 15 December 1934, Burao. This is what my passport shows, although I was told that I was actually born in a flat tree-less rural area called Arori, about 15 km or so south of Burao.

When I was being enrolled for the Boarding Elementary School at Sheikh, I was asked whether I could remember an event that had recently happened. I told the interviewers about the incident of the lost camels, which was a very important event for me. They all laughed, although I could not see what was funny about my story. Anyway, I was accepted for the school.

Much later I learnt that on the night of 5 June 1944, the Camel Corps Company at Burao mutinied. This was not very long before my interview. I was in Burao during the mutiny and was aware of the occurrence, but I was totally ignorant of what it was or what it was about. I remember the people saying "*Askartii baa hubkii la' baxsatay*" (in English: "The soldiers ran away with their weapons"). Perhaps my interviewers expected me to say something about that mutiny! (More about the mutiny later.)

It might have been sometime in late September 1944 when my late father took me, along with two other boys – Mohamed Haji Yusuf (*Dhaw-Dhawle*) and Abdulrahman Haji Deria Shide – to Sheikh, and the three of us, together with others, formed the first class that was enrolled on 6 October 1944 for the Boarding Elementary School at Sheikh. I completed my elementary and intermediate education at Sheikh School. The class that I was in sat for the Intermediate School Entrance Examination in December 1947 and for the Intermediate School Leaving Examination in March 1952.

Before leaving Sheikh School, I was involved in an event concerning the British Royal Family. One afternoon in 1952, while we were hanging around the dormitories, P.H.C. Badham, the Principal of Sheikh School, called me and asked me if I heard that the King passed away. I was not at that time familiar with this euphemistic expression "passed away". I thought the King passed by and went away. Mr Badham realized that I was not with him, and told me that the King had died. He instructed me to fly the flag at half mast at 6 am the following morning. I was not sure whether this was punishment or part of my duties as the Head Prefect of the School. As shown in the picture of the office block of Sheikh School (on page 214), the flagpole was fixed high up onto the front wall of the office block. A ladder was provided for me to carry out the assignment. It was much later that I came to know that the British King died on 6 February 1952.

Secondary education

Even before the results of the Intermediate School Leaving Examination of 1952 became available, I decided to join the Police Force. In those days, there was no career adviser to turn to. The Commissioner of Police in Hargeisa interviewed me. He informed me that I would attend the Police Training Centre at Mandera for a six-month training. I would be provided with free board and lodging and a monthly salary of Sh. 32/ – all told. After training, I would be posted to any Police Station in the protectorate. Regarding promotion, I would take my chance with all the other policemen. I asked the Commissioner if I would be given scholarship abroad immediately after completing my training. The Commissioner's answer was a firm "No". With that, the interview came to an end and we went our separate ways.

The awaited results of the school leaving examination became available. Towards the end of June 1952, six boys from my class, including myself, were sent on a government scholarship to Hantoub Secondary School, Sudan, for a four-year secondary education.

In June 1953, I and a group of my friends at Hantoub Secondary School, Sudan, were on holiday in a small town between Khartoum and Port Sudan called Sinkat. The Sudanese District Commissioner provided us with a large guest house and a radio. One day we were listening to Radio Hargeisa describing, in Somali, the proceedings of the coronation ceremony of the British monarch, Queen Elizabeth II. I told my friends of my flag-raising assignment at Sheikh School and how disappointed I was that I was not invited to the coronation event. The coronation of the British Queen was on 2 June 1953. End of the royal story.

Further study

On completion of our secondary education in Sudan, all the six of us returned to British Somaliland Protectorate in mid-1956. When the results of Hantoub School examination were received – all six of us passed the GCE O-level – I wanted to study history. I was sent to Sheikh School as a temporary teacher, with the handsome monthly salary of Sh. 260/ – (around £13 which was a relatively large sum in those days). After two months or so, I changed my mind and opted for medicine and I was sent to Hargeisa and attached to Hargeisa Group Hospital to familiarize myself with the hospital environment and continued to draw my salary of Sh. 260/-. I was given the designation of Technical Trainee, although there was no training of any sort involved. I just watched operations carried out by Dr Dering, a Polish Jew who survived the Hitler concentration camps. In the afternoons, I used to teach simple English on voluntary basis to junior Dressers.

Since I was not doing much work in the hospital, I was asked to work as an interpreter, for about three months, with I.M. Lewis who was conducting fieldwork on social anthropology in Somaliland Protectorate.

In September 1957, the six of us from Hantoub Secondary School were sent on another government scholarship to the United Kingdom to study for the GCE A-level examinations. After the A-level examinations, we individually joined different higher educational institutions.

Medical studies

I joined the Medical School of Aberdeen University, Scotland, in October 1960. I graduated in medicine (with the degree MBChB) in 1966. I worked in the UK as a Junior Doctor for two years in different hospitals and, in the meantime obtained a Diploma of Tropical Medicine & Hygiene (DTM&H) from Liverpool University in 1968.

In September 1968, I returned to a new country (at least for me) called the Somali Republic. During my absence in the UK, the British Somaliland Protectorate and the Italian Somalia both became independent and united to form the Somali Republic (aka Somalia) on first July 1960.

I started work in Digfer General Hospital in the capital, Mogadishu. On 21 October 1969, the civil government was overthrown in a military coup d'état. In December, I was sent, as a Team Leader of a five-person Technical Aid Mission from Somalia to Equatorial Guinea in West Africa for one year (1970) to help the country after the Spanish colonial government suddenly left the country, without proper preparation for nationals to run the country. The Somalia Team was one of a number of teams from different African countries, under the auspices of the Organization of African Unity (OAU), as it was called at that time.

A group of the mission members from different African countries in the capital of Equatorial Guinea, Fernando Poo, in 1970. Members of Somali Mission are: back row, far left – the author; back row, far right (soldier – sorry, I have forgotten his name); front row, left – Khadija Barre (nurse).

Upon my return to Somalia and before resuming my previous work in Digfer Hospital, I was awarded a World Health Organization (WHO) scholarship and obtained a Diploma in Clinical Medicine in the Tropics (DCMT) in 1971 from London University.

After working in Digfer Hospital as a senior physician for about five years, I was again awarded a WHO scholarship and obtained a master's degree in Community Health (MCommH) in 1976 from Liverpool University. It was after obtaining the last qualification that I decided to pursue public health rather than clinical medicine.

Eradication of smallpox

In March 1977, I became the National Manager, as well as WHO Consultant, for the National Campaign Programme for the Eradication of Smallpox from Somalia. The country reported the last endemic case of smallpox in the world to WHO on 31 October 1977. After intensive surveillance of two years for smallpox, the WHO International Commission for The Certification of Smallpox Eradication certified, on 19 October 1979, that smallpox was eradicated from Somalia.

When we started the campaign programme, we found out that the country had no map showing the boundaries of the regions and the districts. With the help of the districts' and the regions' authorities, we produced manually this simple map (shown below) for smallpox surveillance, showing where the approximate boundaries of the regions and districts might be. The WHO printed the map for the Smallpox Eradication Campaign Programme, Somalia. The Somalia military government neither objected to nor endorsed the map.

Administrative divisions of Somaliland from the "Report on Somalia Smallpox Eradication Programme", submitted by the government of Somalia to the International Commission on the Smallpox Eradication Programme in Somalia, August 1979. The report was later published by the World Health Organization, Ref. WHO/SE/79.145.

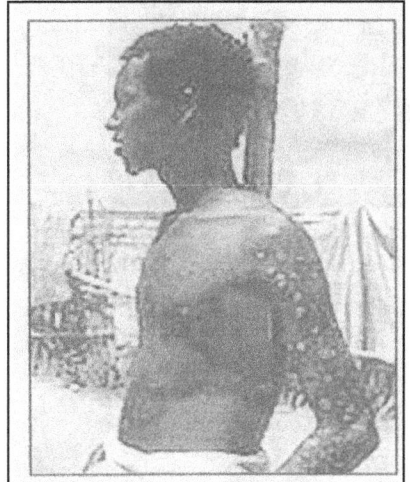

Since the eradication programme closed down, the map took on a life of its own. Different agencies have been using it – for purposes for which it was not designed.

Ali Maow Maalin – the last wild endemic smallpox case in the world. The case was discovered in Marker, with onset of the rash on 26 October 1977, and reported to the WHO on 31 October 1977. Ref. Dr A. Deria, Dr Z. Jezek, Dr K. Markart, Mr P. Carrasco, Dr J. Weikfield, *Bulletin of WHO*, 58 (2): 279–283 (1980).

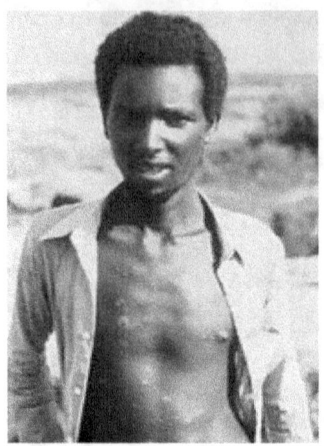 

Left: Ali Maow, after recovery from smallpox. He died of natural causes on 22 July 2013. *Right:* A copy of the plastic cards which were distributed widely in the country in the late 1970s. Anyone who reported a case (or cases) of FURUQA (SMALLPOX) that was not already known to the programme would receive a reward of Sh. 200/-. I saw one of these cards dangling from the neck of a camel in a nomadic area of the country.

The WHO Global Commission (of which I was a member) met in Geneva on 9 December 1979 and issued a statement, certifying that global eradication of smallpox had been achieved.

Members of the WHO Global Commission for the Certification of Smallpox Eradication in session, 9 December 1979. **Front row** (left to right)– Dr Marennikova, Dr Azurin, Dr Burgasov, Dr Fenner, Dr Kostrzewski, Dr Henderson, Dr Koinange Karuga, Dr Zhang. **Back row** (left to right) – Dr Wehrle, Dr Basu, Dr Aashi, Dr Lundbeck, Dr Rodrigues, Dr Dumbell, Dr Netter, Dr Tagaya, Dr Moeti, Dr Kalisa, Dr Shrestha, Dr Deria (the author).

All members of the Commission signed the parchment shown opposite, on 9 December 1979, Geneva, Switzerland.

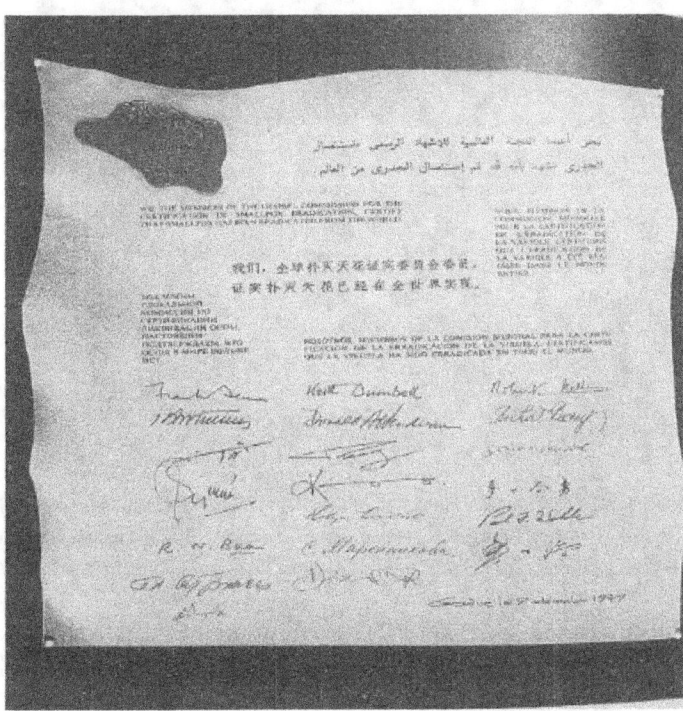

A copy of the parchment containing the WHO Global Commission Statement on the Certification of Global Smallpox eradication. The parchment, in the six official languages of The United Nations, says: "WE, THE MEMBERS OF THE GLOBAL COMMISSION FOR THE CERTIFICATION OF SMALLPOX ERADICATION, CERTIFY THAT SMALLPOX HAS BEEN ERADICATED FROM THE WORLD", followed by their signatures. (The author's signature is bottom left.) The parchment reproduced here was scanned from the author's copy, as a member of the Global Commission for the Certification of Smallpox Eradication.

The author signing the Parchment shown above. Geneva, 9 December 1979.

The author delivering a statement on behalf of the Eastern Mediterranean Region of WHO on the occasion of the World Health Assembly meeting to endorse the conclusion of the WHO Global Commission for the Certification of Smallpox Eradication. Geneva, 8 May 1980.

In its meeting in Geneva on 8 May 1980, the World Health Assembly endorsed the statement of the WHO Global Commission and declared that smallpox had been eradicated from the world.

WHO and other roles

In October 1980, I was appointed, jointly by the WHO and the UN High Commissioner for Refugees (UNHCR), as the Health Coordinator for the Ethiopian Refugees in Somalia, as a result of the 1977–1978 war between Somalia and Ethiopia.

In March 1982, the WHO appointed me as Deputy WHO Representative and Senior Public Health Adviser to the Regional government of the then Southern Sudan and I was based in the capital, Juba. Incidentally, the Region became the new independent county of South Sudan in July 2011.

Towards the end of 1983, there were signs of incipient civil strife in the Region and I was evacuated and appointed as WHO Representative to the Arab Republic of Yemen, based in the capital, Sana'a. I was back in Sudan in 1986 for one year as WHO Health Coordinator for the UN Operations for the large internally displaced population from the Southern Region – as a result of the civil conflict in that Region, as already indicated, and the drought-stricken population in the rest of the country. I was based in the capital, Khartoum.

I ceased being a peripatetic WHO employee in 1987 when the WHO appointed me as the Regional Adviser on Communicable Diseases Control at the WHO Regional Office for the East Mediterranean (EMRO), located in Alexandria, Egypt.

While at EMRO, I took leave without pay in 1989 to attend a five-month (January–May) course on "Health Systems Analysis and Planning" at the Johns Hopkins University, USA.

Retirement

I retired from the World Health Organization service in June 1994. My retirement coincided with a needless civil conflict in Somaliland and I thus retired to the UK where I have been living ever since.

From 1995 to 2006, I was a member of the WHO Global Commission for the Certification of Polio Eradication, as well as a member of the WHO Regional Commission (for the East Mediterranean Region) for the Certification of Polio Eradication. Unfortunately, at the time of writing, polio is still with us and has outlived many of its eradicators!

During my retirement, over the years 1995 to 2006 as a WHO Consultant, I carried out assignments in Communicable Diseases Control, Health Care Planning or Health Programmes Reviews in Iraq, Jordan, Syria, Libya, Kuwait, Tunisia, Somalia and Saudi Arabia.

I presented a paper entitled: "The Emergency Campaign for Smallpox Eradication from Somalia (1977–1979) – Revisited" at the Symposium held at the Oswaldo Crux Foundation, Rio de Janeiro, Brazil: 24–27 August 2010, for the Commemoration of the 30th Anniversary of Smallpox Eradication. In the paper, I reviewed the history of smallpox in Somalia and discussed the approaches the Emergency Campaign adopted in the eradication of the disease from Somalia. All the papers presented at the Symposium were published in the international technical journal, *Vaccine* (vol. 29, supplement 4, 30 December 2011).

Participants in the Smallpox Eradication Commemoration (SEC) 2010 which was held at the Oswaldo Crux Foundation Building, Rio de Janeiro, Brazil. The author is in the front row, fifth from the left.

Section 2: Introduction

I have used the word "formal" in preference to the word "secular" in describing the type of education which forms the subject matter of the book. This is to avoid any possibility of misinterpreting the word "secular".

There is a story to my writing about formal education in British Somaliland Protectorate. I had never entertained the idea that I would one day attempt to write a book until a friend of mine, Ahmed Botan Dhakkaar, who is a retiree like me and lives in the USA, visited me in London, as occasionally happened. Ahmed and I were classmates at Sheikh School, Somaliland Protectorate, and at Hantoub Secondary School, Sudan. We even travelled together to the UK in September 1957 for further studies and we have been in touch ever since. On such occasional reunions, we reminisced about school days and the like. I told Ahmed that, having plenty of time on my hands as a retiree, I often visited different institutions in London as a pastime to skim through some of the documents written by the defunct British Somaliland Protectorate government. He was so excited about some of the things I told him that he urged me to write something about them. I protested that the bits and pieces that I came across were scattered in so many unrelated documents in different institutions, and that I did not take notes or record their references and it was not feasible for me to attempt such a task. Ahmed would have none of it and insisted that I should put something on paper.

I gave in, little knowing what I was letting myself in for. I slept on the "imposed assignment" for a long time, not knowing how to go about it. Eventually, I had to take the plunge. I needed to decide which subject to tackle – for example, formal education or medical services in Somaliland Protectorate. I plumped for the former for two reasons: first, general education is basic to all other fields of study; second, as it so happened, both Ahmed and I were among the first to experience the formal education established in Somaliland Protectorate. Both of us were enrolled into the first government educational programme that was introduced into Somaliland Protectorate in 1944.

I had to start, in earnest, my search for information. My previous casual visits to the different institutions – the British Library, the School of Oriental & African Studies (SOAS) of London University and the National Archives (NA) at Kew Gardens, all in London, became very serious business this time round. Also, in my search, I had to widen the number of relevant institutions to visit. For example, I traced some important documents to the reference libraries of Reading and Oxford Universities. Since I did not know where to look for the specific information that I needed, I had to randomly consult a lot of old books and archival material – a selection of the more relevant ones are in the references. When I refer to one of these sources, I adopt the convention of using the relevant reference number in square brackets.

One of the difficulties I met in my search for information was that, in the National Archives, where most of the relevant documents are housed, the old files about Somaliland Protectorate – in common with other ex-colonial British Dependencies – are kept in cardboard boxes which are given digitalized code numbers. However, the individual files contained in a given box are not as yet all digitalized and cannot be electronically searched for individually. One has to open huge number of boxes to find a piece of information of interest. I must admit that there were moments when the will to continue with the writing temporarily faltered. But I had to convince myself that I reached the point of no return. A mood of despondency set in when it came to assembling, ordering chronologically and making sense of the rough notes – some of them hardly legible – that I culled from so many different sources. Starting the laborious task of weaving the disjointed notes into a narrative was an experience!

It was a relief when I completed the first draft. Revising the draft was no less arduous. Perhaps my moaning only betrays my lack of experience in book writing. All in all, the thought of writing my first book at the tender age of 88 is a great consolation to me.

Education, in any country, competes with other sectors for resources, but in the end it will all depend on what priority is accorded to education. This implies that education reflects the policy of the government of the day. I therefore leave it to the reader to judge for himself/herself, having read the book, as to whether the protectorate government of Somaliland gave due weight to formal education in the country. My views on this are clear in the book.

Scope and framework

As the title of the book indicates, I will confine myself to the period 1884–1960, that is to say, the period that British rule lasted in the country. Being a complete novice as a writer, I needed something to guide me and enable me, as far as possible, to arrange the book in some sort of logical sequence.

Thus, I used the following conceptual framework within which I had to develop a narrative – a random selection of historical events during the British occupation of Somaliland.

Selected historical events

- Beginnings of British government involvement in Somaliland
- 1884–1885: The Berlin Conference
- 1884: British government occupation of Somaliland Coast
- 1884–1920: Hardly any government worth the name in the country. A phase of inactivity interrupted by periodic military expeditions against the Dervishes

- 1920–1940: Some sort of "limited moribund civil administration". During World War II, the country was occupied by Italy for the period 19 August 1940 to 16 March 1941
- 1941–1948: military administration
- 1949 to June 1960: civil administration until independence in June 1960

Key stages in formal education

- 1891–1922: One Catholic mission school in Berbera/Dhaymole area, south of Berbera; three small schools mainly for the sons of resident expatriate traders (Arabs and Indians) – located in the towns of Zeila, Bulahar and Berbera. The Catholic mission school closed down in 1910 and, by 1922, both Zeila and Bulahar Schools also closed down – all the schools were private. The non-mission schools received small government subsidies. Only the Berbera School remained open.
- 1922–1940: The civil administration made feeble attempts to introduce elementary education modelled on the solitary Berbera School, but failed
- 1941–1948: The military administration introduced an educational programme, built a few schools and conducted classes for limited number of male adults, primarily for office work
- 1949–1960: The civil administration tardily built on what the military administration started, but only a little more of the same.

The above expresses in a nutshell what the book is about.

The selected events in **Section 3** are meant to shed some light on the nature of colonial rule and how arbitrary and visionless it was. It is also an attempt at conveying something of the flavour of a colonial government under which the governed were kept in the dark about the policies pursued by the government. By definition, in a colonial set-up, one would not expect independent free media and well-informed public opinion that would hold such foreign government to account.

What the protectorate government did or did not do in the country over the decades is not readily available to the people of Somaliland – that information is not as yet in the public domain. It would take a qualified historian to dig out all that went on in Somaliland Protectorate, evaluate it perceptively and write it up.

To write the history of Somaliland, as distinct from Somaliland Protectorate, would demand even greater effort. I wish to make it clear that it was not my intention, nor was I qualified, to write the history of British Somaliland Protectorate, let alone that of Somaliland. The historical events mentioned above were selected at random.

The formal education surveyed in the book came about within the last 16 years (1944–1960) of the colonial rule in the country. Hence the slimness of the book; and it would have been even slimmer had it not been supplemented with **Section 3.** This testifies to the severe paucity of formal education in the country.

I have told the story of formal education in Somaliland Protectorate in **Section 4,** as it was available in the documents of the defunct government of Somaliland Protectorate. Some of my views on the selected historical events and on formal education in Somaliland Protectorate might not chime with those of some readers of the book. That is not unexpected.

Clanism

The Education Department was minded to maintain fair representation in the student body of all the clans in the protectorate. To monitor that objective, in its annual reports, the Department classified the number of students enrolled at the end of each year, up to 1954, on clan basis. In the interests of history, perhaps I should have kept that classification in the book. However, I decided against it for the simple reason that I am instinctively averse to anything presented in clan terms. Secondly, in this day and age it would be, in my view, inappropriate to document anything that might remotely appear to endow "clanism" with a veneer of acceptability. However, the reader will find that, on a very few occasions, I have kept a document in its original form in which clans are mentioned, or I have named a particular clan or the clan of a particular individual to illuminate a specific point. For example, I have left in its original form where clans were mentioned in the 1920 progress report on the Somali boys who were studying in Sudan or the Ergo (Peace Deputation) sent to Seyyid Mohamed Abdullah Hassan in 1920. It was also the case in the brief account about the background of Seyyid Mohamed Abdullah Hassan. By mentioning clans, I might appear to be contradicting myself. However, I have made a distinction between the clan classifications used by the Education Department and the odd occasions of mentioning clans. Anyway, for my views on clanism, see the **Appendix.**

This book is primarily aimed at the Somalis in the Horn of Africa, as well as the Somali diaspora scattered in the four corners of the globe who are curious enough to know something about a system of education that existed in long bygone age in what used to be called the British Somaliland Protectorate, and who also want to get some rough idea of what the colonial rule in Somaliland Protectorate was like. Incidentally, at Sheikh School in Somaliland Protectorate which I attended, there were Somali students from Djibouti, Ethiopia and Kenya.

Apart from any other considerations, it was important to put on record such past experience before it passes from living memory to history, and to preserve it for the benefit of posterity. It fell to the lot of a member of the first generation, with which the first educational programme in Somaliland Protectorate was started, to document, albeit in a very concise form, the essentials of formal education in British Somaliland Protectorate.

Most of the few pictures included in the book were either provided by friends or were in the public domain (on the internet), or in old out-of-print books on Somaliland, which the author bought via the internet.

Before wrapping up the introduction, I wish to state that I owe to my friend, Ahmed Botan, a debit of gratitude for his sustained encouragement without which this book might never have seen the light of day. I had informative discussions with my late friends Yusuf Ali (Shihari) Abdi and Mohamed Mohamoud Grad on the early stages of the new educational programme, which was introduced into the country during World War II in 1944. Also my friends: Abdullahi Duale (Nile), Osman Hassan Omar (Osman-Badow), Hassan Adan Gudal and Jama Hassan (Jama Gaile) helped me clarify some issues in the educational services in the country in the 1950s. Asha Haji Deria Mohamoud, who was amongst the first girls enrolled into the first government Elementary School for girls in the country, not only clarified for me some aspects of the work in that school, but also allowed me to include in the book some of her published writings, and I am grateful to her for all that. My friend Said Osman Gulaid kindly allowed me to consult some documents in his possession. Except Asha and Said Osman, all the other above-named friends, like me, were among the few lucky boys who were enrolled in the 1944 educational programme at its inception.

I am also grateful to N. Holland, who, as executor of his late father's will, allowed me to make use of the book *Education in British Somaliland*, written by his late father, T.R. Holland, who taught at Sheikh School in the 1940s. A significant part of the early development of the 1944 educational programme is based on this book. Most of the rest is from documents kept at the National Archives, Kew, London, UK.

I am also grateful to Dr Susan and Richard Sills, Executors of the Estate of the late R.R. Darlington, for allowing me to use some documents by Mr Darlington, who taught the class that was in at Sheikh School in British Somaliland Protectorate.

Lastly, I want to make it clear that none of those named above bear any responsibility whatsoever for any shortcomings, be they errors of omission or commission, of the book. The author alone is responsible for any defects in the book.

Section 3:
Randomly selected historical events during the British Somaliland Protectorate

3.1 Beginnings of the British government involvement in Somaliland

It is impossible to consider or understand formal education in British Somaliland Protectorate without understanding a little bit of British colonial policy in British Somaliland Protectorate and the social context, and the British colonial educational policy for British Colonial Tropical Africa. Accordingly, it would be helpful to preface the main subject of the book – in other words, formal education – with a few selected historical events that occurred at different stages during the existence of the British Somaliland Protectorate.

But first, why did the British government embark upon colonizing other countries? Britain, in her colonizing heyday, did not dispatch explorers to all corners of the world for nothing. These explorers were out to discover "virgin countries" (not yet colonized) for British colonization and exploitation. Historians, economists and moral philosophers have been pontificating, for a long time, about the legitimacy of the British colonialism, putting forward all sorts of argument for or against it. Unlike them, as one who lived under colonial rule, my take on the subject is simple. Britain colonized countries mainly for the following reasons:

- To find natural resources in the colonized country for their own exploitation
- To find out the suitability of a country for British settlers
- To explore the possibilities of profitable investment and trade in a country – "trade" embraced trading in humans, by rounding up Africans, transporting them as human commodity and selling them in the slave markets in Britain and America
- To find markets for British manufactured goods
- To spread its culture, especially the English language, as "soft power" for influence, as fronted by the British Council (The BBC World Service is also a potent arm of the soft power strategy)
- To achieve its ends, colonial Britain formed an unholy alliance with Christian missionaries whose main *raison d'être* was to spread Christianity and who acted as an "advance army" to prepare the ground for colonization and exploitation
- To enhance its global presence/power, and for strategic considerations
- Other…

It was not uncommon, in the heydays of the 1960s, when the African countries were one by one becoming independent, for the British government to name

African leaders who had qualifications from British educational institutions – the implication being that the named leaders would be sympathetic to Britain. This was an extension of the soft power (subtle influence) mentioned above.

To be sure, British colonialism was not altruistic, as will be described later under the "Scramble for Africa".

Nowadays, individuals who emigrate in order to improve their lot in life are described as economic migrants. The British colonizers can also be considered to be economic migrants but, unlike the individual migrants of today, the British colonizers had the means to use brutal force to occupy a country to exploit its resources and, in the process, enrich themselves. They even extended such exploitation to trading in humans.

Events which led the British government to involve itself in the affairs of Somaliland included an incident which occurred in 1825 at Berbera or thereabouts [1]. A small British ship was wrecked there and the Somalis plundered the wreckage and molested the seamen. A Somali *Nakhude* (captain) of a dhow who happened to be at the scene intervened and saved the captain of the wrecked ship. The Somali *Nakhude* was called Sharma'arke Ali Salah. As a reward for his assistance to the British captain, Sharma'arke was rewarded with an "Honorary Dress" by the British Political Agent in Mocha in Yemen, which was at that time part of the Ottoman Empire. He was also given a testimonial (its scan shown below), recommending him to Europeans, especially the British, who might visit the Somaliland coast. In 1840, Sharma'arke became the governor of Zeila, which was part of the Ottoman Empire. The story was that, in 1855, he ran afoul of the Turkish government and was fined and discharged. He lived out the rest of his life in Aden. Sharma'arke's clan was given as Habar Yonis. In 1884, his son, Mohamed Sharma'arke, was the *Aqil* (chief of a clan) of the Musa Arreh clan in Berbera.

> 2 The following is a copy of the document :—
> " This Testimonial,
> together with an Honorary Dress, is presented by the British Resident at Mocha to Nagoda Shurmakey Ally Sumaulley, in token of esteem and regard for his humane and gallant conduct at the Port of Burburra, on the coast of Africa, April 10, 1825, in saving the lives of Captain William Lingard, chief officer of the Brig Mary Anne, when that vessel was attacked and plundered by the natives. The said Nagoda is therefore strongly recommended to the notice and good offices of Europeans in general, but particularly so to all English gentlemen visiting these seas."

The testimonial given to Somali captain, Sharma'arke Ali Salah, in 1825, recommending him to Europeans who might visit the Somali coast.

Perhaps it was because of the influence of Sharma'arke in the Somaliland Coast, and later Haji Fareh Musa Igare (adviser to the Somaliland Protectorate government in Burao) and Ahmed Shire (government employee) in Sheikh, that members of their clan became prominent in the civil service of the Somaliland Protectorate government!

The British government had long considered the Somaliland Coast within their sphere of influence – ever since the British established the East India Company in India in 1600 and occupied Aden in 1839, the Suez Canal had opened for navigation (1869), and British government occupied Egypt in 1882. They kept other colonial powers from gaining a foothold in, let alone occupying, the Coast, to protect their interests, including the sea route to the Far East via India, which the British called the Jewel in Crown of the British Empire.

Mr Burton's reconnaissance of the Somaliland Coast [2]

The main objective of the British government was to occupy the Coast of Somaliland and, at that time, they did not show much interest in the rest of Somaliland.

Richard Burton, a British explorer and a military officer of the Bombay government (actually East India Company), carried out reconnaissance missions of the Somaliland Coast in 1854–1855 to pave the way for the occupation of the country. In his book, *First Footsteps in East Africa,* he wrote:

> *The occupation of the port of Berbera has been advised for many reasons: in the first place, Berbera is the true key of the Red Sea, the centre of East African traffic, and the only safe place for shipping upon the western Erythræan [Eritrean] shore from Suez to Guardafui. Backed by lands capable of cultivation, and by hills covered with pine and other valuable trees, enjoying a comparatively temperate climate, with regular although thin monsoon, this harbour has been coveted by many a foreign conqueror. Circumstances have thrown it as it were into our arms, and, if we refuse the chance, another and a rival nation will not be so blind.*

In his second trip to the Somaliland Coast, Mr Burton and his companions were attacked by Somalis, armed with spears, in Berbera in April 1855 and one of his companions was killed. Mr Burton received a javelin through both cheeks, which carried away four teeth and transfixed the palate. Together with his remaining companions, they sailed in a native craft bound for Aden. They took the body of their friend and buried it at sea. Thus, Burton's missions to the Somaliland Coast came to an end. At that time, Somaliland was jointly under the British government in London and the Bombay government (East India Company) in India.

The Berlin Conference and the Scramble for Africa [3]

This infamous conference was for the purpose of formulating new policy for the colonization and exploitation of Africa and was held from November 1884 to February 1885. The following countries participated in the conference: Austria-Hungary, Belgium, Denmark, France, the United Kingdom, Italy, the Netherlands, Portugal, Russia, Spain, Sweden-Norway and the Ottoman Empire. They called themselves, collectively, "the Powers" and entitled the agreement they reached at the conference "The General Act", which was instrumental in the indecent "Scramble for Africa", when the colonial powers carved up the African Continent among themselves for colonization and exploitation.

The Act urged the colonizing powers to implement effective occupation over the areas/territories allotted to them by the Act, which has been the bane of the African people ever since its enactment. The conference was Africa's undoing in multiple ways. The colonial powers contrived the partition of Africa ignoring in the process the cultural and societal set-up of the African people. Clans and families were separated with careless abandon, each part ending up in a foreign territory. At the time of the Berlin Conference there were only two independent African countries – namely Ethiopia and Liberia. Neither of them was invited to the conference, although Ethiopia was there in spirit (to be expanded later).

The colonial powers descended, like hungry vultures, upon the "Virgin Continent" and savagely carved it up among themselves, without the scantest regard for the societal set-up of the people of Africa. Such merciless policy can be described by the Somali expression: *"Qaataye qaado"* ("I took my bit, it's your turn.")

Berlin Conference in session, 1884. The man is pointing to a map of Africa. Source: Wikipedia.

A Brief History of Formal Education in British Somaliland Protectorate

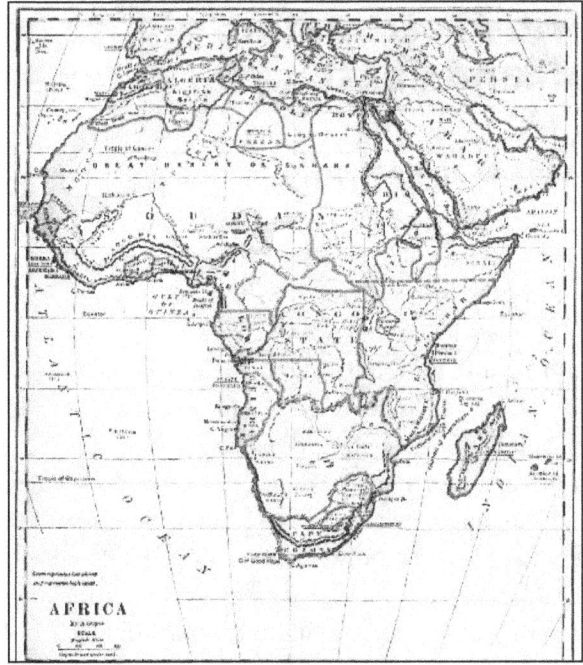

Map of Africa, 1882.

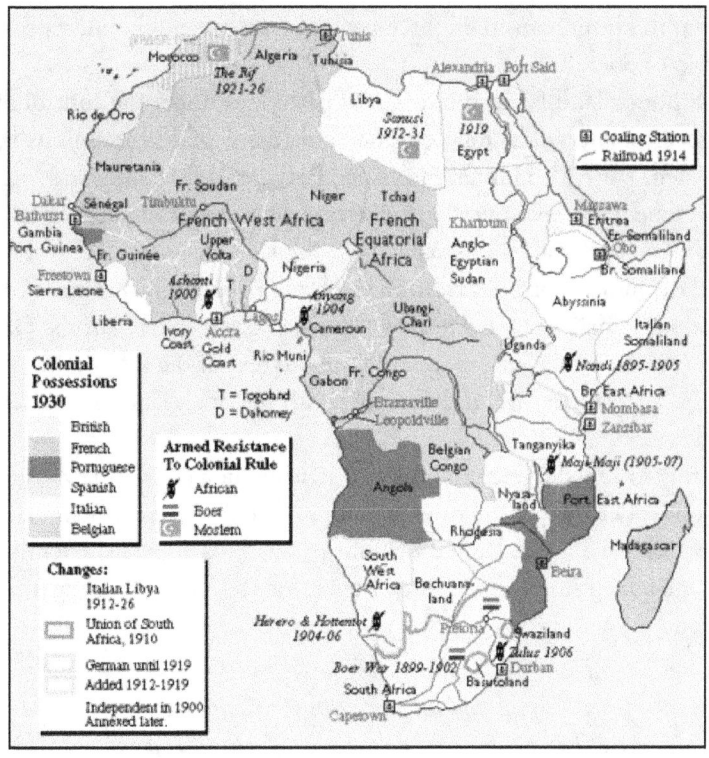

Map of Africa, 45 years after the Berlin Conference.

3.2 The British occupation of the Somaliland Coast

Steps leading to the occupation [4]

By 1874, the Khedive of Egypt declared jurisdiction over the Somaliland Coast, in other words, Zeila, Bulahar and Berbera. (Khedive is the title of the Viceroy of Egypt under Turkish rule). In 1877, the British recognized the Egyptian occupation of the Coast, as the Khedive did not pose existential threat to the British interests. In 1887, the British government formally placed the Somaliland Coast from "Lawya'ado in the West to Bendar Ziada in the East" under "British Protection". The British and the French engaged in tricks and intrigues over Zeila. Eventually, as a result of bundary settlement under the Anglo-French Agreement of 1888, the British abandoned Djibouti to the French and kept Zeila. Egypt became embroiled in the Sudan Mahdiya revolt (1881–1898) and eventually had to abandon the Somaliland Coast. The Egyptian garrisons left their posts at Zeila (1884) and at Harar (1885) for Egypt. Ethiopia occupied Harar in 1887.

Once the Egyptians evacuated Harar (partly populated by Somalis), the town was up for grabs, and either the British or the Bombay government could have easily beaten the Ethiopians to it. Both governments were only interested in the Coastal strip of Somaliland.

In 1884, Somaliland Protectorate was officially put under the control of the Bombay government, which followed the Somaliland affairs through its Political Agent in Aden, Mr F.M. Hunter. He visited Berbera in July 1884 and, on behalf of his government, entered into "bogus" treaty with the Elders of the Habar Awal clan in Berbera. The treaty, in its vagueness, one-sidedness and deceitful intent, was typical of similar worthless treaties which the Bombay government concluded with the other Somaliland clans during 1884–1886, except that of the Dhulbahante clan (more on this later). A scan of the full text of the treaty with the Habar Awal clan, as a representative of the treaties with the other clans, is reproduced opposite.

Would this so-called "Treaty" withstand scrutiny in a court of law? The answer is "no!" No wonder the British government prevented it and other similar treaties from being discussed at the United Nations in 1955 (as discussed later under Ref. 81). After the conclusion of the Treaty, Mr Hunter telegraphed the British government in London, enquiring if:

> ...*it was the intention of Her Majesty's government to make the Somalis pay for the British Agent and his guards in the Coast and other necessary administrative charges; if so, the Customs can be fixed at a rate that will cover such expenses, and yield a fair amount of profit to the Habar Awal*

[clan]. As far as revenues were concerned, the Customs dues [leviable] at the ports of the Habar Awal shall not exceed 5% ad valorem on imports and 1% on exports. All livestock exported to Aden were to be free of import dues of all kinds. No duty was to be charged on articles for the use of bona fide persons in the employ of the British government.

The British and Habr Awal Treaty, 1884

Whereas the Garrison of His highest the Khedive are about to be withdrawn from Berbera and Bulhar, and the Somali Coast general, we the undersigned Elders of the Habr Awal tribe are desirous of entering into an agreement with the British Government for the maintenance, the preservation of order, and other good and sufficient reasons.

Now it is hereby agreed and covenanted as follows:-

ARTICLE I

The Habr Awal do hereby declare that they are pledged and bound never to cede, sell, mortgage or otherwise give for occupation, save to the British Government, any portion of the territory presently inhabited by them or being under their control.

ARTICLE II

All vessels under the British flag shall have free permission to trade and the ports of Berbera, Bulhar and other places in the territories of the Habr Awal.

ARTICLE III

All British subjects residing in, or visiting, the territories of the Habr Awal shall enjoy perfect safety and protection and shall be entitled to travel all over the said limits under the safe conduct of the Elders of the tribe.

ARTICLE IV

The traffic in slaves throughout the territories of the Habr Awal shall cease for ever, and the Commander of any of Her Majesty's vessels, or any other British Officer duly authorised, shall have the power of requiring the surrender of any slave and of supporting the demand by force of arms by land and sea.

ARTICLE V

The British Government shall have the power to appoint an agent or agents to reside at Berbera or elsewhere in the terri-

The British and Habr Awal Treaty, 1884 [4, annex 9, pp. 554–555] – continued overleaf

tories of the Habr Awal, and every such Agent shall be treated with respect and consideration and be entitled to have for his protection such guard as the British Government deem sufficient.

The above-written treaty shall come into force and have effect from the date on which the Egyptian troops shall embark at Berbera, but the agreement shall be considered provisional and subject to revocation or modification unless confirmed by competent authority.

In token of the conclusion of this lawful and honouranble bond, Abdillah Liban and Iamah Yunus (both Ayal Ba-aila), Said Gulaid and Awadh Ali (both Bhandera), Ubsiyeh Jamah and Awadh Liban (both Baho) Ilmi Farah, Yaseen Umar (both ba Eysa Musa), Ahmed Liban and Farah Samanter (both Ayal Shirdon) Hirsi Mahomed, Haid Ahmed, Husain Ali Abokr Ahmed, Ismail Doaly Adan Ismail and Yunus Deriah (all Ayal Gedid), Iamah Farah (Ayal Hosh), Warfah Adowa (Mohamed Yunus), Hirsi Buraid, Ali Mohomed, Husain Gaillay, Magan Said, Mohomed Kabillay and Wais Yusuf (all of the Eysa Musa), Roblay Doblay and Musa Fara (Mikhail), Nur Awadh and Ismail Farah (both of the Awal Hamed),

And

Major Frederick Mercer Hunter, the Officiating Political Resident of Aden, the former for themselves, their heirs and successors and the latter on behalf of the British Government do each and all in the presence of witnesses affix their signatures, marks or seals at Berbera on this twenty-first day of Ramadhan one thousand three hundred and one, corresponding with the fourteenth of July one thousand eight hundred and eighty-four.

(Sd.) F.M. HUNTER, Major,
Officiating Political Resident, Aden.
(Witness) W.J. PEYTON, Lieutenant, Bombay Staff Corps.
(Sd.) RIPON,
Viceroy and Governor-General of India.

This agreement was ratified by the Governor-General of India in Council at Simla on the twenty-third day of August A.D. one thousand eight hundred and eighty-four.

(Sd.) C. GRANT,
Secretary to the Government of India, Foreign Department

As expected, the government replied to Mr Hunter in the affirmative. Such despicable behaviour was characteristic of those who set in motion the Scramble for Africa, and Mr Hunter was of that ilk. He suggested exploitation of the worst kind. He also betrayed the ugly face of colonialism. Mr Hunter's proposal was in line with the exploitative British colonial policy, already mentioned. The British kept Aden at the expense of Somaliland, by getting from the latter tax-free fresh mutton on the hoof for the British garrison at Aden.

Mr Hunter took advantage of the few illiterate Somalis at Berbera, who apparently claimed that their respective clans "owned certain areas" in Somaliland. Mr Hunter, implementing the colonial policy of "divide and rule", separately signed treaties, similar to the one quoted above, with individuals belonging to different clans. Ever since, the British government entertained the wrong idea that the clans owned different territories in Somaliland. This misconception was clearly revealed at the Conference on Somaliland Independence in May 1960, and also the Royal Proclamation of June 1960, as will be described later. This distorted view of the British unwittingly accentuated the clanish sentiments that have plagued the Somalis to this day!

On 4 August 1884, just about three weeks after Mr Hunter's visit to Berber, a small force of about 40 policemen composed of Arabs, Indians, Somalis and others, who were trained in Aden for the purpose, and led by Mr Hunter and L.P. Walsh, crossed the Gulf of Aden and occupied Berbera [5]. There was no opposition from the Egyptians who were subservient to the British.

The Somaliland Coast (and later the whole country) was put under the control of the Bombay government in India in 1884. During that year, Mr Walsh started implementing Mr Hunter's recommendations by taxing all goods exported from the ports of Berbera, Bulahar and Zeila, and used the money for the upkeep of his office, as suggested by Mr Hunter [6]. That was when there was no government, British or otherwise, in Somaliland. No benefit accrued from the locally raised revenue to the Somaliland people.

Mr L. P. Walsh, who became the first Resident British Political Agent in Berbera, Somaliland, 1884. The photo is from his book in Ref. 5.

Mr Walsh states:

> *I kept our custom-houses open for the collection of duties, upon which receipts we were absolutely dependent in order to pay expenses. The British or Indian Exchequer (ie Finance Minister) made no grant whatever to meet our expenditure'. [5, p. 212]*

In other words, the Bombay/British governments started collecting dues from the Somalis from 1884 to finance their presence in Berber, Bulahar and Zeila, without providing any social services to the Somalis. This was, in my view, nothing short of daylight robbery!

The protectorate government of Somaliland made a statement in 1920 that nothing before 1 October 1898 could be verified from the protectorate records

[7]. That date was when the control (as if it existed) of Somaliland was transferred from the Bombay government to the British Foreign Office. The government either did not try hard enough or did not want to reveal the years (1884–1899) in which the British government was collecting taxes from the poor nomadic Somalis, with nothing in return in the form of social services [6].

The British were initially content to collect dues from the trading caravans from the interior of Somaliland and obtain fresh meat on the hoof for their garrison in Aden. In so doing they secured and kept safe from other colonial powers the sea trade route through the Suez Canal and the Red Sea to the Far East.

In 1896, the British declared the whole country of Somaliland as British Protectorate. The southern extent of Somaliland Protectorate at that time was limited by the demarcation line of the Anglo-Italian Agreement of May 1894 [10].

As already mentioned, there was no treaty between the Bombay government and the Dhulbahante clan. According to 1891–1892 correspondence [8] between the British Foreign Office and the Bombay government, the reason given for not having a treaty with the Dhulbahante clan was that the Italians already had some influence in the eastern section of the clan. The Bombay government also thought that the clan would look upon any treaty concluded with it as guaranteeing to it Bombay government protection. The Bombay government, as it put it, did not want to incur indefinite and probably inconvenient responsibilities, even if the government did not find itself involved in difficulties with Italy.

So, there was no treaty between the Dhulbahante clan and Bombay government. Anyway, all the treaties already mentioned were a complete sham and came to nothing. Making the so-called treaties with the Somali clans was a cunning ploy, on the part of the Bombay government, to keep away other colonial powers from the Somaliland coast, by claiming that the Somalis on the coast were under the Bombay government protection. However, such protection was never extended to the Somalis and their land. The reverse was true. The British and Bombay governments signed away a good part of the land of Somaliland to Ethiopia, without the Somalis' consent or knowledge, as will be described later.

3.3 Ethiopia's historical designs on Somaliland territory

Ethiopia was not at the Berlin Conference, yet when it came to the Scramble for the Horn of Africa, Ethiopia had, as it were, an "agent in court" in the form of Italy. The source I consulted states that on 18 July 1890, the Italian Prime Minister, Signor Crispi, instructed his Ambassador in Addis Ababa that King Menelik II of Ethiopia should be informed of the imminent plan to divide East Africa into spheres of influence. Menelik was advised to set out his prior claims and underline them with a reminder that Ethiopia was an ancient Christian kingdom. He was expressly advised to lay down the Ethiopian frontier with the Danakils and the Somalis, and that he should include in the list the tribes of Adal (? Awdal) and Somalis, those of Ogaden, the countries beyond Kafa (see Menelik's map below) and he should always insist on Gildessa, Harar and Lake Assal.

Menelik was not only forewarned but also a long circular letter to the Heads of the State of Britain, France, Germany, Italy and Russia, was drafted for him. The letter began thus:

> *Being desirous to make known to our friends the Powers (Sovereigns) of Europe the boundaries of Ethiopia we have addressed also to you (Your Majesty) the present letter. These are the boundaries:...*

He listed whole number of places, with strange names, embracing not only enormous parts of the lands of the Somalis, but also great tracts of Sudan, Kenya and Uganda. The letter addressed to Queen Victoria of Britain continued [9]:

> *From the Conquering Lion of the Tribe of Judah, Menelik, Elect of God, King of Kings of Ethiopia,*
>
> *To our friend Her Majesty Queen Victoria, Queen of Great Britain and Ireland,*
>
> *Greetings,*
>
> *We ask most especially news of your precious health.*
>
> *I wrote to Your Majesty a letter dated 25 Meskerem 1883; but I do not know if it reached you.[1] The great English power being up to this day the friend of the Ethiopian empire and in recognition of your goodwill to her, we express to you our gratitude.*
>
> *Seeing that we wish to acquaint the friendly powers of Europe in writing with the boundaries of Ethiopia, we hereby write to your Majesty in the*

---

[1] The Ethiopian calendar (EC) year is about eight years behind the Gregorian calendar year. Thus 1883 corresponds to 1891.

same sense, and we are hopeful that you may bestow your benevolent consideration upon what follows:

Boundaries of Ethiopia: In pointing out the exact boundaries of my empire as they exist today I signify my intention, if God graciously grants me life and strength, to re-establish the ancient frontiers of Ethiopia as far as Khartoum and Lake Nyanza (Lake Victoria), with all the Gala territories. I have not the least intention of remaining a disinterested onlooker if powers from a distance come with notion of dividing Africa between themselves, Ethiopia having been, during a course of quite fourteen centuries, an island inhabited by Christians in a sea of pagans.

Just as Almighty God has protected Ethiopia up to the present time, so also, I am confident that he be her guardian today and will also add to her territory in the future,[2] and I have no reason to contemplate that he will divide up Ethiopia amongst other powers.

Formerly the boundary of Ethiopia was the sea. Because of lack of strength on our own part and because of the failure of other Christians to come to our aid, our frontier on the seaward side fell into the hands of the Muslims.[3] Today we make no pretence of seeking to recover our seaward frontier by force; but we hope that the Christian powers, guided by our Lord Jesus Christ, may yield us our frontiers on the sea, or that at least they may give us some points on the coast.

Done at Addis Ababa, 14 Miazia 1883 (corresponding to 10 April 1891).

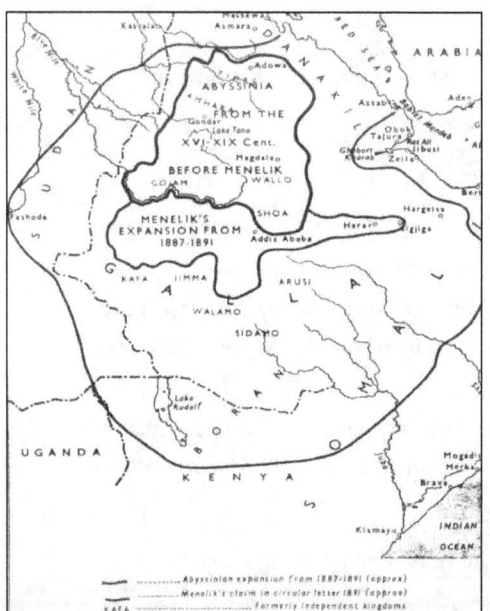

Menelik did not fail to play the Christianity card, as advised by the Italian government. His fanciful map is reproduced here. Hargeisa (Somaliland capital) is to the east. The outside line traces the extent of land which Menelik claimed in his circular letter quoted above. The country known as Abyssinia was the region in the highlands inhabited by the Amhara. When Menelik II became King in 1889, he conquered the neighbouring territories of Oromo, Gala and Somalis, and the country assumed the name of Ethiopia [9].

---

[2] Menelik's prayer for more territory was answered by Mr Rodd (see British Mission to Menelik, later). [3] Muslims probably refer to the Adalite Muslim Sultanate based in Zeila, as recorded by Arab writers of its establishment by the ninth century (see introduction to 4.1).

A Brief History of Formal Education in British Somaliland Protectorate

Following the scramble for the Horn of Africa, Britain and Italy concluded the Anglo-Italian Agreement of May 1894 [10], which demarcated their respective spheres of influence in the Horn of Africa, as shown in the scanned map of the Horn below:

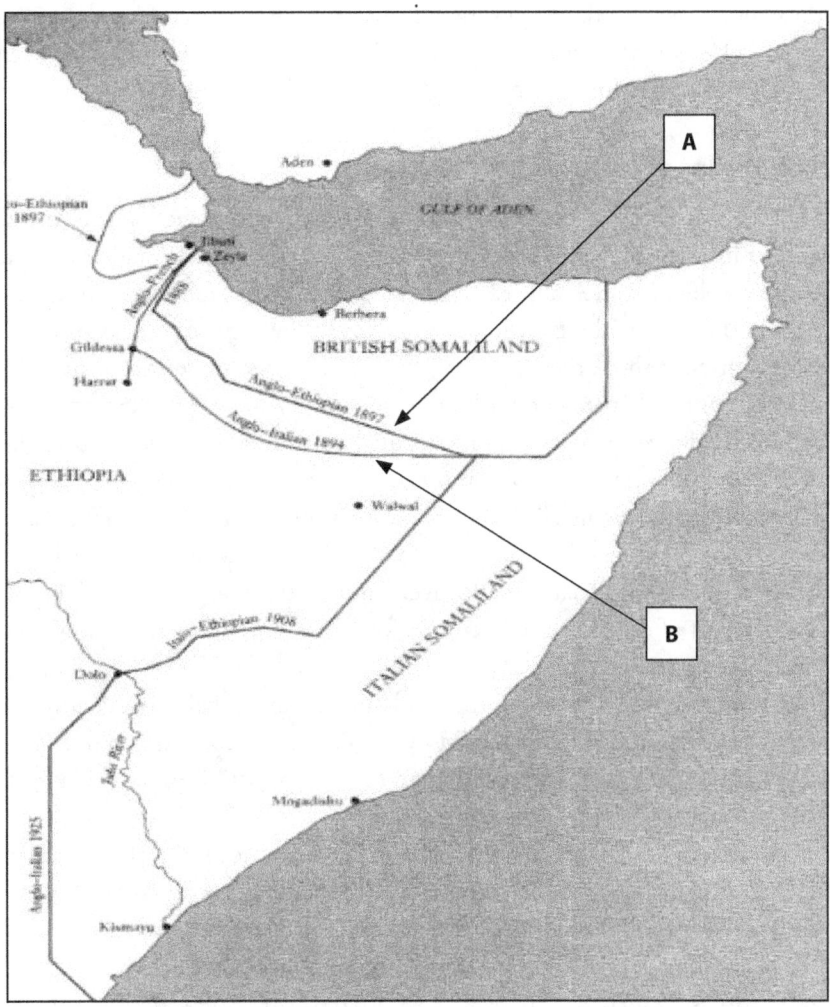

Demarcation of Somaliland boundaries, 1888–1925 [29]. Line A shows the line of demarcation of the Anglo–Ethiopian Agreement of 1897. Line B is the demarcation line of the Anglo–Italian spheres of influence, based on their Agreement of 1894.

In March 1896, Ethiopia defeated the Italian army at Adowa in Ethiopia. Because of this, the European colonial powers came to the conclusion that Ethiopia was a force to be reckoned with and they vied for the goodwill of Menelik, by installing their respective representatives in Addis Ababa. Menelik tried to play off the European powers against each another, to his advantage.

The spectacular Ethiopian victory was a turning point in the course of history of the Horn of Africa, particularly in British Somaliland Protectorate. Ethiopia, well-armed and flushed with pride after defeating a major European army in the field, started to terrorize and kill the Somalis to usurp their lands. In the process, Ethiopia encroached on the Anglo-Italian spheres of influence and tended to exercise military hegemony over the Horn of Africa. Ethiopia was bent on expanding to the East and to the South to occupy the lands of the Somalis.

Sheikh Madar of Hargeisa

Sheikh Madar of Hargeisa was witness to the Abyssinian maltreatment of the Somalis. In his early life, Sheikh Madar Ahmed lived in Harar where he studied the Muslim Religion and Arabic [11]. He established a religious community at Hargeisa in the 1850s. The British sometimes spelt the name of Sh. Madar as Sh. Mutta or Mattar. Perhaps they misheard their Somali interpreters/informers.

In 1891, Lord Delamere, a British big-game hunter, arrived in Hargeisa and built a hunting-lodge there [12]. He was initially planning to settle in Somaliland but then perhaps found conditions in the country not suitable for a European settler. He moved to Kenya in 1896, and Sh. Madar inherited the lodge and made it his home. Lord Delamere did not leave Hargeisa before having one of his legs mauled by a lion. Lord Delamere effectively implemented in Kenya the land exploitation aspect of the policy of Scramble for Africa. His descendants still have holdings in Kenya.

The Ethiopians used to enter the Somaliland territory at will, particularly in the vicinity of Hargeisa and the area settled by the Gadabursi clan, killing the Somalis, looting their livestock and stealing their crops with impunity. Hargeisa was then a watering centre on the bank of the dry river bed of Marode-Jeeh. There was then in Somaliland no authority to curb the excesses of the Ethiopians.

The British Political Agent in Berbera, Mr Merewether, recruited Sh. Madar [14] to report on what the Ethiopians were up to in Harar and the Sheikh, in turn, engaged some Somalis to obtain the required information from Harar.

On one occasion in 1891, Sh. Madar reported to Mr Merewether that the Ethiopians had got wind in their heads and thought because the French and the Italians had given them guns and rifles that they were irresistible.

In the same year (1891) the Ethiopians started to harass Sh. Madar's religious community, claiming that Hargeisa was in Ethiopian land. The Ethiopians maintained that the British were interested only in the Somaliland Coast, and, "as much country as lay within range of ship's guns from the Coast was British". The Ethiopians were not wide of the mark, as far as the British policy on the interior of Somaliland was concerned at that time.

Sh. Madar was very concerned about the Ethiopian activities in the Hargeisa environs. He requested from Mr Merewether, the British Political Agent in Berbera, 30 security men (Biladias). H. Merewether passed on this request to his boss, the Head of the British Agency in Aden, in an undated letter which went like this:

> *Shaik Mattar (sic) is one of the few stipendiaries who has consistently rendered good service to the Agency, and certainly deserves all help the Agency can give him. I presume that given the rifles, he would find the men. As regards the flag it would show the Abyssinians clearly that Shaikh Mattar is our servant, and would, I believe, be a protection to him, for I do not believe the Abyssinians will, at any rate for some time to come, take the initiative against us. [14]*

The response of the British Agency in Aden was that 30 Biladias was excessive. However, 15 Biladias as temporary measure at *Sheikh Madar's* expense could be considered. In addition, the British flag could be handed to the Sheikh to hoist it whenever there was threat from the Ethiopians!

The British government tried hard to avoid any confrontation with the Ethiopians over Somaliland, bearing in mind how the Ethiopians put the Italians to rout at Adowa in 1896. Mr Merewether wrote the following undated letter to Sheikh Madar:

> *After compliments. _____ These are the Sarkar's orders regarding you and your Kariya:*[4]
>
> *The flag which Mr Morrison hoisted you will pull down and keep. Should any spies or single individual visit you to collect information for our enemies, show it to them. Should any large force come near you re-hoist it. Should any large force come against you retire with all speed to Berbera. Do not fear, the Sarkar knows everything and is doing what is best for everybody. Regarding the Biladias let me know if you are prepared to pay and feed so many yourself. May you be preserved!*

The letter makes abundantly clear how completely the British government was in hock to the Ethiopian government and how utterly unconcerned it was about rescuing the land and people of Somaliland from the Ethiopians.

In those days the British government followed what they described as "the policy of complete abstention from interference", in regard to the barbaric tortures inflicted on the Somalis by the Ethiopians.

---

[4] Sarkar – Hindi word for Government.

Right: Sheikh Madar of Hargeisa, c.1910. The British flag was hoisted at Hargeisa on 17 February 1891, near the Masjid and Sh. Madar's house, by Mr Morrison, Deputy Assistant Political Agent at Bulahar. As Sh. Madar was not at home on that date, the flag was left in the custody of Sh. Madar's son, Omar Sh. Madar, to keep it until his father retuned, into whose charge it was to be given. Perhaps the figure with Sh. Madar is that of his son, Omar Sh. Madar! Sh. Madar, on the right, did his bit to keep the Ethiopians at bay, but the British let him down [11]..

The man who was behind the maltreatment of the Somalis was Ras Makonnen, Governor of Harar and father of Emperor Haile Selassie. His image is reproduced here.

Ras Makonnen, from Gleichen's book in Ref. 11. Ethiopia occupied Harar in January 1887. Ras Makonnen (also written as Makunan) became the Governor of Harar. He later styled himself as Ras Makonnen, Amir and Governor of Harar and its Colonies, which, he maintained, used to extend to the sea. No doubt, he adopted the title of Amir to play the Muslim card and lure the Somalis to his side.

British government mission to King Menelik II of Ethiopia [14, 15]

Makonnen claimed the Habar Awal clan in the Hargeisa area as Ethiopian subjects and called on them to destroy Lord Delamere lodge (Sh. Madar's home in Hargeisa) which Makonnen considered to be in Ethiopian territory.

The British government expressed, with tongue-in-cheek, its alarm at the Ethiopian expansionist designs on the Somaliland territory. It was in that context that, in 1897, the British government despatched a mission to King Menelik in Addis Ababa, Ethiopia.

Group photo of the British Mission to Menelik: showing members of the British Mission and their Servants, 1897. Photo from Swayne's book, in Ref. 17.

Menelik II, King of Ethiopia: 1889–1913.

The mission was led by R. Rodd, Special envoy of Queen Victoria and the chief negotiator with King Menelik. It is to be noted that Mr Rodd also participated in the Berlin Conference (1884–1885), as a staff member of the British Embassy in Berlin [16].

Members of the mission also included Mr H.G.C. Swayne [17], at the request of the East India Company (ie Bombay government). He was a big-game hunter in Somaliland and knew the extent of the lands that the Somali nomads of Somaliland Protectorate roamed about with their livestock.

The negotiations between the mission and Menelik lasted from 3 May to 4 June 1897. The mission must have also known Menelik's circular letter of 1891, mentioned earlier.

In his book, *Seventeen Trips through Somaliland and a visit to Abyssinia*, Mr Swayne recorded the atrocities perpetrated by the Ethiopians among the Somalis who, in vain, pleaded for British government protection.

The British government gave Mr Rodd, as the special envoy of Queen Victoria, specific terms of reference, which included:

- To make the necessary concessions in regard to the frontiers of Somaliland Protectorate as defined in the Anglo-Italian Agreement of 1894, provided such concessions were not of a nature to interfere with the main object for which the protectorate was assumed, namely, the securing of adequate supplies for the port of Aden, and the administration of the protectorate itself.
- In the event of agreeing to the transfer to Abyssinia of any clans currently under British protection, Mr Rodd was to secure pledges that they would be well treated with justice and consideration.
- To obtain assurances from Menelik not to allow the passage of arms to the Mahdi in the Sudan.
- To persuade King Menelik not to allow France, which was engaged in furthering her colonial interests: (a) to interfere with the headwaters of the Nile at Lake Tana, (b) to attempt to join her colonies in West Africa to her Colony of Djibouti, through Abyssinia.

At the outset of the negotiations between Mr Rodd and King Menelik, Menelik was quoted as telling Mr Rodd that:

the Somalis had been from time immemorial, until the Muslim invasion, the cattle-keepers of the Ethiopians who could not themselves live in lower countries because of their delicate constitution. The Somalis had to pay their tributes of cattle to their masters, and had been coerced when they failed to do so.

Since there was no Somali at the negotiation table, Menelik was free to say or do whatever he liked about the Somalis, including adding insult to injury, without fear of consequences. As regards the British, before they could ask for justice for the Somalis from the Ethiopians, they themselves should have practised what they preached and should not have given to Ethiopia the best parts of Somaliland! As a result of their negotiations, Mr Rodd and Menelik reached the main Anglo-Ethiopian Agreement of 14 May 1897.

Regarding the Ethiopia/Somaliland frontier, Menelik claimed ignorance of maps and Somali clans and told Mr Rodd that, on his return home, he should negotiate with Ras Makonnen, Governor of Harar, about the Ethiopia/Somaliland boundary. Mr Rodd and Makonnen haggled over where the boundary line between Ethiopia and Somaliland would be – no doubt, both of them knowing that the land for barter was not their own!

The Italians, badly defeated and recently humiliated by the Ethiopians at Adowa in 1896, were demoralized and perhaps they could not bring themselves to participate in the Rodd/Makonnen negotiations. Ras Makonnen thus concentrated on the Anglo-Italian agreement of 1894 (see map of Horn of Africa, below). He demanded that the Anglo-Italian demarcation line be shifted northward and eventually prevailed upon Mr Rodd to make him accept an area estimated at about 25,100 square miles of Somaliland to be added to the Ethiopian territory, as an answer to King Menelik's prayer for more territory in his circular letter referred to earlier!

The area acquired by Ethiopia, as a result of the Italian absence from the negotiation table and Mr Rodd taking indulgent attitude toward the excessive demands of Ras Makonnen, was within the Italian sphere of influence. That was how the Ethiopians usurped what used to be called the "Ogadenia area" and part of Somaliland. The latter area later became known as the Hawd and Reserve Area, and thus an area roughly about three times the size of the area of the Republic of Djibouti (ie 9,000 square miles) was ceded to Ethiopia.

That was the betrayal of the century, as far as the people of Somaliland were concerned!

A whole swathe of the grazing and agricultural southern/south-west parts of Somaliland was signed away to Ethiopia. This was in spite of the treaties which the British entered into with the Somaliland clans, and which pre-dated the 1897 Anglo-Ethiopian agreement.

Mr Rodd was generous in the extreme to his African Christian fellow-colonialist. Mr Rodd could afford to dispense with what was not his own. The Agreement which Mr Rodd reached with Makonnen about the Ethiopia-Somaliland boundary on 4 June 1897 was attached, as an Annex, to the main Anglo-Ethiopian Agreement of 14 May 1897. Queen Victoria was pleased with what Mr Rodd achieved and she suitably decorated him.

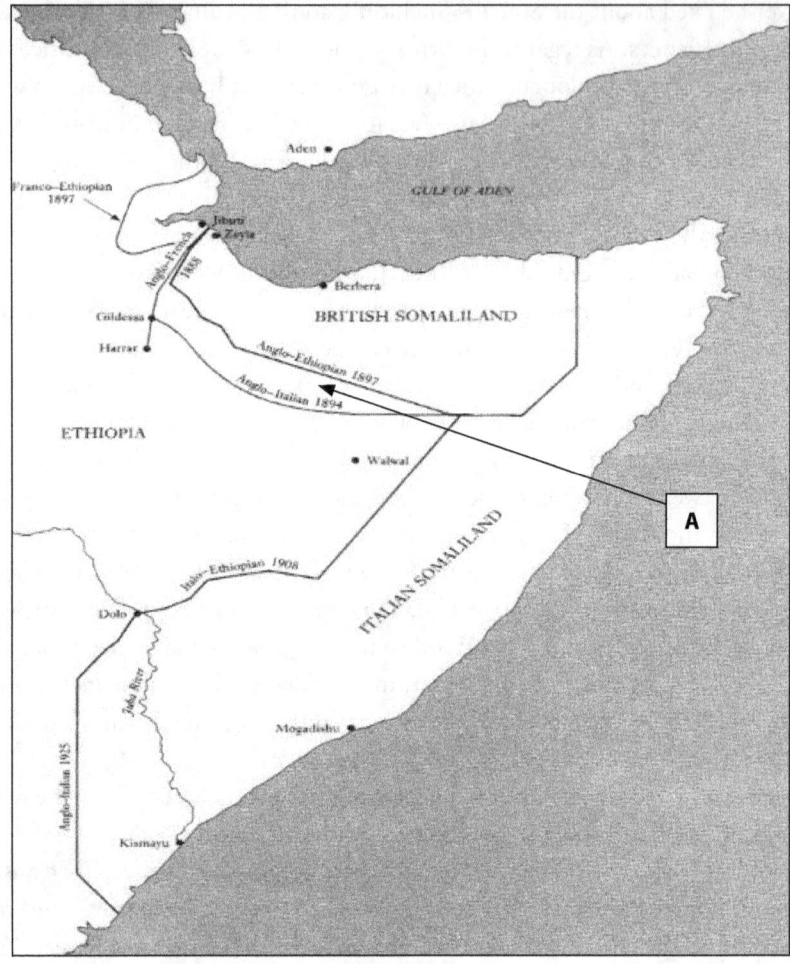

Map of the Horn of Africa, from Beachey's book [29]. Area "A" marks the part of Somaliland given away to Ethiopia by the British Mission to Menelik II in 1897. The part became known as the Hawd and the Reserved Area, arbitrarily dividing up the Horn of Africa, as a consequence of the Scramble for Africa.

3.4 The rise and fall of Seyyid Mohamed Abdullah Hassan and his Dervishes, 1899–1920

The beginnings [18, 19]

Seyyid Mohamed Abdullah Hassan (the Seyyid, for short), also known to the British as the "Mad Mullah of Somaliland", was the son of a father from the Ogaden, Bah Gheri sub-clan and of a mother from the Dhulbahante, Ali Gheri sub-clan. He was supposed to have been born in the 1860s in the Buuhoodle area. He made several pilgrimages to Mecca. While still in his prime of life in 1895, he returned to Berbera from his last pilgrimage where he had lived initially. He wanted to introduce the Salihiya Dariqa (Religious Sect) in Berbera, acting as the representative of the founder of the Dariqa, Mohamed ibn Salah al-Rashidi in Mecca. In the process, he came into conflict with the old established Dariqas, namely, Qadiriya, Dandarawiya and Ahmediya in Berbera. He accused the adherents of these Dariqas of acquiescing to Christianity being planted in the country and tolerating small Somali children being converted to Christianity and running around the Berbera streets, with crucifixes round their necks. The Seyyid condemned the Roman Catholic missionary activities in the country. (The mission school is later described under 4.1).

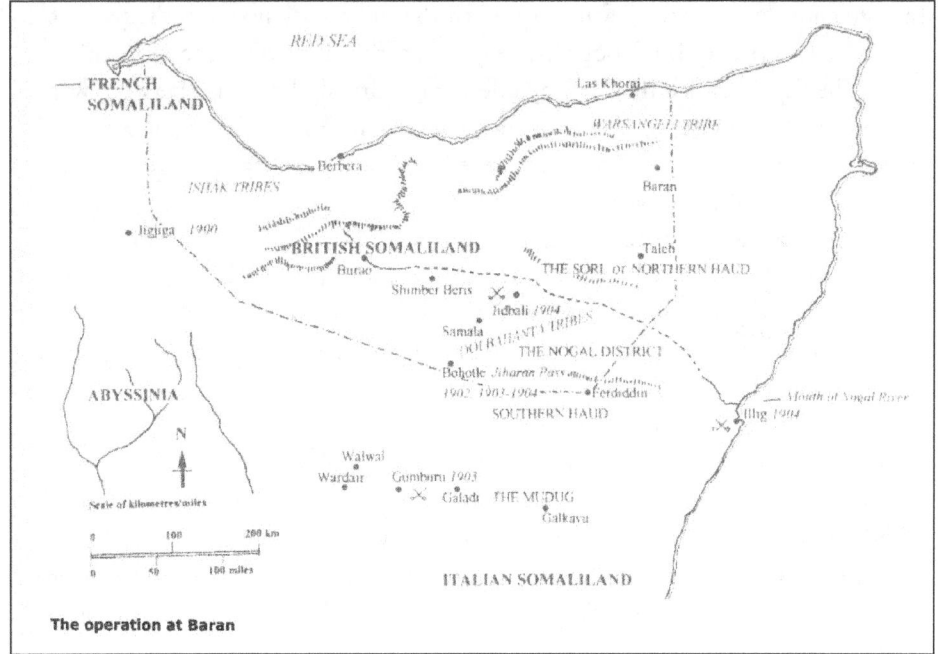

Map of Somaliland during the Dervish revolt

The Seyyid eventually moved to the interior, to a place called Kirid, where his mother's clan traditionally inhabited. He acted as a Somali elder and adjudicated disputes between clans. Meanwhile, a large number of Somalis in that area flocked to the Seyyid's banner. A rifle, said to have been stolen from the camp of the British Vice-Consul in Berbera and allegedly taken to the Seyyid's camp, resulted in fruitless correspondence between the Vice-Consul and the Seyyid, who denied any knowledge about the rifle.

It seemed it was about this time that the Seyyid came to the conclusion that he should make a move against the British in the country. In August 1899, at the head of a large Somali force, the Seyyid arrived at Burao which was, at that time, not much more than a centre for water supply during the dry season, for the Habar Yonis, Habar Je'lo and Dhulbahante clans. On arrival at Burao, the Seyyid declared himself the *"Mahdi", (the expected one)* and called his Somali force the *Dervishes*. He proclaimed holy war against the British Force, calling them the infidels.

The first act of the Seyyid and his Dervishes was to attack the Dariqa at Sheikh and raze it to the ground. Rumour spread that the second target of the Seyyid was Berbera. Some of the Indian and Arab traders in the town fled to Aden. No attack on Berbera took place.

On 1 September 1899, the Seyyid wrote a letter to the British authorities, accusing them of offending against the religion of the people of Somaliland. He mentioned an Aqil named Mohamed who was sent by the British authority to him, to enquire about the Seyyid's arms. The Seyyid mentioned in his letter that Aqil Mohamed's enquiries about the Seyyid's arms prompted him to write this letter. The Seyyid ended his letter by offering the British the choice between war and peace. In response, Mr Hayes-Sadler, the British Consul-General in Aden, immediately proclaimed the Seyyid a "rebel" and warned all against assisting the rebel or communicating with him.

The Seyyid's rebellion was well and truly in the open. The Seyyid, with his force, returned to Burao and moved to Odweine, south-west of Burao, to try to enlist the support of Habar Yonis and Edagale clans in that area.

On their way, the Dervishes drove off a large number of livestock belonging to the communities in the Arori plain.

[I wish to insert in here what I heard from those who were at that time there in Arori. Old relatives of mine, no longer alive, used to tell stories about how the Dervishes carried off their livestock in Arori and roughed up the men, in order to persuade them to join the Seyyid's movement. My relatives did not know the date, which was in September 1899. I doubt whether my late relatives would have endorsed my views about the Seyyid. After all, we lived in different periods of history!]

It was recorded that the Seyyid failed to gain the support of the Habar Yonis and Edagale clans in Odweine area. He returned to Burao, and from there, with his force, he moved to Buuhoodle.

The British government was militarily weak at that time and could not confront the challenge of the Seyyid, thanks to the Boer war in South Africa, which was in progress.

Clan-based militia [20]

There was not then what could be called a "government" in the country. What then passed for a "protectorate government" was nothing more than a small, mobile, occupying Imperial Force, led by a Commissioner, always on campaign footing to fight the Dervishes. No administration or other services of any sort were provided for the people of the country, although this Force used to collect local revenues through taxation at the coastal towns of Zeila, Bulahar and Berbera for the upkeep of the occupying force!

In November 1900, the British government brought Mr E.J.E. Swayne, a British officer in the Indian Army, to Somaliland to organize Somali militia against the Dervishes. He was the brother of H.G.C. Swayne [17]. Every month or so, the British Force used to train units of about 300–400 clan-based Somali militiamen on the type of Martini-Henry rifle shown below, for about a week. The men were recruited from what the British government called the "Friendly clans" – those which sided with the occupying Force – but this was in effect the poorly-disguised usual colonial policy of divide-and-rule. After training, the armed militia units, supervised by two or three British officers, would be sent to the field to face the Dervishes. When not engaged in fighting, the units would be sent to their *Reers* (nomadic hamlets) "as reserves". Some of them were provided with riding-camels or ponies or mules and were ordered to scout about the movements of the Dervishes – hence their Somali name *Ilaalo*. The training centre was initially at Adadley, but later was moved to Sheikh.

Later, when some sort of administration (or control) was introduced into the country, the *Ilaalo*, clan-based as before, were used by the District Commissioners (DCs) to enforce the hated *Xeer* (Somali customary law). The *Ilaalo* were rooted in the scouting Somali militia mentioned above.

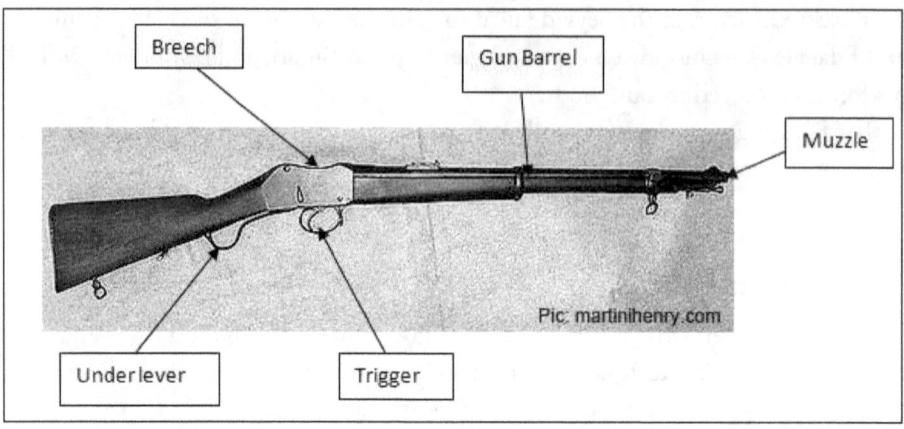

Top: The "Martini-Henry" rifle was in use in Somaliland Protectorate from the 1890s up to the 1940s. The Somalis used to call the shorter barrel version, "Maadhiin-Yare", as shown in the picture and a longer barrelled one, "Hilqadle". ***Bottom left***: Bullets for the rifle. The Somalis used to call the one on the left "Caara-gamuur" (rounded tip) and the one on the right "Caara-dhuub" (pointed tip). The rifle fired one bullet at a time, ("Xabbad-keliyaale" in Somali). ***Bottom right:*** Leather bandolier ("shakad" in Somali) for the bullets.

The Seyyid raised a formidable local force – in other words, the Dervishes – and waged politico-religious war against what he considered as the invading infidels. As to who dubbed the Seyyid the "Mad Mullah" is in dispute. A version I heard, without evidence, runs thus:

The Seyyid was returning from pilgrimage to Mecca. On arrival in Berbera, a British officer asked him, through an interpreter, to show his landing document. The Seyyid wanted the interpreter to ask the officer if somebody ever asked him for his entry document into the country. The interpreter, perhaps finding himself in an awkward position, rather than interpreting the Seyyid's question, instead told the British officer that he (the Seyyid) was a mad *Wadaad* (mullah) who could be ignored.

A different version was quoted in Ref. 18, p. 54, as follows:

> *On 30 July 1899 the Consul-General reported to the Foreign Office that reports from the Dhulbahante, apparently on good authority, are to the effect that the Mullah has gone off his head. It is said that he fired twice at his nephew, killing his horse, and that he was only prevented from doing further damage by being seized by his followers.*

While on this issue, Mr Sadler, the Consul-General for the Somaliland Coast Protectorate, who was based in Aden, was touring the western part of the country in June 1899. On 15 June 1899, in his Camp at Odweine, he received Haji Musa who was returning from the Pilgrimage and was on his way to Hahi settlement. He described Haji Musa as the Head of the Mullah community of Hahi, and the Principal Mullah of the Habar Yonis clan. Mr Sadler mentioned in his despatch of 16 June 1899 that Haji Musa spoke fluent Arabic and was a man of more than ordinary intelligence and education.

At that time the Seyyid was active amongst the clans in the eastern part of the country. Mr Sadler quoted Haji Musa describing the Seyyid as a "religious madman" whose object was to unite the tribes so as to exercise his authority over them [21]. The above version was the only time, in my reading about the subject, that a Mullah well known in that part of the country, was directly quoted as calling the Seyyid "a religious madman".

If the object of the Seyyid was as Haji Musa reportedly said, and the Seyyid succeeded in his mission, it would not have been a bad idea having united clans under a Somali authority. The history of Somaliland would have been different! Also, it could well have been that the British came up with the "mad mullah" title to belittle the Seyyid's struggle. Anyway, what cannot be doubted is that the Seyyid was anything but mad! It was unlikely that a mad man would have been able to mobilize a local force, strong enough to have kept fighting with the British imperial force in the country for 21 years!

The simple explanation could well be the casual way the Somalis use the word "mad" against a man who puts forward controversial ideas. They will say "don"t listen to that man, he is mad', although they realize that he is not actually mad.

The British colonialists in the country, who were not well acquainted with the Somali culture, bought into this loose use of the word "mad", as did Haji Musa against the Seyyid by describing him as *"waa wadaad waalan"* ("He is a religious madman", in English). This description of the Seyyid suited the British narrative. Hence, the "Mad Mullah of Somaliland"!

The first of the five major expeditions against the Seyyid and his followers (Dervishes) was launched on 22 May 1901. The objectives of the first expedition, and indeed the subsequent ones, were given as:

- To capture or defeat the Mullah and put an end to his movement in the

Dhulbahante country

- In the unlikely event of his offering to come in, only an unconditional surrender was to be accepted
- Clans that might actively support him during the operations were to be punished
- Proclamation was to be issued warning the *Daarood* [clans] that only those who continued to assist the Mullah would be considered hostile
- Tribes as a whole would be held responsible for the acts of individuals [22]

It is clear that, even at that stage in the history of the protectorate government, the colonial authority was ready to practise, illegally, collective punishment in the country.

The fighting of the first expedition, which ended in July 1901, took place in the Buuhoodle area. The result was inconclusive, since neither side could prevail over the other. Further expeditions against the Dervishes followed.

To improve communications, in the face of the Dervishes, in 1903 the government proposed to construct railways in the country. For this purpose, 500 "coolies" (manual workers) from India and 200 from Aden were brought into the country. The intention was to construct a railway line from Berbera to Buuhoodle or from Berbera to Habar, with a branch line from Adadley to Buuhoodle. The workers were employed to prepare the ground during the survey which was completed by November 1903. However, construction never started.

Historically, the British government left behind some lasting infrastructure – for example, railways, developed water sources or developed roads in the countries it once colonized, like Sudan, India, etc. However, Somaliland was a different kettle of fish. The government thought better of investing in the country. The government was probably not sure for how long it would remain in the country, or that there were no resources, in the country, for exploitation – more about the government's attitude towards the country is given under 3.6.

Camel carrying Field Artillery for use against the Dervishes. c.1903. Photo from Beachey's book [29].

The British used the Somali camels and men for transport, see picture below.

Somali men carrying British individuals who did not want to get their feet wet! Landing at Zeila, not from a plane or ship, but from the shoulders of Somali men c.1903.
Photo from Drake-Brochman's book [11].

Government taking stock of the situation vis-à-vis the Dervishes [23]

The British government thought that the Dervishes were finished at the end of the fourth campaign which ended in May 1904 at Jidbaale, in the present-day *Sool* Region.

In April 1905, the government took stock of the financing of the non-existent "Somaliland Protectorate Government" and enunciated the policy that would henceforth be followed in the country. The government wrote:

> *In a country which was originally self-supporting, the expenditure on the protectorate has been gradually increasing, thanks to the Mullah's activities,*
>
> *The result of the recent war has – as is usual in such cases – been not only to raise very considerably the annual military expenditure of the protectorate but to cause a temporary expansion of the Civil Department in general which may easily become permanent, unless great vigilance is exercised,*
>
> *The policy of His Majesty's government is now to confine direct administration to the strip of country bordering on the coast, and there is no reason why that administration should be on an elaborate and expensive scale.*
>
> *The case of Somaliland is entirely different from that of certain other*

Protectorates: it neither possesses nor is likely to possess in the future, a large white population. While the native population in 1903 was 153,000, the white population in 1904 was: Officials = 44, non-officials = 13, a total of 47.

Nor again can the protectorate be regarded as a valuable undeveloped possession of this country. However, it possesses a certain importance as a source of supply for Aden.

The Protectorate's total imports and exports in recent years have not exceeded the following amounts, viz

Year	Imports, £	Exports, £
1898	389,961	415,070
1899	452,503	392,375
1900	393,957	364,021
1901	355,175	348,920
1902	294,890	268,887

No statistics appear to be available as to the proportion of this trade which is carried on with the United Kingdom. Owing to the practice of transhipment at Aden, the direct trade is nil. In these circumstances, it would be impossible to justify any heavy civil expenditure from the Imperial funds in the protectorate and that sound policy requires that the country should be administered upon the simplest possible lines.

As regards the military expenditure, on financial ground alone, it would be bad economy to effect reductions which might encourage a recrudescence of the recent war. At the same time, the military position of the country has been entirely changed by the recent agreement with the Mullah, which should remove the only serious source of military disturbance which the protectorate is threatened, and that the result of this alteration may soon become apparent in the protectorate Estimates.

The permanent maintenance of a large force under ordinary conditions could not but encourage the local officers to undertake offensive operations not absolutely necessary for the safety of the settlement – operations which might lead to serious difficulties and to great expenditure in the future, without the prospect of any adequate results.

In view of the alarming growth of its expenditure and the unsatisfactory character of its history in the last few years, advantage may be taken of the opportunity offered by the transfer of control from the Foreign Office to the

Colonial Office to invite special attention to the administrative and financial problems to which recent events have given rise.

The total military expenditure against the activities of the Dervishes for the 4 years, 1901 to 1904, was given as: = £2,450,100.

The total ordinary Expenditure (1898–1899) was: = £66,370

This ordinary expenditure was mainly covered by the revenue raised locally.

If I may briefly comment on the above:

a) The so-called "protectorate government" started collecting revenue from the people of Somaliland from 1884, the year it occupied the Coast of Somaliland, as described under 3.2.
b) 1898–1899 was the earliest period for which the author could find recorded expenditure by the Somaliland Protectorate Government. The expenditure of £66,370 on the mainly Indian soldiers garrisoned at the Somaliland Coast in 1898–1899 was mainly covered by locally raised revenue. The people of Somaliland were unknowingly subsidizing the British government occupation of the Somaliland Coast!
c) The title "protectorate government" was really something of a misnomer, since there was no foreign authority, including the British, which then either protected or governed the people of Somaliland. In fact, that remained the case for many years that followed,
d) When they say that the country was "self-supporting", it was true that the Somalis then led a self-sufficient lifestyle. But it could also be added that they had freedom unfettered by national or foreign authority – one could even say "free in the extreme"! It would be true to describe the conditions then prevailing in the country as being governed by the law of the jungle! Inter-clan raids were the order of the day. Probably the people realized, well before the British involvement in the country, that there was safety in numbers and sought security in groupings — the birth of the clans! That was then. What to do about clanism of today? My answer is in the Appendix.
e) The war mentioned was that of the military operations against the Dervishes and which cost the British government £2,450,100 for the four years 1901–1904. After the defeat of the Dervishes, ordinary expenditure on the protectorate were composed of combined civil and military components, up to and including 1939. The penultimate campaign against the Dervishes and its cost is discussed later.
f) Confining direct administration to the strip of country bordering on the coast was not something new. That was the reason the British occupied the Coast in the first place.
g) It was always the aim of the British colonial policy to introduce British set-

tlers into their Colonies where the "right" conditions existed. In this regard, Somaliland disappointed the British government, as the country did not fit the bill.

h) It is true that the British occupied Somaliland for, among other things, the country's fresh mutton on the hoof for the British garrison already occupying Aden. That was why the British government, on more than one occasion, mooted the idea that, rather than abandon Somaliland, it could be amalgamated with Aden, as Aden depended on the Somaliland trade and it would also be cheaper, economically, to run one rather than two countries. History records the ignominious way the British were thrown out of Aden in 1967.

i) The policy of administering the coastal strip (which they called the settlement) upon the simplest possible lines was eventually applied to the whole country, right up to independence. It was the policy that came to be known as "administration on care and maintenance basis, ie minimal administration to keep and law order; to contain cost and no attempt at development in the country" [23, 37]

j) The mentioned agreement with the Mullah was not with the British, but was with the Italian government, with the knowledge of the British. An Italian Emissary who was also the Italian Consul in Aden, Mr Pestalozzi, signed the Agreement with the Mullah (the Seyyid) on 5 March 1905 at the port of Ilig, on the Indian Ocean coast of present-day Puntland State. In the Agreement, the Mullah promised to keep the peace with all, including the British. The Seyyid was allowed to control a territory straddling the border between British Somaliland Protectorate and Somalia, as shown in the map below, with heavy dots.

A map showing the area that the Seyyid was allowed to control (marked with heavy dots) – a territory straddling the border between British Somaliland Protectorate and Somalia, following the Ilig Agreement signed with the Italian consul on 5 March 1905.

Further details of the Agreement, of which nothing much came, need not concern us here.

It is stated in Jardine's, *The Mad Mullah of Somaliland*, which is wholly about the "Mad Mullah":

> By 1886, the government concluded separate protective treaties with all the Somali tribes now living under the government protection, except the Dhulbahante, with whom no treaty has been made. Thus some 68,000 square miles were added to our African Empire, and an important littoral on the main sea route to India came under British suzerainty. Responsibility for this newly-acquired possession devolved upon the government of India; and, like Aden, the Somali Coast was administered by the government of Bombay.
>
> But on 1st October 1898, owing to Somaliland's intimate connection with the political situation in Abyssinia, and with a view to the development of the resources of the interior, the administration was transferred to the Foreign Office. At the time hopes of peaceful and prosperous development in Somaliland ran high; for it was the only country in our East African Empire that was then self-supporting. But in the following year all such hopes were frustrated by the Somali who soon became known to the world as the Mad Mullah. [18, p. 35]

The British government was relieved by the conclusion of the *Ilig* Agreement, as a result of which, on 1 April 1905, the government transferred the control of Somaliland from the Foreign Office to the Colonial Office. The Colonial Office protested and wanted control to go to the Bombay government which, in turn, refused to accept the "hot potato" and thus the control of the country remained with the Colonial Office right up to the British evacuation of the country during the Second World War in 1940. The Agreement with the Mullah did not last long and the British relief was premature.

The Seyyid fashioned, from his name, his distinct personal stamp which he affixed to the letters he sent to the British officers with whom he corresponded.

The Seyyid's personal stamp [24].

The Seyyid was reputed to stamp his letters not once, not twice, but thrice, perhaps for effect. As a sample, a scan of an undated letter the Seyyid sent to Mr Swayne, then Commissioner of Somaliland Protectorate, is shown below:

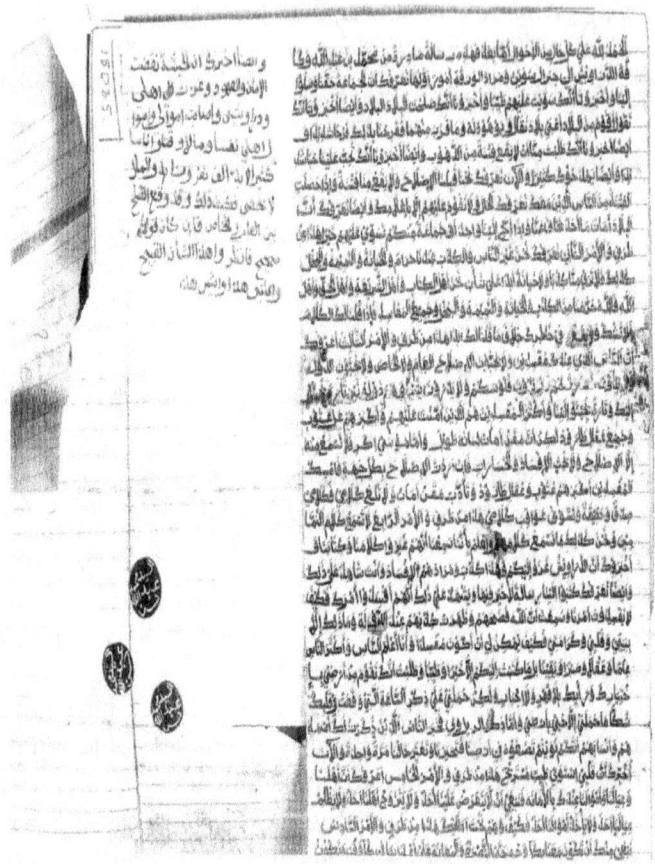

An undated letter sent by the Seyyid to Mr Swayne (then Commissioner of Somaliland Protectorate), stamped three times with the Seyyid's personal stamp [24].

The letter raised several issues, typical of the correspondence he exchanged with the British authorities in the country:

- The Seyyid thought the Somalis around the British Camp (Berbera) were evil-doers and were there for the money.

- He reassured Mr Swayne that he accepted the peace agreement. The letter was written after 5 March 1905, as it referred to the *Ilig* agreement of that date.

- He described the Dervishes as people of the Book (ie the *Qur'an*), of *Sharia*, of God, and bound to avoid lying, deceit, slander and greed.

- He complained about certain individuals in the British Camp, particularly Aqils of certain clans, a man called Magan Amaan and a naval interpreter called Ali Utubi.

- He appeared somewhat apologetic about having asked Mr Swayne to leave the country in one hour on hearing about the proposed railway to be built from Berbera to the interior. This time, the Seyyid suggested that Mr Swayne may leave the country at his convenience and without force being used.

- He urged Mr Swayne to take care of the property and the families and relatives of the Dervishes in the British Protectorate.

- The Seyyid was not shy about asking Mr Swayne for assistance and presents of any kind, according to Mr Swayne's generosity.

- He complained to Mr Swayne about the Ethiopians robbing and killing his Dervishes and his clan people and urged him to do something about that.

The Seyyid's struggle against the protectorate government coincided with the First World War raging in Europe, and the British government could ill-afford the Imperial forces tied up in Somaliland. Some young British soldiers were writing home, complaining that "they were wasting their energy in a God-forsaken little country in the Horn of Africa, while their compatriots were heroically defending the motherland"!

In a tour of inspection of the British Colonies in East Africa, W. Churchill, then Under-Secretary of State for the Colonies, made a stopover at Berbera in October 1907. It took him a whole day to go to and from the foot of the hills, south Berbera. In his minutes dated 28 October 1907, he described Somaliland as "a wilderness of stone and scrub, a land marked by utter poverty, peopled by rifle-armed zealots with more than their share of *Wadaado*." (*Wadaad* is the Somali word for a religious man and the proper plural is *wadaado*). He also painted a pessimistic picture of the Imperial forces facing the Dervishes, arguing that "the country was not worth the expenditure involved." He proposed "amalgamation of the country with Aden." He thought substantial savings would result from administering one country instead of two. He posed the rhetorical questions: "Were not the destinies of Aden and British Somaliland inextricably intertwined? Wasn't it because of Aden that we occupied the coast of Somaliland?" [25] In fact, Aden was then just as poorly developed as was Somaliland Protectorate.

Mr Churchill's recommendations were later given serious consideration, in connection with the following item – Wingate Mission. We will meet Mr Churchill in action again, as the Secretary of State for the Colonies.

Coastal concentration policy – Wingate Special Mission report of 1909 [26]

At one stage, the protectorate government came under increasing pressure from the Dervish movement and the British government was worried and was faced with unpalatable choices. In order to play for time, a fact-finding, two-man mission was sent to Somaliland in 1909. The men were Mr R. Wingate, Governor-General of Sudan and Mr R. Slatin, Inspector-General of Sudan. Both men spoke Arabic. The main terms of the mission were: (a) to advise on the situation in Somaliland Protectorate; and (b) to recommend a policy for the future administration of the country.

In his brief of 15 April 1909 for the two-man mission, the Secretary of State for the Colonies, Lord Crewe, informed the mission of the government's policy that:

> *In view of the cost (some £2,500,000) and inconclusive results of the last expedition, an organised campaign against the Mullah is out of the question. Some alternative policy to that of catching and killing the Mullah must be determined. Faced with the difficulties of the situation as a whole, tired of having to remain indefinitely on the defence, weary with holding a worthless country at great civil and military cost, a great body of opinion is tending more and more to incline withdrawal to certain positions on the coast. Evacuation or such a withdrawal would in themselves be satisfactory to the government if, after consideration of the pros and cons, you could recommend either one or other of these lines of action.*

It is clear that the British government had already decided, in advance, what the recommendations of the mission should be.

The two-man mission arrived in the protectorate in April 1909. They corresponded with the Seyyid but that proved fruitless. It will be recalled that it was largely the sight of young Somali children wearing crucifixes in Berbera that induced Seyyid Mohamed Abdullah Hassan to condemn the Catholic mission and to rebel against the protectorate government.

Members of the mission closely interviewed, without the presence of government officials, some Aqils and other elders in Berbera, Sheikh and Burao. The interviewees were reported to have bitterly complained about Christian missionaries interfering with the religion of young Somali boys. They also complained about the British officers not being able to speak Somali or Arabic. They confided to the mission members that the Somali interpreters told the British officers only what the interpreters thought the officers would like to hear. Those from Sheikh complained about a Somali government employee called Ahmed Shire and those from Burao complained another Somali government employee called Haji Musa Fareh Igare. In both cases, the problem the interviewees from Sheikh and Burao claimed to have faced was that whatever complaints they made to the government were referred to either Ahmed Shire in Sheikh or to Haji Musa Fareh Igare in Burao, with unsatisfactory outcomes, as the interviewees were reported to have maintained. The two-man mission also closely looked into, in detail, the Catholic mission work and this is described under 4.1.

The misguided policy of the protectorate government in allowing a Christian mission to proselytize in the country was further denounced by none other than the two-man mission, who, in their report, severely criticized the protectorate government for:

> …*its insensitivity to the Somali religious feelings by allowing a Roman Christian mission to proselytise in Berbera and the sight of convert Somali children running around in the streets of Berbera with crucifixes round their necks, which was affront to Allah and the Prophet and anathema in Islamic eyes and the tactless exhibition of Christianity in a solidly Islamic society.*

This was a damning indictment against the protectorate government for provoking the Seyyid's revolt and the dire consequences for the people of Somaliland and the British government. It was the sheer political ineptitude of the protectorate government that not only plunged the country into turmoil, but also unwittingly jeopardized the future development of formal education in the country, as will be seen later.

Because the mission severely criticized the British Administrators in the country, the mission report was kept secret and was not published before the Second World War. The mission's recommendations included:

- Complete evacuation of the country
- Defeating the Mullah before considering partial withdrawal to the Coast
- Not offering the Mullah financial subsidy for keeping the peace.

The British government was against sending a large force to Somaliland to defeat the Mullah. Instead, the government opted for the partial evacuation to the Coast – what they called the Coastal Concentration Policy. On 12 November 1909, the Commissioner of the protectorate was instructed to put the policy into effect. By 26 March 1910, the protectorate government withdrew completely from the interior of the country, confining itself to the coastal towns of Zeila, Bulahar, Berbera and Las Qorey, leaving the rest of the country to its own devices. The Roman Catholic mission was also withdrawn from the country. The coastal concentration policy lasted till early 1913.

Zeila, c.1904 [11].

Bulahar, c.1910 [11].

Berbera, c.1904 [11]

Before the withdrawal, the government distributed arms and ammunitions to certain clans which they described as the "Friendlies" and which sided with government and fought against the Dervishes. It was a disastrous measure. The armed clans (the "Friendlies") using the newly acquired weapons soon went on an orgy of killing and looting each other, to settle old scores. A phase of death and devastation, which the Somalis called *Xaaraama-Cune* – eating the ill-gotten gains – ensued. A government that could have maintained law and order did not exist in the country at that time or before, as described earlier.

The distribution of arms and ammunitions (similar to those shown in the earlier picture) to the "Friendlies" at Burao in March 1910, supervised by R. Corfield. He was killed in 1913 in the battle with Dervishes at Dul-Madobe, east of Burao [11].

Abandonment of the coastal concentration policy

By 1913, the so-called "protectorate government" gradually came out from its "coastal shell" and tentatively extended its presence in an ever-increasing radius into the interior of the country engaging, in the process, in skirmishes with the Dervishes. It was at that time that G.F. Archer (*Caarshe-Dheere*, "Archer-the-tall", to the Somalis) became the Commissioner of the protectorate in June 1913.

While the gradual extension into the interior of the country was going on, the First World War ended, and with it the Ottoman Empire. In 1919, the victorious powers held an international conference in Paris, France, to divide up the spoils (in other words, the territories of the defeated Ottoman Empire) among themselves. At that conference, the British Secretary of State for the Colonies, Lord Milner, was disposed to cede the interior, but not the Coast, of Somaliland to Italy – perhaps as a reward for the latter's support in the war. However, Italy became too greedy and demanded the whole of Somaliland Protectorate and Djibouti as well! In the end, Italy left the conference without even the offered part of Somaliland [29].

Perhaps to signify that some sort of government would later be introduced into the country, Mr Archer's title was changed from Commissioner to Governor in 1919, the first protectorate governor to have such title.

Partial defeat of the Seyyid and his Dervishes [27]

The British government launched its fifth campaign against the Dervishes. The campaign by air, land and sea lasted 23 days – from 21 January to 18 February 1920. The government misled the public by describing the crew of the planes as oil explorers. In a similar manner, the government told the public that the members who were demarcating the Somaliland Protectorate/Ethiopia boundary, in the 1930s, were making a road.

For the campaign, the government instructed the elders of the Friendly Clans to muster 5,000 militiamen, on a clan basis. The government would arm them, but the men would take care of their food, water and transport. Here again is the policy of running the country on the cheap. The government forces mined and demolished Taleh Fort in revenge for the daring struggle of the Seyyid who challenged the authority of the foreign invaders. A historical monument that would have informed our history and culture was lost. The cost of the air, land and sea campaign was given as £84,000.

Taleh Fort, surrounded by the government forces, before they mined and demolished it in 1920. Unforgivable vandalism of a cultural and historical building! Photo from Jardine's book [28].

One of the planes which participated in bombing the Seyyid's forts at Midhishi, Jiidale and Taleh. January–February 1920. Photos of the planes, by courtesy of the RAF Museum in London.

This plane was used as an air-ambulance. A casualty was being either loaded or unloaded.

The British government wrote that the reason for using the Royal Air Force against the Dervishes was:

> To test the theory that the moral effect of the new arm, with its power to carry out, without warning, a form of attack against which no counter measures could avail, would so disperse and demoralize the Dervishes following that the troops would be enabled to capture the Mullah's stock and destroy his forts. This object was attained in full [27].

Without fear of opposing enemy aircraft or anti-aircraft ground fire, they could strafe and dive-bomb the Dervishes from a very low height. It was nothing more than a target practice, not worth bragging about.

The Seyyid and some of his Dervish followers fled south into the Ethiopian territory and regrouped in an area called Shinileh, posing a threat to the Friendly Clans.

The final defeat of the Seyyid and his Dervishes – 1920 [28, 29]

Governor Archer attempted to entice the Seyyid from his rebellion, by offering him peaceful settlement, under certain conditions. Governor Archer detailed his offer in a letter, which was hand-carried by an *Ergo* (Peace Deputation), despatched by the governor to the Seyyid.

Summary of the letter (translated from Arabic, as it exists in the source consulted):

- A locality, suitable for stock grazing and farming and where the Seyyid could establish a Dervish Dariqa in the western side of the country, would be assigned to the Seyyid. The Seyyid's children who were in government hands would be restored to him.

- The stock the Seyyid would bring with him would remain his; and if it was not enough, the government would restore to the Seyyid sufficient to meet the requirements of the Seyyid and his followers, stock, pay, etc., so that the Seyyid's Dariqa would be on the same footing as other Dariqas under the protection of the government. The government would not interfere with the Dariqa's religious practice and the Seyyid could make pilgrimages as he wished, with comfort.

- The Seyyid would have nothing to do with the ordering of the tribes by the government, which was a matter dealt with through Aqils, not Sheikhs, who were concerned only with administering the Islamic *Sharia*.

- Any disputes between the Seyyid's Dariqa and the tribes would be referred to the government, and the Courts would be fair to all.

The letter was peremptorily finished off with the following ending:

It is now for you to accept these terms or reject them. There is nothing between yes or no.

If you accept it, come with my Ergo within a space of forty days.
The letter was signed by G.F. Archer, Governor, British Somaliland, Burao, 7 April 1920.

Names and titles of the 10-member *Ergo* were given as:

Sheikh Ismail bin Sheikh Ishaak, Head of the Salihiya Dariqa, Sheikh Abdillahi bin Sheikh Madar, Head of the Dariqa of Qadiriya, Sheikh Mohamed Hussein, Head of the Dandarawiya Daria, Aqil Ali Adan, Habar

Yunis, Rer Sugulleh, baha Deria, Aqil Jama Madar, Habar Yunis, Reer Sugulleh, Rer Robleh Sugulleh, Aqil Haji Ibrahim Warsame, Habar Yunis, Rer Sugulleh, baha Suguleh, Aqil Hirsi Hussein, Habar Yunis, Rer Hussein, Aqil Haji Abdillahi Jama, Habar Toljaala, Rer Dahir, Aqil Ahmed Yasin, Habar Toljaala, Sulamadoo, Aqil Ali Gulaid, Habar Awal, Rer Ahmed.

The Deputation left Burao on 9 April 1920, and reached the Seyyid's Camp at Shinileh on 28 April. After a fruitless meeting with Seyyid, the Deputation left the Seyyid Camp on 12 May and arrived back in Burao on 29 May 1920, empty-handed.

No sooner had the Deputation left the Seyyid Camp than the Dervishes carried out a surprise raid on the Friendlies on 20 May 1920. More raids by the Dervishes followed. What was thought to be a spent force (in other words, the Dervishes) was still very much alive.

The "Friendly clans" were eager to organize a clan-based force (*Col*, in Somali), to finish off the Dervishes. Governor Archer, who had similar ideas, called upon Aqil Haji Mohamed Bullaleh (Haji *Warabe*) who, legend had it, was imbued with the killer instinct. He gave him free hand to raise a clan-based force of 3,000 armed men from the Habar Yonis, Habar Je'lo and Dhulbahante clans. The Force, marching mostly at night, and picking up support on their way from those who had a grudge against the Dervishes, made contact with the Dervishes at Camp Qorahay in late July 1920. The Dervishes were taken by surprise and badly beaten. Many were killed and a few survivors, including the Seyyid, fled further south and settled a place on Webei Shabelle called Imay where, in the end, the Seyyid died of natural causes on or about 23 November 1920. As Mr Beachey put it, a Somali warrior was laid to rest [29].

It was recorded that the rag-tag, clanish force captured 700 rifles and 60,000 head of stock. The sharing of these spoils gave rise to what the Somalis called *Hagoogane*. Those who got the lion's share covered their heads (*hagoog*, in Somali) and triumphantly held them high, while those who got less sulked and covered their heads too, in disappointment. It can be said that the Dervishes were finally defeated in July 1920, by a Somali Force, not by the combined Imperial Force that was fighting against them.

The British consciously belittled the struggle of the Seyyid and his Dervishes. Perhaps they felt that Britain suffered reputational damage, as a result of the country's showing against the poorly-equipped Dervishes. So, they decided that the sooner that struggle was forgotten, the sooner the nation's injured pride would heal!

Left: Photo of the two men who were running the country and oversaw the final defeat of the Seyyid – Risaldar-Major Haji Farah Musa Igare on the left and Governor Archer on the right, c.1919 The photo is from Archer's book [30]. **Right:** I would have liked to juxtapose the photo on the left with that of the Seyyid, but as far as I know, such photo doesn't exist. As an inadequate substitute, I include the Statue of the Seyyid, erected in Mogadishu. I don't know whether it has survived the unfortunate turmoil in Mogadishu.

If we pause for a moment and reflect on what went on in the country in those 21 years (1900–1920), one cannot help concluding that it was, in effect, Somalis fighting against Somalis, with a handful of British officers and their colonial soldiers directing one side of the fight. The bulk of the fighting force was Somalis, the transport used for the military expeditions – consisting of camels, horses and mules – was mainly supplied by the Somalis. The Somalis even supplied some of the weapons used, in the form of spears. And, above all, the land on which the fighting occurred belonged to the Somalis. In other words, it could be said that it was an internecine civil conflict instigated by the British! Others may think differently. Anyway, the conflict in the country had its roots in the uncalled-for introduction of Christianity into the country.

The Somalis have differing ideas about the role the Seyyid played in the history of Somaliland. It is said that religious individuals do not make consummate politicians. (The aphorism "religion and politics don't mix" perhaps holds here!) One of the criticisms levied against the Seyyid is that he considered the Somalis who were not with him to be against him and thus antagonized many Somalis who were indifferent to the whole struggle.

In spite of all that, can't it be said that the Seyyid was a misunderstood prototype nationalist? Contemporary writings about the Seyyid were written by the foreign adventurers against whom he fought. A defeated rebel doesn't receive laurels. It is the victor, not the vanquished, who writes the history. It would be too much to expect objective judgement of the Seyyid's qualities by his foreign adversaries, who grudgingly described him as a fine tactician. He was true to his convictions and resisted falling for the tantalizing peace settlement offer of Governor Archer in April 1920.

As far as the Somali culture goes, he is recognized by those well-versed in this field as one of the greatest Somali poets. Regardless of different views about the Seyyid, the role he played in the history of Somaliland cannot be denied; and the history of Somaliland will not be complete without taking into account the Seyyid's role in that history.

Towards the end of 1921, Mr W. Churchill, this time in his capacity as Secretary of State for the Colonies, invited the governor of Somaliland, Mr Archer, and the Resident and General Officer commanding Aden to Cairo and asked them to work out the financial implications of amalgamating Somaliland and Aden. The discussions, which lasted about three months, were mainly conducted in Aden. In the end, it was on the cost involved in the proposed amalgamation that the plan foundered [30].

On his trip to Egypt, Governor Archer (on the right) took two lion cubs, from Somaliland for London Zoo. Photo from Archer's book [30]. In the days of the British Empire, it was not uncommon for British administrators of the British Dependencies to steal, from the Dependencies, works of art, and samples of fauna and flora and send them to museums, zoos and botanical gardens in Britain.

When Governor Archer returned from the talks in Aden to the country in early January 1922, he stated that:

The Protectorate government was to occupy the county, not to administer it. The country could be run by a political agent, as was the case in the 1880s. An enclave of about 2,500 sq. miles would be carved from the country. The main Centres would be Berbera, Hargeisa and Burao, and instead of DCs, political officers would be in charge of these Centres. The rest of the country would be handed over to Ethiopia or Italy. With regard to education, a few boys could be sent to Gordon Memorial College, Khartoum, Sudan, and the fees would be shared by the boys' parents and the government [31].

While the colonial government was floating such obnoxious ideas about the fate of the country, none of the Somalis in the protectorate had the faintest inkling of what was going on, nor were their opinions sought!

3.5 Attempt at introducing direct stock taxation and murder of A. Gibb, DC of Burao

In February 1922, in order to implement Mr Hussey's recommendations (details under 4.3), Governor Archer conducted consultations about the introduction of stock (sheep) tax with the Aqils (clan chiefs) and other elders in the main towns. He explained to them that he was planning to introduce taxation to raise local revenue to pay for education in the country. But the real purpose of the proposed taxation turned out to be a ploy to find funds for the upkeep of the Camel Corps and the Police, in other words, for the maintenance of law and order which was the major concern of the government.

The governor set the taxation at one sheep/100 sheep [32]. Hargeisa and Berbera elders were amenable to the governor's proposals. Archer then held the usual consultation meetings on taxation in Burao on 24 February 1922. He felt that it was not going to be plain sailing as the participants in the meeting struck a defiant attitude. When Haji Mohamed Bullaleh (Haji *Warabe*), the leader of the ramshackle multi-clan force which finally dispersed the remnants of the Seyyid's Dervishes in July 1920, raised his hand, the governor became despondent, as he did not expect a conciliatory contribution from Haji *Warabe*. Haji *Warabe*, true to form, told the governor that the government could ask the Aqils to collect the taxes, but if the owner of the sheep refused to part with his sheep and crossed the frontier into Ethiopia in order to avoid any payment, what would the Aqils do? He finished his intervention by telling the governor that the proposed taxation was not practical, but that they would consider it and give the governor their answer soon.

The elders, who participated in the meeting with the governor and who were led by Haji *Warabe*, gathered at a spot just outside the main town to discuss the issue of taxation. In the meantime, some hot-headed young men got wind of what the governor had proposed and they armed themselves and demonstrated on the west bank of the Tog (dry riverbed), not far from the Ina Igare "Gob Tree" (see photo below). The governor, together with the District Commissioner of Burao, Mr A. Gibb, and Haji Farah Musa Igare, Chief Adviser of the government, were having tea at a place close to the government fort, on the east bank of the riverbed, opposite Ina Igare Gob Tree, discussing what answer they should expect from Burao elders.

Ina Igare Gob Tree (the largest tree in the photo) on the west bank of the "Tog", under which Haji Farah Muse Igare used to hold court. There used to be a number of wells known as "Burao Wain" in Tog. Burao town was west of Gob Tree, before it was burnt down in 1922.

Burao Fort ("Kilaha" to the Somalis) built in 1902 on the east bank of the "Tog" as the Headquarters of the Somaliland Camel Corps. Photo (c.1910) from Drake-Brockman's book [11].

Then the governor and his advisers heard a gunshot in the direction of the town. When they heard a second gunshot, Mr Gibb rose to find out what was going on and to calm down the situation. The governor asked him to take his (the governor's) car. The governor's driver was Bahnan Hersi (in other words, Haji Bahnan, father of Adan Haji Bahnan, an educator). In the middle of the Tog (dry riverbed), Gibb got out of the car and walked towards the demonstrating young men. He then took fright at the excited gun-toting crowd and returned to the car. As he turned, someone shot him in the back, and he fell dead. Bahnan, who was later rewarded with an MBE, brought the body to the fort.

The governor immediately requested planes from Aden and, on 5 March 1922, after giving the public three hours' notice to clear the town and take with them what they could, Burao was bombed and burnt down to the ground – all except the Mosque. The cost of burning down the town was given as £500. So many innocent families lost their homes. Burning down people's homes was part of the "scorched earth" colonial policy, not only in Somaliland.

Through its informers, the government accepted that Faul Adan, *Habar Yonis*, *Rer Weid* clan, was the man who fired the first shot and Ali Amaan, *Habar Yonis*, *Reer Abdi Hirsi* clan, the man who fired the shot that killed Mr Gibb. Neither man was found guilty in a court of law – nor were the many innocent people who were compelled to contribute to the fine of 3,000 camels mentioned below.

Revenge for the murder of Mr Gibb [33]

To avenge Mr Gibb's murder, as if burning down Burao town was not enough, Governor Archer imposed a collective fine on the *Habar Yonis* clan, of 3,000 camels. This was equivalent to the *mag* (compensation for murder) of 30 Somali men. By burning down the town and imposing a fine of 3,000 camels on the clan, the governor wantonly used collective punishment without legal basis. There was no properly constituted court of law in the country that could hear Mr Gibb's murder case. The governor could make any decision that came into his head. In fact, the governors had almost absolute powers and paid scant attention, if any, to justice and legality in the country, as will be described later.

We will see further travesties of justice perpetrated against innocent Somalis. Along with Mr Gibb's murder died the idea of education and direct taxation; and Mr Hussey's recommendations were conveniently put in abeyance.

There was a story that a well-known Somali *Wadaad* (religious man) in Burao assessed the *mag* for the murder of Mr Gibb. He was alleged to have opined that the *mag* for the murder of a Somali man was 100 camels, and that of a Somali woman was 50 camels. So, the *mag* for the murder of Gibb should be less than that of a Somali woman and be 33⅓ camels, in other words, one third of the *mag* for the murder of a Somali man. The story maintained that the governor heard about the *Wadaad's* assessment and considered it insolent and was very incensed by it. To make his point, the governor imposed the fine of 3,000 on the clan suspected of committing the murder, and the fine was to be paid in 14 days! This was a collective punishment on an industrial scale and it was officially recorded as detailed in the table below.

The government was, rightly or wrongly, convinced that Haji Mohamed Bullaleh (Haji *Warabe*) had instigated the disturbance that led to the murder of Mr Gibb and declared Haji Mohamed a "wanted man". He took refuge on the Ethiopian side of the southern border of the protectorate. Given below, for historical interest, is the breakdown of how the government apportioned the fine, presumably in proportion to the assumed culpability of the different sub-clans concerned. Only Arab, *Rer* Ali sub-clan was not Habar Yonis clan, and *Rer* Ali sub-clan lived among the Habar Yonis clan.

Compensation (*mag* in Somali) per clan for the murder of Mr Gibb, DC of Burao, in Burao on 24 February 1922.

Clans	Fine (denominated in camels)
Reer Ainashe, Burale	500
Rer Tinashe, Bah Mun	500
Reer Ainashe, Bah Bale	250
	Total = 1250
Hirsi Bari, Reer Waraabe	250
Hirsi Bari, Reer Weid	250
Hirsi Bari, Reer Abdi Hirsi	250
	Total = 750
Reer Sugule, Bah Makahil	50
Reer Sugule, Bah Deria	50
Reer Sugule, Bah Roble	50
Reer Sugule, Bah Eili	50
Reer Sugule, Bah Adan Madobe	50
	Total = 250
Musa Arreh	50
Musa Ismail	50
Ali Said	200
Arab, Reer Ali	200
Ba Dhulbahante	50
Reer Hussein	100
Ugaad Omer	100
	Total = 750
	Grand total = 3,000 camels.

When the body of Mr Gibb was brought to the fort, some members of the Camel Corps were ordered to fire into the crowd, and they either fired over the head of the crowd or a short distance from the crowd. The protectorate government concluded that a Somali could not be relied on to fire on a Somali in a riot. The government recommended that some of the Camel Corps should be recruited from outside the protectorate. A contingent was brought from Nyasaland (present-day Malawi) in November 1922. The contingent was periodically replaced. The contingent was known in Somaliland as the "Yao", and was with the Somaliland Camel Corps at the beginning of World War II. The contingent's services were dispensed with when the protectorate government evacuated the country in 1940.

Also after the murder of Mr Gibb, two planes were kept in the country, at a cost of £500 per year. Whenever there was disturbance in any part of the protectorate, the planes were flown low over that area, as a show of force, to frighten the nomads and cause their livestock to stampede.

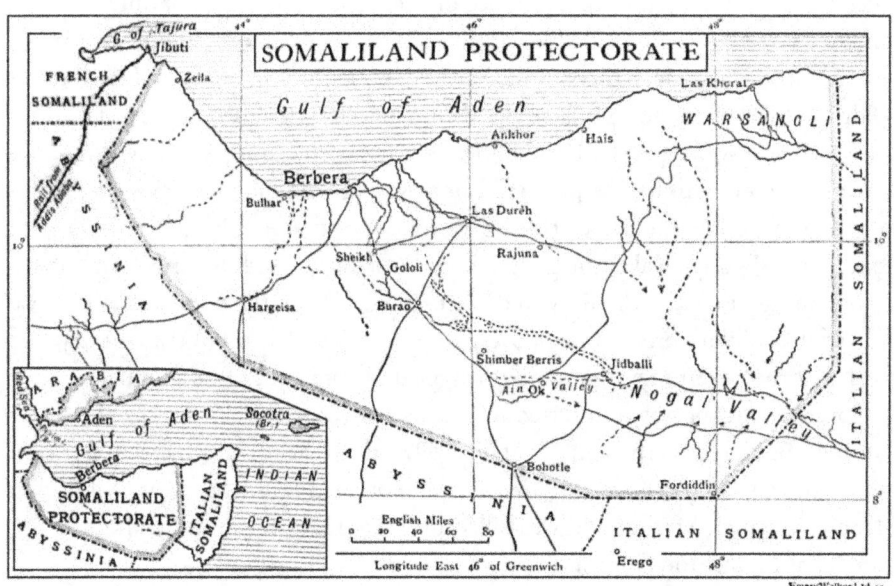

Map of Somaliland Protectorate in the 1950s

3.6 The protectorate government in the doldrums

The Dervishes left the scene in 1920. The Somaliland/Aden amalgamation project failed in 1922. An attempt to introduce direct stock (sheep) tax not only failed but ended in disaster in 1922. No forward-planning policy development of any description was in place. The so-called protectorate government found itself in the doldrums. There was not much of a government administration to talk of in the country. The government had no political vision for the country and was at a loss as to what to do with it. The phase of campaigns against the Dervishes gave way to a situation where the protectorate government drifted into a state of hibernation. When slightly awake, the government busied itself with issuing ordinances for one thing or another, mainly to extract revenues from the poor Somalis. It was only after a military protectorate government assumed control of the country in 1941 that the government hesitantly struggled to come out of its slumber.

Governor Archer was transferred to become Governor of Uganda. G.H. Summers became governor on 17 August 1922 in Archer's place. He was not new to the country. He was in the Army and was wounded in the battle of Dul-Madobe in which Mr Corfield was killed in 1913. He also led one of the campaigns against the Dervishes.

He dropped Governor Archer's stock tax, but raised the customs duties from 15% to 25%, to make up for the supposed local revenue that the failed stock tax might have generated.

On 26 January 1926, Mr Summers was replaced as governor of the country by H.B. Kittermaster (*Kidhmaster* to the Somalis). Fairly soon after his arrival, he realized the absurdity of the Anglo-Ethiopian Treaty of 1897. He could not help commenting on how the British government shamelessly dishonoured all the "treaties" it entered into with the Somali clans. He wrote in 1927:

> *The treaty with Gadabursi signed by Major Hunter in 1884 and the treaty with Ethiopia signed by Mr Rennell Rodd in 1897 are contradictory. In view of the latter treaty, our claim to protection of the whole Gadabursi Clan is legally insupportable. Presumably the latter treaty, being international, will be held as having greater validity than the treaty with a small African Clan. We have placed ourselves in a position in which one of the two agreements signed by us must be abandoned. The same situation pertains with regard to Isa and Habar Awal Clans with whom we also have signed treaties [34].*

The governor's remarks about how the British government had disregarded the treaties were prescient, bearing in mind what the British Colonial Secretary told the Somaliland Delegation in 1955 in London, in connection with the Hawd/Reserved Area. Successive British governments were all along aware of the anomalous situation but they put off the day when their deception would be revealed (discussed later under 3.13).

Creation of districts in the country [35]

The Aden-based political Agent for Somaliland designated Berbera and Zeila as judicial districts under the Order-in-Council of 1899. As time went on, some semblance of limited and moribund administration, run the on the cheap, was tentatively introduced. No meaningful socio-economic development of any kind was attempted at all. Three further districts – Hargeisa, Burao and Erigavo – were established in the country in 1927, under the Ordinance of 1926. Perhaps because of the inclement weather in Zeila, the District Commissioner (DC) of Zeila was headquartered in Borama and travelled to Zeila as his duties required.

Governor Kittermaster decided that a district would consist of the "areas" normally roamed about by the different clans under the administrative control of the DCs of Zeila, Hargeisa, Berbera, Burao and Erigavo. The government mentioned "areas" inhabited by mobile nomadic communities whose movements were (and are) dictated by the weather – in other words, the availability of pasture and water for their livestock. In this sense, the communities could find themselves in different Districts at certain times of the year. In my view, a better way of creating Districts would have been to plan the Districts in such a way that each District would contain a mixture of the different clans, to minimize clan affiliations.

The protectorate government was not inclined to think in this way. And what about the Somaliland governments which, in this day and age, established Districts and Regions in the country on clan basis? They should have known better! They could have restructured the whole internal administrative boundaries inherited from the colonial government, rather than ape it!

During the stagnation period, the protectorate government formalized a regressive and unjust measure which was already in operation for a long time without legal basis. The measure was that of Capital Punishment which was formally legalized in 1928 under Ordinance No. 4 of 1928 [36].

Somaliland for disposal in the international market [37]

Ever since the beginnings of the Dervish struggle in the country at the dawn of the 20th century, on several occasions, the British government raised the question of what to do with the country. The government wished to wash its hands of the country, but the question was, how?

The government toyed with different scenarios for the future of the country. An opportunity was presented by the great depression in the 1930s. During that period, in 1931, when the international financial markets collapsed and trade was depressed, the British government was engaged in cutting expenditure drastically. It was during that exercise that the British government set up an inter-departmental committee of the British government to look into what could be done with Somaliland. Perhaps the government intended to make Somaliland a casualty of the great depression and abandon it! The Committee discussed various options including, but not limited to, the following:

- For the government to remain in the coastal strip – ie Zeila, Bulahar, Berbera and Las Qorey – and offer the rest of the country to either Ethiopia or Italy
- To cede the country to Ethiopia or Italy
- To amalgamate the country with Aden, to effect some economies by running one country instead of two
- To put the country under Mandate of the League of Nations
- To dispose of the country in the most profitable market
- To introduce a forward development policy and possibly annex the country at some future date
- To administer the country at minimum cost and without meaningful development, and they called this the "Stagnation Policy"

The British government opted for the final option in the above list. One can only say that the British government was physically represented in Somaliland Protectorate, but *not in spirit!*

To implement the "stagnation policy", in 1931 the Colonial Office asked the Governor of the protectorate, Mr Kittermaster, to reduce the budget of the protectorate by £30,000. The existing budget was £135,953 (about 60% of it for law and order). In his wisdom, he proposed the following reductions [38]:

- Restricting medical services to save £4,000
- Abolishing the education budget to save £900
- Closing down the Agriculture Department to save £1,808
- Closing down the Veterinary Department to save £2,935
- Closing down the wireless stations at Zeila, Borama and Erigavo to save £200
- Changing the Governor's title to Commissioner to save £3,000
- Closing down Gigjiga Consulate to save £13,000
- Effecting overall contraction of the government to save £20,000

In the end, in his eagerness to cut the budget drastically, he reduced it not by £30,000, as requested, but by £45,843! The governor, rather than prepare a budget for the country, would perhaps have preferred to get rid of the country itself!

In 1931, the annual expenditure on education was given as £465. There were no government-maintained educational facilities of any sort in the country. The only thing the government used to do was to subsidize the small private school in Berbera with a small amount of money. In 1931, two men were sent to Sudan on a two-month course on gum sorting and grading, at a cost of £200. It couldn't have been that the whole amount of £465 was used on education in 1931! The figure of £900 budgeted for education was an exaggeration.

The government took a census of the population in 1931 and the result was as follows:

Government population census of Somaliland (1931)

Nationality	Number
Europeans and other white population	68
Indians	520
Persians	12
Arabs	1,614
Turkish	11
Egyptians	7
Ethiopians	100
Sudanese	89
Natives of Nyasaland (*Yao* in the Camel Corps)	258
Swahilis	4
Native population (ie Somalis) estimated	**344,700**

In the 1911 census population of the coastal towns of Zeila, Bulahar and Berbera, the Indian population was 741, and that of the Arabs was 1857 (see 4.1)

The Somali population was not included in the 1911 census. That was the time the so-called protectorate administration was cooped up in the coastal towns of the country, as already described under 3.4.

3.7 Joint Anglo-Ethiopian Boundary Commission

The British Section final report [39]

Early in the 1920s the British and the Ethiopian governments started preparations for the demarcation of the Somaliland/Ethiopia boundary. The two governments formed a Joint Anglo-Ethiopian Boundary Commission.

When the British government studied the Anglo-Ethiopian Treaty of 1897 closely, it turned out to be like opening a can of worms! The treaty threw up a whole lot of contradictions vis-à-vis the other treaties which the British government entered into with the Somaliland clans. It seemed so hopeless that the Colonial Office suggested scrapping the 1897 Treaty and proposing a new treaty to the Ethiopian government. In 1933, the Colonial Office put forward several scenarios for extending the boundary south, at least, to *Wal-waal* and *War-dheer*, as shown in the map opposite. In return, Zeila would be given to Ethiopia so that it would have an outlet to the sea [40].

In the map, the Colonial Office indicated, with a line of red dashes, where the southern boundary should have been extended. The British Foreign Office objected to the idea, maintaining that the Anglo-Ethiopian treaty of 1897 was between two sovereign States and could not be summarily disregarded. When it came to the treaties, the Foreign Office always prevailed, by siding with the Ethiopians and upholding the 1897 treaty. Discussions on the process of demarcating the Somaliland/Ethiopia boundary continued into the mid-1930s. However, the proposed extension of the boundary to the south never materialized. As the caption of the photograph of the Anglo-Ethiopian Boundary Commission indicates, the Joint Commission had no authority to reinterpret the 1897 treaty.

The people of Somaliland, who were the most affected by the boundary, neither participated in the work of the Commission nor were they consulted about the boundary. For demarcating the boundary, the Commission followed a straight geometrical line derived from aerial photography.

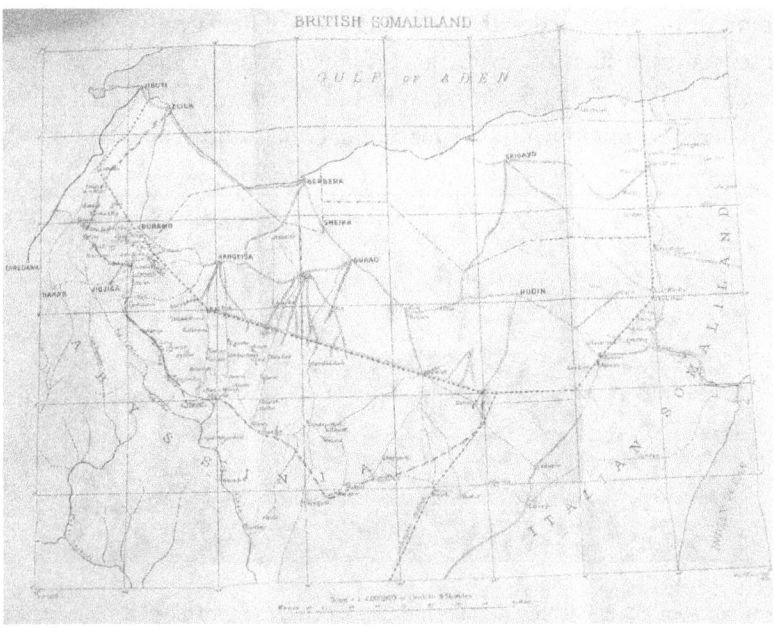

Map (1920s) showing where the British Colonial Office thought the southern border between Somaliland and Ethiopia should have been extended (originally shown by a line of red dashes).

Once the Commission fixed the straight line between two points with their survey instruments, and with the help of aerial photographs, they cleared from the bush about two metres on either side of the line. The purpose of the cleared strip was to serve as a road for their lorries, which carried their field equipment, including tents for accommodation. The cleared strip was also the actual demarcation line of the Ethiopia–Somaliland Protectorate boundary which eventually was used as a road. The Commission signposted the boundary line with hundreds of stone pillars, about two km. apart, as shown by the photo below. Mr D. Walsh, with umbrella and engaged in surveying in the photo on the left, was not only a member of the Joint Commission but was also the District Commissioner of Borama and he knew that part of the country very well.

Some members of the Commission putting up stone pillars (c.1933)

The Commission continued with this straight line of demarcation, regardless of the consequences of such a demarcation, as shown by the photo below. A farm near Borama town was divided into two by the demarcation line, each half ending up in a different country, ie in Ethiopia and in Somaliland Protectorate!

The demarcation line at Dababur, near Borama. Line A points to one of the pillars, indicating the demarcation line. Line B shows how a farm near Borama is divided by the demarcation line, ie half in Ethiopia and the other in Somaliland Protectorate.

The British team of the Joint Anglo-Ethiopian Boundary Commission, 1932–1935. The arbitrary line demarcating the Somaliland Protectorate-Ethiopia boundary divided families and clans, with dire consequences for Somaliland. The original caption to the photograph indicates that the Joint Commission had "no power to adjust the frontier" and no authority to reinterpret the 1897 treaty.

Because of the tract of land being cleared for the Commission lorries to pass through, the protectorate government deceitfully told the public that the Commission was constructing a road.

The actual demarcation work took about three years, from January 1932 to February 1935. The Somali nomads in the areas were ill-informed about the purpose of the "unusual" activities of white men moving around in the grazing areas in the south of the country. Various misleading stories were put out by the protectorate government, for example, as already mentioned, that a road was being constructed. However, when the nomads finally realized that a boundary was being demarcated, beyond which they might not be allowed to take their livestock freely to the south, the nomads in the *Hawd* area started to knock down randomly some of the pillars.

Governor Kittermaster was irritated by the nomads' behaviour and issued a short ordinance to deal with situation. The governors, as a whole, used to issue ordinances without much regard for legal niceties nor for the practicalities of enforcing of such ordinances. To show how the governors exercised absolute powers in the country and the unjust collective punishments they imposed on the Somalis, it would be instructive to note the scan of Governor Kittermaster's short ordinance, issued in September 1931, about the damaged boundary demarcation pillars [41]:

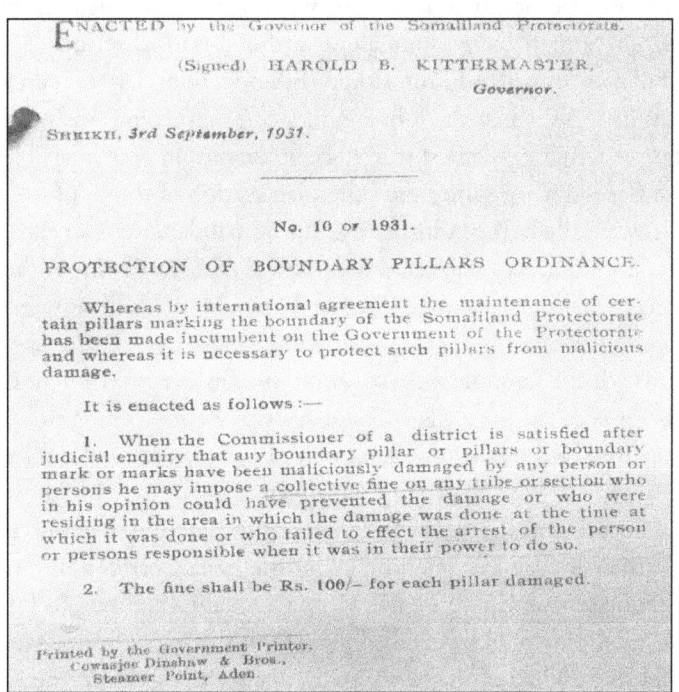

A short ordinance, issued by Governor Kittermaster, in September 1931, concerning the "Protection of Boundary Pillars"

This can hardly be considered a model for enlightened legislation. How could such measures be applied to nomadic communities, continually on the move, in search of water and pasture for their livestock? From where did the nomads derive the power to arrest each other? If anything, that was tantamount to inciting fighting among the nomads!

"Judicial enquiry" in the context of the Ordinance is nonsense. In my research, I did not come across a District Commissioner or a Governor in Somaliland Protectorate who was said to have had legal training, and at that time no national or foreign lawyers practised in the country. The country suffered from legal and judicial deficiency.

In spite of the ordinance, the nomads continued with their protests. It is to be noted that the Ordinance is dated September 1931, while the actual demarcation work started in January 1932. Before this date, there were no pillars in existence. Governor Kittermaster must have issued the Ordinance retroactively! I would not be surprised if this were the case. Regarding the idea that a Somali might arrest another Somali, perhaps Governor Kittermaster was thinking of the legal practice called "citizen's arrest" in Britain, where a citizen might arrest a person accused of wrong doing. But British citizens have rights and duties under the government for which they themselves have voted into office. This was a far cry from the situation in Somaliland Protectorate, which was under the control of a foreign power under which the Somalis had no say in how the government was formed or how the country was run. Somaliland was not alone in this abnormal set-up.

The work of the Somaliland Protectorate/Ethiopia boundary demarcation continued. It was in 1934, when the Joint Boundary Commission was still engaged in the demarcation activities that a disturbance broke out, in which Mr Herr Beitz (the German Chief Technician of the Ethiopian section of the Joint Boundary Commission) was killed. The culprits were the Somali labourers working for the Commission. Some sources suspected that the "coolies" realized that the Commission was actually making a boundary between Somaliland Protectorate and Ethiopia.

In the course of the boundary demarcation, the British government offered Ethiopia what was called the Zeila corridor, a strip of land leading from the Ethiopian territory to the Port of Zeila, to give Ethiopia access to the Red Sea. In return, the Ethiopians were to give up the grazing Hawd Area, which would become part of Somaliland Protectorate. It was at this juncture that a Member of the British Parliament raised a question about the Zeila Corridor and in reply, the Secretary of State for the Colonies, Mr M. MacDonald, (Hansard, 8 July 1935), stated: "Consultation would have taken place with the tribe affected with a view to the transfer to Ethiopia of the necessary rights in the area concerned." No land transfers took place. However, a similar proposed land-swap involving Zeila is discussed later, under 3.12.

Governor Kittermaster was replaced, as governor, by A.S. Lawrance (Laaran, to the Somalis) on 18 June 1932. Governor Lawrance introduced another regressive and unjust measure which had been already in operation for a long time, without legal basis – collective punishment. When the protectorate government was planning to legislate for collective punishment, the government took its cue from the Somali clans' practice of *Xaq* and *Xeer*, a practice that was (and is), in effect, collective punishment. The government reasoned thus:

> *The Somali social structure is based on collective responsibility and collective ownership. The Somali society is composed of mag-paying-groups (mag-wadaag or mag-sharing) which are governed by the Somali Customary Law known as "Xaq and Xeer", in Somali)'* [42]

Collective punishment was eventually legalized in 1933 under the ordinance of 1933 [43]. Just as capital punishment was applied both to the guilty and the innocent so was the collective punishment applied similarly. Both collective and capital punishments were based on the colonial policy of being "guilty by association"! To show how wide, as it was vague, was the net which the government cast in collective punishment, a scan of the second article of the ordinance is reproduced on the next page.

Political cases (ie murder and robbing stock) were settled by the application of *Xaq* and *Xeer*. The Article mentions "area" without defining it. Both collective and capital punishments were introduced to, supposedly, maintain law and order. But in fact they resulted in punishing both the guilty and the innocent alike, in a country where a judicial system did not exist. At times, the British government was alarmed by the way the protectorate government was playing fast and loose with justice in the country. For example, the Legal Secretary was sometimes both the legal adviser to the government and the judge of the protectorate court. It was like an Attorney General advising on a case today and then tomorrow, as the Chief Justice, trying the same case. (Why this was so, see later.)

In this regard, isn't there some truth in the government's reasoning in introducing collective punishment, given the way we practised, and still do, *Xaq* and *Xeer*?[5] Still, I condemn the cruel protectorate government policy of imposing collective punishment on the people of Somaliland. The government should have known better. Two wrongs do not make a right! I believe that any socially conscious Somali would find *Xeer* repugnant.

---

[5] *Xaq* and *Xeer* go together. *Xeer* is the customary law in Somaliland and it is clan-based. It does not take into account natural justice. Both guilty and innocent clan members share the crime committed by an individual member of the clan. *Xaq* (compensation for murder and wounding) as practised in Somaliland is also unjust. Clan members share the compensation for the murder or wounding committing by a member of the clan. *Xaq* should be decoupled from *Xeer* and be dealt with under the enacted laws of the country. *Xeer* has to be abolished (also see the Appendix).

AN ORDINANCE.

ENACTED by the Commissioner of the Somaliland Protectorate.

(Signed) A. S. LAWRANCE.
Commissioner.

SHEIKH, *2nd July, 1933.*

No. 4 OF 1933.

AN ORDINANCE TO MAKE PROVISION WITH RESPECT TO COLLECTIVE PUNISHMENT.

It is hereby enacted as follows:—

1. This Ordinance may be cited as "The Collective Punishment Ordinance, 1933." — Short title

2. The Commissioner may impose fines in money or in kind as he may decide on all or any inhabitants of any township, village, area or district or members of any tribe, sub-tribe or community, if, after inquiry, he is satisfied— — Fines on townships villages, etc. accessory to crimes.

   (a) that they or any of them have colluded with any criminal, or harboured, or rescued, or attempted to rescue, or failed to take all reasonable means to prevent the escape of, any criminal or any person accused of having committed a crime;

   (b) that they or any of them have suppressed, or combined to suppress, evidence in any criminal case or in any political case, investigation, or inquiry, or in any inquest;

   (c) that stolen property, or property which might reasonably be suspected of being the proceeds, or part of the proceeds, of a theft having been traced to within the limits of their township, village, area, district, tribe, sub-tribe or community, they have failed or neglected to restore the property or to take on the track beyond the limits of such township, village, area, district, tribe, sub-tribe or community,

and may order the whole or any part of the fines recovered under the provisions of paragraphs (a), (b) and (c) to be applied in compensation for the injury caused by the offence of which the criminal is accused or to which the criminal case, or the political case, investigation, inquiry, or inquest relates, or in compensation to

An ordinance enacted by Governor A.S. Lawrance in July 1933, making provision for collective punishment in the British Somaliland Protectorate.

It is to be noted that, as far as the protectorate government was concerned, collective punishment was a convenient means of raising local revenue during the colonial rule. If a clan member, usually man, committed an offence against another clan and the culprit's clan couldn't or wouldn't hand in the culprit, the government would send out a detachment of the *Ilaalo* or the Camel Corps (later the Scouts) which would round up a portion of the livestock of the suspected culprit's clan. The government would auction the impounded livestock, pay some of the proceeds to the aggrieved party and keep the remainder in the government coffers! The government usually maximized the number of the impounded stock for this purpose. Sometimes, the portion which the government kept was called "Court Fees", when no Court was held for the case at issue. Perhaps the government meant the cost incurred in rounding up the livestock!

As mentioned earlier, Governor Kittermaster issued a retroactive ordinance in 1931 about damaged pillars, when there were no such pillars along the Somaliland Protectorate/Ethiopia boundary. Governor Lawrance did similar thing in 1935 against a Somali named Mohamed Warsame (described as of *Habar Awal, Makahil* clan). Mohamed used to be an employee of the Ethiopian government and had also acquired American nationality. He was born in Somaliland, had two brothers in the Somaliland Protectorate Police force and had property in Burao. He wanted to visit his mother in Berbera and also to dispose of some of his property in Burao. Governor Lawrance refused Mohamed entry to the country. Somehow, Mohamed entered the country in July 1935 without the governor's knowledge. When the governor came to know about Mohamed's presence in the country, there was no law that the governor could use against the Somali. The governor then immediately revised an Ordinance on Immigration which he had enacted in August 1935 and made it retroactive to 1 July 1935, so that it would be applicable to Mohamed Warsame [44].

Mohamed appealed to the Secretary of State for the Colonies. The Colonial Office's only intervention was that, since the case involved the USA and questions might be asked in the British Parliament, the governor should provide the Colonial Secretary with reason(s) why the Somali was denied entry into the protectorate. I did not find any reply by the governor, nor do I know whether he took any further action against Mohamed Warsame. That was how the colonial governors in the country debased legality and justice in the country. In this regard, British colonial governors in those days were not fussy about the concept of legality.

How the British government legislated in its colonies/protectorates

To legislate in the colonies, the Colonial Office used to bypass the scrutiny of the Parliament. The Colonial Office used a monarchical procedure through a select group, appointed by the monarch and called the Privy Council. The Council advised the monarch on such issues as legislating in the Colonies. The advice of the Council used to be issued in the name of the monarch in a legal form called Order-in-Council. Thus, whenever the Secretary of State for the Colonies wished to issue a piece of legislation for the Colonies, he would first submit his proposal to the Privy Council. The Council would review the proposal, on behalf of the monarch, and the final decision would be published as Order-in-Council. The governors of the Colonies used to base the local Ordinances which they enacted on such Orders-in-Council. It was very unlikely that such Orders would have passed muster had they been subjected to Parliamentary scrutiny.

3.8 Legalized injustice in Somaliland Protectorate

As mentioned elsewhere, Somaliland was under the control of the Bombay government from August 1884 to September 1898. During that period and before, there was no written law applicable to the country. Still the Bombay government illegally raised local revenues from the Somalis to finance their occupation of the Somaliland Coast. It is to be noted that both the Indian and Bombay governments were under the British government. So, Somaliland was a British Dependency under another British Dependency (ie the Bombay government).

In October 1898, the control of the country was transferred to the British Foreign Office. It was in October 1899 that the British government introduced the first Order-in-Council, entitled the "Somaliland Order-in-Council" of 1899 for the administration of the country [45]. The Order also established, *for the first time*, that the Somaliland legal system would be based on the *British India Laws*, for both civil and criminal cases. The Order allowed for the lay British Political Agents for Somaliland (who were based in Aden, Berbera, Bulahar and Zeila) to pass sentences, including the death sentence, on the Somalis. Cases resulting from inter-clan conflicts and away from the Coastal limit, which was not more than a few miles, were labelled as "Jungle Cases" and were treated politically rather than judicially, a service which did not exist. This meant carrying out punitive raids on the clans concerned and impounding portions of their livestock, mainly for the coffers of the occupying coastal authority.

The Order also for the first time made provision for raising local revenue. The Order introduced a whole raft of Indian Acts, including the Indian Penal Code, Land Acquisition Act, Whipping Act, Prevention of Cruelty to Animals Act, etc. Whipping, as part of punishment for both the juveniles and adults, was in practice in Somaliland Protectorate up to the late 1930s. It was a degrading practice. The Prevention of Cruelty to Animals Act perhaps reflected the custom of the vegan Hindus who do not eat animal products and to whom cows are sacred. In those days, the Somalis mainly lived on milk and meat. The government was concerned about cruelty to animals, although Somaliland was then famed for being big-game hunting ground – as a sport – by British officials and civilians! Some officials of Somaliland Protectorate even boasted of selling trophies from the wild animals they killed to supplement their salaries.

Under the 1899 Order, the British government issued the Somaliland Order-in-Council of 1906, which, for the first time, authorized the Commissioner of Somaliland to legislate for the country, by issuing Ordinances for the administration of the country, including local revenue raising [46]. The title of "Governor" of the country was introduced in 1919.

The Order-in-Council of 1929 further elaborated the sanctioned injustices in the country, as follows [47]:

> In all cases, civil and criminal, to which natives are parties, every Court (a) shall be guided by native law, so far as it is applicable and it is not repugnant to justice and morality, or inconsistent with any Order-in-Council or Ordinance; and (b) shall decide all such cases according to substantial justice, without excessive regard to technicalities of procedure and without undue delay.

Article 36 of the Order stated that:

> Subject to the approval of the Secretary of State, the protectorate Court may frame Rules of Procedure and other Rules, consistent with this Order, for the better execution of the provisions herein contained in respect of civil or criminal proceedings, and for regulating the conditions of which persons other than parties may be permitted to practice as advocates or solicitors in any Court, and for suspending or excluding (subject to a right of appeal) such persons from practice in case of misconduct.

"Native law", as far as the Order-in-Council was concerned, meant *Xaq* and *Xeer* – the Somaliland Customary Law which was then practised in Somaliland Protectorate (as it is now!) and which was (or is) *neither just nor moral*. (For my personal views on clanism, *Xaq* and *Xeer*, see the Appendix.)

Since no Law School in the world taught *Xaq* and *Xeer*, the Order-in-Council, in effect, excluded foreign lawyers from practising in the country. There were then no national lawyers and the prospect of their becoming available any time soon was in the distant future.

Even before the Order, lay colonial administrators used to hear court cases, including murder/manslaughter cases. Thus, the Order legitimized what was already going on, and this spared the protectorate administrators the prospect of being legally challenged in the so-called courts in the protectorate. The Somalis, even if they could afford it, were not allowed to engage lawyers to plead their cases in the courts.

The requirement of the Order-in-Council that court cases be decided according to "substantial justice, without excessive regard to technicalities and procedure", clearly indicated that murder or manslaughter cases involving Somalis would be heard by lay colonial administrators who would cut corners and pass sham judgements. As was very clear in the way the Order-in-Council was framed, justice and legality meant nothing in Somaliland Protectorate. This was abundantly confirmed by the following murder case.

In February 1936, under the 1929 Order-in-Council, Mr Plowman, District Commissioner of Burao, who, as far as I could ascertain, had no legal qualification, passed death sentences on four men accused of shooting and murdering Mohamed Khalif of Dhulbahante, *Reer Hirsi Egal* sub-clan [48].

The condemned men were, as usual, not legally represented in their Court trial and their estimated ages ranged from 17 to 25 years. They were listed as:

Abdi Farah,	*Dhulbahante, Reer Wais Adan sub-clan,*
Ali Abdi,	" " " "
Ismaan ALI,	" " " "
Saleyman Ahmed,	" " " "

It was not exactly established who fired the shot that killed Mohamed Khalif. It was mentioned that there was blood feud between the sub-clans of *Reer Wais Adan* and *Reer Hirsi Egal*. It was stated that the four men were avenging the murder of a man of their sub-clan, who was murdered by the *Reer Hirsi Egal* sub-clan. It was, however, stated that Mohamed Khalif himself had nothing to do with the planning and the execution of that murder.

The only authority to which the condemned four men could appeal was the Governor of the protectorate, Mr Lawrance, who also had no legal qualification. In April 1936, Governor Lawrance *alone*, as Judge and Jury of the protectorate Court of Appeal at Berbera, heard pleas and denials from the condemned men; but the governor upheld the death sentences. The men's relatives in Aden engaged a lawyer who drafted an appeal to the governor. The appeal heavily criticized the death sentences and exposed that the whole court procedures were legally flawed. The governor could not defend his decision and commuted the death sentences to 20 years' imprisonment (equivalent to life imprisonment).

Strangely enough, the Secretary to the government was legally qualified, but he was not allowed to get involved in the protectorate Courts, except when the governor was away, in which case he would act for the governor to hear appeals from the District Courts. The Secretary was otherwise engaged in routine administrative work.

The legal adviser of the Colonial Office, Sir Busche, was intrigued by what was going on in the protectorate Courts and found the whole situation comical. He wrote:

> *I still try to see the humour of the remarkable situation in which the one lawyer in the protectorate decodes telegrams and pays the subordinate staff while people who are not lawyers try murder cases in court* [49].

In spite of this damning observation, the Colonial Office would not intervene!

Some Members of the British Parliament came to hear about the murder case. Governor Lawrance suspected that Haji Fareh Omaar, who was a long-standing critic of the protectorate government, might have passed on information about the murder case to the Members of Parliament (MPs). The governor's suspicion was well founded. It was reported in 1934 that Haji Fareh, unknowingly, confided to a Somali "agent" who was spying on him while in Dire Dawa, that he often sent information to the British government about Somalis being hanged without proper trial [50]. Haji Fareh had a Somali contact, named Ismail Telephone, who lived in London. Ismail had his own contacts among the British Parliamentarians whom he used to brief about events in Somaliland Protectorate. That was how it came about that the Secretary of State for the Colonies was occasionally ambushed by MPs who asked him awkward questions about Somaliland Protectorate. These MPs were concerned about the lack of judicial practice in Somaliland Protectorate. In this respect, and in particular the above-mentioned murder case, I present below a few exchanges which took place in the British Parliament, quoted from *Hansard,* (the official record of the proceedings of the British Parliament).

Questions raised in the British Parliament on the judicial practice (or lack of it) in British Somaliland Protectorate [51]

Hansard reports the following Parliamentarian exchanges (*Hansard*, 8 February 1938). Sir Arnold Wilson asked the Secretary of State for the Colonies:

> **Sir Arnold Wilson, MP:** *(1) what, if any, legal qualifications are possessed by judges in British Somaliland who have power, respectively, to pass, and to hear appeals against, death sentences on defendants who are not permitted to be heard by counsel; and whether he has now reviewed the question of judicial arrangements in this Protectorate and has in hand the issue of rules of procedure under Article 36 of the Somaliland Order-in-Council, 1929, (2) whether he has now reviewed the practice of the protectorate Court in Somaliland, established under the Somaliland Order-in-Council, 1929, to refuse to persons accused of criminal offences, who might on conviction be sentenced to death, leave to be heard by counsel; and, if so, what is the present position?*

> **Mr Ormsby-Gore:** *(Secretary of State for the Colonies): At present the members of the courts empowered to pass death sentences, and to hear appeals against such sentences, in British Somaliland are not required to possess legal qualifications. My Hon. and Gallant Friend is aware that the question of amending the judicial arrangements in the protectorate, including the question of representation of accused persons by counsel, has been engaging my attention.*

The questions continued the next day and Sir Arnold Wilson again addressed the Secretary of State for the Colonies (*Hansard*, 9 February 1938)

> **Sir Arnold Wilson, MP:** *How many sentences of death have been passed in British Somaliland during the past 10 years; and in how many of these cases have been reversed or commuted on appeal?*

> **Mr Ormsby-Gore:** *In the 10-year period 1928–1937 inclusive, 30 sentences of death were passed in British Somaliland. Of these 3 were quashed on appeal and 13 were commuted.*

On 13 April, Mr Ammon, MP, asked the Secretary of State for the Colonies (*Hansard*, 13 April 1938):

> **Mr Ammon, MP:** *Whether he is in a position to announce a decision as the result of his inquiries into the judicial arrangements, including the question of the representation by counsel, in British Somaliland?*

> **Mr Ormsby-Gore:** *After consultation with the Governor I have decided on a re-organization of the judicial arrangements in the protectorate. The legal secretary will become a member of the protectorate court when sitting either as a Court of original jurisdiction or as a Court hearing appeals from district magistrates. Advocates will be allowed to appear before the protectorate Court in cases of murder or manslaughter. The re-organization will be put into effect as soon as the necessary arrangements can be made.*

Questions to the new Secretary of State for the Colonies (*Hansard*, 25 May 1938):

> **Mr Ammon, MP:** *How many judges or magistrates with legal qualifications now hold judicial posts in British Somaliland; whether there are any counsel habitually practising in that Protectorate; and whether, in view of the fact that certain Somalis who were sentenced to death in 1936 and whose sentences were later commuted were not defended at their trial, and of the fact that hitherto judges in the protectorate Courts did not have any legal qualifications, he will order a re-trial of these men, with adequate legal representation, before a qualified legal tribunal?*

> **Mr MacDonald:** *(new Secretary of State for the Colonies): The answer to the first two parts of the question is that there are none at present; but, as my predecessor informed the Hon. Member on 13 April, the Legal Secretary, an officer with legal qualifications, is to become a member of the protectorate Court and advocates are to be allowed to appear in cases of murder and manslaughter. With regard to the third part of the question, I have no power to order a re-trial.*

Mr McGovern, MP, asked the Secretary of State for the Colonies (*Hansard*, 6 July 1938):

> **Mr McGovern, MP:** *whether he will consider allowing a fresh trial to Abdi Farah, Ali Abdi, Ismaan Ali and Saleyman Ahmed, who were sentenced to death in February 1936, which sentence was subsequently commuted to imprisonment for 20 years, and who were refused permission to*

be represented by lawyers at their trial, and allowing them to be represented by lawyers at this fresh trial?

Mr MacDonald: *I would refer the Hon. Member to the reply which I gave on 25 May to a question by the Hon. Member for Camberwell, North (Mr Ammon).*

Mr McGovern, MP: *Is there any intention of granting a fresh trial to these men, in order to give them the opportunity of being represented in a proper way?*

Mr MacDonald: *As I said in the answer to which I referred the Hon. Member, and of which I am sending him a copy, I have no power to order such a new trial.*

Mr McGovern: *Cannot the Right Hon. Gentleman recommend that consideration should be given to it, seeing that these people feel that great injustice has been done owing to the fact that they were not properly represented at a proper trial? Cannot the Right Hon. Gentleman make representations on the matter?*

Mr MacDonald: *I have already covered that point in the answer I have already given.*

Mr McGovern: *Will the Right Hon. Gentleman answer my question: Is he prepared to make representations, if he has not already done so?*

Mr MacDonald: *I have no power to interfere in the matter.*

The Parliamentarian exchanges quoted above say it all! Somaliland Protectorate was a place where justice was not served. When the Secretary of State for the Colonies replied that he had no power to interfere in the murder case sentence, he was just reconfirming the Order-in-Council of 1929 under which the death sentence, later commuted by the governor, was passed. So, the Secretary of State for the Colonies had to stonewall direct questioning on the matter. After all, it was the Colonial Office which introduced the Order-in-Council in the first place.

According to the reply of the Secretary of State for the Colonies, Mr Orsmby-Gore, on 13 April 1938, it would be the first time that legal representation in murder and manslaughter court cases was, in principle, accepted. This "concession" applied only to protectorate courts (appeal cases) and did not extend to District Courts nor to civil court cases. In fact, all that changed was that the legally qualified Secretary to the government would hear appeal cases, and, in his absence, the lay governor would act for him. The legal issue really remained unsolved. The successive protectorate governors were in no mood to implement Article 36 of the Order-in-Council. They did not like the idea of having lawyers in the protectorate; they viewed lawyers more as a hindrance than a help. The Order-in-Council of 1929, which legalized *Xaq* and *Xeer*, as practised in the protectorate, was not amended before August 1953.

The senseless murder case (Mohamed Khalif) interested me for no other reason than it was a mockery of justice all round! My purpose of this write-up of the murder case was twofold: first, to put in the public domain the fact that the British government, by issuing the Orders-in-Council of 1898 and 1929 *deliberately legalized injustice* and *illegality* in Somaliland Protectorate. The magnitude of injustice perpetrated against the people of Somaliland during the British Colonial rule is difficult to imagine. Lay British administrators in the so-called protectorate courts passed death sentences, without legal basis, on the Somalis accused of murder, and the defendants could only appeal to a lay governor. The system was devoid of legality. The protectorate government was the *legislative, executive* and the *judiciary*, all rolled into one. There was no separation of power – worse than the worst dictatorship. Few individual Somalis (more accurately, clans) could afford to engage a foreign lawyer who could prepare for them an appeal to the Privy Council against the judgement of the governor on death sentences.

The hanging of the 14 Somalis during the 10-year period 1928–1937 (see Parliamentary exchanges quoted above), and those before and after them who met similar fate, can only be described as extrajudicial killings.

What masqueraded as law courts in the protectorate were nothing of the sort, and the death sentences they passed were no more than laymen's opinions, not based on law. Perhaps this illegal practice was peculiar to Somaliland Protectorate; because of lack of educated public opinion which could protest against such injustice.

The second reason to record the murder case of Mohamed Khalif is to expose, if such was needed, the folly of clan affiliations. Mohamed Khalif, who had no hand in the murder on which the four men were avenging, had the misfortune of belonging to the "accused" sub-clan (*Reer Hirsi Egal*). An innocent man (Mohamed Khalif) was murdered for the criminal action of others. The basis of this tragic murder was the toxic mix of *Xaq*, *Xeer* and collective punishment, which are part and parcel of clanism!

My question is: for how long will the people of Somaliland tolerate the gross injustice inherent in clanism, wherein the innocent suffers for the wrongdoing of others? It is incumbent upon all socially conscious citizens of Somaliland to ponder over this question and decide the best way to respond to it.

3.9 Italian occupation of Ethiopia, 1935–1941

For good or ill, fate ordained that Somaliland and Ethiopia would, geographically, coexist in close proximity – too close for comfort, one might say – and that their histories would be somewhat intertwined. This is one of the reasons why, in October 1898, Somaliland was transferred from the India Office to the British Foreign Office (discussed under 3.4).

In the 1935–1936 war between Ethiopia and Italy, the latter occupied the former in 1936, and Emperor Haile Selassie fled the country and ended up in Britain as a refugee. Also, about 1,400 of his subjects took refuge in Somaliland Protectorate. A relief camp was opened for them at Minje'aseye, between Berbera and Sheikh [52].

The League of Nations in Geneva, Switzerland, imposed an arms embargo on both Italy and Ethiopia. However, Britain and France turned a blind eye to Italy's shipment of military supplies through the Suez Canal (under British control) and Djibouti (a French Colony), and denying Ethiopia to do the same. Britain and France were then wooing Italy, in order that it might not side with Germany.

Italy not only occupied Ethiopia but also absorbed it, in detail, into the Italian East Africa Colonies (in other word, Eritrea and Somalia), as described in the Italian government Decree of 12 May 1936, reproduced below.

[J 4231/3957/1]   No. 130.

Italian Decree No. 754 regarding the Transference of Ethiopia to Italian Sovereignty.—(Communicated by the Italian Ambassador, May 12, 1936.)

(Translation.)

VICTOR EMMANUEL III, by the Grace of God and by the will of the Nation, King of Italy, having seen article 5 of the fundamental statute of the kingdom; having seen article 3, N. 2, of the law of the 31st January, 1926—IV, N. 100; in view of the law of the 9th December, 1928—VII, N. 2693; having recognised the urgent and absolute necessity of taking measures; having heard the Grand Council of Fascism; having heard the Council of Ministers; upon the proposal of the head of the Government, Prime Minister, Secretary of State, we have decreed and we decree:

Article 1. The territories and peoples which belonged to the Empire of Ethiopia are placed under the full and entire sovereignty of the Kingdom of Italy. The title of Emperor of Ethiopia is assumed, for himself and for his successors, by the King of Italy.

Art. 2. Ethiopia is ruled and represented by a Governor-General having the title of Viceroy, on whom the Governors of Eritrea and Somaliland are also dependent. The Governor-General, Viceroy of Ethiopia, has under his dependency all the civil and military authorities of the territories placed under his jurisdiction. The Governor-General, Viceroy of Ethiopia, is nominated by Royal decree, upon the proposal of the head of the Government, Prime Minister, Secretary of State, Minister Secretary of State for the Colonies.

Art. 3. Measures to establish the laws of Ethiopia will be taken by Royal decrees, to be issued upon the proposal of the head of the Government, Prime Minister, Secretary of State, Minister Secretary of State for the Colonies.

Art. 4. The present decree, which has effect from the day of its dating, will be presented to Parliament for conversion into law. The head of the Government, Prime Minister, Secretary of State, is authorised, as proposer, to present the necessary draft law.

We order that the present decree, furnished with the seal of State, shall be inserted in the official collection of the laws and decrees of the Kingdom of Italy, and we command whomsoever it may concern to observe it and cause it to be observed.

Given at Rome, the 9th day of May, 1936—Year XIV.

VITTORIO EMANUELE.
MUSSOLINI.

The Italian government Decree of 12 May 1936, regarding the transfer of Ethiopia to Italy [53].

To add insult to injury, the King of Italy even gave to himself the title of Emperor Haile Selassie. While in exile, Haile Selassie appealed to the League of Nations in Geneva. He addressed the League, in person, in June 1936. It was a long address. Suffice it to say that he catalogued a litany of complaints against both Italy and the League itself. The thrust of his case was that, as a member of the League, his country did not receive the expected support from the League. He felt, no doubt having Britain and France in mind, that Ethiopia was sacrificed on the altar of some members' vested interests.

Haile Selassie ended his address by saying:

Representatives of the World, I have come to Geneva to discharge in your midst the most painful of the duties of the head of a State. What reply shall I have to take back to my people?' [Haile Selassie's address can be found online].

The reply he received was that the big powers lifted the arms embargo from Italy. These big powers, led by Britain and France, were for Italy. Haile Selassie left the hall, as a dejected and broken man.

Haile Selassie addressing the League of Nations in June 1936, Geneva, Switzerland.

Right from the Berlin Conference days, Haile Selassie and his predecessors had been hand-in-glove with the European colonial powers he was addressing. He was rudely awakened to the reality of the opportunistic nature of international politics. Perhaps Haile Selassie forgot the truism: *There is no permanent friendship, but there is permanent self-interest!*

I take no pleasure in Fascist Italy occupying a neighbouring African country ruled, as it was, by an Imperialist African Monarch. However, did the Ethiopians, having experienced what was it like to lose one's country, reflect on their cruel act of helping to themselves a big chunk of the Somali lands?

In 1939, the Somaliland Camel Corps (SCC) was composed of 500 *Askaris* (soldiers) and 14 British officers. This force was patrolling along a border of 750 miles, which Somaliland Protectorate had with the Italian colony of Somalia and the Italian-occupied Ethiopia. During World War II, the British force from Kenya captured Mogadishu from the Italians on 26 February 1941. Also, British forces from Sudan, supported by Ethiopian resistance militia, liberated Ethiopia from the Italian occupation in April 1941 and Haile Selassie was back in Addis Ababa on 5 April 1941 [54].

British government appeasement policy towards Italy

In the 1930s, particularly since the demarcation of the boundary between Somaliland Protectorate and Ethiopia was completed in 1935 and Italy occupied Ethiopia in 1936, the British government was apprehensive and predicted that, if war broke out in Europe, Italy might side with Germany. Thus, while the dark clouds of war were gathering momentum, the British government adopted a conciliatory policy towards Italy, by which the government avoided any word or deed that might provoke Italy – a policy which the government later regretted.

The protectorate government embarked upon a process of persuading the Somali nomads to register or hand in their arms in exchange for money. The government, in collaboration with the Italians, also prevented the nomads from crossing, with their arms, the southern border – for fear that they might come into conflict with the Banda (ie the armed irregular Somali scouts) guarding the Italian side of the border. Eventually, the protectorate government decided to disarm the nomads in 1938, without success [55].

The British government foresaw that the country would be evacuated if Italy entered the "expected war" in Europe on the Axis side (ie Germany and its allies). The government established an office in Aden in late 1938 (what could be called a protectorate government-in-exile in Aden!) for Somaliland Protectorate affairs and put Mr R.H. Smith in charge of the Office [56]. The duties of the office included the following:

- Making arrangements and looking after the welfare of the refugees from Somaliland
- Keeping in touch with the affairs of Italian-occupied Somaliland
- Assisting the intelligence authorities, including monthly reconnaissance to Somaliland
- Acting as political adviser to the G(R) secret mission in Aden (more on this under 3.11)

In September 1939, the government also cleared all the Hospitals of patients.

Governor Lawrance was replaced as governor by V. Glenday (*Faras-Ade* to the Somalis) on 2 March 1939. War in Europe became almost inevitable at that time, and the British government was minded to evacuate Somaliland Protectorate completely before the first shot was fired! After all, if the government was willing to dispose of the country in the international market, it could have equally evacuated it, not defend it.

3.10 Italian occupation of Somaliland Protectorate, 1940–41

In May 1939, the British and French governments held a conference in Aden on the defence of Somaliland Protectorate and Djibouti. They decided that, in the event of Italy joining the Axis side (ie Germany and its allies), Djibouti and Berbera ports would be defended. The rest of British Somaliland Protectorate would be left undefended. It was when the meaning of the word "protectorate" became meaningless.

In July 1939, the British government allotted the miserly sum of nine hundred pounds (£900 only) for the defence of Berbera [57]! That was the measure of how much Britain valued Somaliland! Incidentally, in that same year, expenditure on the office of the governor, Mr Glenday, was £2,994 – three times more than for the defence of Berbera [58]!

War broke out and, in spite of the British government's conciliatory policy, Italy entered the Second World War on the Axis side on 10 June 1940. The first town in Somaliland Protectorate to be evacuated was Borama, on 11 June 1940. The town was (and still is) about four miles from the Ethiopian border. The Italians overran Hargeisa on 5 August and Odweine on 6 August 1940. The order to evacuate the protectorate was made public in Berbera on 16 August and Sheikh Pass was blown up on 17 August, thus the Pass was thereafter closed to wheeled traffic. The British evacuated the protectorate when the Australian warship *Hobart*, with the last evacuees on board, finally sailed away from Berbera harbour on 19 August 1940. Mohamoud Ahmed Ali and the Director of Education, Mr Ellison, were among the evacuees.

Before sailing away, the warship bombarded and destroyed the principal government buildings in Berbera. Such action of vandalism perhaps signalled that the British government was not planning to return to Somaliland and therefore was not prepared to leave behind anything useful. If that was the intention, what an inglorious way of abandoning the country that would have been! The then governor of Aden (who was host to the "protectorate government in exile" during the Italian occupation, as already mentioned, was reported to have discouraged British reoccupation of the country.

It was also said that when the Italians entered Berbera, the *Banda* (irregular army, mostly Ethiopians) looted the town and plundered everything they could lay their hands on, as a reprisal for similar acts allegedly committed by Somali troops (from Italian Somalia) fighting for the Italians during the Italian invasion and occupation of Ethiopia in 1935–1941.

Government justification for evacuating British Somaliland Protectorate

The document mentioned earlier [57] states that: "the policy of not defending British Somaliland was dictated by the general weakness of the position and by the inadvisability of expending resources on a protectorate which had little or no strategic importance".

The defence budget of £900, also mentioned earlier, was in line with the unsurprising assessment given above. From the start, the policy was, in fact, to defend Berbera and not to bother about the rest of the country, reflecting the old British interest in only the coastal strip of the country. But they even failed to defend Berbera!

Is it any wonder that Somaliland was the first country in the British Empire to be evacuated in the Second World War?

It was said that when the then British Prime Minister, Mr Churchill, learnt about what was considered comparatively low casualty numbers (260 out of about 5,500 men or about 5%) among Berbera defenders, he criticized the defending force for abandoning the town (not the country!) prematurely and without putting in enough effort to defend it, a failure, as he was reported to have said, which led to the first British possession to be captured by an enemy force.

When the British government reviewed the way the country was lost, they cited four factors which they claimed were mainly responsible for the loss [57]:

a) The British governments' insistence on running their colonies on the cheap, especially in the matter of defence
b) The War Cabinet's slowness in sanctioning the necessary defence requirements for Berbera
c) The collapse of the French resistance in Djibouti, thus allowing the Italians to concentrate their attacks on Somaliland
d) Almost complete lack of facilities in Berbera as a port, which militated against rapid reinforcement

Obviously, (a) and (d) resulted directly from the "No development policy" in Somaliland, sanctioned by the British government way back in 1905 [23]. That policy, which had been in operation in the country throughout the life of Somaliland Protectorate, came home to roost in 1940! There was nothing genuine in the government's lamentation of the stagnation policy prescribed for the country. The government also rued their appeasement policy towards Italy in the late 1930s, particularly after Italian occupation of Ethiopia.

The Italians installed a military government in the country. They replaced the Indian Rupee with the Italian Lira. The Italians seemed to have done nothing much else during their occupation of the country. However, they robbed the

Somalis of their livestock when, in March 1941, they turned tail and ran away south, instead of facing the British Imperial Forces.

But what can be said about two colonial powers fighting over a country that did not belong to either of them?

3.11 British reoccupation of Somaliland

In the Aden Office referred to earlier, the secret mission mentioned was a combined Somali, Arab and Indian seaborne force code-named G(R), and trained and led by a few British officers. I could not find out what the code G(R) stood for. The G(R) Force sailed from Aden on the evening of 15 March 1941 and reoccupied Berbera early in the morning of 16 March, without resistance from the Italians [59].

It was a throw-back to 4 August 1884 when a small combined Somali, Arab and Indian Force, led by two British officers, sailed from Aden and occupied Berbera, for the first time, without resistance from the occupying Egyptians (see 3.2). The Italians abandoned the country as easily as they occupied it in the first place.

Establishment of a protectorate military government [60]

On 17 March 1941, a protectorate military government was set up in the country and it installed itself in Hargeisa. The military governor was A.R. Chater (*Caga-Yare,* the small-footed, to the Somalis). He was not a stranger to the country, as he used to be the Commander of the Somaliland Camel Corps (SCC) before and during the War. It was decided that the administration of the country would be on the same footing as that of Somalia, which the British forces captured from the Italians. The government, of course, got rid of the Italian lira and reinstated the rupee. The government also introduced the East African Shilling (Sh.) and both the Indian rupee and the shilling remained parallel legal tender until eventually the rupee was phased out, and the shilling continued to be the sole currency of the country until Independence. It was the first time that many Somalis learnt how to convert one currency into another currency. The rupee was equivalent to one shilling and fifty cents (Sh. 1/50).

The Somaliland Camel Corps was also hastily re-formed. The governor was busy with setting up a military government and was not interested in doing anything about education (see 4.6).

A number of *Ilaalos* (ie Scouts) were recruited to guard the large number of the Italian Prisoners of War (POW). These POW, except some who voluntarily decided to remain in Somaliland Protectorate, were evacuated to Kenya. The number of the *Ilaalos* was increased to about 900 men and were renamed the Somali Guard Battalion [61]. They participated in the British operation of blockading the "puppet government" in Djibouti, which declared allegiance to the government installed in Vichy town in German-occupied France. In World War II, France surrendered to Germany in June 1940. The blockade was over at the end of 1942.

Financial contribution by Somalis to the War effort [62]

During World War II, many Somali soldiers, policemen and *Ilaalos* in the service of the protectorate government were made to fight for the British Empire. Some of them fell in the battle fields. However, the Somalis made a different kind of contribution. According to Governor Chater, in September–October 1941 a number of Somalis from Hargeisa and Berbera expressed to the governor their wish to contribute to the war effort. By December 1941, they collected £2,869–11–6 and handed the money over to the government, stipulating that the money should go towards the cost of a *Spitfire,* a British war plane! The governor maintained that it was all the initiative of the Somalis and the government did not bring pressure to bear upon them. I wondered how many Somalis, if any, then knew what Spitfire was! Was this gesture, on the part of the Somalis concerned, a misplaced loyalty? The governor, on behalf of the Somalis, sent an expression of loyalty to the King and a gracious reply from His Majesty was received.

I could not find information about the fate of that money. I was somewhat dubious about the whole thing, but left the matter at that.

However, the cruel irony was that at the time the Somalis were volunteering their money for the defence of the British Empire in 1941, the only government-maintained elementary school in the whole country was closed and turned into a hospital for the troops [157]. Again, just one year before, in August 1940, the British government considered Somaliland not worthy of defending it and abandoned the country to the invading Italians.

It was not long, in my search for information for the book, before I stumbled across a memorandum by Mr Glenday, (Governor of the Protectorate, from 2 March 1939 to 18 August 1940), dated 20 January 1940 [63]. The memorandum (reproduced opposite, for all to see) referred to a telegram of 6 November 1939, in which the Secretary of State for the Colonies, M.J. MacDonald, urged the governor:

> *To introduce simple **non-native income tax** in the protectorate as a means of raising additional revenue to represent the protectorate's **due share of payment for the war**. (Emphasis added).*

The significance of why the Colonial Secretary used the expression "non-native income tax" is discussed below. But before that, it would appear that the non-native income tax was extended to the Somalis, who were, directly or indirectly, made to contribute to the locally raised *additional revenue* for the War effort, as prescribed by the Colonial Secretary. The Colonial Secretary's telegram belied Governor Chater's version of the issue – in other words, his assertion that the government did not have a hand in inducing the Somalis to part with their money.

Compare the sum of £2,869–11–6 which the Somalis collected for the war effort, and the sum of £900 which the British government earmarked for the defence of the country in 1939! That unjust demand – for the Somalis to support a cause with which they had nothing to do – was made about two months after Britain declared war on Germany on 3 September 1939. Governor Glenday worked out elaborate plan for taxation of the Somalis, but events of World War II overtook whatever the governor planned. The names of the key Somali leaders who were behind the financial contribution were not given. That was not surprising, as the key leader was none other than the British Colonial Secretary himself!

Shown below is a scan of the first and relevant part the Governor Glenday's memorandum.

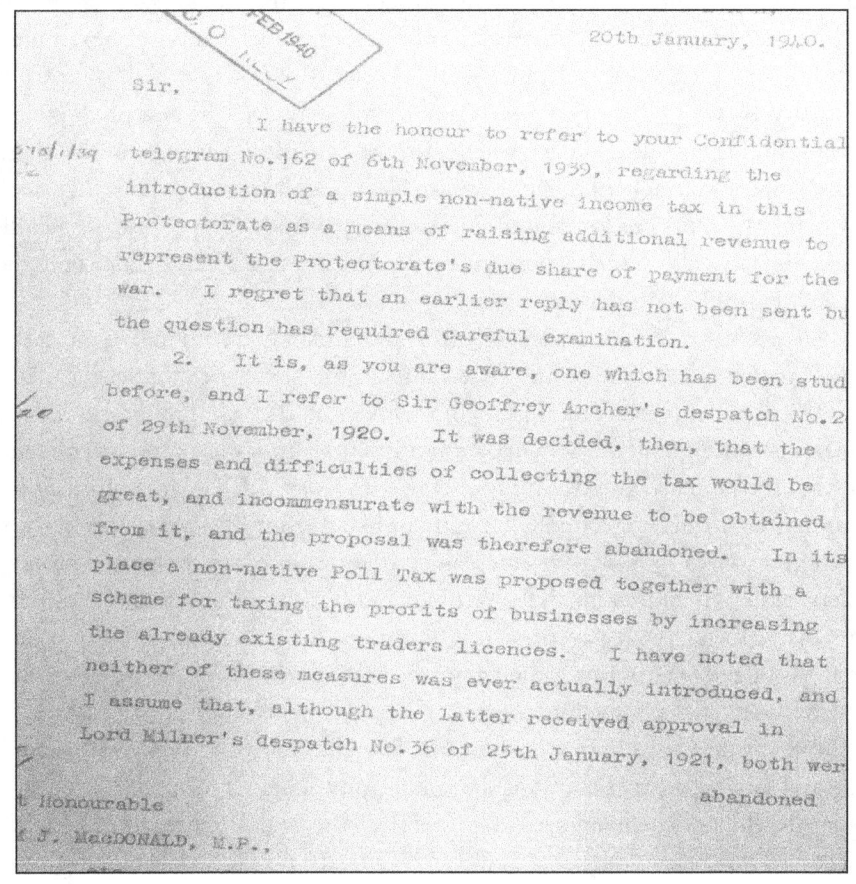

Governor Glenday's response (dated 20 January 1940) to the Colonial Secretary's telegram of 6 November 1939 concerning the introduction of "non-native income tax" in British Somaliland Protectorate [63]

The fact that the Colonial Secretary specified "non-native tax" was significant. There was, from the 1920s, in Nairobi, Kenya, a Somali community from Somaliland Protectorate [64]. The community was politically active and hated and objected to the pejorative term "native" which the British colonial governments of the colonies used for the local people. The Somali community demanded not to be classified as natives, but be given the status of the Asians, so as to pay the same higher tax rate as the Asians. The relevant tax rates in Kenya were:

- for the Europeans, Sh. 40/year
- for the Asians, Sh. 30/year
- for the "natives", ie Kenyans and Somalis, Sh. 20/year

The Somali Community succeeded in gaining several concessions through the courts. The community members were allowed to pay the higher tax rate (Sh. 30/year) as the Asians; and they were exempt from Native Ordinances (for example, those for Native Hut and Poll Tax, Pass Rules, etc). Kenya was then a country dominated by white British settlers, who gave to themselves the best productive parts of the country. The settlers, whether in the agricultural areas or in the main towns, employed a large number of Kenyans as cheap labourers, whom they not only blatantly oppressed but also discriminated against. It was because of such discrimination that the Somalis chose to pay the higher tax and refused not only the native but also the non-native status.

Members of the Somali community in Nairobi mainly traded in livestock. They traded amongst the ethnic-Somali pastoralists in the Northern Frontier District (NFD) – now the North-Eastern Province of Kenya. They used to inform these Somali nomads of how the Somali community in Nairobi was promoting the interests of the Somalis. The Commissioner of NFD was V. Glenday, a future governor of Somaliland Protectorate. He did not like the Somalis from Nairobi who traded in livestock in NFD. He complained that the activities of these livestock traders tended to undermine the government authority and to poison the minds of the natives against the government. On its part, the Somali community accused Mr Glenday of not providing any social services in NFD and being venomously opposed to the Somali interests.

The community was in touch with some Somali elders in Somaliland Protectorate and briefed them about what the community achieved for itself in Kenya, urging the elders to demand better services from the protectorate government. The community even designated Haji Fareh Omaar, an influential and long-standing critic of the protectorate government, as its spokesman in Somaliland Protectorate. It was in the context described above that the Colonial Secretary used the expression "non-native". The influence of the Somali community in Nairobi will also feature in Section 4, on formal education.

NFD was (and is) the least developed part of Kenya. In passing, there were four men who were the District Commissioners of the NFD just before being transferred to Somaliland Protectorate as governors. They were: G. Archer, H. Kittermaster, V. Glenday and G. Reece. It would appear that the NFD provided a suitable training ground for the would-be governor of Somaliland Protectorate, where the declared policy was maintaining law and order and providing no meaningful socio-economic development.

G.T. Fisher replaced, as military governor of Somaliland Protectorate, Mr Chater in March 1943. As was usual for new governors, he toured the country soon after his arrival and was amazed by the lack of development, including education, in the country. He then seemed to have found for himself the reason for such lack of development.

For his first impressions and explanations thereof, see Ref. 174 and for the formal educational programme introduced under his governorship, 1944–1948, see 4.7 to 4.8.

Somaliland Camel Corps mutiny

The Somaliland Camel Corps was primarily raised to fight the Dervishes. Its beginnings date back to the Coastal Concentration period (1910–1912), and it was initially called the Somaliland Camel Constabulary. It was properly constituted in 1912 under the Command of R.C. Corfield, who was killed in the battle of *Dul-Madobe* in 1913.

I mentioned in Section 1 that the Somaliland Camel Corps (SCC) mutinied in 1944. It was not the first time the SCC mutinied. In November 1936, C Company of the SCC was stationed in Borama and it used horses as a means of transport. Lt. Vaux, the Commanding Officer of the company, provided the soldiers with wooden scrapers and ordered them to scrape the horses' dung from the stable. The soldiers felt that such a menial task was not only beneath their dignity but also somehow interfered with their Muslim religion. They mutinied [65]. About 35 of them who were considered as the ringleaders were discharged. Lt. Vaux perhaps concluded that he had precipitated an unwelcome incident and committed suicide. Since the Dervishes in the 1920s, the British officers destined to work in Somaliland Protectorate were briefed to be careful about actions that might offend the religious sensibilities of the Somalis.

The mutiny of the Somaliland Camel Corps (SCC) in 1944 also had religious connotations. The SCC was put under order to move to Kenya for reorganization, re-equipment and training as an armed corps regiment. This conversion was to take place in June 1944. The soldiers requested Asian status and not to be given the Kenyan dress (in other words, collarless shirts). They also heard rumours that their ration in Kenya would contain pork. The authorities rejected the soldiers' requests. On 5 June 1944, C Company in Burao mutinied [66]. A Court of Enquiry into the mutiny was set up. With the exception of just a few of them, the SCC was disbanded in September 1944.

The Somaliland Scouts were formed from the Somali Guard Battalion mentioned earlier, together with the remnants of the Somaliland Camel Corps [67]. From 1940 to 1960, the Somaliland Protectorate Army (ie the Somaliland Camel Corps; later the Somaliland Scouts) was under the British Ministry of Defence, and was part of the British Army. The Ministry of Defence directly administered, equipped and paid the protectorate Scouts. The Somaliland Protectorate government had no control over the Somaliland Scouts. However, the Ministry of Defence charged the annual expenditure on the Somaliland Scouts to the Colonial Office. As this arrangement was between the Ministry of Defence and the Colonial Office, from 1940 to 1960, the protectorate government did not show in its annual expenditure the annual expenditure on the Somaliland Army.

The annual expenditure on the Somaliland Scouts ranged from £200,000 to £330,000 [68]. The annual average figure of £265,000 would be added to the annual government subsidies from 1940 to 1960.

Anglo-Ethiopian Agreement of 1944 [69]

The governments of Britain and Ethiopia concluded an Agreement on 19 December 1944. By this agreement, the British relinquished advantages they hitherto enjoyed in Ethiopia. They returned the Ethiopian section of the Addis Ababa-Djibouti railroad to Ethiopian control and removed their garrisons except from the Ogaden. The agreement further defined the Hawd and the Reserved Areas (see maps below).

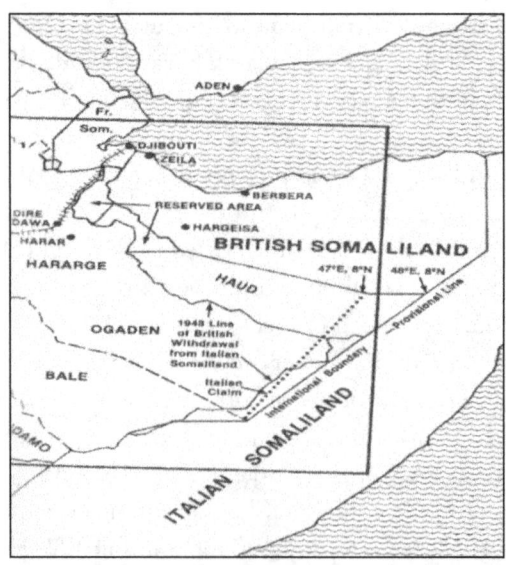

Map based on the Anglo-Ethiopian Agreement of 1944, showing the Hawd and the Reserved Areas, as defined by the agreement. Map was modified from one in Beachey [29].

The map below shows the Hawd and the Reserved Area, as related to Somaliland Protectorate:

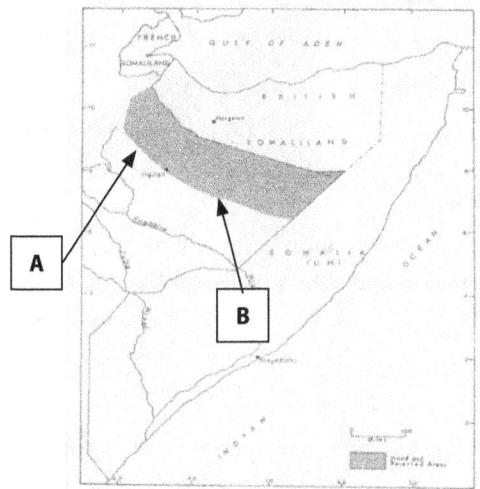

Map showing Hawd and the Reserved Area, as related to Somaliland Protectorate. Disputed Territories are shaded. A is the Reserved Area; B is Hawd

The 1944 agreement also stipulated that the *status quo would be maintained in regard to all schools in the Hawd and the Reserved Areas.*

There were at that time no governmental schools of any sort in Hawd and the Reserved Area – that meant that no new schools would be built in the areas. However, see later (Ref. 189, page 251) about an incident related to this stipulated status.

The 1944 Agreement was subject to termination, by either side giving three months' notice. On 24 July 1948, an Anglo-Ethiopian Protocol was concluded, whereby the British evacuated the greater part of the Ogaden region which was restored to the Ethiopian jurisdiction.

The Colonial Development & Welfare Act (CD&WA) [70]

The Colonial Office partly financed Somaliland from the fund sanctioned under the Act. For the first time, the British government regularized the ad hoc grants which it extended to its dependencies, by-passing the above-mentioned Act and by which the fund was established in 1929. The Act, usually referred to as given in the tittle, was for the period 1929–1940 and subsequent similar Acts for varying periods of five to ten years were passed. The criteria for deciding the grants under the Act included:

- Size and population of the colony
- Its own economic resources and possibilities
- Present state of development
- Development schemes known to exist or to be under contemplation
- Financial resources likely to be available locally

The idea behind the Act was that, by developing the colonies, trade with the colonies would increase and the British people at home would reap the benefits, in the form of employment.

The fund was established for developmental schemes, *not* for recurrent expenditure. Under the first Act of 1929, Somaliland Protectorate received a token grant of £63 in 1929. In 1945, Somaliland Protectorate received a grant of £268,650 under the 1945 Act. The protectorate government allocated the grant as follows:

Allocation of the £268,650 grant received in 1945 by Somaliland Protectorate

Medical department	£ 89,000
Police and prisons	£65,000
Agriculture department	£61,500
Administration	£25,000
Public works department	£15,600
Water supplies	£8,320
Education department	£4,230

Although the Education Department fared badly in the re-allocation of the CD&WF, it benefited from the fund in later years. The distribution of the money reflects the low priority accorded to formal education in the country, in comparison with the police and prisons. The allocation of £4,230 for education became part of the funds used for the initial construction of the educational facilities in different parts of the protectorate in 1945.

In July 1944, the Las Anod District was created from part of the Burao District. It was also in April 1945 that the Colonial Office approved Hargeisa as the capital of the protectorate. The justifications offered for this action were as given below:

- To impress upon the Somalis that the British government was also interested in the interior of the country, as well as the coast, which was the primary concern of the occupation in 1884
- Hargeisa climate was mild and was also on the road from Berbera to Jigjiga

- The majority of the population is in the west of the protectorate
- Agriculture is feasible in the west of the country

The other main reason, not mentioned by the government, for why Hargeisa was chosen on reoccupation of the country was that, during the evacuation, the British forces bombarded and destroyed the principal government buildings in Berbera and there were no suitable buildings available in Berbera for government use. Even in Hargeisa, the government was housed for years in tents and flimsy prefabricated "shelters", since there were hardly any government buildings in Hargeisa before.

A Mahdi again? [71]

One night in 1945, the protectorate government was rudely awakened and startled! It was not because of the countrywide disturbances resulting from the Somali objection to bait-laying for the control of the locust infestation in the country.

According to government documents, Sheikh Bashir Yusuf had been critical of the government. On the night of 2–3 July 1945, armed men, led by Sheikh Bashir, fired on the Police Quarter Guard at the jail, killing one prisoner and wounding another. Then they went to the house of the District Commissioner of Burao and opened fire, killing the *Ilaalo*-man guard of the house. The attackers then fled.

On 7 July, the police force tracked the men to the *Buur-Dhaab* area, east of Burao. Fire exchange followed; Sh. Bashir and another described as his Commander-in-Chief were killed, another wounded and captured. The rest of the group escaped. From the police side, one *Ilaalo*-man was reported wounded. It was reported that 22 men participated in the Burao attacks.

As collective punishment, Governor Fisher gave orders for the seizure of 6,000 camels from the clan concerned, to be released at the rate of 300 camels for each assailant surrendered. In the end, rather than having their camels impounded, the clan paid a lump sum.

Nowhere in the documents consulted was there an indication that the figure of 6,000 camels was arrived at in a court of law. Governor Fisher fixed this figure off the top of his head. I already mentioned Governor Archer's imposition of collective punishment of 3,000 camels for the murder of Mr Gibb, District Commissioner of Burao, in 1922, without due process of law. The governors of Somaliland Protectorate were a law unto themselves.

The government indicated that Sh. Bashir had some family relationship with Seyyid Mohamed Abdullah Hassan and was inspired by the Seyyid. The government described Sh. Bashir as "half-mad Mullah" and suspected that he was attempting to take advantage of the disturbances caused by the locust infestation in the country in that year (1945). The government never took too kindly to any activity likely to rekindle memories of the murder of Mr Gibb, or the Seyyid and his Dervishes. Sh. Bashir was a nationalist in the same mould as Seyyid Mohamed Abdullah Hassan.

Commission for War Claims Settlement [72]

The protectorate government established the Commission for War Claims Settlement in 1943. The compensation period was limited to 10 June 1940 to 16 March 1941. The Commission was required to hear and dispose of all claims for compensation arising out of the hostilities with Italy, and the subsequent Italian occupation of Somaliland Protectorate.

The rules for recommending compensation were that (a) the claimant would come before the Commission to offer sworn evidence in support of his claim, or (b) the claimant would be represented by his appointed agent with full knowledge of his affairs and a Power of Attorney to give sworn evidence on his behalf. The Commission finally reported on its work in March 1945.

- Total claims registered with Commission were given as 4,122

- Total amount of money claimed for the registered 4,122 claims was given as £810,376

- Total amount recommended for compensation was given as £163,474, or 20% of the total amount claimed. Of the total £163,474, £14,635 was paid out to 35 European officials, 6 Somaliland Camel Corps officers and 72 Asian officials. The rest of the money was distributed among civilians. The ex-Director of Education, Mr Ellison, received £250 for a small, old car which he abandoned in Berbera in 1940.

The document referenced above [72] gives details of the dates when the main centres in the country were captured by the Italians.

The Somalis making claims were severely handicapped by their inability to produce documented evidence for their losses. It was recorded that 900 Somalis who registered claims did not come up for interviews. So they lost whatever they claimed by default. The greater proportion of the money was paid out to Indian and Arab merchants.

The interviews were not without their comic moments. A poor Somali, who perhaps misunderstood what the people were queuing for joined the queue. When he was asked, in the interview, what his business was, he replied that he was a street-beggar poor man. Hard luck! It was not mentioned whether the interviewers pitied him and gave him something. The document also mentions that:

> *The Italians were out to ingratiate themselves with the people, realizing the importance of Burao District from the point of view of population and cen-*

tral position, and to impress upon them the justice and benevolence of Italian rule. A conducted tour of Abyssinia was arranged for a party of the leading Aqils in Burao to further this object.

The Aqils were not named.

First Somaliland Protectorate Advisory Council inaugurated [73]

The protectorate government, at last, woke up to the absence of Somali participation in the affairs of the country. The first meeting of the First Somaliland Protectorate Advisory Council was held at Sheikh School, 2–9 July 1946, during the long school summer holiday. Mohamoud Ahmed Ali acted as the Secretary of the meeting. One agenda item introduced by the government proposed that the country be divided among the clans. By such division, the government thought, each clan would carefully look after its own part of the country and, as a result, the grazing in the country would improve!

The Somali members in the council unanimously objected to the proposal. They pointed out that, though the Somalis "quarrel over water, grazing, etc, they soon make up their differences and continue to live together peacefully. The country is a common property and it belongs to all the Somali clans." They rejected any policy that put barriers between the clans, and which would give rise to *fitnah* (their word) amongst the clans. *Fitnah*, in this case, meant destructive inter-clan feuds. The proposal was killed there and then.

Practically none of the Somali members of the council had formal education. However, compare our "uneducated" elders' foresight in those days, with our present-day educated politicians who failed to appreciate what our elders sensed in 1946. Instead, our governments have been creating districts and regions on clan basis, in the process entrenching clanism and sowing the seeds of future *fitnah* among the Somaliland communities. Already some clans claim *de facto* ownership of regions and districts so created! Are we, in Somaliland, socially progressing or regressing?

After World War II, the country was kept under military rule from 1941 to 1948. Reading around the subject, I could not help thinking that one of the plausible reasons why the country had to be run by a military government for so long after the War was that the British government was conflicted about what to do with the country. The government could not come to a decision about whether or not to dispose of the country. Perhaps the assumption was that, should it come to abandoning the country, a local military government would have been superior, logistically, to a local civil government, to extricate the British government from the likely mess that might have ensued!

3.12 Civil government replaced the military government

The military governor, Mr Fisher, was replaced by a civil governor, G. Reece (*Kama-kama*, to the Somalis, mocking the way he talked), on 15 November 1948 [74]. The people of Somaliland did not notice any difference in the administration of the military and civil protectorate governments. They all governed the country in a militaristic fashion. It was all a one-man rule. The governor reigned supreme. When issuing an official proclamation, the governor would style himself thus: "I, (name), Governor and Commander-in-Chief in and over the Somaliland Protectorate, do hereby declare that…" What could be more "one-man rule" than that? Since the establishment of some semblance of a protectorate government in the 1930s, the administration was, in fact, a hybrid of military and civil; hence the title "Governor and Commander-in-Chief" which all the governors of the protectorate had.

In January 1949, the Colonial Office instructed the protectorate government:

> During the next 3 years, it should budget for an expenditure of £1,000,000 per annum. This figure was based on the assumption that local revenues will not fall below £350,000 per annum and that efforts will be made to increase local revenues during that same period. With the above qualifications, the difference between local revenues and expenditure will be met by a grant-in-aid from His Majesty's Government [75].

The emphasis was on maximizing the local revenues, in order to reduce the grants-in-aid. The protectorate government decided that any local revenue increase would not go to the provision of new services; instead, the government subsidy would proportionally be reduced. This policy thus precluded any expenditure on development. It was a colonial administration that was marking time until the people had enough of it and threw it out!

To show how anti-development the Colonial Office was, the War Office, before handing over the administration of the country to the Colonial Office, prepared a rehabilitation project for the major roads in the country and earmarked a sum of £490,000 for the purpose. The Colonial Office perhaps concluded that the War Office was not "on message", regarding the policy established for the county, ie "minimum administration and nil or little development". The project was duly cancelled in early 1950.

Attempts at abolishing the *Xaq* and *Xeer* (Somali customary law)

Some Somalis who had a sense of justice wanted *Xeer* to be abolished. In September 1953, the protectorate district councils meeting in Burao proposed the abolition of *Xeer*; but the protectorate government rejected the idea [76].

However, in July 1956, Governor Pike (who replaced Governor Reece, see later) appointed a two-man commission to review the *Ilaalo* establishment. The *Ilaalo* were a clan-based, quasi-police, armed force which enforced the *Xeer*. Members of the Commission were J.S.R. Cole, the Attorney General of the protectorate government and Chairman of the Commission, and Mr Milson, Officer in the Secretariat. The Commission's recommendations contained the following [77]:

- The *Xeer* (ie the Somali customary law) in its entirety and the *Ilaalo* police force who enforce it should be abolished

- The suggestion that justice could be founded on any other principle than individual responsibility was savagery, destroying all hope of progress

- The role of the government should be to guide the Somali society *away from* division into feuding, raiding and warring tribes who for the purposes of defence have formed themselves into "blood-paying groups"; and *towards* a society of individuals in which responsibility was individual rather than collective

Here is a Colonial Commission with which I agree 100% in its opinion of *Xeer* and its ramifications. I could not have improved on the way the Commission put it. Its analysis was in line with the contents of the Appendix, in which my views about *Xaq, Xeer* and clanism are expressed. Had the authors of the letter of 1958 in the Appendix been aware of this report, they would have referred to it and that would have strengthened their argument against *Xaq* and *Xeer*, as practised in British Somaliland Protectorate.

The response of Governor Pike to the Commission's views was that such radical change could not be foisted on the Somalis in the short time remaining. The government all along supported *Xaq* (compensation for wound or murder) under the Somali customary law (*Xeer*), and hence the establishment of collective punishment in the country. I have commented elsewhere in the book on why the protectorate government saw *Xaq and Xeer* as a means of raising local revenue.

Again, in November 1957, the protectorate Legislative Council meeting in Hargeisa proposed to abolish the *Xeer* [78]. The government vetoed the proposals, arguing that nothing to replace the *Xeer* was put forward. Unfortunately, the Somalis who were trying to get rid of the *Xeer* in 1953 and 1957 could not adequately articulate their case, as did the Attorney General of the protectorate, quoted above. The government was, of course, for the *Xeer*, as it was a main contributor to the local revenue.

Proposed land-swap with Ethiopia [79]

In 1953, the British and the Ethiopian governments were engaged in negotiations on a friendship agreement that would replace the temporary 1944 Anglo-

Ethiopian Agreement, mentioned earlier. During the negotiations, the British government brought up the old question of land exchange with the government of Ethiopia in 1935 (see 3.7). The government proposed swapping the Zeila Corridor of 25 miles wide or wider from the Ethiopian territory and leading to the Port of Zeila, for the grazing Hawd area. The government produced a map showing the shape of the proposed corridor (map reproduced opposite). The government proposal contained scenarios, including financial arrangement of £500,000 in addition to the corridor. A telling statement in the proposal pointed out that:

> ...since Somaliland Protectorate and its people were not British possession or subjects, but only British protected, the transfer or surrender of the whole or part of the protectorate and the people therein were a matter of the Royal Prerogative, not involving an Act of Parliament.

That being the case, the proposal stated that the inhabitants of the Zeila Corridor (overwhelmingly the *Esa* clan) would not be consulted nor their consent sought for the transfer of the corridor. This also indicated that the British government assumed that different clans owned different parts of the country! Not consulting the clan concerned was a departure from the government's position in 1935 (see 3.7), when the then Secretary of State for the Colonies confirmed that the tribe concerned would have been consulted.

The Governor of the protectorate in 1953, Mr Reece, participated in drafting the proposal. He informed his collaborators from the government in London that the *Esa* clan was predominantly an Ethiopian clan and its *Suldaan* was an Ethiopian subject, paid by the Ethiopian government. Mr Reece maintained that the clan was independent by nature and little control was exercised over it either by the Ethiopian government or that of Somaliland Protectorate.

It was very likely that Governor Reece persuaded the British government to adopt the non-consultation position on the Zeila Corridor, to see a "troublesome clan", in the eyes of the governor, bundled off with the corridor to Ethiopia! In fact, Governor Kittermaster had similar ideas in the early 1930s.

Anyway, since the British monarch had the authority to dispose of the country at will, consulting the inhabitants of the protectorate seemed to be pointless! I could not find out whether the proposal was actually put to the Ethiopian government. We now know that no land barter for land came to pass. We also know that Somaliland and its people were, in the judgement of the British government, a commodity to be bartered in the international market!

It is important to point out a British government's misconception about the people of the British Somaliland Protectorate. The British government never accepted that the Somalis in Somaliland Protectorate were a homogeneous nation, commonly owning a country which had internationally recognized boundaries. The British government, all along, maintained that different clans owned different parts of the country. The Royal Proclamation at the country's Independence also showed this misconception.

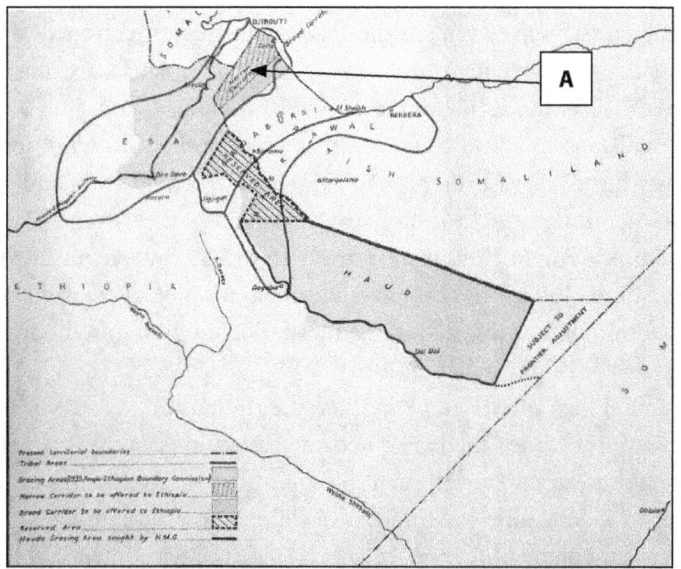

Map showing the proposed Zeila Corridor, marked "A", to be given to Ethiopia in 1953 [67].

Mr T.O. Pike (*Laba-Sac'le*, "he the two-cow owner", to the Somalis, replaced, as Governor of the protectorate, Mr G. Reece in February 1954.

3.13 The Anglo-Ethiopian Agreement of 1954

The friendship agreement to replace the 1944 agreement, mentioned earlier, was the Anglo-Ethiopian Agreement of 29 November 1954, which became effective on 28 February 1955 [80]. The long process of Ethiopian "land-grab", at the expense of Somaliland, and always aided and abetted by the British government, had started with the Anglo-Ethiopian Agreement of 14 May 1897 and culminated in the above-mentioned Anglo-Ethiopian Agreement of 29 November 1954. By this agreement, the Anglo-Ethiopian Agreement of 1897 was re-affirmed; Ethiopia reassumed full jurisdiction and administration of the Hawd and the Reserved Area. Ethiopia was restored to its internationally recognized borders of 1935 (in other words, pre-Italian occupation).

The agreement guaranteed, in perpetuity, the right of the citizens of Somaliland to take their livestock into "the Hawd and the Reserved Area" for grazing and watering. Also, a protectorate government liaison officer was allowed to travel in these territories to look after the interests of these Somaliland nomads.

The agreement entailed, *inter alia*, that as a result of withdrawing the British Administration from the Hawd and the Reserved Area, nomadic Somalilanders who took their livestock into the Hawd and the Reserved Area for grazing and watering would, from 28 February 1955, be subject not only to constant Ethiopian harassment but also to the Ethiopian jurisdiction. The agreement handed, fraudulently, the best grazing and agricultural land of Somaliland to Ethiopia on a silver platter.

The agreement that was to become effective on 28 February 1955 was announced to the people of Somaliland on 5 January 1955 – in other words, with less than eight weeks' notice! The people of Somaliland took the sad news badly and spontaneous demonstrations against the agreement were hurriedly organized in the protectorate – the only weapon at the disposal of the Somaliland public! The protectorate government was expecting violent riots and bloodshed, and took counter measures; but their fears did not materialize.

Somaliland delegation to Britain in 1955 about Hawd and Reserved Area [81]

The delegation was crowd-funded – in other words, the people of Somaliland, spearheaded by the National Somali League Party, contributed to the delegation's expenses.

To pre-empt any hospitality which the British government might, as a friendly gesture, extend to the delegation, Governor Pike telegraphed the Colonial Office on 25 January 1955, informing them that "the delegation will be four in number, arriving in London on 5 February 1955. Grateful reserve accommodation. Period of stay indefinite at present. They are responsible for their own hotel bills and all other expenses."

The Somali delegation (picture below) went to Britain to protest to the British government about the unjust Anglo-Ethiopian Agreements of 1897 and 1954, and to attempt to stop the implementation of the 1954 Agreement.

Some of the reference material used by the delegation included Richard Burton's book [1] in which some description, with maps, is given about the western part of Somaliland, extending to Harar, which was then mainly populated by Somalis.

Somali Delegation to the United Kingdom in February–June 1955: From **left** to **right**: Suldaan Abdillahi Suldaan Deria, Abdirahman Ali Mohamed Dubad (Dube Ali Yare), Michael Mariano and Suldaan Abdirahman Suldaan Deria.

In their discussions with the Colonial Office, the delegation argued that the treaties between the British and the Somaliland clan leaders pre-dated the Anglo-Ethiopian Agreements of 1954 and 1897 and, therefore, the two latter agreements were invalid; also that the British government was in breach of the treaties with the Somaliland clans. The Somali delegation was informed that the agreements which the British government entered into with a sovereign state (ie Ethiopia) would *take precedence* over agreements entered into with clan leaders! The British government, not for the first time, let down the people of Somaliland.

While the Somaliland delegation was still in London, the 1897 and 1954 Anglo-Ethiopian Agreements were debated in the British Parliament (*Hansard*, 23 February 1955). In the debates, the Secretary of State for the Colonies, Mr Lennox-Boyd, stated that he "regretted the 1897 Agreement" and it was "unfortunate". He continued, saying that "the Agreement suffered from his government's limited knowledge of Somaliland at the time."

What he described as *"unfortunate"* was gross understatement and was much more than that. It was unmitigated calamity for the people of Somaliland. Mr

Lennox-Boyd should not have disingenuously claimed in the British Parliament that his government's knowledge of Somaliland was insufficient, for the following reasons:

- The Rodd Mission, which negotiated the 1897 agreement, included Mr Swayne who, for many years, traversed and had intimate knowledge of the territory of Somaliland
- The mission was in possession of the Anglo-Italian agreement of 1894, demarcating their respective spheres of influence in the hinterland of Somaliland (see 3.3)

The Rodd Mission, at the instigation of the British monarch, knowingly breached both the treaties which the Bombay government (on behalf of the British government) concluded with the Elders of the Somaliland clans and the Anglo-Italian Agreement of 1894. The British government informed the delegation that a petition to the United Nations General Assembly would be strongly opposed by the British.

While in London, the delegation contacted the Embassies of Canada and New Zealand, in the hope that one of the countries might sponsor the delegation petition to the UN, but without success. On 5 May 1955 the delegation sent the petition, drafted with the help of British legal experts in constitutional law, to the UN Secretary General and then left for Cairo, Egypt. According to a report of the British Embassy in Cairo, a statement released by the delegation at a press conference in Cairo on 2 June 1955 declared that the Egyptian government agreed to sponsor the delegation petition at the UN General Assembly, with a view to bringing the petition before the International Court of Justice. The report also mentioned that Mr Michael Mariano, member of the delegation, was reported to have said that, in connection with petition, the delegation had been in close touch with Wing Commander Ali Sabry, Chief of the Office of the Prime Minister of Egypt.

However, it was not long before the British Embassy in Cairo reported on 7 June 1955 that Wing Commander Ali Sabry informed the British Embassy that the Egyptian government did not agree to sponsor the delegation's petition at the UN General Assembly, but only agreed that Egypt would support the petition if another member state sponsored it. Was there a misunderstanding between the delegation and Ali Sabry, or was it that the Egyptian government got cold feet at the last moment?

The delegation's situation reminds one of the present-day situation of Somaliland. Whenever the Somaliland government approaches a country which might recognize it, the response it gets is that another country has to do that first! It only shows that Somaliland never had, as an ally, one of the big powers, with sufficient interest in the country and which might take Somaliland under its wing!

The British were pleased with Egypt's action on two counts: (a) they (the British) were spared legal debates on the dodgy Anglo-Ethiopian treaties at the UN and, (b) they hoped that Egypt, by its action, would make itself unpopular with the people of Somaliland. Egypt, on its part, did not want to upset Ethiopia, because of the Nile waters, nor the British who still occupied the Suez Canal which Egypt was planning to recover.

The Somali delegation returned from its mission, empty-handed, to Somaliland in late June 1955. The people of Somaliland were resigned to the fate that recovery of the territories was a lost cause. The November 1954 Anglo-Ethiopian Agreement was a harbinger of the beginning of the end of colonial rule in Somaliland. Eventually, anger, frustration and demonstrations gave way to talk of early independence and union with Somalia. A general mood of elation set in in the country!

Members of the Somali Delegation were an ad hoc group created for the Retaining the Reserved Area and the Hawd, called the National United Front (NUF, for short). Later the NUF transitioned to fully-fledged political party.

Protests against the handover of the best part of Somaliland to Ethiopia were not confined to the protectorate. In 1955, there were 10 students (including the author) studying in Hantoub Secondary School, Sudan. When we heard about the land transfer on Radio Hargeisa, we stopped attending classes and sent a telegram to the Director of Education of Somaliland Protectorate. In it we stated that if the land handover was not stopped within 48 hours (or 72, I can't remember which), we would return home. The following day the director sent us a telegram, through the headmaster of Hantoub Secondary School, Mr Brown, telling us that, if we did not return to classes immediately, he would request the headmaster to send us home – he ominously added that we would regret it for the rest of our lives. We ignored the director's threat. We felt deeply incensed by the British government's injustice. The headmaster was, all the time, advising and urging us to change our minds. Then another telegram, jointly by Mohamoud Ahmed Ali and Yusuf Haji Adan, was received by the headmaster. They told us that we were not helping Somaliland by disrupting our studies and ordered us to resume our classes immediately, and we did. In the end, wiser counsel prevailed over the hubris of youth!

We were on strike for about five days and, in that period, we sent articles to some of the national newspapers; in the evenings we held discussions with the students. Sudan was scheduled to obtain its independence in January 1956 and all the students were politically conscious and active. I remember at least one occasion when all the students in Hantoub Secondary School, including my Somali group, went on "political" strike and the school was closed for two weeks. While I was researching for the book, I tried, to no avail, to find the telegrams and the letter of the Director of Education related to the strike of my group in Sudan.

Delegation member Mr Michael Mariano, accompanied by an unnamed person, was in London in September 1955, with the intention of flying to New York to attend the UN General Assembly and lobby the Arab block about the Somali petition. The British government strongly discouraged him from his mission. They told him that the petition would not come up as an agenda item at the UN General Assembly.

The British government was also so concerned about "the very dangerous possibilities of the Somali petition, from the point of view of all Protectorate Treaties" [81] that the government had to send the urgent letter, scanned below, to their representative at the UN. The government was so rattled by the petition because it feared that, if discussed at the UN General Assembly, the Somali petition would unravel the sham treaties it made not only with the people of Somaliland but also with others in British protectorates. The petition indicated that the Somalis had a strong case, but lacked a UN member state to sponsor their case at the UN. Somaliland was, not for the first time, the victim of high international politics.

```
                        CONFIDENTIAL
                FROM FOREIGN OFFICE TO NEW YORK
           (United Kingdom Delegation to the United Nations)
Cypher/OTP                                              DEPARTMENTAL
                                                        DISTRIBUTION

No. 1152
September 20, 1955              D. 7.48 p.m. September 20, 1955

IMMEDIATE
CONFIDENTIAL

        Somali Petition and the Haud.
            Draft brief enclosed in Marnham's letter to Gidden of
    September 13 is still under discussion between Departments and
    an agreed version will be sent as soon as possible.
            2.  You should, of course, strongly oppose any attempt
    at inscription, but we leave to your discretion how this should
    be done in the light of your tactics over the Cyprus item.
            3.  Somali petition has very dangerous possibilities from
    point of view of all protectorate treaties but we hope inscrip-
    tion can be defeated without going to lengths suggested in draft
    brief.  In particular, specific instructions should be requested
    before any threats of withdrawal are made.


    DISTRIBUTED TO:
    United Nations Department
    African Department
```

Confidential communication from the British Foreign Office to its UN representative concerning the Somali petition, September 1955 [81]

Mr Michael Mariano was not successful in New York. As we now know, the petition was never debated at the UN General Assembly nor was it referred to the International Court of Justice at The Hague.

While the people of Somaliland were smarting from the loss of the best part of their land, the British government was discussing how to evacuate its nationals and others, in the event of rebellion in Somaliland, as described below.

British government deliberations on Somaliland Protectorate, in the context of the Horn of Africa and the Middle East [82]

From the mid-1950s, there was a strong desire in the country for independence and union with Somalia, and the date marked for these two momentous events was 1960, a date like no other, bearing in mind what was to happen in Somalia in 1960. The British government, on its part, was cognizant of the public mood in Somaliland and the events in Somalia. All along, the British government kept the situation in Somaliland Protectorate under continual review.

The British government was much concerned about the future of Somaliland – that is to say, whether the country would become an independent state or join Somalia. Whether the two territories amalgamated or not, the British held out little chance of their success. The British thought that any difficulties in Somalia might impact on Somaliland and Kenya.

Events in the Middle East added to the British concern. These included the coup d'état in Egypt in July 1952; the independence of Sudan from Britain and Egypt in January 1956; and the British invasion of the Suez Canal in October 1956.

To keep the situation under review in the aftermath of these events, and in particular their implications for the future prospects of Somaliland Protectorate, the British government formed a committee composed of the different departments of the British government in London. The committee held series of meetings – at some stages, officials of Somaliland Protectorate, the Governor of Kenya and the British Ambassador to Ethiopia participated in the committee's meetings. By 1957, the committee reached the conclusions summarized below:

1. The Somaliland Protectorate governors should continue to be recruited from outside, so that the governor would consider problems in the protectorate dispassionately and without emotional encumbrance

2. Somaliland is of no particular value to Britain at all and relationship with Ethiopia is of more value to Britain. The destabilizing factor is the British obligation to the Somalis in the protectorate

3. The only British assets in Somaliland are a high-powered relay station under construction at Berbera and scheduled to become operational in 1960. However, the equipment would be portable.

4. Wajer Airport in Kenya is to be developed, in preference to Hargeisa airport
5. Somalia is likely to be ill-administered, bankrupt and intensely nationalistic
6. A united state (ie Somaliland and Somalia) will still remain poor and less stable than Somaliland
7. It would not be desirable to invite Somaliland State or an amalgamated state to join the Commonwealth
8. A contingency plan, kept current and code-named "Operation Grout", is to be prepared; the operation is to be directed to extract British subjects and subjects of friendly nations in Somaliland Protectorate, in the event of a rebellion
9. Somaliland Protectorate will need heavy British subsidies until at least 1960 or perhaps 1965

It becomes monotonous how often the British had to repeat what little value Somaliland was to them. As a whole, the conclusions, as they applied to Somaliland, contained nothing that was not, in one form or another, already mentioned in this book. It was not surprising that the British valued their relationship with Ethiopia much more than that with Somaliland. That was why they gave the best part of Somaliland to Ethiopia in 1897, deliberately ignoring their obligations (and treaties) to the people and country of Somaliland. Then they complained that their obligations to the people of Somaliland was a spoiling factor in the Anglo-Ethiopian relationship. Doesn't this smack of hypocrisy?

The British government predicted that united Somaliland-Somalia would be unstable and that prediction came to pass.

Visit of the Duke of Gloucester

It was the turn of a member of the British royal family to find out what was being done in the protectorate, in the name of the monarch. The Duke of Gloucester visited the protectorate in the twilight of its existence in November 1958. He opened the refurbished Hargeisa Airport and unveiled a plague at the incomplete buildings of the new Secondary School at Sheikh.

At the time, Seyyid Ahmed Sheikh Musa, who lived in Cairo, was a critic of the protectorate government [83]. He was broadcasting on *Sawt el-Arab Radio* (the Arab Voice) in Cairo, urging the Somalis to boycott the Duke's visit and throw off the yoke of colonialism. Because of his hostility to the protectorate government, Seyyid Ahmed was already made *persona non grata* in Somaliland Protectorate and Aden. An exclusion order (preventing him from entering Somaliland Protectorate and Aden) which was signed in March 1958 and which was to run up to March 1960 was already in place.

Such misuse of power by the governors was not uncommon in Somaliland Protectorate.

3.14 Ill-conceived independence offered to Somaliland

In 1958, Governor Pike, together with the Leaders of the Somaliland political parties, had been busying themselves with plans to form a local government, prior to independence. They were working on the assumption that the country would become independent sometime in 1965 or even later.

However, all that was to change abruptly. By the end of 1958, the view of the British government was that rapid constitutional changes had to be introduced into the protectorate. The Secretary of State for the Colonies, Mr A. Lennox-Boyd, was to convey this change in policy to the protectorate government, the Somaliland political parties and to the Somaliland public at large.

Visit of the Secretary of State for the Colonies [84, 85]

The Secretary of State for the Colonies, Mr Lennox-Boyd, visited Somaliland Protectorate in February 1959, as shown in the photo below, inspecting a Guard of Honour.

Alan Lennox-Boyd, Secretary of State for the Colonies, inspecting a Guard of Honour on a visit to Somaliland, February 1959.

Mr Lennox-Boyd must have been depressed by what he found in the country – in others words, the lack of development in all aspects of the socio-economic sectors of the country. He did not see the point of prolonging what was already an embarrassing situation.

The main constitutional changes which Mr Lennox-Boyd broadcast on Radio Hargeisa on 9 February 1959 were as follows [86]:

- By 1960, there would be an elected Legislative Council with unofficial Somalis forming the majority, some of them with executive responsibilities
- The British government would thereafter take the necessary steps which would lead to internal self-government for the protectorate
- If the Legislative Council so wished, the British government would facilitate, after Somalia's independence in 1960, suitable negotiations with the government of Somalia for the formation of closer association of the two territories

The policy change was not sufficient for the Somaliland politicians, who were agitating for early independence.

In March 1959, elections were held. The Somali National League (SNL), the then main political party in the country, boycotted the elections. The party demanded that the majority of elected members should be unofficial (in other words, not in government service), but the protectorate government rejected their demand.

In July 1959, Mr D. Hall replaced, as the last Governor of the protectorate, Governor Pike. Mr Hall was transferred from Northern Rhodesia (present-day Zambia) where he was the Secretary for Native Affairs. He just made it to Somaliland Protectorate before retirement, to get his title of Knight Commander of the Order of St Michael and St George (KCMG), which can also be written out, irreverently, as "Kindly Call Me Governor" (KCMG)! Retiring governors were rewarded with this title. Rarely did a senior colonial administrator seek transfer to Somaliland Protectorate as a career-enhancing move!

In October 1959, the clans of *Esa*, *Gadabur*si, *Dhulbahante* and *Warsangeli* held a conference, chaired by Garaad Mohamoud Ali Shire, in Las Anod. They formed a political party called the United Somali Party (USP), which would provide opposition to the Somali National League (SNL).

Elections were held in February 1960, on universal adult male suffrage. The Somali National League (SNL) and the United Somali Party (USP) won 20 and 12 seats respectively; the National United Front (NUF) won 1 seat, held by Michael Mariano. The SNL and the USP formed a coalition (SNL–USP).

A Somaliland Protectorate Legislative Council composed of the 33 elected unofficial members and 3 official members was established by the governor. From the Legislative Council members, a Somaliland Protectorate Executive Council of 4 unofficial members and 3 officials (all 7 of them to be called Ministers) was formed. The Executive Council was designated as the principal instrument of policy. The purpose of the above-mentioned Councils was to usher in, very late in the day, local government, just about four months before independence. Before this constitutional change, the legislative and the executive powers were solely vested in the governor of the protectorate.

The names and portfolios of the members of the Executive Council were as follows [87]:

Executive Council members (1960)

Mr D. Hall	Governor of the protectorate
Mr R.J. Wallace	Minister of Finance
Mr P. Carrel	Minister of Defence & Foreign Affairs
Mohamed Haji Ibrahim Egal	Minister of Local Government & Leader of Government Business
Ali Garaad Jama	Minister of Public Works & Communications
Ahmed Haji Duale	Minister of Natural Resources
Haji Ibrahim Nur	Minister of Social Services (ie Education & Health)
Yusuf Ismail Samater	Assistant Minister of Social Services

At the request of Mohamed Haji Ibrahim Egal, Minister for Local Government and Leader of Government Business, Yusuf Ismail Samater was later added to the Executive Council as Assistant Minister, Social Services. All the Executive Council members were appointed by the Governor of the protectorate.

The chain of events, since the visit of the Colonial Secretary, was rather chaotic and there was no carefully thought-through plan to guide those who were dealing with situation in the country. Events were moving at an astonishing speed. Both the British and the Somali Officials were in hurry, for different ends – for the British, to get rid of Somaliland soonest possible; for the Somalis, to obtain independence and unite with Somalia at the earliest possible time.

At the meeting of the protectorate Legislative Council on 6 April 1960, the Honourable Member for Bank Division of Hargeisa Town (Mohamed Behi) moved the following motion:

> *That it is the opinion of this House that practical steps should be taken forthwith for the immediate unification of the protectorate and Somalia, That prompt action is essential to achieve this most cherished aim, and can be fully justified by the special importance which popular feeling in this country attaches to its early achievement, That a bold and definite action be taken, and That the date of independence and unification with Somalia must be 1st July 1960, the date when Somalia will attain its full freedom [88].*

The Honourable Member for Abdulkadir (Haji Musa Ahmed Shirwa) seconded the motion, which was unanimously adopted. The rest is fateful history!

The resolution took both the protectorate and the British governments by surprise. Governor Hall, in his letter of 13 April 1960 to the Colonial Secretary [89], put forward what he thought was a plausible explanation for the unexpected resolution, pointing an "accusing figure" at Ahmed (Kaise) Haji Duale, Minister of National Resources, while, in addition, implicating Haji Mohamed Hussein in the resolution.

Haji Mohamed Hussein was from Somalia but he lived in Cairo, Egypt. He was an ardent advocate of Greater Somalia, and he used to broadcast, in Somali and Arabic, on *Sawt Al-Arab Radio* in Cairo. The governor wrote that Haji Mohamed Hussein was in Hargeisa in March 1960 and had a meeting with Ahmed Haji Duale. The governor's suspicion was that it was the influence of Haji Mohamed Hussein on Ahmed Haji Duale that prompted the resolution of the Legislative Council of 6 April 1960.

Be that as it may, the resolution meant, in effect, that the demand of Somaliland for independence from Britain was conditional on joining Somalia. The resolution also risked all the inherent perils and pitfalls such sudden policy change would entail. The Protectorate Executive Council, in turn, sprang a further surprise on the protectorate government when it approved the establishment of the "Northern Region" of the "Somali Republic" at its meeting on 13 April 1960 [90].

A budget had to be prepared to finance the Northern Region and tide it over the period up to the end of 1960, before a budget could be prepared for the united Somaliland and Somalia (in other words, the desired Somali Republic) after 1960. From 1949, the financial year of the protectorate started 1 April and ended 31 March. Thus, the annual expenditure included the expenditure of the first quarter of the following year – January to March. A budget had to be prepared for the period 1 April to 31 December 1960. However, as Somaliland was due for independence on 26 June 1960, preparing the budget proved rather tricky for the British and Somali officials who were engaged in the exercise. Because of the decision of the Executive Council on 13 April 1960, the question was what to call the country, as the country somehow developed some sort of "split personality disorder", as shown by the following three states:

- From 1 April to 25 June 1960, the country would be the "Northern Region" of the "as-yet-unborn Somali Republic" (according to the Executive Council's resolution of 13 June 1960)

- From 26 June to 30 June 1960, the country would be the Independent State of Somaliland

- From 1 July 1960, the country would become the proper Northern Region of the Somali Republic

Although I have drastically shortened and paraphrased the rather confusing document on this issue, I think I have captured the gist of what was going on in the minds of those who were framing the budget. In the end, a budget for the period 1 April to 31 December 1960 was presented to the Executive Council on 16 June 1960, and it was approved. The expenditure for the period April to December 1960 was given as follows:

Expenditure for the "Northern Region" for April–December 1960 [91]

Local revenue	£652,663
Government subsidy	£640,000 (including £265,000 for the Somaliland Scouts)
Total expenditure	**£1,292,663** of which expenditure on education = £70,983 (5.5% of the total expenditure)

The expenditure included £20,000 for establishing an embassy in London, UK. This perhaps meant that the money was the share of the Northern Region of the cost, for the period 1 July to 31 December 1960, of the embassy which the Somali Republic might establish in London; or that Somaliland might change its mind about unification with Somalia and establish its own embassy in London, which was very unlikely!

The Executive Council was extremely keen on early independence and the unification of Somaliland and Somalia. To show its impatience, at its meeting on 26 April 1960, the Executive Council requested the government to find out from constitutional experts in London whether it was necessary for the protectorate to be declared an independent state for a short period before the declaration of union with Somalia. The council was advised that "within the knowledge at present available it would appear that such a short period might be required in which the Provisional government here should take certain necessary legislative actions" [92]. Was the Executive Council jumping the gun or was it that an arrangement of sorts was reached with Mogadishu, in advance of independence and unification?

The last meeting of the protectorate Executive Council was on 18 June 1960.

How many of the Somaliland public were aware that, by 13 April 1960, the country was, in all but name, already part of the non-existent Somali Republic?

To show that Somaliland was, in effect, already part of the "future Somali Republic", on the Somaliland's Independence Day, the Somalia flag was hoisted. It is a five-pointed star on a blue background. The flag, with the mutual agreement of the Somali Youth League (SYL) and the Italian Trusteeship Administration in Somalia, was introduced and presented to the UN Mission in Somalia in September 1954. The flag was adopted via a Decree of the Italian President [93].

It ought to be kept in mind that, here, I am dealing with history which has to be told, without bias, as it was recorded. Commenting on it is another matter. It is a truism that history does not please everybody. With the benefit of hindsight, some might think that the situation could have been handled differently. However, I think it has to be accepted, as I do, that the way the Somali leaders acted truly reflected the current mood in Somaliland Protectorate where "short-term" politics trumped all other considerations.

Somaliland delegation for constitutional talks with the British government [94]

To implement the 6 April 1960 resolution, a Somali delegation (photo below) from Somaliland Protectorate travelled to Britain to conduct constitutional talks with the British government, lasting 2 to 12 May 1960. On the last day of the conference, the independence date of Somaliland was set for 26 June 1960.

The session for signing the document for Somaliland Independence: **Standing** (left to right): Sir D. Hall, (last Governor of Somaliland Protectorate), Ali Garaad Jama, Haji Ibrahim Nur and Ahmed (Kaise) Haji Dulale; **sitting** (left to right): Mohamed Haji Ibrahim Egal, Mr I. Macleod, (Secretary of State for the Colonies). (Egal became the 2nd President of the Republic of Somaliland on 16 May 1993. He died on 3 May 2002, while still President).

The political atmosphere in Somaliland Protectorate being what it was, no Somalilander can doubt the integrity of the delegates or criticize them for the position they took in the negotiations. They really correctly interpreted the current mood of the people of Somaliland Protectorate. What became glaringly obvious was the dismal lack of constitutional development in the country, and that was why the British government, very late in the day, decided to wash its hands of the Cinderella of the British Empire!

Somaliland Protectorate was the odd one out in the British Empire. Historically, the British government used to prepare its African dependencies for local government. Nationals working in local government gained, over time, experience in administration. As independence approached, practically all local government departments would be headed by trained national administrators, experienced in public administration. At independence, a "Government-in-waiting" would move in to take up the reins of the new government of the independent country.

Somaliland Protectorate did not go through that gradual process in which experience in public administration was gained. This was due to the British government's lack of interest in the country – hence the "stagnation policy", described in the book. This neglect resulted in grossly inadequate development, including formal education, in the country. In effect, the country moved from direct protectorate government rule to direct union with Somalia. As discussed later under Ref. 218 (page 320), in March 1959, out of 33 administrative government posts, the Somalis held 8 of them. To this day, the country suffers from the lack of sufficiently trained and experienced public administrators.

Oddly enough, just before signing the Independence Document, Mr Macleod, the Secretary of State for the Colonies, forgetting what his government told the Somaliland delegation in 1955 (about the Hawd and the Reserved Area), required the Somali delegation to agree that they would arrange for the clan leaders to accept the independence of Somaliland and to abrogate all the "treaties" and free the British government from all obligations under the treaties. He stated that the treaties were, in the first place, entered into with the Somali tribes.

That showed that the Secretary of State for the Colonies was not really satisfied that the Somaliland delegation represented the people of Somaliland. The Somaliland delegation agreed that a meeting would be held for the Council of Elders of the protectorate on 24 May 1960 when the policy of independence would be endorsed. The Elders' consent was obtained.

Thus, the British government had it both ways – by considering treaties invalid and valid at the same time to suit its interests. It would appear that the government borrowed the Somali expression *"La jiifsaanna bannaan"* (in other words, bending the rule!), which is applicable to such insincere behaviour. Perhaps when the Secretary of State for the Colonies signed the independence document, he heaved a sigh of relief and inaudibly muttered to himself "good riddance to Somaliland, no more drain on the British Treasury"!

> DATE FOR INDEPENDENCE
>
> 42. The Somaliland delegation proposed that the date of independence be the twenty-sixth of June, 1960. The Secretary of State said that this would be acceptable.
>
> SIGNED this 12th day of May 1960.
>
> *[signature]*
> IAIN MACLEOD
>
> *[signature]*
> D. B. HALL
>
> *[signature]*
> MOHAMED HAJI IBRAHIM EGAL
>
> *[signature]*
> AHMED HAJI DUALEH
>
> *[signature]*
> ALI GERAD JAMA
>
> *[signature]*
> HAJI IBRAHIM NUR
>
> *[signature]*
> H. C. F. WILKS
> Secretary

The signature page of the Independence Document confirming the date of independence for Somaliland, 12 May 1960.

[Just for the sake of argument, what would the situation have been had the Somaliland delegation rejected Mr Macleod's demand or the Elders declared that there were no treaties to be abrogated, as that action had already been carried out unilaterally by the British government? Perhaps the British government would have found itself in the International Court of Justice. Just a thought!]

BY THE QUEEN
A PROCLAMATION

TERMINATING HER MAJESTY'S PROTECTION OVER THE SOMALILAND PROTECTORATE.

ELIZABETH R.

Whereas the territories in Africa known as the Somaliland Protectorate are under Our protection:

And whereas by treaty, grant, usage, sufferance and other lawful means We have power and jurisdiction in the Somaliland Protectorate:

And whereas it is intended that the Somaliland Protectorate shall become an independent country on the twenty-sixth day of June 1960 (hereinafter referred to as "the appointed day"):

Now, therefore, We do hereby, by and with the advice of Our Privy Council, proclaim and declare that, as from the beginning of the appointed day, Our protection over the territories known as the Somaliland Protectorate shall cease, and all treaties and agreements in force immediately before the appointed day between Us or Our Government of the United Kingdom of Great Britain and Northern Ireland and any of the Tribes of the said territories, all Our obligations existing immediately before that day towards the said territories and all functions, powers, rights, authority or jurisdiction exercisable by Us immediately before that day in or in relation to the said territories by treaty, grant, usage, sufferance or otherwise, shall lapse.

> Given at Our Court at Buckingham Palace this twenty-third day of June in the year of our Lord one thousand nine hundred and sixty, and in the ninth year of Our Reign.

GOD SAVE THE QUEEN

The above proclamation from Friday 24th June 1960 begins with the words "the territories in Africa". This indicates that the British government all along considered Somaliland as different territories belonging to the different clans with which it signed the so-called "treaties". Perhaps the Queen was not briefed that the treaties she was cancelling had already been unilaterally dishonoured by one of Queen Victoria's governments, about 12 years after they were entered into!

The British occupation of Somaliland finally came to an end after midnight on 26 June 1960, when the Union Jack was lowered, folded and handed over to the British representative, Mr Carrel, who returned from whence he came, while Somaliland became a Sovereign State – or was it?

The last governor of the protectorate, Mr Hall, perhaps had no stomach for the scene of the Union Jack being brought down for good. He hurriedly left the country on the morning of 25 June 1960. Mr Carrel, Chief Secretary to the defunct protectorate government, became Acting Governor for 14 hours to suffer the indignity avoided by Mr Hall and he took away the folded Union Jack [95].

Perhaps there was more to it than the governor merely avoiding participating in the independence celebrations. The fact that the people of Somaliland, through their elected Legislative Council, opted for independence and union with Somalia, perhaps displeased the British government. To display their displeasure, they not only prevented the presence of the governor but also decided not to field a member of the royal family to "grace" the occasion, as used to be the custom at such events. In a bit of a huff, they ordered their man, the governor, to depart the country post-haste – or could it be that the British government came to the conclusion that, since Somaliland was already part of the Somali Republic, there was not much of an independence to celebrate?

Anyway, the people of Somaliland were totally absorbed in their celebrations and were oblivious to the sudden departure of the governor. They were listening, on Radio Hargeisa, to the uplifting poem called *"Kaana siib Kanna saar"*, composed and recited in his distinctive voice by the late nationalist poet Abdullahi Suldaan Mohamed (aka *Tima'adde*). Although the poem was for the occasion, it was, in particular, for the Somali Flag.

In memory of Tima'adde, I quote below the four lines which form the refrain of the poem. I am not endowed with the ability to compose poems, let alone rendering them into another language. I can only try to give a rough translation of the meaning of the lines:

Saaxirkii kala guuray 'e	We split with the sorcerer (Saaxirkii, ie sorcerer, is a metaphor for the colonialist)
Sareeyow ma nuqsaamow	The ever-high-up, the-ever-complete (ie the Somali Flag)
Aan siduu yahay eego 'e	In order to admire its sight (ie the Somali Flag)
Kaana siib Kanna saar	Lower that (the Union Jack – below left), <u>Hoist this</u> (the Somali Flag – below right)

 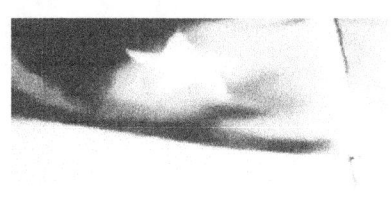

I could have pictured brand new flags, but I kept the old ones used for that momentous occasion of 26 June 1960, for historical interest. The translation of the poem leaves much to be desired, but I hope it conveys the drift of what the lines mean.

About the ceremonial proceedings in Mogadishu, on the occasion of the unification of the State of Somaliland and Somalia on 1 July 1960, the British Representative in Mogadishu reported to his government on 8 July 1960 and wrote:

> *At 8.30 am on 1st July 1960, the combined former Legislative Assemblies of Somalia and Somaliland met to ratify the Act of Union between Somalia and Somaliland. Union was acclaimed by show of hands, but no document was signed. Members went on to confirm Adan Abdulla as Provisional President of the Somali Republic and oaths of loyalty were taken [96].*

These randomly selected historical events, by a non-historian, cannot by any stretch of the imagination be taken as the history of the British Somaliland Protectorate. The events are meant to provide context for the development (or lack of it) of formal education in the country during the British occupation.

The selected historical events (1884–1960) end here. Good riddance to colonialism! [6]

---

[6] For the record: The position of Colonial Secretary was first created in 1768 for the North American colonies, and the position was abolished in 1966. The British government stopped, by law, the use of the term 'Colony' in 1981. The sun effectively and finally set on the British Empire when, in 1997, Hong Kong was transferred to China. The UK still has a few overseas territories (not described as colonies). As someone put it, the Commonwealth represents the ghost of the British Empire!

Section 4:
Formal Education in British Somaliland Protectorate

All the names and dates of when the individual commissioners/governors first assumed their duties in the protectorate have already been given in the appropriate places in Section 3. In Section 4, on formal education, only some commissioners and governors are named, as required.

Scholars debate when and how Islam reached the people of Somaliland. The general view is that Islam reached the Coast of Somaliland, through proselytizers / traders/Muslim Arabs, sometime after the Hijra (ie seventh century).

Since that time, until fairly recently, the only traditional institution in the country for learning had either been the *Mal'amd* (*Qur'aanic* schools), some of them also taught basic Arabic in settlements; or the "itinerant religious Classes" (*Xerr*, in Somali), a mobile group of young men led by a learned Sheikh and dependent for their livelihood on the hospitality of the nomadic communities among which they moved.

Young boys studying the *Qur'aan* in the traditional way, by using roughly hewn wooden boards and twig pencils ("Loox" and "qalum", respectively, in Somali). The ink ("khad" in Somali) is prepared by rubbing charcoal into either small amount of water or fresh milk.

4.1 Small private schools in coastal towns

The Roman Catholic mission school [97]

In April 1891, the Rev. Louis de G. Lasserre, Bishop of Morocco and Vicar Apostolic of Arabia, applied to Mr Sealy (the British Political Agent and Consul for the Somali Coast in Aden) for permission to establish a branch of his French Catholic mission "in the Somali country". His intention was to have a farm in the interior. In May 1891 he was permitted to go to *Suqsade* and *Wagar* areas in the Golis Range Mountains to look for a suitable location. But the Mohamed Esa Clan which lived in these areas refused point-blank to allow him to settle there.

Mr Lasserre returned to Aden and it was thought that was the end of the matter. However, between 1891 and 1894, the Lasserre Mission was permitted to rent a house in Berbera, with the philanthropic object of feeding, housing and educating abandoned children in Berbera. In March 1894, Mr Lasserre applied to the British Assistant Political Resident in Berbera for a site in Berbera where he could build a permanent mission station. The application was rejected. In September 1894, Mr Lasserre renewed his application, and this time a piece of land (Shac'ab area) in Berbera was given to him for the purpose mentioned above. The Berbera community was not consulted on the concession granted to Mr Lasserre.

In 1909, some Aqils and other Somali elders complained to the Wingate mission members (see page 62) about Christian missionaries interfering with the religion of the young Somali boys and girls [26]. The concession and the conditions attached to it read thus:

Concession No. 1274 of 1894: Somali Coast Agency, Aden, 29 December 1894

Permission is hereby given to the Right Reverend Dr L. de G. Lasserre, Bishop of Morocco and Vicar Apostolic of Arabia, Superior of the Roman Catholic Mission at Berbera on the Somali Coast, to occupy the building site in Berbera, bounded on the north, south, east and west by Government occupied ground, for the erection of a Chapel, School-House, Residence, Quarters for the missionaries and other Outhouses, on the following conditions:

That the Mission shall conform to the British law and procedures,

That no flag of any kind shall be flown on the premises,

That the Mission or any of its officials or employees shall not interfere or act as agents in political matters, and if any such official or employee is found to be so acting, he shall be removed by the Bishop, on the request from the authorities at Berbera,

> *That proper sanitation measures shall be adopted, as approved by the Government Officer-in-Charge, Berbera,*
>
> *That the right of occupancy is not transferable without previous permission in writing from Government; and after transfer the Roman Catholic Mission shall not occupy the premises as tenants.*

The Rev. Lasserre accepted the above conditions attached to the concession granted to him. In Berbera, the mission took in abandoned children and pauper adults to feed, house, clothe, educate and teach them the doctrine of Christianity. After some complaints of some relatives, no child was to be received into the Mission, unless by the consent of his/her relatives or the Aqil of his/her Clan. The mission was permitted to convert the children to Christianity, but the mission would only preach within the Mission's precincts. The converted children wore crucifixes round their necks. The mission did not have on their staff health professionals of any kind and relied on the government Medical Officer for medical assistance.

In 1904, the mission requested Colonel Swayne – Consul-General and Commander of the Imperial Forces in the protectorate – to allow them to establish a mission Station in the interior. Instead of a mission station, they were allowed to establish a camp at Shimbirale which the mission could use as a health resort for missionaries who required a change from Berbera, and for gardening purposes – on condition that *no missionary work should be undertaken at Shimbirale nor should buildings of a permanent nature be erected there.*[1]

The mission kept flocks of sheep and herds of cattle at Shimbirale. They employed children and others in gardening and tending the flocks. The mission ignored the conditions attached to Shimbirale camp and carried out missionary work there, and built houses (they called them "shelters") for their staff and pupils.

During the withdrawal from the interior and concentration in coast (see section 3.4), the Roman Catholic mission was ordered, for their safety, to close down on 13 March 1910. By 22 March, the Mission's activities at Shimbirale and in Berbera came to an end. The government never recognized Shimbirale as a mission station. However, the mission admitted that they had 110 pupils there – boys and girls. This was against the concession granted to them.

The mission claimed compensation for losses at Shimbirale and in Berbera. The government awarded the mission 40,000 rupees as compensation for their buildings in Berbera (which the government took over) and rejected any compensation for losses at Shimbirale, as the mission did not adhere to the conditions that had been mutually agreed. The mission sent some of their pupils to their mission

---

1 Shimbirale, about 30 miles south of Berbera, is a fertile valley extending westward from the detached mountain called Dhimole [1, p. 77].

station in Aden – including some who were older than 18 years and could give their consent, and younger ones who had the consent of their relatives or the Aqils of their clan. All the staff of the mission left Berbera for Djibouti on 3 May 1910 [98].

Just about a year after the mission had left the country, the Branch of the mission in Aden applied to the government in August 1911 for permission to re-start missionary work in Somaliland. The application was rejected. Dating from that rejection in 1911, Christian missions were never allowed to carry out missionary work in the country, in spite of frequent applications from different Christian missions (for further details see 4.4).

A few Christian Somalis who were taught by the mission in Berbera or at Shimbirale were perhaps the first Somalis to receive some sort of formal education. Some were employed by the protectorate government as clerks or telegraphists.

Small *Qur'aanic*/Arabic Schools [99]

In 1898, a small *Qur'aanic*-cum-Arabic School was opened in Berbera. By 1905, similar small schools were opened in both Bulahar and Zeila. All the three schools were built by private initiative and were run by their owners. Apart from the *Qur'aan*, basic Arabic and arithmetic (in Arabic) were taught. Most of the pupils were the children of Arab and Indian traders. The very few Somali pupils who attended these schools were the sons of government employees.

The government subsidised the schools with small annual amounts. The enrolment at the schools in 1907 was given as: Berbera School – 71 pupils; Bulahar School – 34 pupils; and Zeila School – 74 pupils. The composition of the pupils reflected the permanent population in the three towns.

The total returns of a non-Somali census [100], taken in 1911, in the three towns of Zeila, Bulahar and Berbera, were recorded as follows: Arabs – 1,857; Indians – 741; Europeans – 26; mixed population – 798. The composition of the mixed population was not further classified, but none was Somali. It is apparent that what little education existed was for the resident Arabs and Indians. It would also appear that, at that time, the coastal towns were permanently populated by non-Somalis.

In addition to the information about formal education, I was also interested in the *total* annual expenditure on the protectorate. As described under 3.4, expenditure on the campaigns against the Dervishes (1901 to 1904) was given as £2,450,100 (a portion of which was locally raised revenue). At first, I was inclined to disregard this expenditure. However, as the expenditure was incurred in Somaliland Protectorate, I reluctantly left it in. The £2,450,100 was apportioned over four years – in other words, £612,525 was added to the annual government subsidies of each of the four years, 1901 to 1904. These campaigns which the British Government conducted to occupy Somaliland by force brought nothing but death and destruction to the people of Somaliland.

The annual expenditure published by the Somaliland Protectorate Government consisted of the revenues raised locally and the British Government subsidies. This expenditure was the combined routine military and civil expenditure, up to and including 1939. The expenditure was reported to the Colonial Office in sterling pounds, although the currency of Somaliland Protectorate was initially the Indian Rupee.[2]

The published and available annual expenditure on the protectorate for the years 1900 to 1960 is summarized in six tables, each of which covers a 10-year period, as a convenient way of viewing the relative expenditure on formal education at different periods. The audited annual government expenditure figures are used throughout the book.

Table 1: Annual expenditure (in sterling £) on Somaliland Protectorate, 1900–1909:[3]

	1900	1901	1902	1903	1904	1905	1906	1907	1908	1909
Local revenues	22,402 (43.1%)	28,878 (4.3%)	24,968 (3.8%)	39,842 (6%)	35,188 (4.8%)	39,477 (34.2%)	38,388 (50.9%)	28,607 (27.2%)	30,326 (25.4%)	31,382 (14.1%)
Government subsidies	29,557 (56.9%)	642,897* (95.7%)	635,014* (96.2%)	627,333* (94%)	690,994* (95.2%)	76,000 (65.8%)	37,000 (49.1%)	76,593 (72.8%)	89,000 (74.6%)	190,500** (85.9%)
Annual expenditure	51,959	671,775	659,982	667,175	726,182	115,477	75,388	105,200	119,326	221,882
Expenditure on education	...	...	...	103 (0.02%)	104 (0.01%)	102 (0.09%)	164 (0.2%)	103 (0.1%)	105 (0.09%)	107 (0.05%)

* Government subsidies in 1901–04 were inflated by the £2,450,100 on campaigns against the Dervishes: thus sum of £612,525 is added to each annual government subsidy (1901 to 1904).

** Ain valley occupation and evacuation operation from the interior increased the expenditure in 1909 and 1910. No money on education was recorded for the years 1900–1902.

Even the three small schools in the coastal towns and the paltry subsidies spent on them were not mainly for the benefit of the Somalis. Perhaps such ridiculously small sums of money were shown in the annual expenditure to give the illusion that educational services were being provided in the country!

---

2 The rupee was later replaced with the East African Shilling – after World War II. The Shilling ceased to be legal tender after the independence of the country in 1960, and the Somalia Shilling was adopted for the two united countries of Somalia and Somaliland.

3 For expenditure data, see the following references: 1900–1905 [101]; 1906–1908 [102]; 1909 [103].

As a result of the building of the Djibouti–Addis Ababa railway by the French in the 1890s and 1920s, trade in west of Somaliland coast shifted to Djibouti. Consequently, attendances at Zeila and Bulahar schools dwindled to insignificance and the schools ceased to function by 1920. Apart from campaigns against the Dervishes, nothing much else was then happening in the country. The so-called "Protectorate Government" existed in name only.

The second table of the 10-yearly annual expenditure follows:

Table 2: Annual expenditure (in sterling £) on Somaliland Protectorate, 1910–1919[4]

	1910	1911	1912	1913	1914	1915	1916	1917	1918	1919
Local revenues	30,862 (23.4%)	26,472 (100%)	29,735 (71.1%)	30,482 (61%)	30,307 (38.3%)	29,270 (23.5%)	40,008 (31.6%)	42,008 (36.3%)	54,497 (37%)	81,870 (25.3%)
Government subsidies	101,000 (76.6%)	Nil*	12,103 (28.9%)	19,440 (38.9%)	48,859 (61.7%)	95,197 (76.5%)	87,409 (68.4%)	73,815 (63.7%)	92,831 (63%)	241,119 (74.7%)
Annual expenditure	131,862	26,472	41,838	49,922	79,166	124,467	127,417	115,823	147,328	322,989
Expenditure on education	112 (.08%)	112 (0.4%)	112 (0.3%)	112 (0.2%)	112 (0.1)	92 (0.07)	96 (0.08%)	132 (0.1%)	98 (0.07%)	391 (0.1%)

*During Coastal Concentration. The so-called government raised enough local revenue for its presence in the coast.

Six Somali boys sent to Sudan for education [110]

On 19 December 1919, six Somali boys, some of whom attended one or other of the three schools mentioned earlier, were sent to Gordon Memorial College, Khartoum, Sudan. One of the boys was Mohamoud Ahmed Ali – he was about 16 years old at the time; he would later become the pioneer in the field of formal education in Somaliland Protectorate.

The names of the other boys were given as: Mohamed Gabobe, Adan Burale, Ahmed Sh. Musa, Ibrahim Adan (? Qalab-Jaan) and Omer Mohamoud. The first three, who were expected to return by 1923, were supposed to be Arabic teachers. The last two and Mohamoud Ahmed were to complete a full course in the literary section of Gordon College and return by 1927. The parents of the boys paid part of their sons' fees and the other part was considered as a Protectorate Government scholarship. The boys were the sons of Somali notables and/or government employees – for example, Mohamoud Ahmed's father was a government employee interpreter in Berbera; Adan Burale's father was a policeman in Zeila; and the

---

4 For expenditure data, see the following references: 1910 [104], 1911 [105], 1912 [106], 1913 [107], 1914 [108], 1915–1919 [109].

father of Ahmed Sh. Musa was a *Qaadi* (judge in Shariah) and a prominent leader of the *Qaadiriya Dariqa* (a religious sect) in Burao.

Scanned below is a report on the progress of the six boys, submitted by the Director of Education, Sudan, in March 1920 to the Somaliland Government [111]:

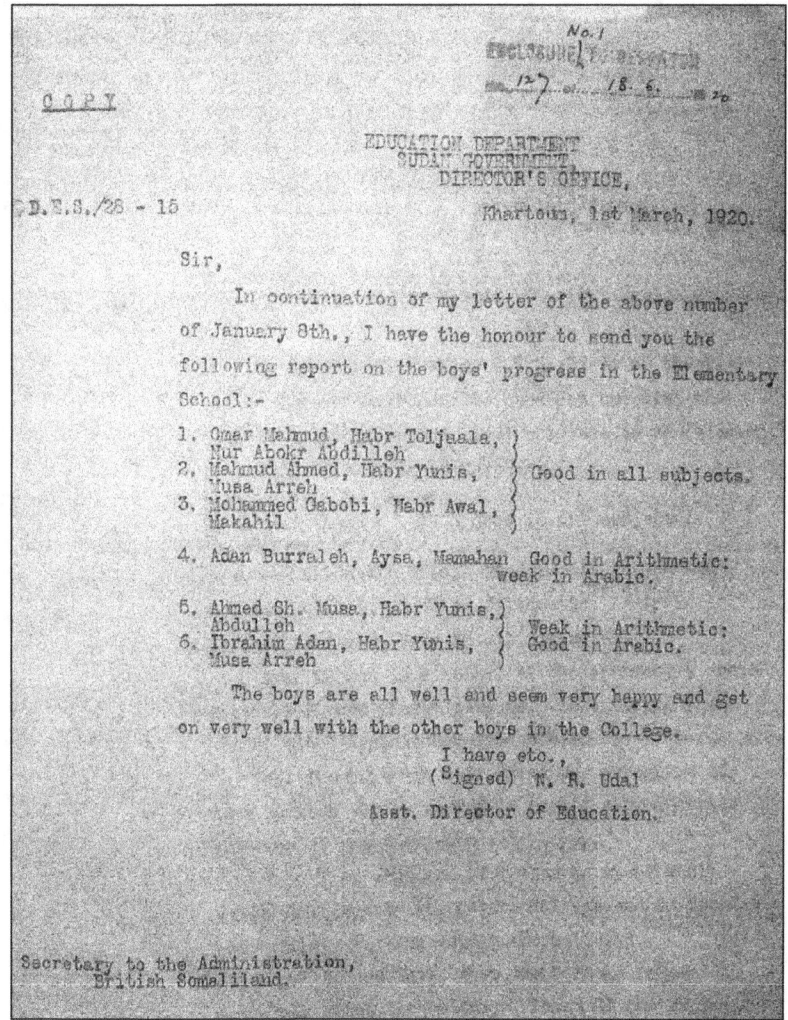

Progress report of six Somali boys from Director of Education, Sudan (March 1920): the first three are described as being "Good in all subjects"; the next is apparently "Good in Arithmetic, weak in Arabic"; the final two are "Weak in Arithmetic, Good in Arabic". The report concludes: "The boys are all well and seem very happy and get on very well with the other boys in the College."

4.2 The Genesis of British educational policy for British Colonial Tropical Africa

So far, there had been no government effort to initiate a formal educational programme in the Somaliland Protectorate. Before proceeding any further, I will briefly review how education for the British Tropical African Colonies originated. This type of education was foreshadowed by a Privy Council memorandum of 1847 on "industrial schools for the coloured races", setting forth a number of ideas which were later incorporated into colonial provision for education in Africa. The structure of the Indian education was considered rather top-heavy, following the establishment of universities whose students became leaders in the movements of political discontent – a type of education (ie academic) that was therefore to be avoided in Africa [112].

Phelps-Stokes Fund influence in the education for Colonial Tropical Africa [113]

At the beginning of the 20th century there were, in the USA Southern States, Christian missions which provided basic education for the poor Afro-American manual workers who worked on the farms owned by white Americans. One of the Christian missions was known as Phelps-Stokes Fund. This mission thought that the type of education offered to the Afro-Americans was also suitable for the British African colonies.

In 1920, the Phelps-Stokes Fund, in collaboration with multi-national missionaries, sent a Commission to the British West African Colonies, with the following terms of reference [113]:

1. To enquire as to the educational work being done at present in each of the areas to be studied,
2. To investigate the educational needs of the people in the light of the religious, social, hygiene and economic conditions,
3. To ascertain to what extent these needs are being met,
4. To assist in the formulation of plans designed to meet the educational needs of the native races,
5. To make available the full results of this study.

The report of the Commission was published in 1922; and it made specific recommendations for each country visited. The Commission also issued general policy recommendations containing core ideas, as listed below, which permeated the country-specific recommendations. The Commission envisaged that the core ideas would form a blueprint for the future education of the British Tropical

African Colonies. These core ideas were:

1. Teaching of industrial education and agriculture as the core basis of Colonial African education, ie vocational and technical training
2. Africans to be given education which would equip them for rural life
3. The vernacular to be used for lower primary classes
4. That there would be a uniform system of education in all government and missionary schools
5. Employment of untrained teachers
6. Establishing teacher training centres
7. Less emphasis on "literary or bookish" education of Africans, as it was considered to be irrelevant to their needs
8. Education to be run on racial segregation line
9. Setting up District Education Committees
10. The aim was to train the African for manual work – in factories or on farms; adult education was to form part of such education
11. Women's education was to be based on domestic science, which consisted of personal hygiene, caring for infants, food preparation and nursing the sick

It seemed that women were merely to "supply" the future healthy manual workers! The Commission argued that the type of proposed education for the African colonies was designed to meet the needs of both labour development and the Christian civilizing missionaries. It was clear that literacy for Bible reading and spread of Christianity was the Christian mission's education priority objectives.

The Colonial Office reacted to the Phelps-Stokes Fund Education Commission's report, by appointing, in November 1923, an Advisory Committee on Native Education in the British Tropical African Dependencies [114]. The Secretary of the Committee was Mr Hanns Vischer, who was based at the Colonial Office. Expenditure on the Committee was covered by the Colonial Governments of the African Dependencies. The terms of the Committee were:

1. To advise the Secretary of State for the Colonies on any matters of "native education" in the British Colonies and Protectorates in Tropical Africa which he may from to time refer to them
2. To assist him in advancing the progress of education in those colonies and protectorates

Of the ten members of the committee, at least two were identifiable as representing the churches. However, what was the background of the Secretary of Committee, Mr Vischer? He was Swiss, educated in Britain, and 1899 he joined the Church Missionary Society (CMS) in Britain. In 1900, he sailed to Nigeria to join the Christian missionaries to the Hausa in Northern Nigeria. He resigned from CMS in 1902. In 1903, he was naturalized as a British subject. In 1908, the Commissioner of Northern Nigeria, Mr Frederick Lugar, tasked Mr Vischer with organizing elementary education in that territory. In 1914, when the Southern and Northern parts of Nigeria merged into one country, he became the Director of Education for Northern Nigeria. As already mentioned, he was the Secretary of the Advisory Committee for Native Education for British Colonial Africa. He later became the Secretary General and Founder Member of the International Institute of African Languages and Culture based in London [115]. Mr Vischer had significant influence in the education for Colonial Tropical Africa in the 1920s and 30s.

The Colonial Office invited the Phelps-Stokes Fund to co-sponsor – with the Colonial Office – a Commission to visit East, Central and South African colonies, using the terms of reference for the Commission which had visited the British West African Dependencies. The sponsored Commission carried out its studies and reported on its work in 1924.

Mr Vischer participated in the Commission. Again, the Commission made country-specific recommendations (for example, for Kenya) and endorsed the general recommendations of the previous Commission to the West African Dependencies.

The report of the Commission to East/Central/South Africa was published in 1925, and it was discussed at a conference held in Belgium in 1926, attended by multi-national missionary societies. The object of conference was that the missionary societies would coordinate their future educational efforts in colonial Africa.

The above-mentioned Commission did not visit Somaliland Protectorate, and it is not difficult to guess why that was the case. The recent religious/political Dervish struggle of Seyyid Mohamed Abdullah Hassan was still fresh in the minds of the British Government. Also, the type of education which the Phelps-Stokes Fund was advocating for the British African Colonies was to be largely implemented by Christian missions. Somaliland Protectorate had, therefore, to be left out from the Commission's itinerary. The people of Somaliland would not have anything to do with Christian missionaries and they would have probably objected to the Somali language being written in Roman script.

The attempts to introduce formal education in 1922 and 1938 – as well as the educational programme introduced into Somaliland Protectorate in 1944 – all mirrored, to a large extent, the Phelps-Stokes Fund philosophy on education for British Colonial Africa.

The first Director of Education of Somaliland Protectorate – R.E. Ellison, appointed in 1938 – had taught in schools in Northern Nigeria, schools set up by Mr Vischer. A later Director of Education of Somaliland Protectorate, C.R.V.

Bell, taught at schools in Kenya in the 1930s – Kenya being one of the countries for which specific recommendations were made by the Phelps-Stokes Fund Education Commission in 1924.

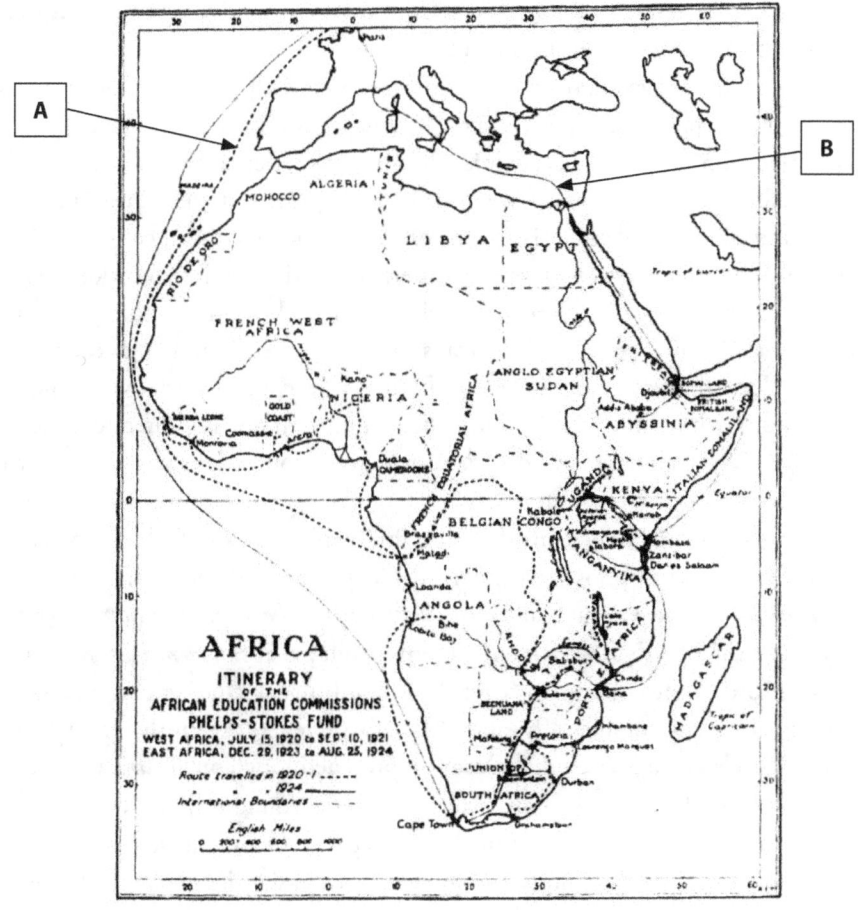

Itinerary of the African Education Commissions, Phelps-Stokes Fund (1920–21 and 1923–24)
Line A: Route taken by the Commission to West Africa, 1920–21.
Line B: Route taken by the Commission to East/Central/South Africa, 1923–24.

Colonial Education Policy for British Tropical Africa [116]

The Advisory Committee on Native Education for Colonial Tropical Africa prepared a Memorandum in which they outlined their views about the form the education for Colonial Africa should take. They submitted the memorandum to the Secretary of State for the Colonies in March 1925.

The Secretary of State for the Colonies accepted the contents of the Memorandum and published them in a document which carried the title: Colonial Education Policy for British Tropical Africa. It was modelled on the general policy recommendations of the Education Commissions of Phelps-Stokes Fund. Mr Hanns Vischer, Secretary of the Advisory Committee on Native Education at the Colonial Office, played a crucial role in this.

This Colonial education policy guided the Colonial Office in the interwar years and beyond. The policy favoured "practical" education within the context of African "tradition" in place of academic education, as stated in the Commissions' recommendations. The document was also an attempt to unite the Christian missionaries and the colonial administrations of the individual African colonies. The origin of this educational policy was the experience derived from education designed for the poor Afro-Americans, described earlier. The notion underlying this thinking was that the poor Afro-Americans – and, by extension, the Africans – lacked intellectual capacity and were merely suited for manual work, which did not demand much brain work! This attitude conjures up the semi-literate, if not illiterate, oppressed and segregated Afro-American cotton-pickers in the Southern States of USA in the 19th century.

The British Colonial policy on education for Tropical African Colonies was also predicated on the assumptions that the British colonies would allow *Christian missionaries into the colonies* and allow the *vernacular to be written in Roman script*.

It was also the British Government Colonial policy that *sufficient local revenues* would be raised in the colonies to cover the expenditure (including that on education) on running the colonies. The above three basic tenets of British colonial education policy characterized the education provided for colonial Africa.

The Colonial Office and the Christian missionaries found it that it was to their mutual advantage to work together in partnership – in other words, the colonial government would run the colony and maintain law and order; while the Christian missionaries would provide education and medical care to gain the confidence of those with whom they came into contact and create an environment conducive to effective proselytization. To achieve this, the missions would write the vernacular of the subjects of the British African colonies, so that they could read the Bible in their local languages.

Some Christian missionaries estimated that, in 1938, about 90% of education in British Colonial Africa was in the hands of Christian missionaries.

Northern Nigeria [117]

Before leaving this general survey of the British Government colonial education policy for Africa, I would like to describe briefly in here a case study which has some relevance to how the Somalis viewed Christian mission education in Somaliland Protectorate.

Mr Hanns Vischer's background and his involvement in the education in Northern Nigeria has already been described. The Commissioner of Northern Nigeria, Mr Frederick Lugard, decreed that English should be taught in the mission schools (the only schools then in the provinces) to produce junior office workers for the government. He also ordered that the Roman script be substituted for the Arabic (*ajami*) characters – in other words, that the Hausa language should be written in Roman script rather than in Arabic. Commissioner Lugard demanded that the children be sent to the mission schools to learn English. The Muslim communities (Hausa-Fulani tribes) did not readily accept the mission-based education (which echoes the experiences of the Berbera school mission in Somaliland Protectorate). They were reluctant to send their children to such schools, viewing western education as a fraudulent deception being imposed upon the Hausa people by a conquering European force. The Emirs, who kept slaves, rather than send their own children to the mission schools, instead, sent the children of their slaves! Perhaps this was unintended liberation of the slave children!

The Hausa pejoratively called the Roman script "*boko*", an indigenous Hausa word which originally connoted "sham", "deceit" or "lack of authenticity". The word came to acquire its current meaning of "Hausa written in Roman script and western education in general". The emergence of the fundamentalist group "*boko haram*" originated from this extended meaning of *boko*. My source, who authoritatively writes about the etymology of *boko*, categorically refutes the notion that the word "*boko*" was borrowed from the English word "book" [118].

There was even a Mahdi rebellion against the missionary work in Northern Nigeria in 1906. A religious man named *Mallam* (teacher) Isa, Headman of a village called Satiru, was reported to have claimed to be a Mahdi. The British Government was very sensitive to any movement involving religious discontent in Muslim countries – the Mahdi revolt in Sudan and the Dervishes in British Somaliland Protectorate were two cases in point. Commissioner Lugard, who was reputed to be cruel in the conquest of Northern Nigeria and who brooked no opposition to his rule, ruthlessly destroyed the village of that "Mahdi" and almost annihilated the people in that area [119].

Religion-wise, the situation of the Hausa people in the Northern Provinces of Nigeria was not dissimilar to that of the situation of the people of Somaliland Protectorate. Thus, one can draw a parallel between these two Muslim communities' reaction to mission-based education and writing the vernacular in Roman script.

Also, there was a direct link between the colonial formal education introduced in the Northern Provinces of Nigeria and the one attempted to be introduced in

Somaliland Protectorate in 1938. From 1928, Mr Ellison was the Superintendent of Education for the Northern Provinces of Nigeria. He used to supervise the mission-run elementary schools previously established by Mr Vischer, as described earlier. Mr Ellison was seconded to British Somaliland Protectorate and was appointed as Director of Education in 1938. He tried to transplant the mission approach to education (including, for example, writing the local language in Roman script) to another Muslim country – in other words, Somaliland Protectorate, with dire consequences for formal education in Somaliland Protectorate.

Having considered the genesis of British Colonial education policy for Tropical Africa, we will now turn to the attempted introduction of elementary education in Somaliland itself.

4.3 Attempts at introducing elementary education in Somaliland

In 1920, after the Seyyid and his Dervishes left the scene and the dust settled, Governor Archer found that the country – much to his chagrin – was, if anything, in no better state than it was in 1884. British occupation and the ensuing Dervish struggle had brought about death and destruction upon the country.

The Vatican did not forget the Catholic mission school at Berbera, which had closed down in 1910 (see 3.4). In 1920, the Vatican requested that it should be re-opened [120]. Governor Archer rejected the request and the Christian missionaries were barred from the protectorate, as they had been since 1911.

The remaining school in Berbera was, for the first 21 years, run by a Sudanese teacher named Seyyid Khayralla (who died in 1919). A Somali teacher took his place and ran the school. Although the author has no definite evidence for it, it is likely that the Somali teacher concerned was Haji Hussein Haji Duale. We will meet him again later. The tuition at the school was free and that was why the government subsidized it. The average annual enrolment was 40 boys. Yet, out of the 40 or so boys, the number of the Somali boys did not usually exceed 10 boys – the rest were classified as Indians, Arabs and Sudanese. It seems the government did not consider Sudanese as Arabs!

At the school, the *Qur'aan* and the 3 Rs (ie reading, writing and arithmetic, in Arabic) were taught. The boys were enrolled or withdrawn at the wish of their parents.

Governor Archer turned his attention to what could be done about education and how to raise local revenue to pay for the education. He sought information on a suitable way of approaching the education issues and, for the purpose, paid a visit to Sudan [121]. In Khartoum, the governor met Mr E.R.J. Hussey who was the Chief Inspector of Education of Sudan and sounded him out about his interest in going to Somaliland to advise on an educational scheme in the country. Once the governor obtained Mr Hussey's acceptance, the Colonial Office recruited him.

Consultancy of E.R.J. Hussey on formal education [122]

Mr Hussey visited the country in 1920. In his report of 5 December 1920, he recommended six elementary schools to be built – three in the coastal towns of Berbera, Bulahar and Zeila, the other three in up-country (but exactly where was not specified), and one intermediate school at Sheikh. The medium of instruction would be English. In his report, Mr Hussey stated that the people wanted Arabic and English, although he recommended English for the government schools. He recommended the local language (the vernacular) for the private schools. However, there was no role for the vernacular, since then the Somali language was not written. The issue later became a source of discontent among the Somalis, who strongly objected to writing it in Latin script. Hussey also suggested that a Sudanese headmaster be seconded to Somaliland Protectorate for three years in order to train teachers for the elementary schools and help with the initial organization. To pay for the educational scheme, he recommended that the government might impose direct taxation on stock for the partial payment of his recommended scheme. Mr Hussey's recommendations were abandoned when Governor Archer failed to implement taxation on stock in 1922 (see 3.5).

It used to be said that a college meant for Somaliland Protectorate in the 1920s was, instead, built in Khartoum, Sudan. In my search for information about formal education in Somaliland Protectorate, I did not come across any evidence which substantiated this story. Perhaps people misread or misunderstood what Governor Archer wrote in his covering letter of Mr Hussey's report on the educational scheme recommended for the country. In the letter dated 23 December 1920, the governor mooted the idea of a small college, modelled on Gordon College in Khartoum, for Somaliland Protectorate. He put it in a rather rhetorical form (in other words, wouldn't it have been better if a small college…?) He did not recommend a college for Somaliland Protectorate, and nothing came of the governor's throw-away remarks in his letter. The British Government never intended to build a college in Somaliland Protectorate. We will see that, during World War II, when the military protectorate government initiated a formal educational programme in 1944, the government then ruled out secondary schools, let alone college, for the foreseeable future.

Gordon College, Khartoum, was built with private money raised in the UK, in memory of Mr Gordon who was killed in Khartoum in 1885 by the Dervishes of Mohamed Ahmed bin Abdullah (in other words, Mohamed al-Mahdi of Sudan).

It would have been a forlorn hope to have expected the British citizens to contribute to the building of a college at Dul-Madobe in memory of Mr Corfield, who was killed at Dul-Madobe in 1913 by the Dervishes of Seyyid Mohamed Abdullah Hassan, the Mahdi of Somaliland!

In 1928, Governor Kittermaster's contribution to the discussions, about starting some form of basic education in the country, was seen as a novel idea! He suggested that:

> *An elementary schooling could be introduced by teaching convicted juveniles in small rooms (ie reformatories of a sort) attached to the main prisons [123].*

A reformatory was a residential school for the rehabilitation of children under 16 who had committed crimes punishable by imprisonment, as was the practice in Britain. The Governor included the negative remark:

> *The Somalis themselves are asking for education though I am doubtful as to how far their demand is genuine [123].*

How can one tell whether or not the Somalis' demand for education was genuine if the service was not provided? The people expressed a felt need for education. In spite of the Somalis' demand for education, successive protectorate governments maintained that the Somalis opposed formal education introduced by the government. As will be seen later, the protectorate government deceitfully interpreted rejection of written Somali in Latin script as rejection of formal education.

Anyway, the Colonial Office, instead of replying to Governor Kittermaster, minuted at one of its internal meetings in 1936: "as agreed, Kittermaster's reformatory school project had better remain in decent oblivion". Judging by the time elapsed since his proposal, it would appear that the governor did not follow it up with the Colonial Office. Perhaps he did not mean it in the first place, given his negative remark mentioned above!

The Colonial Office failed to suggest any better education, yet discouraged a project which could have at least kept delinquent children not only out of further mischief, but could also perhaps have enabled them to learn some trade.

Mohamoud Ahmed Ali (1903–1983), the doyen of formal education in Somaliland Protectorate, was sent to Sudan for education in 1919 and returned from his studies in Sudan to Somaliland Protectorate in 1927. He was employed by the protectorate government as a clerk in Berbera, since there were no other openings for educated Somalis. While still a clerk, he joined the Berbera School. It is stated in the Education Department Annual Report on Education for 1952 (see later):

> *Mohamoud Ahmed Ali after returning from Sudan in 1930 made successful representation for the payment of grants to selected Qur'aanic and/or Arabic schools in the county, in the hope of encouraging them to take a more progressive attitude.*

The most likely date of return of Mohamoud Ahmed from Sudan seems to be that given by Mr Ellison [149], as the introduction of Grants-in-Aid for *Qur'aanic* and/or Arabic Schools were in 1929, as shown below.

Governor Kittermaster accepted Mohamoud's suggestion about grants to *Qur'aanic* and/or Arabic Schools. It was decided that, for the selected schools to qualify for grants, they would teach the *Qur'aan* and/or Arabic and basic Arithmetic in Arabic, and would be open for inspection. The payment rates were given as below:

- 10 rupees/month for schools of 10–19 boys
- 20 rupees/month for schools of 20–29 boys
- 30 rupees/month for schools over 30 boys

This policy of government assistance to the private *Qur'aanic*/Arabic Schools was first implemented in Somaliland Protectorate in 1929 [124].

Perhaps the governor accepted Mohamoud's suggestion out of embarrassment, because there was no school in the country that was built and maintained by the government. The only educational facility subsidized by the government was the small school in Berbera.

The policy instigated by Mohamoud Ahmed Ali was the beginning of the assisted private *Qur'aanic*/Arabic schools which later supplied pupils for the mainstream of the future formal elementary education in the country. Apart from grants, the schools were also given a few books and articles of school equipment. The grants were paid direct to the teachers, who were also paid something, in cash or in kind, by the parents of the boys. Supervision and approval for grants before 1938 were carried out by the District Commissioners.

It became the policy of the Education Department, since the inception of the formal educational programme of 1944, which was introduced during the Second World War, to enrol boys for the government elementary classes from the aided *Qur'aanic* and/or Arabic schools in the country.

Table 3: Annual expenditure (in sterling £) on Somaliland Protectorate: 1920–1929[5]

	1920	1921	1922	1923	1924	1925	1926	1927	1928	1929
Local revenues	90,116 (25.3%)	121,980 (58.2%)	82,316 (32.2%)	78,542 (54.4%)	83,400 (53.3%)	89,057 (53.0%)	90,569 (60.7%)	67,738 (51.6%)	157,487 (84.1%)	105,781 (53.2%)
Government subsidies	266,072* (74.7%)	87,723 (41.8%)	173,530** (67.8%)	65,842 (45.6%)	72,967 (46.7%)	78,898 (47.0%)	58,556 (39.3%)	63,556 (48.4%)	29,750 (15.9%)	93,178 (46.8%)
Annual expenditure	356,188	209,703	255,846	144,384	156,367	167,955	149,125	131,294	187,237	198,959
Expenditure on education	332 (0.09%)	332 (0.2%)	498 (0.2%)	201 (0.1%)	340 (0.2%)	293 (0.2%)	135 (0.09%)	29 (0.02%)	34 (0.02%)	199 (0.1%)

* Includes £84,000 for the air campaign against the Dervishes in 1920. **Includes £500 for burning down Burao for the murder Mr Gibb in Burao in 1922.

Attempt at reviving Hussey's recommendations

In the 1930s, a few Somali parents sent their sons to Sudan to be educated. The government partly covered the cost of their tuition. The pupils included Ali Sh. Mohamed Jirdeh, Yusuf Haji Adan, Mohamed Shire Gaab, Abdisalam Hassan Mursal and Yusuf Ismail Samater.

---

5 For expenditure data, see the following documents: 1920–1921 [125], 1922 [126], 1923–1924 [127], 1925 [128], 1926–27 [129], 1928 [130], 1929 [131].

In 1935, Governor Lawrance declared his policy on education, the contents of which were:

> *Giving the Somalis and others a capacity and taste for employment in stock raising [ie animals], agriculture, industry and commerce, to enable them to appreciate realities and become more useful members of the society into which they have been born and to lead public opinion (particularly tribal) in the right direction of good government, friendship and peace. The curriculum, in addition to religious instruction, would aim at primarily providing a thorough grounding in reading, writing and arithmetic, together with some elementary knowledge of geography, hygiene, stock raising, agriculture and handiwork [132].*

He dusted the ill-fated Mr Hussey's report of 1920 report on education and extracted the main points from it. He proposed that six elementary schools be built in various unspecified parts of the country; the existing Berbera School was to be re-housed and additional funds be found for Somalis' education in Sudan.

The governor submitted his proposals to the Colonial Office. A sub-committee of the Advisory Committee on Education in the Colonies considered the proposals and advised that, to begin with, only one new elementary school should be opened and other schools to follow whenever that became practicable.

In 1936, Governor Lawrance formed a 4-man Commission [133] chaired by the Secretary to the Government, Mr C. Ploman, to advise on:

- The site of the proposed elementary school at Berbera
- The teaching staff
- The curriculum
- The language of instruction

The Commission, which did not include Somalis in its membership, recommended, among other things, that written Somali should be the medium of instruction in the school. That was what the governor was hoping for. The recommendations were sent to the Education Department of Sudan for their comments. In response, they said that the governor would be well-advised, before anything else, to recruit a European Superintendent of Education for the country. However, rather than first recruiting a European Superintendent of Education, as recommended, the governor built a new proper school building in Berbera in 1937 at a cost of £925. It was the *first* school the British Government built in the country, up to that time [134]. However, the new school would not be opened before recruiting a European Superintendent of Education. It would appear that the recruitment of the Superintendent and building the new school were not coordinated. It was like putting the cart before the horse! The Superintendent of Education should have been recruited first, to advise the local Commission that the governor formed for the new school.

Mohamoud Ahmed Ali was then the Headmaster of the old *Qur'aanic*/Arabic Berbera School, while still drawing a clerk salary. His assistant was Haji Hussein Haji Duale.

The government, in its wisdom, thought that a two-class Elementary School, where the medium of instruction was in Arabic, and managed adequately by Somali teachers, warranted the appointment of a European Superintendent of Education and the creation of a new Department of Education. If this is not making a mountain out of a molehill, I do not know what is! It was a risible attempt, on the part of the government, to raise, in that manner, its profile in the field of formal education which did not then exist in the country.

It would have made sense if the recruitment of a European Superintendent of Education and creating a Department of Education had been part and parcel of introducing national programme on formal education.

The first Director of Education for British Somaliland Protectorate [135]

Eventually, the Colonial Office recruited Mr R.E. Ellison for Somaliland Protectorate, as Superintendent (soon changed to Director) of Education. He was working in the educational services in Nigeria and arrived in Berbera on 11 April 1938, thus becoming the first Director of Education of Somaliland Protectorate.

But what about the religious background of Mr Ellison? At his memorial service at Westminster Abbey, London, in 1984, his brother, the Revd. G.A. Ellison, the former Bishop of London, described him as a great Church of England man who valued whence he came – his father had served as chaplain to Queen Victoria and King Edward VII. His grandfather was also a Bishop. When in Nigeria, according to his brother, Mr Ellison frowned upon non-church-going Europeans [136]. Mr Ellison's involvement in the Christian missionary-run educational services in Northern Nigeria has already been discussed under 4.2.

Mr R.E. Ellison, the first Director of Education of Somaliland Protectorate: April 1938 to August 1940.

Sometime after his arrival in Berbera, Mr Ellison toured the country, visiting – as well as Berbera – Burao, Hargeisa and Borama, in order to familiarize himself with the situation in the country and to have discussions with the District Commissioners and some Somali elders.

Mr Ellison expressed his opinion about education for the Somalis even before the new Berbera School opened. He wrote in his annual report on education for 1938 that:

> *The primary stage of education should be considered as an end in itself and it should be designed with regard to the needs of the majority of Somali boys who would come from rural areas and who would not normally pass beyond the primary stage [137].*

This illiberal attitude towards education in the country was not surprising, as he was reflecting Governor Lawrance's educational policy, already mentioned.

The Somalis' objection to written Somali, not to formal education

Then arose the question of what medium of instruction to be used in the new school in Berbera. (I use the terms "Latin script" and "Roman alphabet" interchangeably.)

Mr Ellison, Governor Lawrance and the Colonial Office were all keen on writing the vernacular (ie Somali language) in the Latin script. Governor Lawrance was intent on using written Somali in the school. However, since the Sudan Education Department did not comment on the governor's Commission recommendation for written Somali, the governor sought further advice from the Education Department of Sudan. The Department recommended Arabic to be used since, in their opinion, like other unwritten languages, unwritten Somali would have no cultural value and would eventually disappear and Arabic would take its place. However, the Education Department of Sudan also suggested that written Somali would be useful for district administrators [138]. That was how ignorant some people were about a living language used by a thriving society.

Mr Ellison was lukewarm about the Arabic language as the medium of instruction in the school and he much preferred the written Somali. He argued that Arabic was not a language known to the people and it was not one which could feed into any subsequent education programme of interest to the protectorate. Mr Ellison's experience in the education introduced in the Muslim Northern Provinces of Nigeria has been described earlier, especially replacing the Arabic alphabet with Roman script *"boko"*.

Mr Ellison failed to appreciate that the *Qur'aan* is in Arabic and the children have to learn how to read and write the *Qur'aan* in Arabic. Secondly, Arabic, rather than being unknown to the Somalis, was the main non-Somali language in which some Somalis were literate, although a few Somali government employees also used a little English. There was evidence that Mr Ellison could not relate to the Somaliland community. In a letter to his father he wrote, in part:

> *Somali Muslims are very different proposition from our nice, respectful, obedient and well-behaved Muslims of Northern Nigeria.*

Mr Ellison was not the first British Colonial Administrator to complain about the Somali disdain for unearned obedience.

Mr Ellison was not sure how to go about the education in the country. He wondered how education could be introduced into a country where 95% of the population was nomadic, and he wrote home saying, in part:

> *…population consisting of herdsmen who are constantly on the move and know no settled village or town life at all. About half a dozen mushroom townships, excluding Berbera, have grown up around district HQs and the Somalis who become townsmen are generally agreed to be an unpleasant and uncharacteristic lot. If we open schools we shall be bringing up the Somali youth in an environment that is quite unnatural and likely to be harmful to him. Modern education theory is that school life must be closely associated with home life and the educational programme must be adapted towards the kind of life which the pupils are going to live when they leave the school. If we educate them in the towns they will grow up as horrible little townees and will despise the nomadic life of the bush. Govt. rightly deprecates this, but at the same time opens its first school in Berbera. The reasoning seems to be incredible [139].*

It is obvious that, if Mr Ellison had had his way, there would have been no schools in towns. He also admits that the population was predominantly nomadic, constantly on the move, and fixed educational facilities for them were then impracticable. He was against opening schools in the town, and schools could not be built in nomadic areas – then how on earth could formal education be provided for the country? Mr Ellison steeped himself, while in Northern Nigeria, in the British Colonial policy for education in Tropical Africa – the aim of which was to keep the colonized Africans in the rural areas and deliver limited literacy for manual work and for reading the Bible. He could not think of any other educational policy for Somaliland Protectorate.

The educational system that might have satisfied Mr Ellison's idea about starting formal education in the country was a beefed up *Xerr* (itinerant religious classes, in Somali), described at the beginning of Section 4. Had Mr Ellison's views prevailed, formal education in the country would have suffered enormously.

If I may digress for a moment: I personally observed, at different periods in two different countries, education (or more accurately, literacy) specifically designed for nomads. The first was in Somalia in 1973. The Government of Mohamed Siad Barre, after adopting the Latin script as the official orthography for the Somali language, launched a literacy campaign for the nomads in 1973 (more of this later). The second was in Iran in 1976. The Shah of Iran introduced in 1976 what he called the "White Revolution" – in other words, a literacy campaign for the nomads. The "white" referred to the fact that the secondary school and college students who were teaching the nomads how write and read were provided with white tents. In the open areas where the nomads inhabited, one could see the white tents scattered in different distant places. I was there in Iran to study primary care, as part of my MSc Degree Course on Community Health at Liverpool University. Such literacy campaigns were unthinkable in Somaliland Protectorate in 1938!

The Somali elders in the main towns of the protectorate were against writing the Somali language in Latin script, but they were *not* against formal education.

The elders of Borama beseechingly asked the protectorate government to open an elementary school in the town. Suldaan Ali and the Aqils in Borama handed a petition dated 14 March 1938 to the Under-Secretary of State for the Colonies, Lord Dufferin, who was visiting the protectorate [140]. In the petition, they complained bitterly about the lack of education in their area "where there was not even a single petition-writer or interpreter"! They informed Lord Dufferin that they would accept written Somali in the *Qur'aanic* and/or Arabic Schools. The Borama elders felt neglected, having neither a petition-writer or interpreter in Borama – important services in those days. Lord Dufferin told the petitioners that he would discuss the letter with the Secretary of State for the Colonies and would reply in due course. I did not find a reply to the petition, and I assume that the petition was ignored.

Mr Ellison visited Borama and had discussions on education with the elders of the town. He confirmed to the governor that the people of Borama were prepared to accept written Somali as a compulsory subject for all pupils.

In August 1938, Governor Lawrance, quoting Mr Ellison, wrote to the Colonial Office:

> *It is most gratifying to hear that Borama stands forth like an oasis in the desert of general opposition by the Mullahs to the writing of Somali in the schools of the county.*

The governor requested the Colonial Office that an Elementary School be opened in Borama [141]. Both the Borama elders' plea for education and the governor's request for an elementary school in Borama appeared to have fallen on deaf ears. Unlike the Borama elders, the reaction of the other elders in the other main towns to the proposal of introducing written Somali in Latin script was distinctly unfavourable.

It was much later, and the country under a different governor (in other words, Mr Glenday), that the reply to Borama elders' petition surfaced. As was the practice, the petition was referred to the governor for his observations before the Secretary of State for the Colonies could reply to it. The governor wrote to the Colonial Secretary thus:

> *The petitioners raise the question of education. You will appreciate that this petition was written before the Berbera School was opened, and I suggest that in your reply you should draw attention to what has been already achieved in the way of education and add that you hope that it may be possible after some years to open a school at Borama also..*

The achievement in education, which the governor referred to, was the two-class elementary school at Berbera. What use was that school to Borama? Or to any other town, for that matter, except Berbera? The governor's advice to the Colonial Secretary showed how governors of Somaliland Protectorate used to send misleading information to the Colonial Office. This was a game that the governors and the Colonial Office played, both parties knowing that the information they were exchanging was not wholly true!

Mr Ellison, at last realizing that rural education was not feasible in Somaliland, wrote in his annual report on education for 1938:

> *It is the comparatively small urban population which at present forms the section of the community which most eagerly asks for education [142].*

It was, of course, natural that the urban section of the population, engaged in commerce and thus interacting with foreign traders, would need education and demand it. This sector was also articulate enough and was in touch with the protectorate government. One would not have expected that the nomads would have asked for formal education in 1938 – if anything, they would have preferred to keep safe distance from government interference.

It has to be remembered that the type of rural education advocated by the Phelps-Stokes Fund and then adopted by the Colonial Office was based on the assumption that there would be settled agricultural communities in any given British African Colony. Mr Ellison was familiar with that type of rural education. In Somaliland Protectorate there were hardly any such communities. The Somalis were predominantly pastoral nomads who were continually on the move with their flocks and herds, from one grazing and/or watering area to another. Thus, at that time, rural formal education was not a viable proposition for Somaliland Protectorate.

By then enough evidence had been adduced for the fact that the urban Somalis were *for* – not against – formal education. In spite of that, successive governors of Somaliland Protectorate used to say, without shame, that the Somalis rejected formal education introduced by the government.

On 10 September 1938, to express their objection to written Somali in Latin script, the opinion leaders of Burao, composed of Aqils and other elders, asked for a *Shir* (meeting) with the District Commissioner of Burao, R.H. Smith. They told the District Commissioner that they were against written Somali for the following reasons:

- Written Somali would lessen the importance of Arabic in the eyes of the children and would thereby tend to weaken religious teaching
- It would reduce the Somali people to the status of other East African tribes whose languages were written and who were then made to learn the Bible and, as a result, had Christianity imposed on them

They did not discuss formal education as such. At the end of the meeting, they requested the District Commissioner to convey their position on written Somali to the governor, and he did [143]. Perhaps the second point raised by the elders betrayed some influence of the Somali Community in Nairobi (see later).

Just a few days after the Burao elders' meeting with the District Commissioner, support for the Somalis' objection to written Somali came from unexpected quarter. On 14 September 1938, E.N. Park, District Commissioner of Hargeisa, broke ranks and uncharacteristically reported to Governor Lawrance that the Somali objection to written Somali was not without justification. He mentioned in his report that a Dr Gurney issued some leaflets in Somali, written in Latin script, and informed some Somalis that, if they learnt to read their language, they would be able to read the Bible [144]. It transpired that Dr Gurney was a member of the Bible Churchman's Missionary Society and was a Doctor for about 1,400 Ethiopian Refugees in Minje'aseye Camp (between Berbera and Sheikh). The refugees were there as a result of the Italian invasion and occupation of Ethiopia in 1935–1941 (see 3.9).

The refugee camp was within Berbera District and the District Commissioner of Berbera probably heard about Dr Gurney's missionary activity, but chose to keep quiet about it. The government discreetly removed Dr Gurney from his duties in the refugee camp and sent him home to the UK, on medical grounds, as he was actually not feeling well. Governor Lawrance informed Dr Gurney's society that he should never be sent back to Somaliland. From 1911, Christian missionaries, in spite of their repeated requests, were never allowed in the country – the only policy consistently followed by the protectorate government of the country.

The new elementary school in Berbera

Governor Lawrance belatedly recanted his former attitude to written Somali and declared, in December 1938, that written Somali would not be compulsory, but would remain optional and that no child would be compelled to use written Somali [145]. But the damage was already done. The proposal to write the Somali language muddied the waters! Objection to written Somali created in the minds of a few vociferous religious individuals strong prejudice against formal education.

The old Berbera School was closed down in June 1938, and the pupils were to be moved to the new school building. The plan was to open the new school in October 1938. However, the intensity of opposition to written Somali (which the governor did not completely withdraw) was such that the school could not be opened on the appointed date.

The root cause of the delay in opening the new school was touched upon under 3.11. It has also to be pointed out that, from the 1920s, in Nairobi, Kenya, there was a small Somali community from Somaliland Protectorate. Members of the community were vocal critics of the protectorate government of Somaliland. They regularly contacted the Somali elders (some of them religious) in the protectorate, and apprised them of such issues as poll tax, discrimination and how the Kenyans were despised by the Europeans in Kenya. They used to tell the Somali elders in the protectorate that the local languages of Kenya and Uganda were written and then the Christian religion was imposed on the citizens of these countries.

There was little doubt that the Somali community in Nairobi greatly influenced the thinking of some Somali elders in the protectorate, when controversy about writing the Somali language was raging. A few religious men in the protectorate, especially from the *Dariqa* of Qaadiriya, continued to criticize the school. They demonized the school and questioned Mr Ellison's actions. They interpreted his presence in the country as nothing short of a proselytising mission agent in disguise and called him the "Padre", a description which Mr Ellison resented. They lost trust in him. Old memories of the Christian mission school in Berbera, which not only wrote the Somali in Latin script but also converted young Somali children into the Christian religion, were revived. There was a feeling among the Berbera community that the new school represented the thin end of the wedge and that the religion of the Somali people was being subverted. The elders were not happy with Mr Ellison and they petitioned Governor Lawrance that Mr Ellison should be removed from the country, since he could not teach Arabic and refused to teach English in the school [146]. The first complaint of the elders was obviously true and the second one was documented to be true [147].

Mr Ellison could have satisfied Berbera elders' wishes, if he introduced the alphabet and a few English words in Class II. With such compromise, perhaps further unnecessary controversy and prejudice against the school might have been avoided. But when Mr Ellison refused to teach English in the school, he was making a statement! The Somalis rejected his "beloved written vernacular", which was one of the pillars of British Colonial education policy.

Some militant religious elements mixed up written Somali with formal education and "misled" some of their followers. They went so far as to declare that writing the Somali language was "*Haraam*" (forbidden, in Islam), and warned parents about the consequences if their children learnt the written Somali language. Given below is an example of what some religious men were reported to have said, as reported by E.N. Park, the District Officer of Hargeisa, on 16 July 1938 [148] (see opposite). The occasion was the festival of *Aw Barkhadle*, whose tomb lies near a dry riverbed about 30 km to the north-east of Hargeisa.

```
ENCLOSURE TO DESPATCH    ORIGINAL
Secret    of 20-7- 1938.

COPY.

                                    No. 816.
                        DISTRICT OFFICE, HARGEISA,
                        BRITISH SOMALILAND,
                        16th July, 1938.

Secretary to the Government,
     At the festival of Jam Aw Burkudleh which
took place yesterday two Wadads spoke against the
teaching of written Somali in the schools.  They were
Sheikh Abdillahi Aw Adan, Mijertein, and Sheikh
Abdillahi Gaileh, Aidigalla Ba Delo - the Sheikh of
Aw Burkudleh.  Sheikh Abdillahi Aw Adan said that
their children must not learn it and if they did they
would become Kafirs.  He said that Somalis were Arabs
and if they learnt to write Somali they would be
classed as natives of Africa and be in the same
category as the Yaos of East Africa.  He referred to
the fact that now the Somalis in East Africa were
classed with Indians and Arabs and paid the same tax.

                        (Signed) E.N. PARK,
                        District Officer, Hargeisa.
```

Report from E.N. Park, District Officer, Hargeisa, about objections to written Somali in schools, 16 July 1938.

On such festivals, some religious men are prone to go into religious ecstasy and to make outlandish statements, as Sheikh Abdillahi Aw Adan was reported to have done in E.N. Park's report. Sheikh Abdillahi gave vent to the feeling then prevalent among a few extremists (religious men) in Somaliland Protectorate. They were product of their time. Their confusion of formal education with written Somali was ill-founded. But they were acting out of ignorance. I think they were neither hypocrites nor opportunists, as the protectorate government described them. It is not unnatural for people to react negatively to the introduction of something which is not familiar to them; and the proposed written Somali was such a thing. These religious men who were reported on were no doubt under the influence of the politically active Somali Community in Nairobi, as Sheikh Abdillahi was reported to have stated that the Somalis in East Africa were classed with Indians and Arabs and paid the same tax. That was the case, at least for the Somalis in Nairobi, as described in section 3.11.

A further digression: I myself had a brief encounter with a religiously excited *Wadad*, 19 years after the scene described in the letter mentioned above. It so happened that it was also at a festival of *Aw Barkhadle*. In 1957, while I was waiting for a scholarship to the UK and whiling away the time at Hargeisa Group Hospital, I was asked to work as an interpreter for about three months with a Mr I.M. Lewis, who was engaged in field research on social anthropology in Somaliland Protectorate. We used to visit nomadic communities in Hargeisa District. Mr Lewis used to ask old men and women about Somali customs and nomadic life.

One day, Mr Lewis told me that the *Aw Barkhadle* Festival (*siyaaro*, in Somali) was on and that we would visit there the following day. When we arrived at the *Aw Barkhadle* tomb, the congregation was performing the Friday prayer. My first impression was the sheer number of sheep sacrificed. From practically every tree in sight, a carcass was hanging – sometimes more than one. After the prayer, the congregation moved towards the tomb, where we were. At the front of the crowd, there was a man in white robes, swirling and brandishing a scimitar and reciting something. He walked briskly towards us, shouting in a menacing voice, "*Waar muxuu gaal kani halkan ka qabanayaa*"? (In English, "Hey, what is this infidel doing here?"), pointing his sword towards Mr Lewis. For a moment, we thought we were in danger and took refuge behind a tree. Before the exited man could do any damage, a man from the crowd came forward and, to our relief, calmed down the man. Our saviour advised us to move a little distance from the tomb to a big shady tree, and soon he sent us a big dish of freshly cooked mutton. We returned to Hargeisa, none the worst for the antics of the man who was behaving like a whirling dervish. Later, Mr Lewis told me that the visit had been a useful experience for him. In my case, I enjoyed the festive scene in spite of the excited man.[6]

In case written Somali would become a compulsory school subject in the future, in 1938 the governor sought advice from the International Institute of African Languages and Culture, London, UK, for suitable orthography and the Institute worked out one for Somaliland Protectorate. The Secretary General of the Institute was none other than Mr Hanns Vischer, who featured in the education introduced into the Hausa Land in Northern Nigeria, and also in the work of the Phelps-Stokes Fund Education Commissions for Colonial Africa (see 4.2).

---

6 Mr Lewis mentions the incident in a footnote of his book, *Saints and Somalis,* London: Haan Associates, 1998, p. 97. My name, among others who worked with him, appears on p. xviii.

While the controversy about written Somali was going on in the country, Mr Ellison busied himself with collecting Somali stories which were to be translated, using the new orthography, and the collection was to be sent to the UK for printing. I could not find a sample of the recommended orthography nor the translated Somali stories.

At last, the new school opened, without fanfare, on 1 December 1938, with 45 pupils divided into two classes: Class I of 17 pupils, composed of beginners who had been to *Qur'aanic* schools for a few months or not at all, and Class II of 28 pupils who were mainly boys from the former old Berbera School and who could read and write a little Arabic.

But the hostility towards the school continued and the Somali teachers experienced some social inconveniences because of their connection with the school. Such negative attitudes from a few individuals to formal education continued to the early 1940s. Mohamoud Ahmed Ali was the Headmaster of the new school. Because of the inclement climate in Berbera during the *Kharif* (the hot season), the school closed from mid-May to mid-September of each year – in other words, it had only one term yearly. The new Berbera Elementary School, in effect, followed the old school curriculum. Apart from the *Qur'aan*, basic Arabic and arithmetic (in Arabic) were taught in it. English was not taught, as confirmed to me by my friend, Abdullahi Duale (nicknamed Nile), who attended the school. As already mentioned, Mr Ellison refused to teach English there, even when the Berbera elders requested him to do so.

At the end of December 1938, the number of boys enrolled at Berbera School was still 45 boys. The expenditure on education in 1938 was given as £2,173, including £212, as grants to 14 approved *Qur'aanic*/Arabic schools. The annual salary and official expenses of the Director of Education, Mr Ellison, was £715 and accounted for 33% of the expenditure on education.

Mr Ellison submitted his first annual report on education for 1938 (dated March 1939) to Governor Glenday [149]. The report was also the first of its kind to be submitted by a Somaliland Protectorate Government to the Colonial Office.

No regular salary scale for the Somali teachers was laid down. Mohamoud Ahmed Ali and Hassan Dhoore Fareh retained their salary scale as clerks. Mohamoud Ahmed's salary scale was at Grade I. Since he had already passed the Grade I examination for clerks, he could not be promoted beyond that grade. There were no further higher positions for Somalis in the protectorate government service.

The staff of the school was composed of Mr Ellison, Mohamoud Ahmed Ali, Hassan Dhoore Fareh (Government interpreter) and Haji Hussein Haji Duale. The name of Hassan Dhoore was given to me by my friend Abdullahi Duale (Nile), who attended the school in 1939–1940. One of the children of Hassan

Dhoore Fareh was the late Hussein Hassan (Badag), who was one of the 16 students with whom the first secondary school in British Somaliland Protectorate was opened in 1953 at Sheikh.

Strangely enough, Mr Ellison often referred to Mohamoud Ahmed and Hassan Dhoore as "the clerks" – not by their names. Yes, they were clerks, as far as salary scales were concerned, but they were also members of the "infant" Education Department. It would have been common courtesy for him to address his Somali colleagues properly. Mr Ellison states in his report that Mohamoud Ahmed Ali returned from his studies in Sudan in 1927.

From some sources, it was described how much Mohamoud Ahmed tried to reason with those who were hostile to the school, but Mr Ellison never acknowledged the role Mohamoud Ahmed played in the issue of formal education in the country. He even gave Governor Kittermaster the credit for the initiative of government assistance to some approved *Qur'aanic*/Arabic schools, not to Mohamoud Ahmed who, as earlier mentioned, brought up the issue with the governor, in the first place.

It was about this time that the ridiculous side of his appointment as Director of Education dawned upon Mr Ellison, when he wrote home in April 1939 saying in part:

> *4/5th of my official time went on supervising an Elementary School with two Classes – it is certainly not a full-time job for a European officer, and not much fun or much experience for me.*

In Northern Nigeria, he was Superintendent of Education, responsible for about twenty elementary schools and a junior secondary school of seven classes [150]. In the last paragraph, in his annual report on education for 1938, about the staff of the Education Department, Mr Ellison wrote:

> *Apart from clerical and menial posts, the Director of Education is the only official on the Administrative Staff of the Department.*

He himself did not actually take part in teaching the pupils in the school. He lumped the teaching staff and the cleaners together. By presenting the Somali teaching staff in that manner, he betrayed the ugly face – the only face it had – of British Colonialism in the country.

Burao School Incident [151]

The Berbera School broke up for the long summer holiday on 15 May 1939. Mohamoud Ahmed and Mr Ellison travelled to Burao to inspect the assisted *Qur'aanic*/Arabic schools, reaching Burao on 17 May 1939. Two policemen accompanied them during the inspection of the schools, to control the crowd around the schools being inspected. They inspected several schools without a hitch. On 20 May, while inspecting a school run by Haji Ismail Farah and which was close to the Qadriya Mosque, young men crowded in front of the school and started throwing stones at the school door and at Mr Ellison's car, which was parked in front of the school. One of the two policemen was hit and he fell to the ground. Mohamoud Ahmed and Mr Ellison, together with the pupils and the teacher of the school, barricaded themselves in the school and closed the door. The remaining policeman blew his whistle. More policemen and the District Commissioner (DC) of Burao, R.H. Smith, arrived at the scene. The DC warned the crowd to disperse, but it did not, and more people joined the rioting crowd. The DC then ordered the policemen to open fire into the crowd and three civilians were killed. The DC alleged that the riot was incited by Sheikh Osman Nur, Head of the Qaadiriya Dariqa, and Haji Farah Omaar, an influential Somali elder. Both men were, for a long time, a thorn in the side of the protectorate government, and they were detained.

During the Burao riots, Governor V. Glenday, who replaced Governor Lawrance on 2 March 1939, was in Aden to attend Anglo-French Conference [152] on the defence of Berbera (*not* Somaliland!) and Djibouti. When he heard about the riots, he was reported to have told the Colonial Office: "It is that wretched education again. The Burao riot would happen whilst my back was turned."

Board of Enquiry into the Burao School incident [153]

Shortly after the incident, Mr Ploman who was acting for the governor, set up a Board of Enquiry into the cause of the incident. The Board membership, which did not include Somalis, was composed of:

- R.A. Haig, Judge of the protectorate court
- A.R. Chater, Officer Commanding, Somaliland Camel Corps, King's African Rifles
- B.H. Horsley, District Officer

At the enquiry, Governor Glenday, who was then back in his post, suggested that:

> *It would be best if the outbreak of war were used as an excuse to end the experiment in education. The Protectorate Government by going in for Education Policy, was putting the cart before the horse in that in anything to help the Clansman nutrition should have preference. And since our funds are so small we should do one thing at a time. Education to an empty belly breeds sedition only or, at its highest, paranoiacs like Hitler, Stalin and Mussolini. All our spare money should therefore be spent on improving their water supplies and grazing.*

Practically nothing was done on water resources development and the grazing policy amounted to periodic closures to grazing of small areas in the protectorate, during the main rainy season – a practice which started in 1935.

It should be remembered that Governor Glenday, before he was transferred to Somaliland Protectorate, was Commissioner of Kenya's Northern Frontier District (NFD), populated by ethnic Somalis, where there were practically no educational services. He could not comprehend why the Colonial Office would concern itself with educating the Somalis in British Somaliland Protectorate – and not treat them as those in NFD!

In his covering letter to the report of the Board of Enquiry to Colonial Office of 7 October 1939, Governor Glenday stated the following [154]:

> *With the outbreak of war, rigid economy is imperative. All new and unessential services will have to be severely curtailed and among these, education must be included. Moreover, in view of the Education Department's short and stormy history, I am convinced that it would be politically prudent at the present juncture to reduce its services and return to the position which existed before the appointment of the Director of Education.*

The Enquiry Board concluded that no particular person was behind the riots, but the whole thing broke out spontaneously. The two detained Somali elders were immediately released. I did not find the full report of the Board; I only saw short extracts quoted by the governor and also by Mr Ellison in his annual report on education for 1939.

As far as the governor was concerned, the protectorate government should not have wasted British taxpayers' money on educating the Somalis. While the Somalis were objecting to written Somali, the governor was objecting to formal education altogether. Such was the attitude of the man who was running the county! That was the lot of Somaliland! The British Government classified the governorships of the British colonies: from Class IV (bottom) to Class I (top). The governorship in Somaliland Protectorate was Class IV – the bottom rung in the hierarchy of governorships in the British Colonies.

Following the reoccupation of Somaliland in the Second World War, Mr Glenday was almost *persona non grata* in both Somaliland and Aden, because of his feud with the military authorities before and during the evacuation of the country. He was notorious in those days for being the governor who ran away from his post. In July 1940, when the Italians already overran Borama and Hargeisa was about to fall, he requested leave to Nairobi to be with his wife who was about to have a baby [155]. After reoccupation of the country, the authorities in the country sent telegrams to the War Office in London, urging them to "keep out" Glenday from Somaliland and Aden.

Before leaving the deliberations of the Board of Enquiry for the Burao school incident, I wish to repeat here what the Board Members said about the Somali

Wadads (religious men) and the *Wadads*' attitude to formal education. Members of the Board were intrigued by the way the *Wadads* went about their businesses. They wondered what the *Wadads* were and the hold they had over the people. They implied that the *Wadads* employed some manipulative techniques to impress those naïve enough to believe whatever the *Wadads* told them. The Board Members' views about the Somali *Wadads* shown below is quoted from Mr Ellison's annual report on education for 1939:

> *Although the Somali may be described as a fanatical adherent to his own conception of the Mohamedan religion, it is impossible to regard that conception as entirely orthodox. In the past the teaching of religion has remained exclusively in the hands of certain leaders known as Wadads, who, we believe, not infrequently display ignorance of the accepted doctrines of Islam. How these people, who are no more than semi-literate, come to be accepted as religious leaders it is not easy to say: they may be described, however, as elders of various sects who, although without any recognized qualification, have in one way or another gained a reputation for possessing a special knowledge of the Koran, and the right to guide others in all matters appertaining to religion. We cannot doubt that they have in the past exerted, and still exert, a wide influence over the people.*
>
> *In accordance with a long-standing custom, the Wadads have the right to collect from members of their sects a tribute known as 'siyaaro', the sum thus collected being applied partly to charitable purposes and partly to the remuneration of the Wadads themselves. It is, however, notorious that persons who have acquired some education, such as clerks and others employed by the government, are less susceptible to the influence of the Wadads; and that the latter have in recent years experienced difficulty in collecting the 'siyaaro' from the more educated Somalis. It will therefore be readily appreciated that any movement, having as its object the enlightenment of the people, would tend to detract from the prestige of the Wadads and would soon meet with the opposition of the more ignorant and unscrupulous of them.*

If I may briefly comment on the above: I have no problem with the Board Members' idea that the Somali *Wadads* can be considered as elders. In my view, that is what they are. Once a Somali man has the prefix "Aw" tagged to his name, he is deferred to and becomes one of the opinion-formers in his community. Only a tiny fraction of the *Wadads* earn their living by wholly devoting themselves to religious matters – for example, running *Qur'aanic* Schools (*Mal'aamado*, in Somali), managing mosques, becoming Heads of *Dariqas*, etc. The rest conduct their businesses either in towns or in the interior, like any other Somali men.

The Board members maintained that the educated Somalis were not susceptible to the *Wadads'* views, citing the Somali clerks and others. Perhaps "others" meant the interpreters, as other educated Somalis. Many of the interpreters graduated from being "boy servants" of British officers who, on the way, picked up some English words, some of them swear words, and could hardly read or write.

That was then the level of educated Somalis in the country! The *Wadads*, as well as the Somali commercial men (as mentioned earlier) were, by default, filling a void. There was no other section of the Somaliland community which could question the government actions in the country.

The Somali clerks were very junior and were themselves working under Indian clerks, who were sometimes accused of working against the Somali clerks' promotions, perhaps for self-preservation! By the nature of their status, the Somali clerks would not – nor were they expected to – question the actions of the protectorate government, in spite of their being described as the "educated Somalis" by the Board members.

The Board members mentioned that the *Wadads* lacked qualifications. The members knew very well that, in the country, there was no religious institute from which the *Wadads* could graduate with qualifications. However, it was unwise for the Board members to bring up the question of qualifications. Mr Ploman – who as an Acting Governor had set up the Board – was a District Commissioner of Burao only three years before, in 1936. He held a court there for a murder case, as a result of which he found four men guilty of murder and passed death sentences on them. There was no lawyer to represent the accused men nor a properly constituted jury. Mr Ploman did not have legal qualification of any kind when he was acting in that manner. In fact, there was not a single legally qualified officer in the protectorate government in 1936, and none before that date. As the saying goes: "People who live in glass houses should not throw stones!" Thankfully, the *Wadads* did not hold criminal courts and passed death sentences! I have discussed, under 3.8, the injustice and illegality perpetrated against the people of Somaliland, including Mr Ploman's lack of legal qualification, and more.

The Board members stated that the *Wadads* were against education. As has already mentioned, *Wadads* and others were against written Somali, not formal education. A very few *Wadads* of the Qaadiriya *Dariqa* in Burao, Berbera and Hargeisa confused written Somali with formal education. Even these *Wadads* did not specifically object to formal education, as evidenced by those in Berbera who requested English to be taught in the school – a request that was rejected by the Director of Education.

I think the Board members found it convenient to blame the *Wadads* for something that was actually the government's responsibility: the root cause of the Somalis' objection to written Somali was the admission of the Roman Catholic mission into the country in the first place. That action proved to be prejudicial to the introduction of formal education in the country.

The reader will no doubt also form their own opinion on the Board Members' views about the Somali *Wadads*.

After giving evidence to the Board of Enquiry, Mr Ellison went on a long home leave on 31 July 1939. He advised that the school should not be opened, pending his return. The Somali teaching staff were all there, and Mr Ellison was not among the teaching staff. But he could not trust the Somali teachers to run, even for a few months, the two-class elementary school without him. The implication is that the school was built by the government and had to be under the control by a British officer at all times.

During his leave in London, Mr Ellison met the Sub-Committee (for Africa) of the Advisory Committee on Education in the Colonies for discussions on his annual report on education for 1938. At that meeting, Mr Ellison informed the Sub-Committee that:

> It is not correct to say that the Somalis as a whole are hostile to education. On the contrary, the majority really want education. The hostility is purely from a few uninformed Wadads [156].

That statement – again – from someone in the know belied what the protectorate government used to say often: that the Somalis rejected the education introduced by the government.

There was antipathy between Governor Glenday and Mr Ellison. While Mr Ellison was on leave, the governor considered that it might be best if Mr Ellison did not return and was replaced by someone whose temperament and general outlook were likely to be more successful in dealing with the Somalis. The governor's characterization of Mr Ellison was similar to the *pot calling the kettle black*. Both men were indifferent to the Somalis' need for education. The governor also thought that the education of Somaliland could be supervised by the Director of Education of Aden. The governor was not the only one to suggest such an idea, as will be seen later.

The following extract is from Mr Ellison's annual report on education for 1939:

> In 1940, there were seven Somali teacher trainees in Bakht el-Ruda. Two boys from a Mal'amad (Qur'aanic/Arabic School) in Hargeisa, run by Sh. Ali Ibrahim, were sent to Bakht el-Ruda, Sudan, to be trained as Arabic teachers for Elementary Schools. The boys, as confirmed to me by Abdillahi Duale (Nile), were Ali Megag Samater and Yusuf Sh. Madar. They were to join their course at the beginning of 1939.
>
> Mohamoud Haji Duale and Hassan Jama Trike, who completed the first term at the new Berbera School, were sent to Bakht el-Ruda Teacher Training Centre, Sudan, to be trained as Arabic teachers for Elementary Schools. They were to join their courses at the beginning of 1940. Abdisalam Hassan Mursal completed his intermediate school course in Sudan; did one

year's teaching, under supervision, at an Elementary School and he was to go to Bakht el-Ruda for a teacher training course and return to Somaliland early in 1941. Mohamed Shire and Yusuf Ismail Samater who started their teacher training course at Bakht el-Ruda in 1937 were expected to complete their training by 1941 and return to Somaliland, and they did in 1941.

They were all following a course, at different stages, on Arabic teaching in elementary schools. They were the only Somali students then being educated outside the country. Part of the cost of their education was borne by their parents, and the other part was considered as a government scholarship.

During the long school holiday in 1939, the Government arranged for Mohamoud Ahmed to spend three months at Bakht el-Ruda Teacher Training Centre, to follow a refresher course on teaching Arabic to primary boys. While in Sudan, Mohamoud Ahmed met the other Somali students studying in Sudan. One of them was Yusuf Haji Adan (1914–2005) who was planning to continue his studies and become a lawyer. Mohamoud Ahmed suggested to Yusuf to return and join the Education Department. Yusuf Haji Adan agreed and returned to Somaliland in December 1939, secured government employment as a clerk and, as a teacher, joined Mohamoud Ahmed at the Berbera School.

By the time Mr Ellison returned from his long home leave on 24 December 1939, the pupils were already on holiday for more than seven months. This was because Mr Ellison directed that the school should not be opened in his absence. The second term of the school started on 1 January 1940.

In addition to the new school at Berbera, Mr Ellison proposed another elementary school to be opened in Borama, as Governor Lawrance had made a similar recommendation to the Colonial Office in 1938. This time round, Governor Glenday did not welcome the proposal. He justified his opposition to the proposed school on the grounds that the Italians were just across the frontier and it was possible that they might enter the war on the German side. As it happened, the Italians did declare war on Britain and its allies on 10 June 1940.

The Berbera School closed for the long summer holiday on 16 May 1940 and never reopened before the end of the Second World War. The school was turned into a hospital for troops. Mr Ellison was transferred to Sheikh to help with ciphering government telegrams [157]. The Berbera School was the first and the only government-maintained school in the country up to and including 1940. It functioned for two terms only – from 1 December 1938 to 15 May 1939 and from 1 January to 16 May 1940. On 4 August 1940, Mr Ellison went to Berbera to wind up the Education Department.

Mr Ellison and Mohamoud Ahmed Ali were among the last evacuees on board the warship *Hobart* that sailed away from Berbera harbour to Aden on 19 August

1940, as described earlier under 3.10. Mr Ellison abandoned a small car in Berbera, for which he was awarded £250 – under the War Claims scheme, described under 3.11. It was recorded that 10 boys from the school were sent to Aden to continue with their studies there. I could not find any further information about the boys – for example, their names, or whether they returned from Aden. I cannot be sure but I have a feeling that the late Ahmed-Kaise Haji Duale was one of them. My friend Abdullahi Duale (Nile) who attended the school was at that time too young to remember about the boys.

At the end of 1939, the number of boys enrolled at Berbera School was 43 boys. The expenditure on education in 1939 was given as £1,714, including grants to the approved *Qur'aanic*/Arabic Schools. The salary, and other official expenses, of the Director of Education was given as £725, accounting for 42% of the expenditure on education. Mr Ellison submitted to the governor his second and final annual report on education for 1939 in March 1940 [158].

Although the Berber School was meant to cater for the whole protectorate, only a few boys who had homes in Berbera could attend the school, since it was a day school. Arab and Indian boys were also among the pupils.

Had the protectorate government been serious about education for the Somalis, it would, at least, have built a boarding elementary school at a central place like Sheikh town, to which children from the five existing Districts could be sent; and the parents of these children would have contributed to the cost of their children's education.

In fact, it was in 1920 that Mr Hussey, a consultant on education in the protectorate, recommended a few elementary schools in different places of the protectorate and a boarding intermediate school at Sheikh, as described under 4.3. Mr Hussey's recommendations were not lost on the military government, when introducing the first educational programme in the country in 1944.

The fourth table follows overleaf.

Table 4: Annual expenditure (in sterling £) on Somaliland Protectorate: 1930-1939:[7]

	1930	1931	1932	1933	1934	1935	1936	1937	1938	1939
Local revenues	108,829 (53.2%)	92,840 (48.1%)	159,745 (94.4%)	140,297 (89.5%)	162,044 (100%)	105,209 (59.5%)	96,065 (54.9%)	204,449 (96.6%)	206,074 (91.7%)	175,000 (70%)
Government subsidies	95,906 (46.8%)	100,303 (51.9%)	9,517 (5.6)	16,464 (10.5%)	No Govt. subsidy	71,519 (40.5%)	78,826 (45.1%)	7,105 (3.4%)	18,770 (8.3%)	74,944** (30%)
Annual expenditure	204,735	193,143	169,262	156,761	162,044	176,728	174,891	211,554	224,844	249,944
Expenditure on education	631 (0.3%)	465 (0.2%)	575 (0.3%)	500 (0.3%)	500 (0.3%)	397 (0.2%)	559 (0.3%)	1,585* (0.7%)	2,173* (1%)	1,714 (0.7%)

* Each year of 1937/1938 includes part of £925 for building the new elementary school at Berbera. The expenditure on education in 1938–1939 was inflated by the relatively high salary of the new British Director of Education. **Includes £900 for the defence of Berbera in the WW2.

4.4 Ban of Christian missions from Somaliland Protectorate

The ban on Christian missionary work in the country dated back to 1911, when Christian missionary work was stopped, following the government's withdrawal from the interior of the country, as already discussed under 3.4 and 4.1. From 1911, many Christian missions pestered the protectorate government with requests for admission into the country. They proposed all sorts of projects to develop the education and medical care in the country. It was recorded that some of the requests of these missions were with the protectorate government, unanswered, at Independence. Some of these missions are mentioned at different places in the book. However, I thought it might be convenient to bring them together in one place. The missions most persistent in their requests included:

- The Vatican, who wanted to finance some schools in the country
- The Bible Churchmen's Missionary Society
- The National Free Church Council, who wanted to use Somaliland as a base for their efforts to assist relief work in Ethiopia (then occupied by Italy in 1936–1941)
- The Mennonites, who were already established in Somalia
- The Sudan Interior Mission, already active in Sudan, Aden, Somalia and the Ogaden area (ie the present-day Somali Region of Federal Ethiopia)

---

7 For expenditure data, see the following references: 1930 [159], 1931 [160], 1932–1934 [161], 1935–1936 [162], 1937 [163], 1938 [164], 1939 [165].

The last two missions argued that they were already involved in Somali-inhabited territories and it was illogical to bar them from working in Somaliland Protectorate, which was part of the British Empire! One of the vociferous British missions, namely The Bible Churchmen's Missionary Society wrote in 1937, saying, in part:

> *The Somalis obviously get their fanatical ideas from the Arab. It would therefore seem good policy to isolate them as far as possible from Arabia. Instead of that, the exact opposite is being done. An Elementary School was started recently and Arabic character was taught for reading and writing. This is done in spite of the fact that the Somali language is much more easily rendered into Roman character than into Arabic. Since Turkey, the erstwhile leading Muslim power, has abandoned the Arabic character in favour of the Roman, it does not seem very unnatural or outrageous for our Government to follow suit. If a Mosque was built at Woking [a town in England] why should not a Christian service be held in Somaliland? If religious freedom is a real thing in the British Empire, then the Somali has the right to hear the gospel and to read the Bible [166].*

The small school mentioned by the mission referred to the Elementary School built in Berbera in 1937, and in which the medium of instruction was Arabic, as the Mission, disapprovingly, stated.

The most consistent policy of the protectorate government was that of keeping out the Christian missions so that they would not impose their activities onto the Somaliland people. The protectorate government had a short ready answer to the frequent requests from the Christian missions: "No, thank you!" This exclusion policy was in line with the expressed wish of the people of Somaliland.

Governor Glenday who, in 1939, vividly described how strongly the people of Somaliland objected to Christian missionary activities in the country, opined that, 'The best way to ensure that Somalis avoided hospitals forever was to permit a mission to open one.'

However, there was serious consequence of banning the missions from working in the country. In the absence of the potential contribution of the Christian missions to development – specifically in education and medical care in the country – the responsibility for such development devolved to the protectorate government, which miserably failed to make any meaningful progress in these fields. The symbiotic relationship which existed between the British Colonial Office and the Christian missions has already been described under 4.2.

In 1937, an official in the Colonial Office, Mr Lee, lamented the ban of Christian missions from the country, and expressed his views in this manner:

> *We are able to do so little for the Somalis in the way of medical and educational work that it is, to say the least, a great pity we are unable to avail ourselves of the services which missionaries are ready to provide [167].*

4.5 The vexed issue of the unwritten Somali language

Before leaving the issue of written Somali, it is important to explore further why the government was insistent on the issue of writing the Somali language in the Latin script. The government was attempting to repeat in Somaliland what the British people themselves had experienced in the dim and distant past. In 597 CE, Pope Gregory in Rome sent his emissary, St Augustine, to Britain (in other words, to the Anglo-Saxons) to convert the pagans there to Christianity. With some modifications, the British people had to adopt the Roman alphabet in order to be able to read and study the Bible and other Christian literature.

The people of Somaliland, without knowing how Christianity was introduced into Britain, suspected that writing their language in the Latin script was the prelude to the imposition of Christianity on them. Thus they rejected the suggestion that their language should be written in the Latin script, but they did *not* oppose the introduction of formal education in the country – contrary to the myth that the protectorate government created and perpetuated.

Way back in 1885, the British government had ruled that spoken Somali would have to be made obligatory for officers in the Aden Residency who would also work in Somaliland. It was proposed that a reward of 360 Rupees would be given to the military officer who passed a colloquial test in Somali. The candidate would converse on general subjects with a Somali. Later, in 1905, a written test was also introduced. The maximum number of marks obtainable was 100 in each of the written tests, the pass mark in each test was 50%, and the total pass mark was 60%. The test was considered as elementary standard and the reward was reduced to 180 Rupees [168].

The rules were updated in 1920 [169] and all those British Administrators whose work brought them in constant direct contact with the "natives" had to pass oral and written tests in Somali at ordinary and advanced levels – for (much reduced) financial rewards and/or promotion. What was called R.S.G.II System of Spelling was used for the written Somali and this system remained the "official orthography", although it was never taught in schools during the existence of the protectorate. A sample scan from the original document, which contains the type of tests set for the soldiers in 1927 is shown opposite.

QUESTION PAPERS

Somali Translation. Army Candidates

Time allowed, 1 hour

Translate the following passages into idiomatic English:—

1

Nin Marehanah, maga'isi Abi-Guled, wuhhu laha afar nagod u gursadei. Nag waliba wil hei d'ashei, afarti wil yei heshin wayen. Had iyo gor yei iss layen. Abahod yu gor badan u waniyei, wahhba makhli wayen. Abahod yu yid'i, "Nin waliba ghori i ken." Afarti wil yei afar ghori abahod u kenen, markasa abahod afarti ghori iss ku hed'ei. Kolkasu ghorihi iss ku hed'na mid u dihei, wuhhu yid'i "Kala jabi." Inanki yu ghorihi ghadei, kolkasu jabin kari wai.

2

Sban iyo toban ka hore, safar Ogaden u Berberah ka bahhai boghol aur, dadka wa boghol iyo konton ahayen. Kolkei lehh asho Berberah ka so'oden, wa kun iyo sideton nin o Habr Yunis ka daba dulen, safarki bei u tegen o da'en. Nimanki Ogaden wa bahhsaden o Habr Yunis holihi wa la tagtei. Jidkasa bei aurti ka ghalghaleyen o wa 'unen. Ogaden ba yimaden, gel kaleh bei ka so da'en, laba kun iyo lehh boghol gel bei so da'en.

Somali. Set Composition. Army Candidates

Time allowed, 1½ hours

Translate the following into idiomatic language such as you would use to a party of Somalis; write in the R.G.S. II system.

1

The authorities accepted Nixon's proposal to advance up the Tigris to Kut al Amara and early in August Townshend began pushing forward and drove an advanced Turkish force out of a position on the right bank of the Tigris. In September he completely defeated the enemy a little further on, taking 1,650 prisoners, 13 guns and much war material. Kut was occupied and the cavalry pursued the fleeing Osmanlis halfway to Baghdad.

2

There was a merchant in Baghdad who had a son named Abu Hassan the "Wag." This merchant died leaving his son vast wealth, whereupon Abu Hassan divided his property into two equal portions, one of which he laid aside, and the other he expended. He entertained the sons of other merchants, and when his money was finished he repaired to these friends and explained his case, showing how little remained, but none of them paid any regard to him, or uttered a word in reply. So he returned to his mother and told her of the treatment he had experienced from his associates.

Example of a written language exam for soldiers, 1927.

I did not come across evidence showing that the spelling system recommended by the International Institute of African Languages and Culture in 1938 was either similar to or different from the R.S.G. System.

The written Somali language was not merely for the Berbera School curriculum. Written Somali was also needed for the British Administrators in the protectorate to communicate with the Somalis. It was the British Colonial policy that Colonial Administrators should learn the local languages.

The British evacuation on 19 August 1940 brought to an end – albeit for a short period (19 August 1940 to 16 March 1941) – the British occupation of Somaliland.

4.6 Reviving formal education during World War II, 1942–1943

As mentioned above, there was a seven-month hiatus before the British reoccupied the country on 16 March 1941 – on 17 March, a military government was established in the country. The Somaliland Camel Corps was hastily re-formed. The Military Governor, A.R. Chater, was preoccupied with building up a military government from scratch [170]. For him, education was not a burning issue that merited his immediate attention [171].

In 1941–1942, Somaliland Protectorate was put under the Political Headquarters, East Africa Command, Nairobi, Kenya. The country was included in the "Administration of the Occupied Enemy Territories" and was controlled from the above-named Headquarters, through which Governor Chater communicated with the War Office in London. In February 1942, the East Africa Command in Nairobi wrote to the War Office, London, a short document in which they proposed some form of education for Somaliland [172]:

> *…it is important that the policy agreed upon now should be one that can be accepted and developed when British Somaliland returns to the Colonial Office rule…*
>
> *For the present it is not recommended that a subsidy to the Koranic schools be reinstated. The policy adopted before the war of subsidizing Koranic schools proved so unacceptable to sections of the population that no attempt should be made at this stage to revive it. Before it is tried again, Government schools should be opened and Muslim teachers encouraged to come to these schools at appointed times to teach the Koran. When education officers gain the confidence of the Koranic teachers, the question of subsidizing Koranic schools can be reconsidered…*
>
> *Meanwhile, it is necessary and urgent that elementary education should be provided for selected personnel of the Police Force, the Somaliland Camel Corps, the Post Office and the Medical Services. Two schools, of which one would be established at Hargeisa and the other at Burao, would at present be sufficient…*
>
> *It is estimated that the cost of these elementary schools, for which no buildings are yet required, will be as follows:*
>
> *Annual salaries, £120*
>
> *Annual expenditure on text books and materials, £60*
>
> *Equipment (non-recurrent), £120*
>
> *…The two schools will accommodate eighty pupils.*

As had been the case all along, any attempts to design education for the Somalis never advanced beyond training a few for junior office work. The above "plan" is no exception.

Since school buildings were not required, and no such buildings existed either in Hargeisa or Burao, where would the suggested 80 pupils be accommodated?

It seems that those who wrote the above document were concerned about the sensitivities of those Somalis who confused written Somali with formal education.

In my research, I did not come across any evidence that supported the statement that *Qur'aanic* schools' subsidies were unacceptable to some sections of the Somaliland people. Perhaps advice against subsidies to *Qur'aanic* schools was one way of cutting costs on education.

The content of the educational plan (if it can be labelled a plan), reflected the Colonial Office educational policy of training a few number of people for office work. What was proposed above was short, hands-on training to meet the already limited needs of the government.

The police and military men would, for their drills, have to understand and react to such commands as "Attention! Quick march! Left turn! Right turn! About turn! Halt! Stand at ease! Dismissed!" The Postman (telegraphist) would learn the alphabet so as to be able to send messages in Morse Code, without being able to read or understand the messages he was transmitting! For the Medical Services, dressers would learn by observation, since they would be illiterate, how to clean ulcers and dress them, to fetch bed-pans for bedbound patients and perhaps would also be shown how to dispense a few tablets identifiable by colour. I know that in Omdurman, Sudan, there used to be a small school for the nomadic, illiterate, female birth attendants. There they were trained to dispense tablets by colour, and by touch in the dark. Perhaps the first Somali dressers were similarly trained. I think the above pretty well sums up the syllabus for the would-be students who might attend the proposed Hargeisa and Burao schools.

I must, however, make it clear that I do not intend to belittle or denigrate the noble careers for which the so-called educational plan was meant. Far be it from me even to imply such a thing. I am simply caricaturing the risible attempt at devising an educational system for Somaliland.

In fact, during World War II, before the 1944 Educational Programme was introduced, others tried their hands at planning some sort of education for Somaliland Protectorate. In this regard, the Somali proverb *"Nin buka boqol u tali",* in English: "A sick man has hundred advisers" was, metaphorically, applicable to the educational situation in Somaliland Protectorate.

There was no indication as to whether or not the document on education referred to above was discussed with Governor Chater before it was sent to the War Office, or whether he had it in mind when he dismissively wrote in 1942:

> *Education is to wait until such time as the Somalis themselves ask for it. When they begin to want schools, there will be time enough for the responsible officers to put together a scheme.*

Governor Chater was in denial. The Somalis wanted education – as confirmed by the ex-Director of Education, Mr Ellison, as well as other evidence already described in the book.

The expenditure on education in 1940 was given as £1,415 (including the salary of Mr Ellison, Director of Education, fees of Somali students in Sudan and Aden and grants to some *Qur'aanic*/Arabic Schools). No expenditure on education was recorded for 1941. The expenditure on education in 1942 was given as £230.

Initiative of five Somali educators during World War II

Mohamoud Ahmed Ali returned from Aden, where he and other Somalis were refugees. He was given a job as a clerk in a legal office of the military government in Hargeisa. Yusuf Haji Adan, who was already in Hargeisa, also had a clerk job in the Hargeisa District Office and was in charge of a store where the government ration and fuel were kept. The monthly salaries of Mohamoud Ahmed and Yusuf Haji Adan were 200 rupees and 120 rupees respectively.

In 1942, Mohamoud Ahmed recruited the support of Yusuf Haji Adan and decided to revive formal education in the county, modelled on the Berbera School, but adding basic English as a subject. From their resources – by pooling their salaries – they instructed an Indian builder to construct an *"Arish"* (a primitive structure of daub and wattle) at the site where, later, Fisher Elementary School in Hargeisa stood. They encountered difficulties in the building and, by the time they took in the first boys, the Arish School was still incomplete.

By 1942, Mohamed Shire Gaab, Yusuf Ismail Samater and Abdisalam Hassan Mursal returned from Sudan. The government was planning to recruit them into the police force. However, Mohamoud Ahmed briefed them about the lack of education in the country and persuaded them to work with him and Yusuf Haji Adan.

A Brief History of Formal Education in British Somaliland Protectorate

Lest we forget. Here are the five Somali educators who, on their own initiative, launched formal education in Somaliland Protectorate in 1942. From *left to right*, top: Mohamoud Ahmed Ali, Yusuf Haji Adan, Mohamed Shire; bottom: Abdisalam Hassan Mursal, Yusuf Ismail Samater. The people of Somaliland owe them a great deal. **We will remember them!** All of them taught me at Sheikh School. Photograph modified from Ref. 173.

They were recruited as clerks, as was the practice, but joined Mohamoud Ahmed and Yusuf Haji Adan. Thus came about a nucleus of five trained Somali teachers. With Mohamoud Ahmed as their leader, they planned how best to approach the onerous task of reactivating the educational activities in the country.

A few die-hard religious men were still agitating against government schools. But the difference between the 1930s and 1940s was that those involved in initiating formal education in the country in 1942 were Somalis and also the controversial issue of written Somali was no longer an issue, as it had been shelved. The public gradually came round to the benefits that education would bring. As already described, the public on the whole was not against formal education, but was against written Somali in Latin script.

The teachers decided to start the first class of the Arish School. In order not to arouse any animosity towards the school and to encourage parents to enrol their sons, each of the five teachers took it upon himself to bring to the school a boy from his family, to set an example to the rest of the Somalis:

- Mohamoud Ahmed brought Abdirahman Ahmed (nicknamed Tur)
- Yusuf Haji Adan brought Suudi Haji Adan, who was older than the other boys and later joined the adult class and became an instructor
- Yusuf Ismail brough Mohamed Ismail (nicknamed Kebed)

- Mohamed Shire brought Yusuf Adan Bowkeh
- Abdisalam Hassan brought Ibrahim Salah Indhagod

As they hoped, some elders started enrolling their sons. Sheikh Ibrahim Sh. Omer Sh. Madar (Chief Qadi – judge in *Shariah* – of Hargeisa) brought Ali Sh. Ibrahim (Ali Qadi); Hashi Abdi, policeman, brought Mohamed Hashi; Haji Ibrahim Egal, businessman, brought Mohamed Haji Ibrahim. The first class of the Arish School in Hargeisa started with these eight boys. More parents followed suit and more boys were enrolled.

By October 1942, the teachers succeeded in starting three elementary schools in the three towns of Hargeisa (Headmaster: Abdisalam Hassan Mursal), Berbera (Headmaster: Mohamed Shire) and Burao (Headmaster: Yusuf Ismail Samater).

Mohamoud Ahmed, supported by Yusuf Haji Adan, when not teaching, spent time travelling to support and encourage the other teachers at the schools. At that stage, Mohamoud Ahmed and his colleagues were, for all practical purposes, running a nascent Education Department (see later on page 195 what the future British Director of Education, C.R.V. Bell, said about Mohamoud Ahmed's efforts in education in the country). The government eventually started supporting the three elementary schools which became known as the government schools. Later, the government built a proper elementary school within the vicinity of the Hargeisa Arish School.

Fawzia Yusuf Haji Adan, relating what she learnt from her late father, gives a short account of the problems the five Somali educators encountered in their efforts, in her book entitled *Geedi Nololeedkii Yusuf X. Adan* [173]. The book is in Somali and its title translates as *The Biography of Yusuf Haji Adan*. The above details about how the five Somali educators set about their initial work of opening the three schools are mainly based on this book, which I gratefully acknowledge.

In March 1943, G.T. Fisher replaced Mr Chater as Military Governor. Within a few days of his arrival in the country, Governor Fisher opened the new school mentioned earlier and, as expected, named it "Fisher Elementary School". The boys moved from the Arish School into the newly built school. After Independence, the school was inevitably re-named once more and was called Sheikh Bashir School. The irony was that the killing of Sh. Bashir was ordered by Governor Fisher in 1945 – an incident already described [71]. Some British Colonial governors could not resist the temptation to give their names to buildings they opened in a British Colony (knowing, perhaps, that their names would not survive after Independence).

As was the habit of new governors, Mr Fisher toured the country in May 1943. Expressing his first impressions, he sent an uncharacteristically candid despatch to the War Office, which said it all, about the hopeless situation in the country. Lamenting the pitiful socio-economic life in the country, he said, in part:

There is little education in the country. Annual expenditure on education seldom exceeds £300. The result of this neglect of education is now most embarrassing to the Administration which must depend even in the subordinate ranks of its services on assistance imported very expensively from outside. ... We are impeded at every turn by lack of trained and educated Somalis in all branches of Government activity. Since the reoccupation, comment in the coffee shops and elsewhere compares unfavourably our lack of achievement in this sphere with the activity of the French and the Italians in the neighbouring territories. Whatever may have been the case in the past, there is now an urgent and pressing call for education, which comes not only from those in charge of the Administration, but from large sections of the people as well. There cannot now be many countries in the Empire where the population is 99% illiterate. It is this state of affairs which it is hoped to remedy, and indeed which must be remedied before there can be substantial progress in other directions. **During the year there was, for a variety of reasons, an increase in the popularity of education in the protectorate.** *A sum of £230 was allotted for the purpose (Emphasis is the author's) [174].*

The governor was spot on in his assessment! But he also found for himself the reason for the lack of development in the country and wrote about the same time of the above despatch as follows:

Since occupation of the country in 1884, it has been the policy to have as little as possible to do with the affairs of the interior and maintain a minimum administration just sufficient to keep active our imperial rights of occupancy for strategic reasons.

Again the governor was correct in reiterating the already known policy [23]. The governor mentions an increase in popularity of education in 1943. This was because formal education in the country was in the hands of five Somali educators. The governor simply disclosed the shameful failures of previous governors who took refuge in the myth they created – that the Somalis rejected education, when, of course, it was the idea of writing the Somali language in Roman script and all that that implied that was rejected. But he also reminded the government in London of the consequences of its policy of running the country on the cheap – in other words, the policy of "care and maintenance and without development", as already described in section 3.

Governor Fisher's concern about lack of development, including education, in the country was in stark contrast to the view of his immediate predecessor, Governor Chater, who was not at all worried by the glaring dearth of education in the country. The differing attitudes of the two governors can perhaps be explained by the fact that Governor Fisher was new to the country and saw things with a fresh mind. Governor Chater, by contrast, had spent many years in the country and had become inured to the lack of education in the country. In fact, previous protectorate governors accepted the lack of development in the country as being nothing out of the ordinary!

Governor Fisher, having acquainted himself with the sorry state of the country, called for a meeting of the District Commissioners. A 10-year plan for education was proposed for the country, to get educated Somalis for all government posts and even raising the standard of the traders – at an annual cost of £50,000. Note that the Somalis were to be educated for government posts – in other words, as junior civil servants, as there were no other opportunities in the country for the educated Somalis! As will be seen later, the future Director of Education had similar idea.

The proposal is briefly described below:

> *Recruiting large number of training staff of Europeans for ten years, at the end of which the country might be made almost independent of outside assistance. Training for five years up to the age of thirteen/fourteen of specially selected boys in general education and knowledge of English. After this, on passing a Board Examiners, they would be allowed to enter a special Medical School in the protectorate where their interests in medical subjects would proceed. The Medical School would supply Dressers of 3 Grades and opportunities would be given to the best boys to be trained as Sub-Surgeons and one or two of the most brilliant students might be allowed to proceed to England to obtain a Diploma in Medicine at one of the Universities.*

It was the fate of the British Colonies to be at the mercy of perhaps well-meaning amateur planners and the Somaliland Protectorate was no exception. A military man, without medical background of any sort and who cut his teeth on services in the Indian Army, tried to plan education for the country! Because he was the governor and the Commander-in-Chief, he thought he could do anything and everything in the country.

How many would be a "large number" of European trainers? What would they do exactly? Where was the "general education", when there were only three small elementary schools in the whole country, each school staffed by one teacher? And how about the non-existent medical school plucked from thin air? Since no buildings existed for the purpose, where would all that proposed training be carried out? In short, there was no rhyme or reason to the governor's proposal and it was nothing more than an exercise in futility. He sent the proposal to the War Office, which did not think much of it and conveniently ignored it.

In spite of my criticism of Governor Fisher's attempts, I sympathize with him for the dreadful situation in the country which he described. He could not fathom the amount of ignorance and lack of development in the country.

Consultancies on education

Governor Fisher abandoned venturing into fields for which he was not qualified and sought expert advice on education for the country. He contacted the Governor of Aden, requesting that the British Council should give some advice on education in Somaliland. In response, the British Council sent a two-man mission – Messrs Emerson and Meyer – to Somaliland in June 1943. The team submitted a short report to the governor, mainly recommending that Aden and Somaliland could share a Director of Education! We have already met with a similar recommendation, not just sharing a Director of Education but amalgamating the two countries into one country, as discussed in Section 3.

The governor also sent Mohamoud Ahmed Ali to Aden towards the end of 1943 for discussions on policies and syllabuses with Aden's Director of Education. When Mohamoud Ahmed returned from Aden in January 1944, he was accompanied by Abdi Said and six boys, two of whom were Abdi Said's sons. Some of the boys had attended the Berbera School in 1939–1940, and continued their studies, with partial financial support of the protectorate government, at Marist Brothers' School, Aden. Apart from Abdi Said's sons (Yusuf and Mohamed), I could not find the names of the other boys. Two Somalis who attended the Berbera School in 1939–1940 could not remember the ten boys who were sent to Aden, at the closure of the school in 1940.

Fauzia Yusuf Haji Adan names in her book the late Ahmed-Kaise Haji Duale and the late Mohamed Abokor Haji Fareh among the boys who came from Aden with Mohamoud Ahmed and Abdi Said in January 1944.

Report of A.T. Lacey [175]

Governor Fisher requested further opinion on education and the Director of Education of Kenya, A.T. Lacey, was invited to advise on education for Somaliland Protectorate. In his report of October 1943, he made the following recommendations:

1. He did not think that it was a good idea for Somaliland to share a Director of Education with Aden.
2. Since Mr Ellison, first Director of Education for Somaliland, was not available, he recommended Capt. C.R.V. Bell, in the service of Kenya Education Department, as the future Director of Education for Somaliland Protectorate and Mohamoud Ahmed Ali as Secretary. *(It was not explained what the title "Secretary" denoted).*
3. He advised that, because of severe shortage of Somali teachers, the beginnings should be small.

4. He advised that the number of foreign teachers, even Muslims, must be strictly limited. *(In this respect, perhaps Mr Lacey was alarmed by the governor's large number of European trainers, referred to earlier.)*
5. He proposed a primary education of six years' duration, followed by secondary education; Arabic would be the first language to use; English would be introduced in the second year and would become the medium of instruction in the fourth year; the Somali language would be used for oral work, but never written *(a complete reversal of Mr Ellison's policy on written Somali)*; a Central Boarding Primary School in Hargeisa, with a European Headmaster.
6. He advised against secondary schools for years to come and proposed evening classes for adult education. *(Unhelpful advice.)*
7. In addition to the three existing elementary schools, he recommended elementary schools for Borama and Erigavo. All elementary schools would have a boarding wing to accommodate 20 boys from the interior.
8. He advised against leather and metal work in the schools.
9. He recommended that Somali teachers should be on the same grade as the clerks. *(An unhelpful recommendation!)*
10. He advised to continue the small grants, with the conditions attached, given to approved *Qur'aanic*-cum-Arabic Schools.
11. For female education, he advised that girls be limited to *Qur'aanic* studies and domestic science (for women who attended clinics).

(The insertions in italics in the recommendations are the author's.)

Recommendation (6) had damaging effect on the development of education in the country, as will be seen later. Recommendation (11) unfortunately reinforced prevalent prejudice against female education in the country.

At the end of 1943, the number of enrolled boys in the three government elementary schools was 99 and the total expenditure on education was given as £2,631, including the cost of the Consultancies of the British Council mission and Mr Lacey, as well as the fees of the students in Sudan, in Aden and grants to the approved *Qur'aanic*/Arabic Schools. (In 1931, the population was estimated at 344,700 people. The protectorate government was still using this figure in 1940 – no proper census was ever done in the country.)

4.7 Mr Bell's report of 1944 on introducing formal educational programme

As recommended by Mr Lacey, Captain C.R.V. Bell (later promoted to Major) was appointed as Superintendent (later changed to Director) of Education of Somaliland Protectorate and he arrived in Hargeisa on 23 December 1943.

As to Mr Bell's background (described in his obituary in the *Journal of the Anglo-Somali Society*, mentioned later) – he taught in schools in Kenya in the 1930s, up to the beginning of World War II. Kenya was one of the East African countries visited by the Education Commission of the Phelps-Stokes Fund in 1924, and for which country-specific recommendations on education were made (see 4.2). Mr Bell thus had experience in the educational philosophy advocated by the Phelps-Stokes Fund for the British African Colonies, from the 1920s.

Mr Bell was put in touch with Mohamoud Ahmed Ali and together they toured the country, and conducted discussions with the District Commissioners (DCs) and elders in the main towns. On 24 January 1944, Mr Bell submitted to the governor his report including recommendations [176] on the educational survey he jointly carried out with Mohamoud Ahmed. In it, he outlined an educational programme, as detailed below. Mr Bell mentioned the only three elementary schools which then existed in the country – in Hargeisa, Berbera and Burao. Each school contained from 15 to 25 students in class I, and 15 to 20 in class II. At Hargeisa, there were 18 boys in Class III. There were also 16 *Qur'aanic* schools in various parts of the country, which received government grants. Just as Mohamoud Ahmed did before him, Mr Bell appreciated the importance of assisting the *Qur'aanic*/Arabic schools. He thought that if they taught nothing but the *Qur'aan*, they served the purpose of keeping a number of children off the streets for a large part of the day. Neither Mr Lacey nor Mr Bell mentioned in their reports that the government grants to *Qur'aanic* and/or Arabic schools were unacceptable to some sections of the Somali community, as was suggested in the document on education of February 1942 [172].

Mr Bell's recommendations closely followed those of Mr Lacey's before him. He put flesh on the bones of Mr Lacey's ideas and developed an educational programme with the requisite budget for its implementation. Mr Bell unfortunately stuck to Mr Lacey's recommendation against secondary schooling for the foreseeable future. As will be seen later, the education for the vast majority of the boys who reached the intermediate level ended there, because of a lack of secondary schools in the country until 1953. The exception was that of a very few boys who were sent abroad for secondary education. Mr Bell ignored Mr Lacey's recommendation that all elementary schools should have a boarding wing to accommodate 20 boys from the interior.

The regressive Colonial Office policy on education for Tropical African Colonies described earlier permeated the individual reports of Mr Lacey and Mr Bell. Both had access to Mr Hussey's report of 1920 and Mr Ellison's annual reports on education for 1938 and 1939. They must have also seen the short 1942 document on education for Somaliland Protectorate.

Mr Bell's recommendations contained the following two main points which suggested that there would be two parallel schemes to attack the educational problem of the country:

- Adult courses in English to meet the immediate needs of the government
- The usual school system, ie elementary, primary, secondary, etc

Mr Bell imported the idea of adult courses from Kenya, where he used to teach Kenyan Non-Commissioned Officers (NCOs) who would act as instructors, in Swahili, in their units. Also, as already described under 4.2, the Phelps-Stokes Fund advocated adult education in the British Colonies.

One of the reasons why adult courses were given high priority was that, following the British evacuation of the country during the Second World War, the Indian clerical staff who formed the bulk of the civil servants were pensioned off and sent home. In the early stage of the British reoccupation of the country, a few of the Indian clerks initially returned to Somaliland Protectorate and the number returned could not cover the acute shortage in clerks. This made it necessary to train Somali male adults quickly. This expedient policy gave a spur to some sort of early Somalization. In fact, the protectorate government was keen to employ Somalis in these junior categories because a Somali was much cheaper to employ than an expatriate Indian and also the government could make a Somali work for much longer before he could qualify for pension, by raising the efficiency bar of the salary scales which the Somalis, with their low salaries and promotion prospects, would hardly reach.

Mr Bell's main recommendations in his report of 24 January 1944 were:

1. There would be two parallel lines of approach: a) Adult courses in English, b) the usual school system – elementary, primary, secondary.
2. The Adult scheme would be temporary and if the first course was successful, it could be repeated for a further two to three years, each course lasting up to one year. Men of 17–25 years old would be selected for the adult courses and they would be made literate in English and they would also be taught civics and would undergo physical training (PT) as well. *(As far as I can remember, commercial subjects were not included in the adult courses. Perhaps that was left to be done by the departments as in-service training).*
3. It was expected that after 1946, the normal school system would be working, so that there would be no need for further adult courses.
4. The usual school system would follow the orthodox lines; the elementary school course would last three years; the primary school course would last

three years; later a secondary school would be needed. By January 1945, all District Headquarters should have elementary schools; a small boarding elementary school attached to a boarding primary school would be used as a practice school for teachers in training and for experimental work. *(In other words, they were trying out modifications in the syllabus before rolling out to the rest of the elementary schools.)*

5. The normal annual intake in each elementary school would be 20–25 boys, aged 8–9 years (for the 25 places at Hargeisa School, chosen on 3 January 1944, there were 112 candidates.) *(That showed how much need there was for education in the country.)*
6. The elementary schools would feed the central primary school. Eighteen boys at Hargeisa School completed the elementary course and would form the nucleus of the primary school. In January 1945 and January 1946, there would be intakes of 20 boys; later the annual intake would be 35–40.
7. As the policy of the Administration was that British Somaliland was part of the British Empire and not part of the Arab world, English would take a much higher place in the syllabus. *(To dilute somewhat Mr Lacey's emphasis on Arabic.)*
8. From July to December 1944, six courses in Elementary Teacher Training would be run, but they would be a makeshift expedient.
9. The Primary syllabus would include literary, technical and commercial subjects. The first year would be a general course, with the chief emphasis upon English. Later the school would be split up into different courses with three main divisions:
    - boys intended for government service – specializing in civics and elementary law
    - boys intending to be traders – specializing in book-keeping, typing, etc – who would mainly come from the coast
    - boys intending to be artisans – specializing in carpentry, masonry, mechanics, etc., with some commercial training to help them run their own businesses
10. Secondary schools would not be needed for many years yet. Some boys would be sent to Sudan. There would be a need for further training of Somali assistants; the departments may train men each in its own way, as the Education Department trains teachers.
11. Juvenile vagrants:
    - A small number of these were being trained in crafts under the PWD Scheme, but the number was to be limited to avoid flooding the country with semi-skilled labour.

- Agricultural settlements would need much labour and would become self-supporting. Education should be in the care of a teacher, and would consist of instruction in the *Qur'aan*, physical training and hygiene.
12. The Somalis in the army could attend the adult courses at Sheikh, instead of being sent to the Jeanes School in Kenya *(where Mr Bell used to teach).*

(The insertions in italics in the recommendations are the author's.)

As already said, Mr Bell, unfortunately, retained Mr Lacey's idea of no secondary schools for a long time to come – and it took a very long time for that time to come! He also proposed in his report to classify the schools as partly or wholly financed by Government, under three headings:

- **Grade "A" schools**: Entirely financed by government; in buildings constructed by government; staff paid by government; furnished and equipped by government. Examples – existing schools at Hargeisa, Berbera and Burao. *(Not true at the time that Mr Bell submitted his report. No government building was in use for education in January 1944. Even the government school in Berbera was occupied by the District Commissioner of Berbera.)*
- **Grade "B" schools**: Housed in local buildings; locally made furniture where possible; one or more staff paid by government; stores from the government. Examples – Las Anod, Hahi (near Odweine), Sheikh Town, Hargeisa Town.
- **Grade "C" schools**: In the past, 15 *Qur'aanic* Schools received a small quarterly grant and he proposed to continue this. The schools were also encouraged to teach Arabic and arithmetic (in Arabic) and no grants would be made unless the schools were prepared to teach these subjects.

Teaching staff

In his report, Mr Bell reviewed the teaching staff needed for the educational programme, which he proposed to the governor. He listed the posts he thought would be filled by European educators: Principal of the Primary School; Inspector of Elementary Schools; Officer for Teacher Training Centre and Wireless; Technical Officer in charge of School of Technical Education.

The Somali teachers then available were the five already mentioned – in other words, Mohamoud Ahmed, Yusuf Haji Adan, Abdisalam Hassan, Mohamed Shire and Yusuf Ismail. None of them, except Mohamoud Ahmed, had full secondary education. In those days, the only opening for the educated Somali was becoming a clerk and to work his way up, potentially reaching the top Grade 1 and no further. Mohamoud Ahmed already passed the Grade I clerk examination early after his return from his studies in Sudan in 1927, but he could not be promoted above that level as there was no level above Grade I.

This situation clearly betrayed the chronic lack of education in the country. The other four teachers were at Grade 4, with no prospect of promotion without passing the clerical examinations. The clerk level became the yardstick with which to gauge the level of education of the Somali.

To decouple teachers from clerks, Mr Bell suggested to the governor new scales for teachers, based on Departmental examinations in teaching methodology and school subjects. The governor approved the new salary scales as proposed. In each grade, the starting salary was as follows:

- Ungraded – 50 rupees/month
- Grade 4 – 80 rupees/month
- Grade 3 – 120 rupees/month
- Grade 2 – 180 rupees/month

When they reached the top of their respective scales, promotion to upper scale was by department examination, except Grade 2 to Grade 1, which was by merit.

With regard to the position of Mohamoud Ahmed, Mr Bell explained that:

Except when Mr Ellison was in Somaliland for 18 months, Mohamoud Ahmed had been in charge of the education in the country; progress had been entirely due to him and his local knowledge and contacts were invaluable to the Department.

The significance of that valid assessment of how Mohamoud Ahmed's efforts to foster formal education in the country was not lost on those who benefited from the formal education for which he worked so hard. He also bore the scars for which those who happen to be head of their community are liable. He was stoned at the Burao School incident in 1939. He was held in high regard in the country and the appellation "The Father of Formal Education" in Somaliland Protectorate was bestowed upon him. In recognition of Mohamoud Ahmed's special case, Mr Bell proposed a new post for Mohamoud Ahmed, that of Supervisor of Education. Later, this title was changed to Inspector of Elementary Schools, at the scale of Grade I, which started at 305 rupees/month.

Construction of school buildings

The report of Mr Bell included the budget for the financial year July 1944 to June 1945. He budgeted, among other things, for the following buildings:

- Primary and elementary boarding schools at Sheikh
- Elementary school at Erigavo

- Elementary school at Borama
- Elementary school at Burao
- Renovating the elementary school at Hargeisa
- Latrines for all the schools
- Accommodation for the teachers of the schools

The budget for the above buildings was set up thus:

School budget, 1944–1945

Buildings	£20,200
Personnel emoluments	£6,155
Other running costs	£10,604
Total	**£36,959**

This sum of £36,959 was the budget, but the expenditure was given as £20,200. Since the educational services in the country were practically being started from scratch, the greater part of the budget was taken up by the construction of the new schools and houses, which took two or more years to complete.

Justification for building Sheikh School at Sheikh

While Mr Bell and Mohamoud Ahmed were, together, touring the country, they came to know about government buildings in Sheikh which were not in use. Before the Second World War, the capital of Somaliland Protectorate was Berbera. During the hot summer season (the *Kharif*), the governor and his entourage (ie the Secretariat) used to retire to Sheikh, with its mild climate. Since the reoccupation of the country, the military government installed itself in Hargeisa and the government buildings at Sheikh became vacant.

These unused buildings (locally referred to as the *Sha'ab* area) included, apart from the governor's house, five houses for the senior members of the governor's staff, an office block and two blocks of smaller houses for clerks and other employees. There was also a small post office. Near the Sheikh town was also an old Fort (*Killaha*, to the Somalis) with a hangar for an aeroplane at one end of a wide open area once used as the airfield during the aerial campaign against Seyyid Mohamed Abdullah Hassan in 1920. Just about equidistant from both Sheikh town and the empty government buildings was the *Dariqa* (a religious settlement), with its own defined area.

Both Mohamoud Ahmed and Mr Bell were not keen on Mr Lacey's recommendation that the primary school be built in Hargeisa or in any other big town with all its undesirable attractions. Mr Bell, tempted by the empty government buildings, decided to persuade the governor that the school be built at Sheikh, and his justifications were as follows:

1. There were available, unused government buildings which could be used to start a boarding primary class immediately, followed by one boarding elementary class.
2. It would be possible to build the new Sheikh School within two to three years and move in as the new buildings become ready.
3. Sheikh was on the main Berbera–Burao road and was connected by telephone to Berbera and Hargeisa.
4. The rainfall, about 20 inches/month at Sheikh was good, and vegetables and *jawari* were cultivated.
5. There were wells and a pump already installed.
6. A good supply of milk and meat was available and it would be possible to teach veterinary work.
7. The school would not be near a big town, which was a great advantage, nor was Sheikh connected with a District Headquarters, making it neutral ground.
8. The Sheikhs of Sheikh town were well disposed to education. The religious community (the *Dariqa*) was not a centre of political intrigue and the establishment of the school at Sheikh would be favourably viewed by other *Wadaads* (ie religious Somali men).
9. Sheikh was central and journeys to the other main towns would be shortened.

On the other hand, Mr Bell maintained that Hargeisa was not suitable for establishing the primary and elementary boarding schools and the teacher training centre there, because of inadequacy of water supply as well as non-availability of a site fit for such educational facilities.

Elders of the Dariqa Community, Sheikh, c.1920 [18].

Governor's House, 1938. The first primary and the first elementary boarding classes started in small buildings nearby the governor's previous house in July and in October, respectively, in 1944. The author was in the elementary class [222].

Mr Bell proposed the handover, temporarily, of the empty government buildings to the Department of Education and also for the school to be built at Sheikh. Governor Fisher agreed to the Mr Bell's proposal, and his budget for 1944–1945 was later approved.

Meanwhile, a few British teachers, all in military uniform and known to and recommended by Mr Bell, were recruited during 1944 and they arrived at Sheikh in this order: Lieutenant Nicholson arrived on 21 May, Captain Badham on 4 June, and Lieutenant Lloyd on 4 August. Also Mr J. Pushpa Raj was recruited from India and he arrived at Sheikh on 6 October, as the first Chief Clerk of Sheikh School.

To upgrade not only their general knowledge but also their teaching skills, Teacher Training Courses for the *Qur'aan* and/or Arabic teachers from the approved private schools were held at Sheikh in June 1944. Similar courses were held later in the year for these teachers and also for some junior teachers at Sheikh School. Some of the best students who graduated from the adult courses (see later) who were kept as teachers attended some of the teacher training courses. The essential books for the primary and the elementary schools were brought from Sudan, East Africa, India and Britain.

4.8 The early stages of the formal educational programme

Subsequent details of the 1944 formal educational programme, from 1944 to 1948, are substantially based – except where indicated otherwise – on the book *Education in British Somaliland* by T.R. Holland, Reading University, UK, 1949, pp. 61–157. I have assigned a single reference number [177] to the book.

Mr Holland taught at Sheikh School in 1945–1946. In collaboration with K.D. Lloyd, a British educator at Sheikh School, Mr Holland documented the early development of the 1944 educational programme. The book presented the evolution of the programme in rather a haphazard way. I have attempted to present the progress of the programme in the sequence in which its different elements were introduced.

Sheikh Boarding Schools [177, p. 61]

In April 1944, Mr Bell sent a circular letter to all the District Commissioners (DCs) about boarding primary and elementary schools that were due to be opened at Sheikh. The elementary school was to cater for boys from the interior, and for boys from districts without elementary schools. The course would last three years and the upper age limit at entry would be 10 years old. The school fee per pupil would be 60 rupees/year for the elementary boarding school. The school fee per student at the boarding primary school would be 150 rupees/year. The responsibility for these fees would lie with the parents – and the government undertook to feed, clothe and educate the boys for this amount. The DCs were advised to send the boys from the interior to Sheikh, even if they were late in applying for a place.

Mr Bell advised that more boys should be sent to the elementary school from Erigavo and Zeila Districts, which were not well represented in the existing elementary schools. At that time, Las Anod was not a District – it was still a sub-District of Burao District.

As already mentioned, Mr Bell proposed to attack the educational problem in the country on two fronts: English courses for adult males on the one hand and the usual educational system for children on the other. The first approach – in other words, adult education, will be dealt with first.

Adult Courses [177, pp. 146–153]

Lieutenant Lloyd was in charge of the first Adult Course – and all the subsequent courses were under the general supervision of Mr Bell, who also taught some English lessons. The first four Adult Courses were held at Sheikh School. The first Adult Course, a special class, was held for a small group of Somali men from the

Somaliland Camel Corps (SCC). It started in November 1944. As if it was a military secret, no information is available about the number of the students or about the duration of the course. Had this course not started, perhaps some of the men from the army would have otherwise been sent to Jeanes' Military School in Kenya, as had been the case before. Training Somali military men locally was in line with Mr Bell's recommendation in his 1944 report. If memory serves me right, the adult trainees included Musa Galal, Mohamed Jama Badmah, Ali Mire, Adan Isaq, Mohamed Adan (Sheef) and Mohamed Burale. Apart from Mohamed Burale, they became English teachers in the Education Department, and some of them later taught the elementary class that I was in.

The second course, which was limited to junior employees of the government departments, started on 4 September 1944. The adult trainees (a total of 30 men) came from the following departments: Administration (6); Agriculture (2); Education (3); Deputy Controller of Finance & Accounts (2); Information (1); Legal (2); Medical (3); Police (7); Public Works Department (2); Survey (1); Veterinary (1).

The requirements for attending the course were as follows: the candidates would be between the ages of 17 and 25 years and would be men of good character. Each man was to bring with him: bedding, a knife, fork and spoon, two blankets (or one blanket and one greatcoat), a box and, if possible, a lamp. Each man would also bring with him his last pay certificate. The men were housed in the old Fort and they were not allowed to bring families to Sheikh.

The course would include instruction in the 3 Rs (reading, writing and arithmetic), school discipline, games, personal and social responsibility and civics. Civics included an explanation of how government functioned, services provided by the government, community development, grazing-land management, impartiality in dealing with the public, etc. Some men might be kept on for further instruction after the end of the course. No previous education or ability to speak English was necessary. The aim was to teach the trainees enough English to make them able to undergo further training and eventually become instructors in their own departments or to work as overseers or interpreters. The aim was not to produce educated men.

Mohamoud Ahmed conducted the civics lessons. The teachers of the Adult Courses were always on the lookout for those trainees who behaved well, worked in class, and who showed aptitude for leadership and initiative. Trainees with such characteristics were selected for further training, with a view to recruiting them as teachers and/or instructors. The course ended in May 1945.

According to Mr Lloyd, within about six weeks, men who had never handled a pencil before in their lives were able to produce legible writing. Of the 30 men who started the course, 23 stayed to the end and they were graded by examination results. Nine men stayed on for a further one month to attend the Teacher Training Course and four of them were subsequently employed as instructors during the third Adult Course.

The third Adult Course started on 22 September 1945 and was, more or less, run on similar lines as the second course, except that the number of men was doubled to 60 and their distribution was as follows: Administration (3); Districts (14) (in other words, at least two from each district); Agriculture (2); Deputy Controller of Finance & Accounts (3); Education (5); Information (4); Legal (2); Medical (3); Pasture (2); Police (12); Post & Telegraphs (2); Public Works Department (4); Survey (2); Veterinary (2).

They were housed in some of the new dormitories that were completed and became available for use. They were divided into three classes of 20 men in each, under three instructors who graduated from the second course, while the fourth instructor had a roving commission. All the instructors were under close supervision. The course ended in April 1946. Many men did well, as judged by the departments to which they belonged.

Mr Bell indicated to the government that the school would find it difficult to run Adult Courses for the ever-increasing number of men being sent to Sheikh. He suggested that it would be more practical to build a school for the adults in Borama, but the government rejected the idea. The policy of "minimal administration and no meaningful development" was in force [23].

The fourth and the last Adult Course, as far as the Government was concerned, started on 17 July 1946 and ended in February 1947. Sixty men attended, of whom 20 had already attended a previous Adult Course. Thirty-eight of the men were government employees and the other 22 were fee-paying private trainees who each paid a fee of 180 rupees to cover the cost of tuition, board and lodging. The vacancies for the private citizens were allocated on the scale of three per district, although Zeila district was offered three more vacancies.

In 1948, the government officially declared that there would be no more Adult Courses. The given reason was that the purpose for the courses was to fill vacancies urgently – and that purpose had been achieved. The Adult Course experiment exposed, if that were needed, the virtual absence of formal education in the country until that point. Perhaps the government realized that it had opened Pandora's Box, since there were more male adults asking for English courses than the government was willing to accommodate. Clamping down on this demand, the government abandoned adult education. That was inevitable because adult education was conditional on producing the required number of clerks and interpreters, and a few literate police and military men for the Administration. (As will be discussed later, the government subsequently changed its mind).

However, some good came out of the adult courses, the teacher training courses and the Army class. Some of the trainees who did very well in the English Courses became trained teachers and thus eased the acute shortage of trained Somali teachers somewhat. As a result, a few more District Elementary Schools of one class or more could be opened.

District Elementary Schools [177, pp. 131–132]

As already mentioned, three elementary schools each containing Class I only were opened in October 1942 – in Burao, Berbera and Hargeisa. By January 1944, in spite of severe shortage of teachers, Burao and Berbera each had Classes I and II, while Hargeisa had Classes I, II and III.

From August 1944 to September 1947, the following new district elementary schools were opened:

- At Borama, on 20 August 1944 (in a loaned private house, the new proper school was opened on 5 March 1945)

- At Las Anod, on 24 September 1944 (in a rented private house, the new proper school was opened in 1947)

- At Erigavo, in August 1945

- At Zeila on 1 October 1946 (in a loaned house, the new proper school was opened at the end of 1947)

The boarding elementary school at Sheikh will be separately dealt with later. It is worth pointing out that the District Commissioner of Erigavo proposed that the elementary school at Erigavo be made a boarding school to cater to the educational need of the nomadic children in the East. That was also in line with what Mr Lacey recommended in 1943, but Mr Bell turned down the proposal. An opportunity was missed. The government was bent on cost-cutting rather than expanding education in the country.

The Berbera Elementary School finally moved from the Berbera *Nadi* (Club) to its proper school premises, after the DC of Berbera had completely vacated it in May 1945.

None of the boys' government elementary schools started in a building designed as a school. But as there was only one class at each school, the premises, for the time being, served the purpose. However, this showed the non-existence of formal education in the country in the past.

The communities' initiatives in formal education [177, pp. 137–140]

Some communities in the country were encouraged by the fact that Somali teachers, not European ones, started schools in 1942 in Hargeisa, Berbera and Burao for educating the Somalis.

- **Hahi:** A religious settlement, situated a short distance south of Odweine, sent their own teacher in 1943 to Hargeisa elementary school to be trained, and afterwards to the teacher training course at Sheikh School. While the teacher was away, the Hahi community built a school which was opened when the teacher returned from Sheikh School. The *Qur'aan*, Arabic and arithmetic (in Arabic) were taught in the school, as well as physical training (PT) some mornings. In addition, the boys were impressed upon helping their parents and the community in general. The school was managed by a committee which guaranteed the teacher's salary of 35 rupees/month. The boys paid 1 rupee/month each and when the monthly collection was less than the teacher's salary, the Committee made up the difference. Mohamoud Ahmed who inspected the school at the end of 1945, reported that some mornings the boys cleared out the mud from the village *balli* (small shallow reservoir) and were also responsible for the trees around the school.

- **Beerato**: a small village near and to the east of Hahi emulated the school at Hahi and built its own school. In 1945, 25 boys were attending the school and the subjects taught were more or less similar to those taught at Hahi School.

- **Burao town**: in 1944, a religious teacher opened a co-education school in which boys and girls aged 12–13 studied together and the girls were in the majority. The teacher informed Mohamoud Ahmed who was inspecting the school that the boys and girls worked peacefully together in one room, and he thought that the girls seemed to be more intelligent than the boys.

- **Burao,** again: in 1944, Burao *Nadi* (Club) decided to open a school for girls and sent the letter (its scan shown overleaf) to the Director of Education. The signatory of the letter, Farah Abdi (Haji Farah Susle Abdi) was a prominent Aqil in Burao, whose daughter was later to join the proposed school. The Director of Education, Mr Bell, positively responded to the request, with a small financial grant to pay for the repairs of a school building already owned by the Nadi and he also agreed that the Education Department would pay for the teacher. The girls' school opened on 23 February 1945 with 18 girls and were mainly taught the *Qur'aan*, Arabic, arithmetic and few other subjects of a domestic nature suggested by Mr Bell.

> BURAO.
> 9th October, 1944.
>
> To the Director of Education.
>
> Salaams,
>
> We thank you very much with regard to the schools and now we wish to open a school in the town of Burao to be run under the supervision of the Nadi.
>
> We shall let you know very soon the details, but we have already a suitable building belonging to the school of the Nadi which we shall be able to use for the purpose. We request you to assist us, if possible, with regard to necessary repairs, whilst your own school is being built.
>
> We wish also to write to you about the establishment of a school for girls.
>
> We all thank you for this great favour.
>
> (Signed) FARAH ABDI.
> President of the Nadi.

Letter from Farah Abdi to Mr Bell, the Director of Education, about the opening of a school in the town of Burao, 9 October 1944.

- **Las Anod**: In March 1946 the community in Las Anod opened a small girls' school in a rented private house. The school opened with 10 girls. The school followed the syllabus of the Burao Girls School. The rent of the house was paid by the girls' parents, but the teacher, Jama Yusuf, was paid by the Education Department.

- **Sheikh**: A story I heard, later confirmed to me of its veracity, went like this: the elders of the *Dariqa* and Sheikh town contacted the Director of Education and, while affirming their support for educating the boys, complained of the Education Department forgetting about girls' education. They pointed out that when the boys now educated grew into manhood, they would think of marriage and they would prefer educated girls to uneducated ones. So, the elders requested a small class for girls. It was as a result of the elders' intervention that in 1947 Mrs Bell (wife of the Director of Education, Mr Bell) started, in her garage, a class for a small group of girls from Sheikh town and the *Dariqa*. In early 1948, Mrs Whitehead (wife of a British teacher at Sheikh School) volunteered to assist Mrs Bell. The girls were taught the *Qur'aan*, English, arithmetic and domestic subjects. Mrs Bell left Sheikh in 1948, but Mrs Whitehead continued to teach the girls until Mr Whitehead and his family moved to Uganda in 1953. One of the girls in that class, Amina Ma'alin Qasim, later became an assistant teacher in the first government Girls Elementary School, which opened in Burao in January 1953. The story of the elders seemed to have been reflected in the justification for building the government elementary school for girls (see later).

Education Department lukewarm about girls' education [177, p. 140]

The Education Department, realizing that the Somali communities up and down the country started to embrace education – in particular girls' education – put out the following statement in 1947:

> *In view of the scarcity of European female teachers in Somaliland, it would be difficult to run Girls Schools. Thus, at present it seems likely that the education of girls will for the most part be confined to private and Qur'aanic Schools. Whenever a community expresses a desire to have a girls' school, it will be encouraged to go ahead, but for the time being it is impossible for the Education Department to start a Government School for Girls. Religious opposition to female education is by no means dead, although it is far weaker than it was, and a premature attempt by Government to introduce education for girls would certainly lead to trouble.*

The above statement flew in the face of the facts on the ground. Where was the religious or any other opposition to girls' education? The *Dariqa* at Sheikh, Burao *Nadi* (Club) and Las Anod community demonstrated their willingness to have their daughters educated in schools similar to the government elementary schools for boys and be taught the subjects taught to the boys. There was even a private co-education school in Burao, mentioned earlier, without any religious objection. The assertion that the girls could not be educated for lack of female European teachers was a lame excuse. It would have meant something if, instead, lack of Somali female teachers was cited. Anyway, the Education Department was not at all minded to open, any time soon, a new third front (ie girls' education) to attack the education problem in the country.

The boarding primary school at Sheikh [177, pp. 98–99]

The first boarding primary school in the country, of one class, was opened in the old government buildings at Sheikh on 21 July 1944. Captain Badham, who also taught Mathematics, was made Principal of the Primary School. Some of the names of the students who formed the first Form IV are listed below (courtesy of my late friend, Mohamed Mohamoud Garaad):

Ahmed-Keyse Haji Duale
Abdi-Rahman (Tur) Ahmed Ali
Mohamed Ali Magan
Mohamed Hashi Abdi
Ahmed Mohamoud Qayir
Ali (Qadi) Sh. Ibrahim
Mohamed Mohamoud Garaad
Abdullahi Duale (Nile)
Farah Mohamed (Farah-Dhere)
Yusuf Abdi Said

Abdullahi Jama-Dalab
Hassan-Nairobi …?
Mohamoud Ali Said (Swahili)
Abdi-Rahman Adani
Yusuf Adan Bowkeh
Adan (Wambi) Omer Ileye
Mohamed (Kebed) Ismail Samatar
Ibrahim Saleh (Indhagod)
Mohamed Hassan Liban
Warsame (Awr-liqe)

Some of the named students are in the photo below.

Left to right: Back row: Mohamoud Ali Said, Abdi Ali Liban, Mohamed Hassan Liban, Yusuf Abdi Said; Middle row: Abdirahman Ahmed Ali (Tuur), Abdullahi Jama-Dalab, Farah (Dheere) Mohamed, Abdi Shiil, Ahmed Mohamoud Qayir (Laba-quwadle); Front row: Mohamed Omer Hashi, Ahmed Bile. Abdulrahman Ahmed Ali (Tuur) – middle row, far left – became the first President of the Republic of Somaliland (28 May 1991 to 16 May 1993).

The class consisted of the Class III transferred from Hargeisa and a few boys who were brought from Marist Bothers' School in Aden, totalling 26 boys. The boys from Aden were some of the ten boys who were sent to Aden when the Berbera School closed down in May 1940, because of the Second World War.

My friend Abdullahi Duale, who was in Class III transferred from Hargeisa, informed me that the families of the transferred boys were each paid 70 rupees.

There was no explanation for the payment – perhaps the gesture was meant to reassure the parents that nothing untoward would happen to their children! He also informed me that they were given the impression that they were being sent to Sudan! As it happened, they ended up in Sheikh.

The elementary and primary education of the class was condensed into just about four years. In the first term, the class underwent intensive teaching in English to a point where they were able to receive the major lessons in English. The initial idea was to divide the class into literary and technical forms.

However, on 10 February 1945, a technical class, with 28 boys, was inaugurated, and Lieutenant Nicholson, assisted by two Somali instructors – Mogeh Mohamed and Adan Warsame – was put in charge of the class. Captain Smith replaced Lieutenant Nicholson in November 1945. Mr Smith, a Scot, confused us when he came to the school kilted! We did not know what to make of the figure, man or woman? In March 1947, J.N. Clark (a civilian) took charge of the technical class and Captain Smith left the country. The technical class was composed of a few boys from the primary class and the majority who previously attended *Qur'aanic*/Arabic schools. To distinguish the technical form from the literary form, the former was called Form T. Later, the policy was to enrol only boys with elementary education for the technical form. These two streams of academic and technical classes continued till 1952, by which time a trades school was opened in Hargeisa (to be described later).

The main purpose of the technical class, according to the Education Department, was to prepare the boys to become self-employed or government-employed artisans. It was not initially in the plan of the department to send artisans abroad for further education. The first time some boys from the technical form were sent abroad for further education was in 1951.

In fact, initially Mr Bell budgeted, in 1944, for a separate technical school to be built in Hargeisa or some other place. A sum of £3,390 was earmarked for the purpose. He then changed his mind and put the two forms in one school and used the money for two additional dormitories at Sheikh.

Boarding Elementary School at Sheikh [177, p. 64, pp. 100–102]

On 6 October 1944, the first boarding elementary school in the country, of one class was enrolled in the old government buildings at Sheikh, with 32 boys (the author was one of them).

Abdisalam Hassan Mursal who was transferred from Hargeisa became the Headmaster of the boarding elementary school and he was responsible to the Principal of Sheikh School, Mr Badham. Later, Yusuf Haji Adan replaced Abdisalam Hassan who became Headmaster of Hargeisa Elementary School.

The boarding elementary school was initially intended to cater mainly for boys from towns without elementary schools yet or from the interior (the author was from the interior).

My friend and classmate, Ahmed Botan, and I put our heads together to try to remember the names of the rest of our classmates, as well as the districts from which they were enrolled and we came up with the following:

Erigavo (8): Mohamed Ahmed Tafadal, Saleh Hussein (Jinniy-aale), Musa Hassan (Musa-Baruur), Abdi Mohamed (aka Sahar-Deed, (later Abdi-Dhiboo), Ali Warsame (dropped out), Qawdhan (full name forgotten, dropped out), Abdi Ibrahim (Aga-Balaadh), Salah-Dibi (full name forgotten, dropped out). **Berbera (2):** Hussein Ahmed, Qalib Musa. **Zeila (5):** Salah Haji Farah, Hussein Burale (dropped out), Farah Wa'ais (Farah-Faras), Jibriil Yaabe (dropped out), Musa Ahmed (not Musa Ahmed Bore), dropped out)	**Las Anod (2):** Ahmed Botan Dhakkaar, Ina Nur Halaag, nicknamed "Bakayle" (full name forgotten, dropped out). **Burao (3):** Abdi-Rahman Haji Deria Shide, Mohamed Haji Yusuf Dhaw-dhawle, Abdullahi Deria Abdi (the author) **Sheikh (6):** Ibrahim Haji Nur (Baanday), Musa Ali Ma'aleesh, Ali Mohamed Hersi (Ali-Aar), Mohamed-Nur Abdi-Rahman, Ibrahim Mohamoud Ahmed Ali, Ahmed Mogeh (Bas-Baas) (all day boys)
We could not remember the names of the following two boys: Shoodhe Jadami (dropped out); a very young boy, enrolled from either Las Qorey or Hubera or Erigavo (dropped out). We could not account for four boys, bringing the total to 32. As far as we could remember, no boys came from either Hargeisa or Borama, unless they were among the four boys who were unaccounted for.	

The first day of attending the class, we were each given a blanket, a towel, a plate, a mug, knife, fork and spoon. In the days that followed, we were each measured for two pairs of khaki shorts and two white shirts. Lost knives and forks were not replaced and it was not uncommon to find some boys eating with their fingers – the way we were accustomed to. Each of us was given a specific school number and mine was 77. For some time, we slept on the floor since beds were not available. Those of us who really felt cold were given an extra blanket. Sheikh was cold, misty and rainy in those days. Before long, once the wooden framework was prepared by the technical instructors in carpentry, simple beds were made by us, under supervision. Later, bed-making became part of the practical work, in the workshop of the technical form who started work, as already mentioned, in February 1945.

For some time, we were not issued with writing materials because they were not available. To practice writing, we were used to being taken outside the class and practising writing on a smoothed area on the ground, using our fingers. Eventually, one day, Mohamoud Ahmed Ali came into our class and said that he had presents for us. We were excited about what they would be. He then called in a messenger standing outside the class, carrying a box. To our delight, each one of us was handed a smooth flat sheet of slate in wooden frame, about 8–9 inches square, and a slate-pencil (photo shown below). However, Mohamoud Ahmed warned us that there would be no replacements for losses or breakages. From then on, we started writing on the slates using the slate-pencils (called in Somali *looxxajjar and qalam-xajjar* respectively,) – and that saved our fingers from the dust. The origin of both *xajjar* and *qalam* is Arabic.

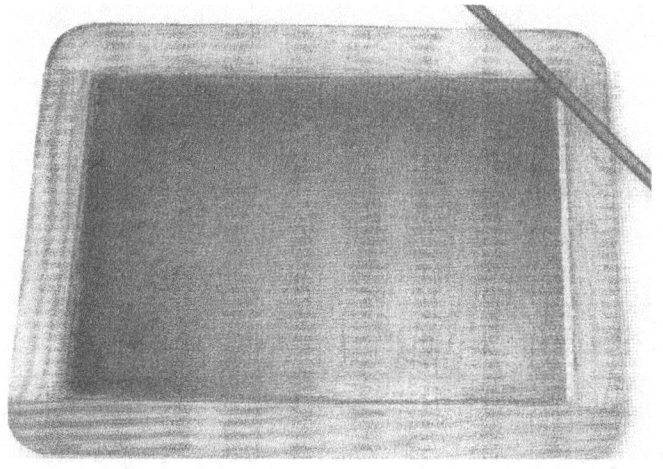

Slate pencil (Qalam xajjar); Slate (Loox-xajjar) Chalk could also be used to write on the slate.

For hand writing, we were trained on a method called Marion Richardson System for Writing. This showed us how to form the letters in upper and lower case and how to join up the letters when in the lower case.

Specimens of the system mentioned above are shown below.

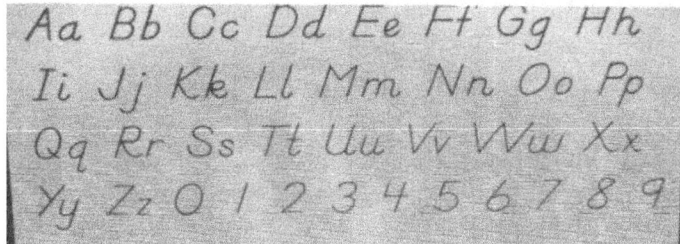

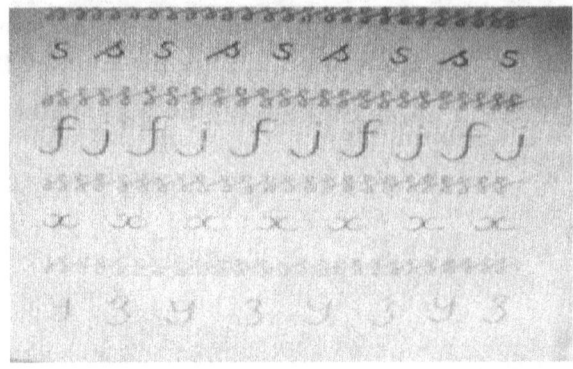

The Marion Richardson System for Writing taught at Sheikh School

In those days, papers and pencils were scarce. I cannot exactly remember the date they were introduced into my class, but perhaps it was in mid-1945.

In the shops, old British newspapers imported from Britain, via Aden, served as the plastic bags of today! At the time of writing, it seems the days of plastic bags are numbered, and the sooner they disappear from the scene, the better it will be for the environment. That fossil fuel will suffer a similar fate is on the horizon!

The elementary boarding class was also used as a "practice class" for teachers in training. To make this possible, it was arranged that the class would start the long summer holidays one month later than the rest the schools and return from such holidays one month later. During the month, the class remained in Sheikh School, all the Somali teachers attended the Annual Teacher Training Course at Sheikh School.

The Teacher Training Course consisted of first giving the trainee teachers lessons in teaching methodology, Arabic, arithmetic (in Arabic), and English, after which they were asked to put what they learnt into practice by giving lessons to us – that was what was meant when Mr Bell recommended "a practice Boarding Elementary Class" in his report of January 1944, by which the educational programme was introduced.

Usually, Mohamoud Ahmed, Yusuf Haji Adan, Abdisalam Hassan, Mr Bell, Mr Badham and Mr Lloyd would sit at the back of the class to observe how the trainee teacher conducted the class. At the end of the period, the observers would give their comments, sensitively, in the presence of the trainee teacher. Even Yusuf Haji Adan and Abdisalam Hassan did not escape, because sometimes they had to give demonstration classes, when the main observations would come from Mohamoud Ahmed.

Pessimistic view of the Director of Education about education in the country [177, p. 68]

In his brief annual report on education for 1944, Mr Bell reviewed what had been done so far. He saw the Education Department re-established on firmer foundation. He mentioned the teachers' training and adult male courses conducted in the year. Several new elementary schools were also opened in the country.

However, after his first full year as Director of Education, in 1944, Mr Bell was very pessimistic about the future of education in the country. This was at a time when the Somaliland elders were urging him to expand the educational facilities so that more boys and girls could be enrolled into the schools. Mr Bell's report included the following:

> There was really little permanent need for large number of educated men in Somaliland. Government Departments and merchants were the only employers of clerical workers and the number of posts available was not very large. The bulk of the population would continue to depend for its livelihood upon stock-raising for many years to come. Technical education was important to train boys as artisans, for whom there was a great demand.

> It was realized that only comparatively few boys from the Elementary Schools would go on to the Primary and Technical Schools, at least for some time to come. Entry to these Schools, after 1945, would be by examination and any boy failing to qualify would have no further education. This would mean that every year about 100 boys would be leaving School after only three years' education. The shortage of suitable staff made it impossible to enlarge the Primary and Technical Schools, which could take only the best of the boys from the Elementary Schools. It was a pity that nothing further could be done for the boys whose education finished at twelve of age; but considering that the vast majority of Somalis had no education at all, their plight did not call for very much sympathy. Most of them would be able to obtain work and all would have received grounding sufficient to enable them to benefit by evening classes and correspondence courses.

The above supports my understanding, as mentioned earlier, that the protectorate government was so used to the lack of formal education in the country that they accepted the situation as normal!

It was true that there were difficulties in the country, including severe shortage of sufficiently educated Somali teachers – this resulted from lack of formal education in the country in the past. However, Mr Bell, rather than being visionary, expressed, right from the start, his views about the education in the country in the usual soulless colonial manner. He expounded that education in the country would aim to turn out clerks and artisans, and educated men were not a priority or not needed at all. He seemed to be out of touch with reality: what possibility was there for a young boy with elementary schooling to engage in correspondence course in Somaliland in, say, 1946? And where were the educational facilities that could provide the correspondence services? It was cruel to say that, because the majority of the population had no education, young boys whose education stopped at elementary schooling, for lack of the second level of education, deserved no sympathy! Certain things are better left unsaid! It will be seen later how Mr Bell's pessimistic outlook negatively impacted upon the development of education in the country.

The total enrolment of the three district elementary schools (at Hargeisa, Berbera and Burao) at the end of 1944 was 147 boys. The enrolment at Sheikh Boarding Elementary School was 30 boys and at the Boarding Primary School was 26 boys. The grand total enrolment at all the schools was 203 boys. The expenditure on education was given as £9,338. The bulk of the expenditure was on building the schools and on personnel emoluments.

Completion of the first phase of the new Sheikh School [177, Appendix 3a]

Construction began in September 1944. By January 1945, the office block, three classrooms and the latrines (all in italics in the table below) had been completed. The buildings formed the nucleus of what became known as the Sheikh School, which catered for the whole Somaliland Protectorate.

The breakdown of the expenditure on all the buildings listed below was given as follows:

Office Block	£620
Block of three classrooms	£620
Three dormitories	£1,050
Mess (Eating) room	£350
Kitchen	£170
Store	£40
Tailor's shop	£35
Ablution (Bathing) block	£60
Latrines for pupils	£40
Latrines for teaching staff	£42
Total	**£ 3,027**

Ali Sheikh Mohamed Jirde of the Public Works Department (PWD) was the Overseer of the construction site, under the supervision of the District Engineer at Berbera District Office. Ali Jirde was one the boys sent to Sudan for education (see 4.3), and studied basic engineering at Gordon College, Khartoum. Ali Jirde himself told me in 2002 that he returned to Somaliland Protectorate in 1937. He joined the PWD as an Overseer. He was later sent, on a scholarship, to the UK in 1948 to join the Brighton Technical College from which he obtained a Diploma in Civil and Structural Engineering in 1951, the first Somali from British Somaliland Protectorate to obtain such qualification.

The houses for the Somali and Sudanese teachers in this new site were built a little later.

At the beginning of January 1945, Class I of 25–30 boys was chosen for each Elementary School. The ages of the boys ranged from 8 to 9 years and they were selected by Mr Bell, Director of Education (in some cases Mr Badham, Principal of Sheikh School), Mohamoud Ahmed Ali, Inspector of Elementary Schools, and the District Commissioners. The new class of 30 boys for the boarding elementary school at Sheikh was distributed as follows: Hargeisa (2); Berbera (2); Burao (2); Las Anod (3); Erigavo (3); Zeila (5); Sheikh (day boys) (4); Somaliland Scouts children (4); special places (5) (at the discretion of the Director of Education). The five special places were reserved for Somali boys from Aden, Djibouti, Kenya, etc.

The fathers of the four boys for the Somaliland Scouts were members of the defunct Somaliland Camel Corps who were killed in the Second World War in either Somaliland Protectorate or in Burma. The government thinking was that the boys would receive free education, since their fathers died while defending the British Empire.

As already mentioned, by January 1945, the office block of Sheikh School, three classrooms and the latrines were ready for use. The two boarding elementary classes and the boarding primary class moved into the three classrooms. The dormitories were not yet ready and so the old government buildings had still to be used.

In the classrooms, there were two big pictures – one was that of the British King, the other was that of Mr Churchill, then the British Prime Minister. When a Somali teacher tried to explain to us who Mr Churchill was, it seemed to some of us that he was a "Chief of a Clan"! We did not know at that time about political parties or governments. Perhaps our understanding of Churchill's job was not all that absurd, given the clan characteristics of all political parties!

Official opening of the new Sheikh School [177, p. 71]

On 20 January 1945, the Military Governor, G.T. Fisher, officially opened Sheikh School. Before the actual opening ceremony, the governor and the accompanying dignitaries were shown round in the classes. In Class I that was in, our teacher,

Abdisalam Hassan, instructed us that if Governor Fisher said "Good morning" when he entered the classroom, we were to shout aloud, "Good morning, Sir!" These were the only three English words we knew at that time. However, it so happened that, instead of Governor Fisher, his wife entered the classroom first, with two young children in tow. Not knowing what Mrs Fisher would say, some of us who knew a little Arabic did not wait for what Mrs Fisher would say and shouted loud "Good morning, Sira", to show that we were greeting a female, by attempting to Arabize the word "sir". I do not know whether Mrs Fisher realized our predicament.

The governor, together with the dignitaries accompanying him, entered the classroom. The governor had a few words with the teacher. In the meantime, we and the young British children stared at each other, bemused, not knowing what to make of each other and unable to exchange words! For some of us, it was the first time we had seen white children, and at close quarters. The governor and his accompanying group then left the room. Our teacher later explained to us when to use the two words "sir" and "madam". This was the first time Class I was taught in English. We all then went out to watch the opening ceremony.

In opening Sheikh School, Governor Fisher unveiled two plaques with inscriptions: one carved in Arabic and the other in English. The plaques, shown in the picture below, were on the front of the office block, which formed the centre piece of the school frontage. The flag (the Union Jack) was fixed between the two plaques. The open space in front of the office block (below the raised wall) was used for school assembly, with which the day's work began.

After the opening ceremony, we returned to our respective classrooms. Sweets were distributed to us, the high point of the day for us, and we were let free for the rest of day. A botched greeting, distribution of sweets and a half-day holiday are the clear memories, which remain with me, of the occasion of the official opening of Sheikh School.

The Office Block (front view) of Sheikh School, opened in 1945, with the flagpole in the centre, and two plaques either side – one in Arabic, one in English.

By 1946, all the Phase 1 Sheikh School buildings were built. The boarding elementary and primary classes moved in from the old government buildings and occupied the new dormitories; the adult classes also did the same. The old buildings were released to the government.

Lion House assembled in front of Sheikh School office block, with the house cup, 1946 [177].

The first three houses were given the names of Lion, Kudu and Leopard. The picture above shows Lion House boys assembled in front of the office block. I was a member of Lion House and I am in the above picture – although it is hard to identify myself! We won a cup, but I can't remember what it was for. There used to be inter-house competitions to win the silver cup – for house cleanliness or neatness, sports and athletics.

The dormitories were of military type (barracks) and each housed about 25 boys. Points were awarded in the inter-house competitions for games, schoolwork and inspections. Great keenness was shown in preparing for Saturday's inspection and the boys spent hours every Friday in tidying up and making as good a show as possible. The dormitories were carefully swept out, the beds made neatly, clothes folded, and eating utensils symmetrically arranged on the beds. In fact, the whole activity was militaristic in character!

The school used to have an uninvited nocturnal visitor in the form of a lion. Its footprints could be seen around the office block and on the hockey ground. Some pupils with "acute hearing" occasionally reported that, during the night, they heard the beast snuffling at the door or the windows. Perhaps because of the lion's presence, I remember the nights that Mohamoud Ahmed went round the houses, as he often did, to ensure that things were in order, carrying a gun and a torch. One night, a lion killed a camel at a spot about one mile from the school. So, two British teachers sat up one night in an attempt to shoot the lion but, as if forewarned, it did not show up that night. One of the teachers later remarked that it was just as well, for the Education Department's rifle was none too accurate.

Meals at Sheikh School

The ration for Sheikh School used to be brought from Mandera, north-east of Hargeisa, where the military ration was stored. Abdi Said, the Quartermaster, and one of the British teachers used to take a truck every month to fetch the ration.

Daily expenditure on food per boy at Sheikh boarding school (in cents) (1945)

Item	Elementary school	Primary school
Rice	5.83 cents	7.77 cents
Flour	2.45	4.86
Ghee	28.12	35.16
Jawari (for making Laxoox)	8.86	15.51
Dates	11.45	11.45
Sugar	3.01	7.51
Tea	1.98	3.95
Salt	0.12	0.15
Milk (¾ pint)	29.88	29.88
Meat	19.33	25.78
Total	111.03	**Total** 142.02
or	12 Annas	or 15 Annas

One rupee = 16 annas (an Indian currency which was also the currency of Somaliland Protectorate); or one shilling and fifty cents (Sh. 1/50).

Abdi Said managed, among other things, the school ration and sports equipment store. The meals were taken as follows:

- **Breakfast** – *Laxoox* and tea (*Laxoox* is like a flat pancake made from *jawari*)
- **Mid-morning break** – dates were issued
- **Lunch** – stewed mutton with rice, drizzled over with ghee, milk (and vegetables sometimes)
- **Supper** – *Laxoox* and dates drizzled over with ghee

- **One-off ostrich egg** – the school authority perhaps wanted to increase the protein content in our diet.

One morning we were served fried ostrich eggs for breakfast. I think few of us, if any, had eaten eggs before – I had definitely never tasted any sort of egg before that. Just as we were tentatively trying to taste it and asking each other what it was, the school cook, Mr Barre, shouted from the kitchen and told us what it was. We dropped the knives and forks which we were clumsily using and walked out of the dining hall. That was the end of ostrich eggs for breakfast. I think this was in February or March 1945. Those of us from nomadic background (the majority of us, including myself) knew the ostrich eggs with the shell intact and we used to play with them by smashing them to see what would come out! But it never occurred to us that they were edible. A nutritious food was lost through ignorance on the part of the pupils, and through the insensitive introduction of a novel food item on the part of the school authority. The rice was usually infested with weevil (*Daaniye*, in Somali). We used to add the milk to the rice, the weevil would float and we would skim them off from the surface of the milk and enjoy our rice. After all, it was a war time!

The school boys' heights and weights were measured yearly and, generally, their health was good and most of them put on weight, perhaps because of the regular meals! Sports and athletics were part and parcel of school life. Abdi Said played an important role in the life of Sheikh School and was very much involved in the organization of these activities. He was a qualified football referee and hockey umpire. Apart from other duties, he used to organize sports in the afternoons. The sports were mainly football and hockey. Cricket was introduced but it did not catch on. Athletics included track events, for example, running a number of times (usually 10) round the football pitch; and running from a place called Hamarta (a valley near Hudiso) and up the mountain to the front of the school office block, covering a distance of about four miles. Tug-of-war was another event which created great excitement.

As already stated, the annual school fees levied on the boys at the elementary and primary boarding classes at Sheikh, were as follows: primary and technical boys: 150 rupees/per pupil; and elementary boys: 60 rupees/per pupil. In all cases, a limited number of free places were allowed. No tuition fees were charged at District elementary schools (see later fee changes).

Question about using the Somali language in Italian Somalia [177, pp. 75–76]

In April 1945, the Education Officer of the British Military Administration, Somalia, sought the views of Mr Bell, Director of Education, Somaliland Protectorate, about the Somali language in the schools. Unlike Somaliland, there was no problem using the written Somali language in the first year in the elementary schools in Somalia. The Education Officer was not keen to use Arabic and gave the following reasons for not using it: (a) Arabic was a foreign language to the Somalis, (b) Arabic was useful only to a point and English must be used and (c) written Arabic differed widely from spoken Arabic.

In spite of that, the Education Officer preferred using Arabic in the first year elementary classes "owing to the great variety of dialects in Somalia"! He indicated that he was prepared to work in agreement with the education policy in Somaliland Protectorate. The Education Officer's arguments against the Arabic language were similar to those put forward, in 1938, by Mr Ellison, first Director of Education of Somaliland Protectorate, who was not keen on the Arabic language (see 4.3).

Mr Bell replied that in the three-year elementary course in British Somaliland, Arabic was used as the medium of instruction, with some oral English in the second year and reading and writing in English in the third year. English as a medium of instruction was started in the second year of the Intermediate School (in other words, the fifth year in school). Mindful of the history of written Somali language in Somaliland Protectorate, Mr Bell added that he would have preferred to have the first-year work entirely in Somali, but that was impossible at that stage of development, owing to the fear of riots!

VE Day – 8 May 1945 – was a public holiday. (VE stands for Victory in Europe). That was when the Second World War ended in Europe, with the defeat of Germany and its allies. On that occasion at Sheikh School, games were arranged for both the pupils and the staff. Sweets were distributed to the pupils – the part we enjoyed most!

We, the pupils, had hardly any comprehension of who was fighting with whom and what the fighting was about. Some nights, short films about the war were shown to us. We enjoyed the pictures, without understanding what was going on.

The year 1945 was also notorious for the invasion of huge swarms of locusts in the country. Even the Sheikh School garden, managed by Ali Maa'alesh, from where the school used to get fresh vegetables, was not spared by the pest. Mr Lloyd, who was in overall charge of the garden and the water pump, was almost in despair, as nothing much could be done about the locusts.

Also, during the long school holiday, many of the Somali teachers were voluntarily drafted into the campaign against the locust and they supervised gangs of "coolies" as they were called (daily workers) who were temporarily hired to lay the poisoned bait for the immature locusts before they were able to fly. There were widespread disturbances against the anti-locust campaign and in Erigavo the situation was so serious that the troops had to be called in to keep the peace; the opening of the elementary school in the town – which had been set for July 1945 – had to be delayed until August.

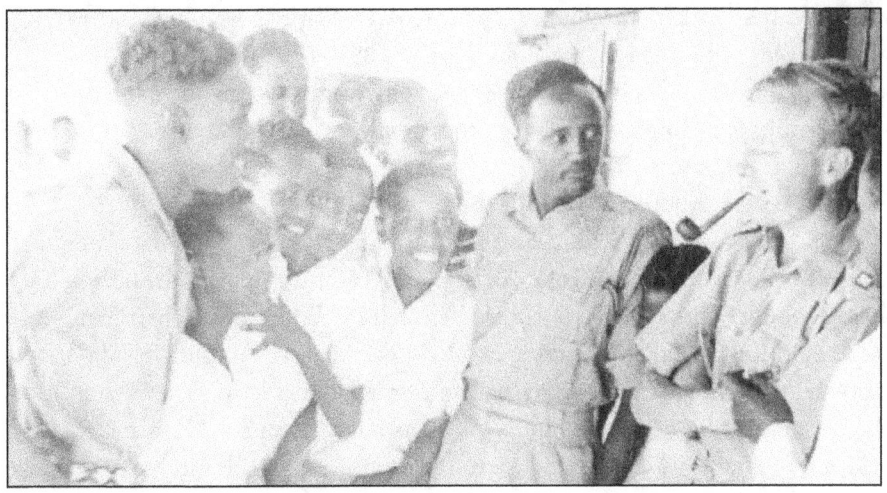

Around 1945. Mr Lloyd, with pipe and in military uniform, having chat with pupils and a man from the adult class. Mr Lloyd had the Somali nickname "Ayah" – locust, in Somali, because his body was slightly tilted to one side when walking and he had silken hair. The locust flies slightly sideways and has silken wings [177].

Scouting at Sheikh School [177, p. 79]

In June 1945, Captain T.R. Holland joined the Education Department and, as well as teaching English in the primary class, he started scouting activities at Sheikh School in November. Mohamoud Ahmed, who was involved in such activities while he was at the Gordon Memorial College in Khartoum, was appointed as Scoutmaster; Abdi Said as Assistant Scoutmaster; and Abdisalam Hassan as Cubmaster. As was the custom in Colonial Africa, Governor Fisher consented to accept the post of Chief Scout of Somaliland Protectorate. Mr Holland left the country the following year, in October 1946.

Boys scouts at Sheikh School, February 1946: Flanked on the left by Mohamoud Ahmed, with fez, and on the right by Abdi Said; Abdisalam Hassan is in the foreground, with safari hat, crouching [177].

A note about the man who started the Boy Scout Movement in 1908: his name was Mr Robert Baden-Powell, one of the archetypal British Empire builders. He was involved, as a soldier, in the Boer Wars of 1899–1902. He based the Boy Scout Movement on his military experience of engaging young men and even boys in military reconnaissance which means, more or less, scouting. The Movement is thus militaristic in character. His real aim was to prepare hardy men who were well-versed in survival skills for the British Empire.

The Scout Movement became an essential ingredient of the syllabuses of government primary schools in Colonial Tropical Africa. It is incredible the amount of correspondence that went to and fro between the Education Department at Sheikh and the Headquarters of the Scout Movement in London, UK, about how to go about starting scouting in Somaliland Protectorate. It appeared that a British Colony that did not embrace scouting was not a "complete Colony"! In fact, a teacher, Ali Mire, was sent to the UK to study scouting, in addition to other subjects (see later).

Oddly enough, the country had at that time three entities carrying the name "Scouts" – the Scouts movement at the Education Department, the *Ilaalo* (Somali name for Scouts) and, because of lack of imagination on the part of the protectorate government, the Somaliland Scouts – an Army which could have been called the "Somaliland Defence Force".

On 15 August 1945, there was another public holiday – VJ, Victory in Japan – when Japan surrendered and the Second World War came to end. One of the British teachers later told the story that when some of the Somalis learnt about the defeat of Japan, their reaction was "now we shall get plenty of rice!", but he added that their prophecy did not come true!

In October 1945, the Director of Education, Mr Bell, announced that all elementary school boys who had reached Standard III and any other boys from *Qur'aanic*/Arabic Schools which received government grants and whose work was good enough should be eligible for entry to the primary school, through competitive examination.

Visit of the Director of Education to Sudan [177, pp. 79–82]

In August 1945, Mr Bell, Director of Education, made a proposal to the governor that he should be allowed to visit Sudan, giving the following reasons for his visit:

- To see the Somali boys in training at Bakht el-Ruda
- To obtain a quota of vacancies for boys at secondary schools and teacher training colleges
- To learn more of the syllabuses in Sudan and to obtain supply of textbooks

- To try to obtain teachers from Sudan

Mr Bell, perhaps realizing that the educational policy against secondary schools, which he had advocated in 1944, was after all wrong, stressed that a decision regarding post-primary education was urgent. But he then, strangely enough, at once stated that it would be uneconomical to start a secondary school in Somaliland for some years to come! He added that in the past, Somalis had gone to Aden or Sudan for secondary education and considered that this should still be the practice, although he maintained that there was some risk of the boys coming into contact with unsuitable political ideas, which would lead to unrest!

Despite all the justifications Mr Bell put forward for his proposed visit to Sudan, the governor turned down his request and advised Mr Bell to visit India, which would be more profitable, and that he should find there what he was looking for in Sudan. More correspondence followed and Mr Bell argued that Sudan would be more acceptable to the Somalis as all the senior trained Somali teachers already obtained their education in Sudan. In the end, the governor relented and allowed Mr Bell to go ahead with the Sudan visit in December 1945.

Major Bell (as he was then) told a funny story about what he experienced when he disembarked a Nile Ferry at Kosti in Sudan. A driver of a large truck sent to collect him was first reluctant to pick him up, because he was under the impression that he had to collect "a major bell"!

Mr Bell reviewed the educational system of Sudan and discovered the set-up as follows:

1. Elementary schools (from age 8) for a four-year duration
2. Intermediate schools for a four-year duration
3. Secondary schools (two only) for a four-year duration, with two junior secondary schools having a two-year course with a vocational basis
4. Gordon Memorial College: Diploma: BA (London); Schools of Administration, Medicine, Engineering
5. Teacher Training Centre at Bakht el-Ruda. Candidates for the centre were recruited as follows:
    - 5a   For elementary schools, recruited from elementary stage, for a six-year course
    - 5b   For elementary schools, recruited from intermediate stage, for a two-year course
    - 5c   For intermediate schools, recruited from secondary stage
    - 5d   Senior teachers – one year at Bakht el-Ruda, after three years at the School of Arts or Science at Gordon Memorial College
6. Two Technical Schools – one reserved for the railways

The intermediate schools in Sudan were more or less equivalent to the primary school at Sheikh. Following Mr Bell's negotiations, the following places were offered to the boys from Somaliland Protectorate:

- January 1946 – two first-year students at Bakht el-Ruda, as in 5a above
- January 1947 – two fifth-year students at Bakht el-Ruda, as in 5b above; three places at secondary school, as in 3 above
- January 1948 – as in 1947, and the situation would then be reviewed

Mr Bell and Sudan's Director of Education compared work done in the primary school, Somaliland Protectorate, with the corresponding work done in Sudan. They agreed that the Somalis compared well with Sudanese in written Arabic but were weak in oral work, and this was to be expected. After all, Arabic was not the mother tongue of the Somalis.

The two Directors agreed that Sheikh Primary School would follow the syllabus of Sudan intermediate schools in English, Arabic and mathematics, so that Somalis would take the same examinations as the Sudanese in the three mentioned subjects. However, they agreed that Sheikh School would develop its own syllabus for Geography, History and Science and examine the candidates in these subjects. They stressed that boys from Somaliland Protectorate would not receive any special consideration for places but would be accepted on their merits.

As the intermediate course in Sudan lasted four years, while that in Somaliland Protectorate was planned to last three years only, to conform to the system of education of Sudan, Mr Bell decided that the primary class which would start in January 1946 would take a four-year course, as by that time there would be sufficient number of teachers available. The primary class then at Sheikh School could not spend a fourth year at the school before some of them could go to Sudan, as they were already over the age of entry into a secondary school or Bakht el-Ruda in Sudan. That was why a Primary Leaving Examination was held in December 1946 (see later). The elementary school course ought to have been extended to four years too, but that was not done (see later for some sort of justification for not doing so).

The Education Department of Sudan could not release any of its teachers, but assisted Mr Bell in recruiting three private Sudanese teachers on a two-year contract. One of the teachers (Mohamed el Bashir) who was to teach Arabic in the primary class at Sheikh School, completed the full secondary course, but the other two only completed the full intermediate course. None of them had teacher training, although they had some teaching experience. The teachers arrived at Sheikh in February 1946.

One would have thought that the educational development in Sudan was then much more advanced than what is described above. However, it has to be remembered that Sudan was then a Condominium, under both British and Egyptian rule, although the British ran the show. In spite of that, the Sudanese used to get the greater part of their education from Egypt, either in Egyptian educational institutions in Sudan or in Egypt. This was greatly facilitated by the fact that the two countries had a common language – Arabic. Mr Bell reported only on the limited section of education in Sudan for which the British Government was responsible.

During his visit in Sudan, Mr Bell thought of sending some boys to Gordon College on a five-year course. The annual cost per student was estimated at £100 and that at Bakht el-Ruda was £50. Mr Bell mentioned that in his calculations while negotiating with the Director of Education of Sudan in 1945, he weighed the advantage of sending three or four boys to Hantoub Secondary School and/or Bakht el-Ruda, against building a secondary school in Somaliland Protectorate (then estimated at £20,000). Mr Bell opted for the former option. The secondary school at Sheikh, which was opened in 1960 cost £142,760. It was not surprising that Mr Bell stuck to what he had already advocated in his first report on education in Somaliland Protectorate in 1944 – in other words, no secondary school for Somaliland Protectorate for many years to come. That short-sighted vision at the outset of the educational development in the country created, right to the end of the colonial rule, ever-present and severe "bottle necks" at the elementary–intermediate–secondary educational levels for lack of sufficient number of places at each level. Mr Bell's decision was, more or less, in line with the educational policy proposed by Governor Archer in 1922 (described under 3.4).

To digress, Governor Fisher made the following statement in his annual report for 1945 [178]:

> *The first step in the development of education is aimed at raising the schools to a level comparable with a nominal African Territory about 1930.*

The statement showed, in blunt terms, how far behind the people of Somaliland were in formal education.

General acceptance of formal education in the country [177, pp. 86–87]

The Education Department's brief report on education for 1945 included the following observations:
1. A few isolated attempts to stir up opposition to the Education Programme had been reported, but they had come to nothing,
2. Even the participation of some of the teachers in the anti-locust campaign had not involved the Education Department in the disturbances which followed the laying of the bait
3. The reasons for the failure to arouse opposition were:

- Almost all the influential men of the towns were in favour of education and many had sons in the schools
- Every chance had been seized of inviting influential Sheikhs and *Wadads* from the interior to come to Sheikh and see for themselves
- Sheikh Adan Hassan (aka Sheikh Kulmiye), the Religious Instructor to the Department whose reputation as a religious leader was high in the country, had toured the country and had met and answered a number of irresponsible rumours

The Education Department was anxious right from the time Sheikh School started. It was feared that, because of the few British teachers at the school, opposition might be directed against the school. Sheikh Adan Hassan, as well as being a religious instructor at Sheikh School, was also employed by the Department for the purpose of travelling around in the country and reasoning with those who might oppose formal education on religious grounds. The Education Department need not have worried. The people of Somaliland Protectorate, on the whole, already accepted formal education as evidenced by the Somaliland communities up and down the country opening schools, as already mentioned.

At the end of 1945, there were seven elementary schools and a one-class primary school. The enrolment of all the government schools at the end of 1945 was: 47 combined literacy and technical boys; 305 elementary boys; 63 adult trainees. The expenditure on education was given as £12,012. Construction of the schools and salaries accounted for the bulk of the expenditure. The cost of board and lodging for the boarding elementary and primary classes at Sheikh School for the year 1945 was estimated at £1,200.

Introduction of Primary School Entrance Examination [177, p. 89]

In December 1945, the Primary School Entrance examination, the first of its kind in Sheikh School, was held for all the boys who had completed Class III elementary schools in the protectorate, and some boys from the government-aided *Qur'aanic*/Arabic schools also sat for the examination. The examination was composed of simple English, Arabic, arithmetic (in Arabic) and some special intelligence and general knowledge tests. The Education Department recorded that about 100 boys sat for the examination and only 28 were admitted into the primary Form IV class in January 1946. That meant about 72% rejection or "waste"! Out of the rejected boys, perhaps a sufficient number to form a second primary Form IV class could have been accepted, had it not been for the lack of spaces in the primary school. In other words, the education of about 72% of the boys, except those known to have actually failed, ended at the elementary level!

Henceforth, I will label as "wastage" the number of students who sat the Primary School Entrance or Primary School Leaving Examinations (where such information is available) and who did not proceed to the next level education, unless they were officially declared as having actually failed in the examinations. In this context, by "wastage" I mean "boys rejected for lack of places in the next level of education".

My late friend Yusuf Ali (Shihare) Abdi, who was a member of that primary Form IV class informed me that, except for one, all of the 28 boys in that form came from Berbera and Hargeisa and he remembered all their names. At that time, there were only three elementary schools, one in each of Hargeisa, Berbera and Burao, which could sit for the examination. Was it that only one boy came from Burao Elementary School? Yusuf could not remember where that boy came from, but he named the boy as Musa Deria Afhakame. I know Musa Deria and his family used to live in Burao, but I could not be sure that he came from Burao Elementary School. The last time I saw Musa, some eight years ago in London, he told me that he lived in Germany, but I did not ask for his contact details. Anyway, at that time I was not thinking about writing this book.

Some boys from Hargeisa Town School sat for the Primary School Entrance Examination – two of them who passed the examination were sent to Bakht el-Ruda in 1946 to be trained as Arabic teachers. I could not find information about their names or if and when they returned.

The boys in Form IV (1946) included: Yusuf Ali (Shihari) Abdi, Hassan Adan Gudaal, Idris Yahye, Mohamed Jama Urdoh, Hassan Megaag Samater, Mohamoud Esa Jama & his brother Abdullahi (Dayah), Mohamed (Sanyare) Haji Ali Guhaad, Abul-Karim Ali Yare, Mohamoud Haji Warsame (Baag), Ali Haji Adan, Rashid Abdi-Rahman (Sumuni, with fez on) [177].

Departmental directive on Government Elementary Schools [177, pp. 140–141]

In 1946, the Director of Education issued a directive about how the government elementary schools would be managed. Given below is a summary of it:

1. The syllabuses were at an experimental stage and each teacher was asked to help the department by sending in notes of any difficulties met and any suggestions so that syllabuses could be revised.
2. The school year would begin in January and new classes would be accepted late in December or early in January. The selection would be made by a committee. No entries would be accepted except at the correct time, but a waiting list should be kept. Standard I would be promoted to Standard II at the end of the year. Boys who were too weak to be promoted would normally be dismissed. Only in exceptional cases, to be reported to the Headquarters, would promotion be made during the year. Dismissals should always be reported to the Headquarters.
3. The hours of work would vary according to the age of the boys. The morning session would consist of five periods of 40 minutes each. One period of 20 minutes would be for physical training (PT). There would be a break of 25 minutes in the middle of the morning. The afternoon session would consist of two periods: one of 40 minutes and the other of 30 minutes. In Standard I there would be no formal afternoon lesson, but in Standards II and III there would be one. At least two afternoon periods in the week would be allotted to games.
4. Friday would be a whole holiday, Thursday and Sunday half holidays. The normal public holidays would be kept. The boys should arrive at least ten minutes before school began in the morning and this time should be used for an inspection of cleanliness and for finding out which boys needed medical attention.
5. Physical training (PT) should be taken in the first period of the morning or in the period immediately before the morning break.
6. The hour of assembly and dismissal depended upon local conditions and each Headmaster would decide this for himself and also make up his own timetable. The periods shown in the table opposite should be given to each subject.
7. Details of the dates for the beginning and end of the school term would be sent to all the elementary schools. There would be only two terms a year – from January to mid-May, and from the end of July to mid-December.

The reason for the two terms was to avoid undue travelling for the boys (nomads) who had long distances to cover, often on foot, to reach their *"Reers"* (nomadic hamlets).

Periods given to each subject at all elementary schools, from 1946

	Standard I	Standard II	Standard III
Qur'aan	6	6	6
Arabic	12	10	10
Arithmetic	7	8	7
Handwork	3	2	2
Somali stories	2	1	1
Geography	-	2	2
Nature study and Hygiene	-	2	2
English	-	3	4
Total per week	30	34	34

Timetable for the Boarding Elementary Classes at Sheikh School, 1946

7.00 am	8.30 am	Lessons
8.30 am	9.00 am	Breakfast
9.00 am	11.15 am	Lessons
11.15 am	11.45 am	Tea break
11.45 am	1.15 pm	Lessons
Lunch & rest		
4.00 pm	5.30 pm	Preparations in the classrooms Games (at least three days a week)
7.00 pm		Supper
7.30 pm	9.30 pm	Preparations (after the school acquired a generator in 1948)
9.30 pm		Bedtime

To signal the end of a period, an old Italian bomb-case suspended in front of the office block was struck with a metal rod two or three times. Normally, the Principal of the School, Mr Badham, was the timekeeper; but any officer who happened to be available gave the signal. Since the school area was normally quiet, the bell could be heard from all the different classes.

Mohamoud Ahmed Ali – as educator and adviser [177, p. 112]

In 1946, the Department of Education made the statement reproduced below. It rang a bell when I read it. It was about how Mohamoud Ahmed Ali endeavoured to inspire the schoolboys and instil a sense of responsibility into them. I would like to think that I might have subconsciously absorbed some of Mohamoud

Ahmed's advice while at school. The statement went like this:

> *Sheikh Town was out-of-bounds to the boys except by special permission, but the boys were allowed to visit one or two coffee-shops after they had been warned by Mohamoud Ahmed of the dangers of the coffee-shop habit. In fact, Mohamoud devoted much time to fostering a spirit of service to the country as a whole; he frequently warned the boys of the folly of exaggerated tribal feeling and told them that it was necessary for the good of the country to renounce their tribal aspirations and think only of the welfare of Somaliland. He denounced the evils of chewing Kat, of smoking, of strong drink, and set before the boys a high standard of personal conduct and of honesty in the service of their country; a standard which he himself maintained by example as well as by precept.*

Mohamoud Ahmed's advice made an indelible impression on me. The Appendix reflects, to a large extent, the advice Mohamoud Ahmed Ali used to give us, as schoolboys at Sheikh School, against the negative influence of clanism.

Introduction of Primary School Leaving Certificate [177, p. 111]

At the end of December 1946, the Primary School Leaving examination, the first of its kind in Sheikh School, was held for 19 boys in the primary Form VI class. This examination differed from subsequent similar examinations in that those who did not qualify for secondary education stayed on for a further one year to continue with their studies. (For the reason for this practice, see Mr Bell's visit to Sudan in 1945, described earlier.)

As a result of the examination, and in line with the arrangements which Mr Bell had made with the Education Department of Sudan, five students were sent on government scholarships to Sudan: three to Hantoub Secondary School, the other two to the Teacher Training Institute at Bakht el-Ruda – all of them to join their respective classes in January 1947.

The rest of Form VI (14 boys) became primary Form VII class in 1947 and continued with their studies. From 1946, the primary course lasted for four years, as arranged by Mr Bell with the Education Department of Sudan in 1945.

In the first week of January 1947, the Primary School Entrance Examination was held for Class III of all the elementary schools. No details were recorded for the examination results – at least, the author could not find any. Among those who sat for that examination were Abdi-Rahman Elmi and Seyyid Mohamoud Abdullah from Borama; Mohamoud Sh. Ahmed and Adan Haji Bahnan from Burao; the late Mohamed-Saleh Haji Hassan from Berbera. The five boys, together with the others who passed the examination formed the primary Form IV class in January 1947.

The single boarding primary school at Sheikh catered for the *whole* protectorate. Small wonder, education for so many boys ended at Standard III elementary schooling!

The total enrolment of government schools at the end of 1946 was given as 408 boys (ie combined elementary and primary boys) and 60 adult males on the English course. The expenditure on education was given as £14,683.

In August 1947, Mohamoud Ahmed went on a one-year course at the Institute of Education of London University. In his absence, Yusuf Haji Adan acted as Inspector of Elementary Schools, while still remaining the Headmaster of the Boarding Elementary School at Sheikh.

The Class III that I was in, in the boarding elementary school at Sheikh School, together with all the other Class IIIs in the district elementary schools, sat for the Primary School Entrance Examination at the end of December 1947. I was amongst the lucky boys who passed the examination and formed the new Form IV primary class in January 1948. I – or more accurately my late father – had to pay my annual school fees of 60 rupees only for the first full year of my elementary education of 1945. The rest of my elementary education followed my intermediate education at Sheikh School (1946–52) were free. Since that time, and until I completed my university education, I had luckily studied on scholarships.

As was also the case in December 1946, I could not find the enrolment at the government schools at the end of 1947, or the results of the examination. The Education Department was not consistent in its documentation. The Protectorate Military Government, under the War Office, was in the process of handing over the protectorate to the Colonial Office; and was perhaps too busy to bother with writing a few pages about the educational activities. Probably this reflected the priority given to education in the country.

In December 1947, the 14 boys in primary Form VII class sat for the Primary School Leaving Examination. As a result, five boys were sent on government scholarships to Sudan: three to Hantoub Secondary School, one to the Teachers Training Institute at Bakht el-Ruda and one to the Agriculture Institute, Duweim. They were all to join their respective classes in January 1948. The wastage – in other words, boys who were rejected for lack of educational places and whose education thus ended with primary school – was 64%. The annual expenditure on education for 1947 was given as £22,373.

In December 1948, no Primary School Leaving Examination was held at Sheikh School and no students from Somaliland Protectorate were sent to Sudan. Instead, two boys (Elmi Ahmed Duale and Abdul-Aziz Haji Deria) from Mogadishu, Somalia, were sent on government scholarships to Hantoub Secondary School, Sudan. This was because, during World War II, the British Government captured Somalia, Ethiopia and Eritrea from Italy.

I digress again: the Primary School Leaving Examination was, more or less, similar to what was known in the UK as the 11-plus examination for the 11-year-old British boys and girls which was introduced into UK in 1944. However, the Somali boys who sat for the Primary Leaving Examination were older than 11 years, because formal education in Somaliland Protectorate had only just started and age was not critical for the boys who were enrolled in the early part of the 1940s for the government elementary schools. For example, I was ten when I was enrolled into Sheikh boarding elementary school in 1944 – I just made it, as the upper age limit was set at 10 years.

A few years ago, I watched the 1940s 11-plus syllabus taught to a class in a village outside London for one month, filmed by a British TV channel. I noticed that practically all the Sheikh Boarding School activities from the 1940s were similar to what the children in that 11-plus class were doing. In other words, the British 11-plus system, suitably adapted for the situation in Somaliland Protectorate, was imported into Sheikh Boarding School. In the UK, the top 15–20% of the boys and girls were selected for the top academic government secondary schools, called "Grammar Schools". There were other avenues for the academically less endowed boys and girls to continue with their education, eg at colleges for vocational training and at other academically less demanding secondary schools.

In the case of Somaliland Protectorate, there were at that time no educational facilities for the many boys who completed primary education but did not qualify for scholarships abroad.

At the time of writing, the British Parliament was still debating the merits and demerits of the 11-plus examination which was in effect abolished in the mid-1970s, although some survived. Some thought that it was socially divisive and was stunting children's potential. Others thought otherwise and advocated the 11-plus type examination and Grammar schools, to give bright children the chance to shine at such examinations.

The Military Administration achievement in formal education [177 p. 157]

By 1948, the situation of education in the country stabilized somewhat – in contrast to the period 1944–46 when the educational programme was being built up from scratch. The limited planned schools and other buildings were almost complete. The year 1948 marked a transitional period. The country reverted to the control of the Colonial Office on 15 November 1948. Since the reoccupation of the country in 1941 until 1948, the War Office, like the Colonial Office before the war, had been subsiding the expenditure not only on education but also on the protectorate as a whole.

At this juncture, it will be of interest to have a look at the progress made, so far, by the educational programme planned by Mr Bell, Director of Education, in 1944.

There was one elementary school at each of the eight main centres – namely, Zeila, Borama, Hargeisa, Berbera, Sheikh, Burao, Las Anod and Erigavo. There were also, at Sheikh, one elementary and one primary boarding school, which were for the whole country.

In 1944–1947, about 150 male adults passed through an eight-month training course in English, Arithmetic and Civics. Those who did very well at school underwent further training and were recruited by the Education Department as teachers. Annual teacher training courses were held for the junior teachers of the Education Department. Also teacher training courses were occasionally held for the teachers at the grant-aided *Qur'aanic* and/or Arabic schools.

The teaching staff of the Education Department grew from 5 in 1943 to 45 in 1948. A few boys were sent on government scholarships to Sudan for four-year secondary education and for two-year teacher training courses. An annual tuition fee of 30 shillings per boy was introduced into the District Elementary Schools in 1948. No studies could be done at Sheikh School at night, for lack of electricity. However, in late 1948, the United Nations Educational, Scientific and Cultural Organization (UNESCO) donated £500 to Sheikh School. With the money, a generator was bought for the school. Thus, the students could study in the classrooms at nights when the generator was switched on for about two hours.

Mr J.B. Whitehead joined the Education Department in January 1948 and taught History and Geography in the Primary School.

To cap it all, the Military Government enacted the 1948 Education Ordinance, the text of which is reproduced below.

Ordinance on Education, 1948 [179]

To secure complete control of education in the country, the Military Government enacted the following Ordinance, the first and the only one of its kind, as far as I could ascertain, ever issued by a Somaliland Protectorate Government on education. Given below is the Ordinance, in its entirety and without any alteration, in its original form:

> *1) The Ordinance may be cited as the Education Ordinance, 1948, and shall come into operation on 1st May 1948.*
>
> *2) In this Ordinance, unless the context otherwise requires: "Assisted school" means a school which for the time being is in receipt of a grant – in-aid from the public revenue. "Boarding school" means a school in which boys are received for board and lodging as well as for formal instruction. "Director of Education" means the officer appointed by the Governor to be in charge of the Education Department and includes the officer appointed to act for the Director of Education. "Government school" means a school under the entire control of the Government. "Grant-in-aid" means a grant*

made out of the public revenue in aid of any school. "Prescribed" means prescribed by any regulations made under this Ordinance. "School" means an institution at which boys receive a regular course of formal instruction and includes a training institution but does not include any institution at which the instruction is wholly of a religious nature or at which only the minimum of formal teaching needed for religious instruction is given. "Teacher" means any person engaged in formal instruction at a school. "Training institution" means an institution approved by the Director of Education for the training of teachers.

3) The Director of Education shall have charge of education in the protectorate.

4) The Director of Education shall in such places as he shall think fit, establish District Advisory Committees for education consisting of such number of members not less than three as he shall deem necessary.

5) It shall be lawful for the Director of Education to pay from the public revenue to the governing body or the person in charge of any school a grant or grant-in-aid of such amount, at such times, on such conditions and to be applied in such manner as may be prescribed or, in default of such prescription, as the Governor may approve.

6) Before payment of any grant-in-aid under this Ordinance the Director of Education may require that security be given to his satisfaction for the proper application of the grant.

7) In every school such records as may be prescribed or, in default of such prescriptions, as the Director of Education may determine shall be kept by the person in charge and shall be open to inspection when required by the Director of Education or his representative.

8) a) No person shall open any school after the date of the commencement of this Ordinance or maintain the same thereafter unless such school is registered in accordance with the provisions of this section,

b) Application for registration of a school shall be made in such manner and shall contain such particulars as might be prescribed or, in default of such prescription, as the Director of Education may require,

c) The person in charge or the manager of every school in existence at the date of the commencement of this Ordinance shall within three months thereof apply to the Director of Education for registration of such school,

d) Any person proposing to open a school after the date of the commencement of this Ordinance shall apply for the registration thereof in like manner at least one month before the date upon which it is proposed to open such school,

e) Upon receipt of an application for registration, the Director of Education, if satisfied that the requirements of this Ordinance have been complied with, shall enter the particulars thereof in a register of schools to be kept by him for the purpose: provided that the Director of Education may refuse to register any school for the reason that, in his opinion, other sufficient educational facilities exist or for other good and sufficient reasons whether of a similar or different kind,

f) An appeal to the Governor shall lie within sixty days from a refusal of the Director of Education to register a school under the provisions of this section and the decision of the Governor thereupon shall be final.

9) The Governor shall cause a list of all schools registered in the protectorate under the provisions of section 8 to be published in the Gazette in the months of June and December of every year.

10) a) The Director of Education shall cause to be kept a register of all teachers and no person shall teach in a school unless his name is contained in such register,

b) The conditions upon which a teacher may be registered and the conditions upon which the name of a teacher may be removed from the register shall be such as may be prescribed: provided that, in default of such prescription, the Director of Education may determine such conditions and may for any good and sufficient reasons refuse to register any person as a teacher or for the same reasons may remove the name of any teacher from the register after giving such teacher sixty days' notice of his intention to do so,

c) An appeal to the Governor shall lie within sixty days from the date upon which the Director of Education, in exercise of the powers conferred upon him by the proviso to the preceding sub-section, gives notice to the person or teacher affected of his refusal to register him or of his intention to remove the teacher's name from the register as the case may be, and the decision of the Governor shall be final.

11) A list of teachers shall be published in the Gazette in the months of June and December of every year.

12) The Director of Education may forbid the use in any school of any text book or other material intended for formal instruction which, in his opinion, is unsuitable by reason of inferior academic standard, for use in such

school: provided that, the Governor may, by order in writing, prohibit the use of any book, material or subject of instruction in any school for any reason which he may think proper.

13) The person in charge of any assisted school shall be bound to receive for formal instruction such pupils as may be assigned thereto by the Director of Education after consultation with the District Advisory Committee of the District in which such school is situated.

14) In Government and assisted schools such fees shall be paid as may be prescribed or in default of such prescription may be determined by the Governor.

15) The Director of Education shall appoint in every District a School Fees Committee consisting of such persons as he may think fit and such Committee shall have the power to reduce or waive the fees payable in respect of any pupil residing within its District.

16) a) If the Director of Education is satisfied by such evidence as he may deem fit that any school is being conducted in such a manner as to contravene the provisions of section 8 or 10 of this Ordinance, or the terms of an order made by him or by the Governor under section 12, he may, by notice in writing, require the person in charge of the school to take such steps within reasonable time as will ensure that the conduct of the school shall comply with such provisions or with the terms of any such order,

b) The notice mentioned in the preceding sub-section shall specify in what respects the Director of Education believes that the provisions of any of the said sections or any such order have been contravened, and the time within which the steps necessary to secure observance of such provisions or order are to be taken,

c) If at the completion of the time specified in the notice mentioned in sub – section (a) of this section or such extension thereto as the Director of Education may allow, the person in charge of the school shall fail to satisfy the Director of Education that the conduct of the school has been made to comply with the terms of any of the said sections or any of such order as aforesaid in the particulars mentioned in the notice, the Director of Education may, subject to the approval of the Governor, order the School to be closed,

d) No person shall continue to maintain a school which has been ordered to be closed under this section, and the name of such school shall forthwith be removed from the register of schools.

17) Any person contravening the provisions of sections 8, 10, 12, 13 or 16

(d) of this Ordinance shall be guilty of an offence and shall be liable to a fine not exceeding one hundred rupees, and in the case of a continuing contravention, to an additional fine not exceeding twenty rupees in respect of each day during which such contravention has continued: provided that no proceedings shall be taken against any person in respect of an offence against this Ordinance without the consent of the Director of Education.

18) Any of the persons hereunder mentioned may at any reasonable time visit any school and may examine records kept therein in accordance with the requirements of this Ordinance and also to listen the formal instruction: Any European Officer of the Education Department, Any member of a District Advisory Committee within his District, Any District Commissioner within his District, Any person either generally or specifically authorized by the Director of Education: provided that the examination of any accounts shall only be carried out by the Director of Education or any other person authorized by him for the purpose.

19) Nothing in this Ordinance shall be taken to prevent the establishment or maintenance of Government schools by the Director of Education in such numbers and in such localities as he shall think fit.

20) The Governor may make regulations for the following purposes:

a) To prescribe the conditions upon which grants-in-aid may be paid in respect of any school, the amount of such grants, the time and mode of payment and the manner in which grants may be applied,

b) To prescribe the duties and regulate the proceedings of District Advisory Committees,

c) To provide for the payment of teachers, for their examination for the purposes of registration under this Ordinance and for the grant of Certificates to teachers and to prescribe the conditions upon which such Certificates may be revoked,

d) To provide for the inspection of schools,

e) To prescribe the records and amounts to be kept at schools and the statistics to be furnished to the Director of Education by the person in charge of any school,

f) To prescribe anything which this Ordinance requires to be prescribed and generally to carry out the purposes of this Ordinance.

The Ordinance shows the tight grip that the protectorate government had on education in the country. It was all left to the discretion of the Director of Education to decide what was or was not acceptable in the education of the country. The Ordinance enabled the Director of Education to regulate the formal – and, to some extent, the non-formal – education in the country as he thought fit. Under section 18, the Inspector of Elementary Schools was not included in the list of authorized officials who could freely enter schools, without the permission of the Director of Education, and inspect them. Instead, he was amongst those whom the Director of Education had to authorize to inspect the schools. Of course, that would not have been the case had the Inspector of Elementary Schools been European. Above all, in education, as in almost all other affairs of the country, the governor of the protectorate was practically the final arbiter.

Under the Ordinance, District Advisory Committees for Education were formed and those already existing were formalized in all the District towns of Borama, Hargeisa, Berbera, Burao, Las Anod and Erigavo. The functions of the committees were:

- To assist in the recruitment of boys for the elementary schools

- To put forward applications for grants from *Qur'aanic* and/or Arabic schools

- To assist the headmasters of the district elementary schools in their relations with the district communities.

Also, under Section 15 of the Ordinance, every District School Fees Committee had the power to reduce or waive the fees payable in respect of any pupil residing within its district. The committees were encouraged to hold monthly meetings and to keep records of their proceedings and recommendations. At the headquarters of the education department, Sheikh, was a Scholarship Committee which was responsible for the award of overseas scholarships to post-intermediate courses, and a Fees Committee which dealt with applications for the remission of boarding fees.

R.R. Darlington (*Gacma-dheere*, the long-armed, to his students) joined the Education Department in August 1949. He taught English and Geography in the primary school (more about him later).

To accord them the recognition they deserve, the Somalis, British and Sudanese educators listed below built up the formal educational services in the country from scratch. The list is not exhaustive, because I have named only those whose names I could remember – but I don't think I have missed many of them. As I started and finished my elementary and intermediate education at Sheikh Boarding School, all the educators named, except the few technical instructors, taught me at one stage or another at Sheikh School between 1944 and 1952. The Somali educators trained locally, except the four religious instructors and the first three technical instructors in the list, graduated from the adult courses. Suudi Haji

Adan (Technical Instructor) attended the adult courses. Hashi Abdulla Farah was a member of the teaching staff, but he had his education in Aden. Abdi Said, although not a member of the teaching staff, played a crucial role in the building up of the Education Department, particularly in the fields of logistics and sports. Ali Sh. Mohamed Jirde, who was employee of the Public Works Department, was the overseer of the construction of Sheikh school buildings. He was subsequently closely associated with Sheikh School, probably as the resident-engineer at Sheikh School.

The names of the educators are listed as below:

Some of the multi-national educators in the early stage of the formal educational programme

Somali educators trained in Sudan	Somali educators trained locally	British educators	Sudanese educators
Mohamoud Ahmed Ali Yusuf Haji Adan Mohamed Shire Abdisalam Hassan Yusuf Ismail Samater Seyyid Abdirahman Ali Mohamoud Haji Duale Mohamed Hashi Abdi Ahmed Mohamoud Qayir Yusuf Sh. Madar.	Omer Arte Qaalib Omer Mohamed (Omer Dheere) Ali Mire Mohamed Shihari Musa Haji Ismail Galaal Mohamed Adan (Sheef) Mohamed Jama Badmah Adan Isaq Hassan Adan Wadaadiid Daud Dahir **Religious instructors:** Sheikh Adan Hassan, Sheikh Ali Ibrahim, Haji Hussein Haji Duale, Ma'alim Qaasim Haji Mohamed. **Technical instructors:** Mogeh Mohamed Adan Warsame Ali Ismail Suudi Haji Adan	C.R.V. Bell P.H.C. Badham K.D. Lloyd J.B. Whitehead R.R. Darlington Lt. Nicholson Captain Smith J.N. Clark.	Mohamed el Bashir Hamza Ahmed Mubarak el Khidir. Omar Hassan Mohamed Takana.

The educators listed above were in the vanguard of building up the Education Department. They blazed a trail for their many worthy successors who were no less deserving of recognition. But there were also others, not in the limelight, who in their own ways, contributed to the effort. There was Barre, the school cook, who used to call us "my boys"; Ibrahim Musa, the school tailor; Adan Bowkah, the school security guard, and his brother Duale Jabuti, who ran a small teashop in the middle of the School, where we used to buy a cup of tea for two cents; Ali Reygal, with the prosthetic leg, whose job it was to switch on and off the school generator at certain hours at night. There was the man whose proper name escapes me, but we used to call him *"Ferman"*, perhaps this was a corruption of "foreman", as he was in charge of a group which was responsible for both the sanitation at the school and for collecting fire wood from distant places, using a big truck. I better stop here before I take a stroll too far down memory lane!

At the end of 1948, the Education Department made the statement that the eight elementary schools and the primary school catered for about 653 boys and about 25% of them would be eligible for further education! Perhaps the figure of 653 was exaggerated. Anyway, it meant a wastage of 75%. This signified how limited the educational facilities in the country were. The expenditure on education in 1948 was given as £22,468.

From 1949 to Independence in 1960, the country was under the control of the Colonial Office.

4.9 The Civil Government built on the 1944 Educational Programme

Sir Thomas Lloyd's visit [180]

In 1949, Sir Thomas Lloyd, Permanent Under-Secretary of State for the Colonies, visited the country. A group of Somali notables presented a memorandum to him. Among the issues raised in the memorandum was a demand for the expansion of education in the country. This demand was really timely, because then the number of government elementary schools (eight in all) grew out of all proportion to the only one government primary school in the country. About 120 boys were yearly competing for about 30 places in the only primary school in the country, which meant that about 75% of the boys would be rejected for lack of places – in other words, "wastage".

As ever, the reply of Sir Thomas Lloyd was typical of the colonial officers' mantra that the country was run on British taxpayers' money. He claimed that the British Government gave the country £2 for every £1 raised in the country as local revenue. Sir Thomas Lloyd was not wide of the mark (See Table 7 later, for details). He added that the cost of educating a Somali in Britain was about £500 per year. Sir Thomas Lloyd gratuitously remarked that there were about 40 colonies which the Colonial Office was looking after. A charitable interpretation that could be put on this uncalled-for remark of Sir Thomas Lloyd is that, because the Colonial Office was supporting so many colonies, the people of Somaliland should content themselves with whatever was offered to them!

When Sir Thomas Lloyd mentioned the cost of training a Somali in Britain, perhaps he had in mind a group of senior clerks who were sent on scholarships to Britain in 1947–1948 to upgrade their knowledge of public administration. They were: Abdirahman Abby Farah, Abdirahim Abby Farah, Iman Dhore and Anthony James who joined Exeter University, UK, and obtained Diplomas in Public Administration. And Abdillahi Abby Farah who attended the Police Training College near Coventry City, UK.

By 1950, all of the above-named returned to Somaliland. Those who studied public administration were employed as Assistant Administrative Officers. Abdillahi Abby was employed as Pay and Quartermaster of the Somaliland Police Force.

I mentioned earlier that Mohamoud Ahmed Ali and Ali Sh. Mohamed Jirde were sent to Britain on scholarships in 1947–1948. These seven mature students were, as far as I know, the first Somalis sent on government scholarships to the UK for studies. Others, in different fields, followed later.

While Sir Thomas Lloyd was still in the country in 1949, the Education Department prepared a small project for the expansion of the educational services and an application for grants under the Colonial Development & Welfare Act of 1945. The project was submitted to the Colonial Office. The proposals approved included provision for:

- A second intermediate school at Borama
- A junior secondary school at Borama
- Girls school at Burao
- Trades school at Hargeisa

When the protectorate government was requesting funds from the Colonial Office to build the girls elementary school, the government justification included the following:

> *The only possible use that could be made of these girls would be as teachers in subsequent girls' schools and as nurses in female and paediatric clinics. Educated wives might exercise a significant effect on uneducated husbands and children. The aim of the school is to raise the standard of living by training girls who may thereafter be expected to take part in the medical, social or educational services for the community or to marry men whose own living standards have been raised by education.*

Why should the scope of an educated girl be so restricted, when that was not the case for an educated boy? Such justification for girls' education reflected the prevalent attitude towards the Somali female. The government's demeaning portrayal of the girls' education only reinforced the ideas held by unenlightened Somali males.

In the Primary School Leaving Examination of December 1949, 25 boys sat for the examination. Eight boys were sent on government scholarships to Sudan: four to Hantoub Secondary School, two to the Agriculture Institute, Duweim, and two to the School of Commerce, Omdurman, all to start their respective courses in January 1950. The wastage was 68%. These boys usually entered either in the government services or in private businesses. The urgent need for secondary educational facilities in the country was obvious.

The total number of students and the names of those who were sent abroad for secondary education on government scholarships, from 1947 to 1953, is given in Ref. 199.

The total enrolment of the eight government elementary schools and the primary school at the end of 1949 was given as 469 boys. The expenditure on education was given as £24,036.

A Brief History of Formal Education in British Somaliland Protectorate

Table 5: The annual expenditure (in sterling £) on Somaliland Protectorate, 1940–1949:[8]

	1940	1941	1942	1943	1944	1945	1946	1947	1948	1949
Local revenues	127,475 (22.9%)	10,081 (2.9%)	121,357 (30.8%)	207,475 (33.2%)	282,949 (35.4%)	335,935 (29.3%)	480,736 (56%)	487,250 (56.7%)	383,626 (42.5%)	338,261 (25%)
Government subsidies	429,243 (77.1%)	342,236 (97.1%)	272,500 (69.2%)	418,061 (66.8%)	517,203 (64.6%)	811,805 (70.7%)	378,392 (44%)	372,394 (43.3%)	518,865 (57.5%)	1,016,779 (75%)
Annual expenditure	556,718	352,317	393,857	625,536	800,152	1,147,740	859,128	859,644	902,491	1,355,040
Expenditure on education	1,415* (0.2%)	**	230 (0.06%)	2,631† (0.4%)	9,338 (1.2%)	12,012 (1%)	14,683 (1.7%)	22,373 (2.6%)	22,468 (2.5%)	24,036 (1.8%)

NB. The annual expenditure of £265,000 on the Somaliland Scouts are added to the annual government subsidies [68]. * Includes the salary of the Director of Education, Mr Ellison, fees for students in Sudan, Aden and grants to *Qur'aanic*/Arabic Schools. ** Figure for education not available. It was the year the British reoccupied the country. The only government school in the country was closed in May 1940. Perhaps no government grants were paid to the few *Qur'aanic*/Arabic Schools which used to get such grants. † Includes fees for students in Sudan, Aden, grants to *Qur'aanic*/Arabic Schools and the Consultancies of the British Council two-man team and Mr Lacey, Director of Education, Kenya.

The 1938 and 1939 annual reports on education were the first standalone reports of their kind published by the protectorate government. From 1944 to 1949, reports on education consisted of a few sheets which formed part of the annual reports of the protectorate governor. During this period, the main activities were concerned with the construction of educational facilities and the accompanying infrastructure. There were not many educational services to report on – but a start was made. It was from 1950 that the Education Department issued separate annual reports on education. By contrast, the Public Works, Veterinary and Medical Units (there were no Departments at that time) started issuing reports by at least 1900. The functions of these Units assumed greater importance when the Seyyid started the Dervish rebellion.

The Public Works Unit was there to develop water resources and build accommodation for government staff. The government transport consisted of camels, horses and the mules. The health of these animals had to be taken care of. Hence the veterinary health unit. The medical unit was mainly for the Colonial adminis

---

8 For expenditure data, see the following references: 1940–1941 [181], 1942–1944 [182], 1945 [183], 1946–1948 [184], 1949 [185].

trators and junior government employees, mainly Indian clerks, who were allowed to bring their families to Somaliland. It was through such veterinary and medical units that "western medicine" was introduced into the country. The services of the three units were usually confined to the settlements which the government used as bases from which to operate.

Annual report on Education for 1950 [186]

In the final decade (1950–1960) of Somaliland Protectorate, at the beginning of almost every year, the protectorate government made somewhat ominous annual policy announcements about education in the country. The statement in the annual report on education for 1950 went like this:

> *Since the protectorate cannot at present support a large urban population without widespread unemployment and poverty, it is not the intention of the Department to provide formal education on a large scale nor to aim at Mass Literacy, but to limit the output of the Schools to those who may reasonably be expected to find suitable employment. Community development and mass education, as distinct from mass literacy, both in towns and in the interior are to be the concern of the Information Department.*

The statement is not surprising. It only re-enforced the education policy enunciated by Mr Bell in his first report in 1944, when he became Director of Education of the protectorate. That policy was to train, not necessarily to educate, functionaries to meet the government's need for clerks and the like, and for artisans to make furniture for the schools and the European bungalows! Mr Bell implied that talks on Radio Hargeisa were sufficient for "mass education", which, in my view, were for general information for the public!

The Director of Education was responsible for policy matters concerning the Information Department, which was, in turn, had responsibility for:

- organizing evening classes for the adult population
- community centres
- providing broadcasting services
- supplying newspapers and periodicals to clubs and societies
- issuing film strips
- issuing monthly newsletter

Classification of government schools

The government schools were reclassified in 1950 in order to bring the nomenclature more in line with what was then in practice elsewhere, (ie the rest of the

British Empire). As a result of that classification, the term "primary school" was adopted for all schools up to the end of the intermediate stage (Standard VII), and primary schools were sub-divided as follows:

1. Elementary schools
   - *Qur'aanic* and other grant-aided Private Schools (Sub-standard and Standard I)
   - Government elementary schools (Standards I–III)
2. Intermediate schools (Standards IV–VII)

There were then no secondary schools in the protectorate, but it was decided that the term "secondary school" would be applied to all schools providing facilities beyond the intermediate stage.

The school year was also altered during 1950, in accordance with similar change in Sudan. It was necessary to align the school year of the protectorate with that of Sudan, as that country was the main destination for secondary education and Arabic teacher training. Sudan decided the school year was to start in July rather than in January. Accordingly, the Education Department decided that, from 1951 onwards, the school year would begin in July instead of January. As a result of the change, there was no Intermediate School Entrance examination at the beginning of 1951.

This disruption in the school year was caused by the lack of educational facilities beyond the intermediate stage. Planning for formal education in the country became dependent on what happened in another country. The solution should have been to make available in the country what was needed so that formal education in Somaliland Protectorate would not be at the mercy of changes in another country.

The government continued to build on the modest educational programme initiated by the Military Government. Overwhelmed by the demand for adult education, the government reversed its earlier decision in 1948 on adult education and revived the adult courses. In 1950, a fifth eight-month adult course for 40 trainees was held in Borama. Subsequently, the form of the adult courses was replaced by civic courses, lasting ten days, for members of the district councils and local authorities. The first such course was held in February 1952.

In the Intermediate Entrance Examination held in January 1950, only 77 boys were accepted out of 128 candidates. The wastage was 40%. There was acute shortage of intermediate school places for boys who completed Class III elementary education.

The class I was in – Form V – engaged in mosquito control nearby Sheikh School. We were checking for the presence of mosquito larvae and spraying pools with DDT (insecticide), 1949 [177].

A weather station at Sheikh School, around 1951.

There used to be a small weather station in front of Sheikh School. The geography master, Mr Darlington, was in charge of the station. As practical lessons in geography, we used to record, under supervision, the minimum and maximum temperatures, the humidity and rainfall.

Refresher courses for the different grades of Somali teachers were held in May/June 1950. The subjects focused on were: Method in Teaching Mathematics, Elementary Science, and Arts/Crafts. Following the courses, promotion examinations to the different grades were held and the results were as follows:

Grade	Number of entries	Number of passes
Ungraded to Grade IV	11	5
Grade IV to Grade III	8	4
Grade III to Grade II	3	1
Total	22	10

Second Intermediate School for boys opened at Amud

In September 1950, a second boarding intermediate school was opened at Amud, just outside Borama town, for 47 boys in Standards V and VI, who were transferred from Sheikh, and 30 new boys taken into Standard IV. Mr Lloyd was appointed as the Principal of the intermediate school.

The Hargeisa community, not content with the slow pace of the government in providing more educational facilities, built a day elementary school in 1950 and the Education Department agreed to run it.

At the end of 1950, apart from a few British teachers, there were 51 Somali and Sudanese teachers and assistant teachers, including 4 technical instructors, in the department. Of the Somali teachers, 10 had completed teacher training course at the Institute in Bakht el-Ruda, Sudan; 10 completed a one-year course at Sheikh School; 4 Sudanese teachers serving in the department on short contracts had completed a secondary school course up to School Certificate and were trained as teachers. The rest of the Somali teachers had no professional qualifications, but benefited from one-month annual courses held for all teachers since 1944. It was the policy of the Department to post all teachers, in rotation, to the boarding intermediate schools or the boarding elementary school at Sheikh, where they could receive help and close supervision from senior members of the teaching staff.

The Education Department reported that Hassan Adan Gudal was one of the four boys who started their studies in Hantoub Secondary School, Sudan, in January 1950. At the end-year examination at Hantoub School in 1950, he came top of the 119 first year students and won the Ahmed Mohamed Salih Prize.

At the end of 1950, there were eight government elementary schools with an enrolment of 515 boys and two intermediate schools with enrolment of 226 boys (total enrolment of 741 boys). The annual expenditure on education in 1950 was given as £31,078, including £1,000 grants to *Qur'aanic*/Arabic schools.

In the 1950 Annual Report on Education, the Education Department did not include the elementary school built by the Hargeisa community, but run by the Education Department.

About the Somali teachers, I could not put it in any better way than the Director of the Education Department, Mr Bell, put it when he wrote in the November 1950 issue of *Corona* (a journal for the British Officials who were working in the British Colonies) that the Somali teachers:

> ...*with little education, nevertheless had made themselves into good teachers by their own diligence and zeal. The teachers from Bakht El Ruda [the Teacher Training Centre in Sudan] proved a credit to the Institute which trained them. The teachers deserve great praise for the schools they have built up [187].*

The last part in which Mr Bell mentions the teachers from Bakht el-Rudha mainly refers to: Mohamoud Ahmed Ali, Yusuf Haji Adan, Mohamed Shire, Abdul-Salaam Hassan Mursal and Yusuf Ismail who, as already mentioned, opened three elementary schools in 1942, before Mr Bell arrived in the country in December 1943. The first part of Mr Bell's appraisal applies to all the Somali teachers. The Somali educators richly deserve such clear seal of approval by the Director of the Education Department.

The annual reports of the Education Department were more or less a copy-and-paste affair, since nothing much in the way of educational development was happening. The government thought that the cost of the elementary schools was prohibitive, especially the boarding elementary school which, in the view of the government, was a luxury at that level! The government estimated that, in 1951, the gross cost per boy in the intermediate grade and elementary boarding school would approximately be £64 per year, while the cost per boy in the district elementary schools would be £11 per year.

Annual report on education for 1951 [188]

The government, ever so reluctant to meaningfully expand the education, announced the following policy statement in the 1951 annual report on education:

- No new elementary schools would be built unless the community was prepared to fund at least 50% of the cost
- The government would accept responsibility for staffing and running the schools when they were built
- In the smaller centres, one class school will be built, catering for an intake of about 25 boys every third year – these schools could be extended if necessary
- A lower standard of building was to be accepted, ie a "native-type" structure with proper doors and windows

It was a sinister poly to curb the public demand for the expansion of the educational facilities. Most probably, the government calculation was that the Somalis would not bother to spend money on education, nor would they build schools. But that turned out to be not true, as demonstrated by Hargeisa community, building an elementary school in 1950. Even before Hargeisa's initiative, other communities had built schools in the early 1940s, as already described. Enrolling children into the one-class elementary school every third year in smaller centres (small towns) was a drastic rationing of education in the country! The idea of native type structure for school buildings was to go back to the "Arish" School type built in Hargeisa by Mohamoud Ahmed Ali and his colleagues in 1942. Development of any sort in the country was anathema to the government!

In 1951, Form VI (the class I was in) of the boarding intermediate school at Sheikh was taken to Erigavo to observe the *Ta'ba* Road which was under construction. The road, which was 50 miles long and opened in October 1952, was in a mountainous terrain and it was constructed to link Erigavo and Maidh on the coast. The engineers were Italian ex-prisoners of war who chose to remain in Somaliland Protectorate after the occupying Italian forces were driven out of the country in March 1941. The Public Works Department depended, to a large extent, on the technical skills of these Italian ex-prisoners. The country was also in the grip of a severe drought in 1951. En route to Erigavo, we were shown how the drought-stricken, destitute nomads in Gar'adag Relief Camp were being cared for. We had to write short essays on our trip to Erigavo. This type of field trip was part of education in Civics. The schoolboys had to be kept in touch with what was going on in the country.

In March 1951, 35 boys in Form VII, including a few boys from the Technical School, sat the Intermediate School Leaving Examination. The examination was held at that time, because of the change of the school year in both Sudan and Somaliland Protectorate, from January to July, as already mentioned. Out of the 35 boys, four were awarded government scholarships to Hantoub Secondary School, Sudan, and would join their classes in Hantoub in July 1951. Two other boys were given government scholarships to Mombasa Institute of Muslim Education (Technical), Kenya. The wastage was 83%.

The educational activities of the technical school were hardly mentioned in the annual reports of the Education Department, but I could not find any explanation for this.

Ali Ismail, Technical Instructor at Sheikh School, was sent to the UK, on a British Council scholarship in 1951, to join Brixton School of Building, to follow a six-month course on woodwork.

The Education Department reported (wrongly, I think!) that four boys were sent to Bakht el-Ruda in 1951. All the boys who were sent to Bakht el-Ruda or Hantoub Secondary School used to know each other and often met during the school holidays. I made some enquiries about the four boys but could not find anybody who could remember four boys from Sheikh School being sent to Bakht el-Ruda in 1951!

Form VII (the Class I was in) was due to sit for the Intermediate School Leaving Examination at the end of 1951. However, the examination was postponed to March 1952, because of the change in the school year.

In September 1951, Musa Galaal (1917–1980) who was well known for his knowledge of the Somali folklore and culture, as well as being an English teacher at Sheikh School, was sent on a scholarship to the UK to join B.W. Andrzejewski, the Polish linguist at the School for Oriental and African Studies (SOAS), London University, UK. Musa Galaal assisted in the research into the Somali Language, which Mr Andrzejewski was conducting in Somaliland Protectorate for about a year and a half up to the end of August 1951. Musa Galaal was also to learn phonetics. He researched into a suitable script for writing the Somali language.

Finally the saga of writing the Somali language came full circle when, on 21 October 1972, the Somali Government adopted the slightly modified Roman alphabet as the official orthography for the Somali language. Musa Galaal's input was instrumental in the adoption of this orthography.

Musa Haji Ismail Galaal, educator and folklorist. He played a significant role in advancing the Somali culture.

Introduction of written Somali

Following the approval of the written Somali language, a flurry of educational activities designed to eliminate mass adult illiteracy in the country ensued. In 1973, all the government employees were compelled to sit for a 15-minute dictation test in Somali, after three months of introduction on written Somali. The Military Government of Siyad Barre used the results of the test to weed out those of very low educational level and who did not do much useful work and, perhaps, also got rid of some politically awkward individuals! That was the only test on the Somali language for which I ever sat – and I passed. For me, that was not all. The fact that I was tested on written Somali was important for me, bearing in mind what I had read about the controversy that had raged over the idea of writing the Somali language since 1885. But that was a different period altogether!

All the secondary schools in the country were closed for the whole year of 1974 and about 25,000 secondary school boys and girls and their teachers were sent out to the rural/nomadic communities to teach them how to write the Somali language. The slogan of the Literacy Campaign was "Teach or Learn" (*"Barr Ama Baro"*, in Somali). What, however, had not been planned for the boys and girls was for them to be, of necessity, engaged in assisting to move the communities they were educating to relief camps, as a result of the severe drought and famine of 1974–75 in the country.

[My intention was not to go beyond the cut-off date of 1960, which I set for myself; but it would have been going against the grain not to touch on the introduction of the official written Somali language. It was a landmark in the Somali cultural development. To give credit where credit is due, the Mohamed Siad Barre regime, by finally introducing official orthography for the Somali language, bequeathed to the Somali people an enduring legacy.]

In 1951, the Education Department clarified the nomenclature used to indicate the qualifications of the Somali Teachers, as shown below:

Qualifications of Somali teachers, 1951

Grade I	Eleven years of teaching. Promotion from Grade II to Grade I was by merit, not by examination
Grade II	Seven and a half years of teaching. Promotion from Grade III to Grade II was on examination and on satisfactory performance in Grade III.
Grade III	Three and a half years of teaching. Promotion from Grade IV to Grade III was on examination and on satisfactory performance in Grade IV.
Grade IV	One and a half years of teaching. Promotion from Ungraded to Grade IV was on examination and on satisfactory performance as Ungraded teacher.
Ungraded	Teachers from the VTC (opened in 1952) were promoted, without examination, to Grade IV after completion of one year of satisfactory service as Ungraded teachers. Teachers with School Leaving Certificates were appointed as Ungraded teachers.

A departmental examination for the Somali teachers was held in June 1951 and the results were as follows:

Departmental examination for Somali teachers, June 1951

Grade	Entries	Passes	Failures	Failed in one subject
Ungraded to Grade IV	6	2	1	3
Grade IV to Grade III	4	2	0	2
Grade III to Grade II	1	0	1	0
Total	11	4	2	5

In July 1951, about half of the class that I was in (Form VI), including me, were kept at Sheikh School for one month during the long summer school holiday, to assist about 15 British officers who were learning the Somali language. The course in Somali for the officers was run by Mr Bell, the Director of Education, Musa Galaal and Mr Andrzejewski (Guush). After each period, the officers would pair up with one of the boys, and the two would sit someplace outside the school in the open air or under a tree. The officers would converse with the boys in Somali, putting into practice what they had just learnt in the class. The boys would correct the mistakes the officers made. After the course the boys were each richer by 20 shillings thanks to their students, the officers. The course was of mutual benefit for both the officers and the boys – the officers were practising their limited Somali language on the boys and the boys, in turn, were practising their limited English language on the officers, although the boys were instructed to limit to talking to the officers in English.

Because the school year was changed to start in July, in June 1951, 129 boys sat for the Intermediate School Entrance Examination and 82 were accepted. The wastage was 36%. Some of the boys were rejected for being over-age.

The enrolment at the end of 1951, at Sheikh and Borama Intermediate Schools was 172 and 102 boys respectively, a total of 274 boys. Enrolment of all the eight elementary schools was 639 boys. The number of aided *Qur'aanic*/Arabic Schools was 38. The annual expenditure on education in 1951 was given as £38,215, including £616 grant to the approved *Qur'aanic*/Arabic Schools.

From 1951, the school year ended in June, in the middle of the financial year of the government. The annual expenditure on education was taken, as was the case before, from the audited annual expenditure on the protectorate, at the end of the financial year.

Annual report on education for 1952 [189]

In the 1952 annual report on education, the Government reiterated, almost word for word, the educational policy which it had announced in 1950. However, this time they included the gloomy picture the government painted about the economic development of the country, by stating:

It is considered that, with the improbability of industrial and commercial development in the protectorate, any such large-scale educational expansion would lead inevitably to a steady drift to the towns with consequent widespread unemployment and poverty.

Put in another way, this meant that education in the urban areas should be limited so that the rural/nomadic population would not drift to the towns, in search of education! It was an absurd way of justifying the deliberate limitation of formal education development in the country.

The Intermediate School Leaving examination was held in March 1952 and 52 boys sat for it. The results were as follows:

- Six boys were sent on government scholarships to Hantoub Secondary School, Sudan, to start their course in July 1952. This was the last group to be sent to Hantoub and the author was in this group.
- Four boys were sent on government scholarships to Aden College (Secondary), Aden.
- Three boys were sent on government scholarships to Aden College (Technical), Aden.
- Fourteen boys joined the Vocational Training Centre (VTC) – ten to be trained as teachers; three to be trained as clerks; one to study basic agriculture.
- Ten boys were accepted for apprenticeship scheme under the Public Works Department (PWD), to be trained in the mechanical and building trades with which the PWD was officially concerned.
- The wastage was 29%.

Also, 150 boys sat for the Intermediate School Entrance Examination and 85 were accepted in the two intermediate schools and 35 in the new trades school (which was not yet built). The wastage was 20%.

Vocational Training Centre [190]

In February 1952, Mr Bell, Director of Education, unveiled a plaque at the buildings of the new Vocational Training Centre (VTC) at Amud, Borama.

Director of Education, Mr Bell (front left) unveiling a plaque at the VTC Buildings in 1952. Inscribed on the plaque was: "This stone was laid by C.R.V. Bell, OBE, Feb. 1952." (Photo from *Journal of the Anglo-Somali Society*, No. 49, 2011. Reproduced with permission.)

When the VTC was budgeted for in 1949, it was described as a "junior secondary school", but it was later re-named the Vocational Training Centre. The centre cost £21,500, once fully furnished and staffed. In February 1952, Mr Bell was transferred to Uganda, as Deputy Director of Education, having been Director of Education of Somaliland Protectorate since 1944.

Mr Bell, perhaps, realized that development of formal education in Somaliland Protectorate had reached a plateau and that he had nothing more he could do in the Department – he would have known that to be the case, as he was the one who had devised the educational programme of 1944 in the first place. On transfer, he first became Deputy Director of Education in Uganda in 1952 and later Director in 1958. He retired to the UK in 1962. Mr Bell (1912–2006), died on 20 September 2006. His obituary written by his son, Michael, is in the *Journal of the Anglo-Somali Society*, No. 41, 2007.

The aim of the VTC was to give further education to potential employees in various government departments – for example, the Education Department, Agriculture and Veterinary Departments, Administration, etc. The centre opened in October 1952 with an intake of 30 boys who were boarders and the individual courses would last two years. Mr Darlington was the first Principal of the VTC. The VTC obviated the need to send students to Bakht el-Ruda for training as teachers for the elementary schools. However, Bakht el-Ruda was still needed for students to be trained as Arabic teachers in the intermediate schools and the secondary school. It was then time to upgrade the knowledge of the senior teachers for higher posts.

New Trades School [191]

A new Trades day school, fully furnished and staffed, was built in Hargeisa at the cost of £13,130. It was opened with 35 boys in September 1952. Thus, the two-stream system of academic and technical education was abandoned – *and about time too!* The existence in one school of two streams side by side – academic and technical – tended to create the impression among the students that the academic stream was for the selected few and the technical stream was for the academically less able.

Candidates for the trades school were recruited from those who completed elementary schooling (Standard III) and the course lasted four years. Apart from such academic subjects as English and mathematics, the boys majored in building and mechanical trades. The reason the school was built in Hargeisa was because it was run by the Public Works Department, on behalf of the Education Department.

It was a day school and the students from the districts – other than those from Hargeisa District – faced severe difficulties in accommodation in Hargeisa. Perhaps some students who qualified for admission into the school decided otherwise because of the accommodation problem.

Governor Reece (right) opening the Trades School in Hargeisa, 1952. The interpreter (left) was not named. Probably he was Mohamoud Ahmed. *Journal of the Anglo-Somali Society*, No 68, 2020. Reproduced with permission.

Under the existing arrangements, the boys would complete their training as apprentices at the PWD under the control of the Director of that Department.

Mr Bell was replaced, as Director of Education, by C. Sykes Thompson, who was transferred from Kenya, and he arrived in Somaliland Protectorate on 6 August 1952.

As a matter of policy, the government decided in 1952 that the boarding elementary school at Sheikh should be run down at the rate of one class per year and cease to exist by 1955. The thinking behind the policy was that, since all the district towns had elementary schools and one was built in Sheikh in 1952, the boarding school outlived the purpose for which it was first built – in other words, mainly for boys from the interior and from districts which did not have elementary schools. The last class for the boarding elementary school at Sheikh was enrolled in 1952.

Since the Director of Education could neither speak Somali nor read or write Arabic, Mohamoud Ahmed Ali was responsible, in addition to the elementary schools, for the supervision and inspection of grant-aided *Qur'aanic* and/or Arabic schools. This entailed a lot of travel in reaching the few far-flung educational facilities in a country where communication by road, let alone by air, was inadequately developed. Still, such supervision and inspection were crucial because the teachers at the district elementary schools, as well as of those of the *Qur'aanic* and/or Arabic Schools, were insufficiently trained and their close supervision was critical for maintaining the standard of the schools.

The aided *Qur'aanic*/Arabic schools were considered to be in the mainstream of the educational system in the country. In fact, the boys in these schools were classified as being equivalent to Standard I of the elementary schools. That was why, unlike other British Colonies, the elementary school in Somaliland Protectorate was kept at a three-year, instead of a four-year duration. The cynic might interpret this as a smart way of cost-cutting, by saving one year's expenditure on the fourth class!

These aided *Qur'aanic*/Arabic schools also played another role. In submitting annual reports on education, all the Departments of Education in British Colonies had to use a standardized format, with sections for different items to be reported upon. The format was devised by the Colonial Office and it had about nine sections. Under one section, the Directors of Education had to report on "Collaboration with Christian Missions". Since there were neither Christian nor Muslim missions in Somaliland Protectorate, the Director of Education of Somaliland Protectorate had to report, under the mentioned section, on the grant-aided *Qur'aanic*/Arabic Schools. The Somaliland Protectorate Government found that practice useful because the number of aided *Qur'aanic*/Arabic schools boosted the small number of the governmental education institutions. However, this was to change (see later).

In 1952, Yusuf Haji Adan was sent to the UK on a government scholarship for a two-year teacher training course at Exeter University. His daughter, Fawzia, describes in her book [173] his nationalistic activities and the unusual circumstances surrounding Yusuf's scholarship. It was well known that Yusuf Haji Adan was a nationalist; and was very much involved in Somaliland politics from the early 1940s. He was advocate of union not only with Somalia but also with Greater Somalia. He composed nationalistic poems, in Somali, against colonialism. It was common knowledge among the senior Somali Government civil servants that

Yusuf Haji Adan was neither in the good books of the Education Department nor those of the protectorate government. He was one of the few senior Somali teachers, yet I did not find his name mentioned in the Education Department's reports either when he was sent to the UK, or when he returned after completing his course. In the annual report on education for 1952 [189], it was just mentioned that "a teacher was awarded scholarship at Exeter University for a teacher training course".

In 1952, four more elementary schools were built: at Sheikh, Hargeisa, Aw Bare (in the *Reserved Ar*ea) and Aware (in the Hawd), bringing the total number of elementary schools to 12, 10 of them in Somaliland Protectorate proper. In this connection, the Somaliland Protectorate Government overlooked the stipulation in the Anglo-Ethiopian agreement of 19 December 1944 which forbade the building of schools in the Hawd and the Reserved Area (see 3.11). In 1952, questions about the schools in Somaliland Protectorate were raised in the British Parliament – P. Freeman, a Member of the British Parliament (MP), was an ardent supporter of Ethiopian interests and he used to urge the British Government to withdraw the British Military Administration from the Hawd and the Reserved Area. The Aw Bare School caused some friction between the Foreign Office, which always supported the Anglo-Ethiopian Agreements (concerning Somaliland Protectorate), and the Colonial Office, which was not enthusiastic about these agreements.

At the end of 1952, the enrolment at the 12 elementary schools was 942 boys and at the three intermediate schools (including the trades school) was 327 boys – a combined total of 1,269 boys. (I excluded two elementary schools and their expenditure: one for the European children and the other for the children of the Indian government civil servants.) In 1952, there were 42 assisted *Qur'aanic* schools, 6 of them for girls. The expenditure on education in 1952 was given as £48,385, including £2,000 grant to the *Qur'aanic*/Arabic schools.

At the end of 1952, the total enrolment at all the government-maintained schools was 1,269 and the estimated population was 640,000 [192]. The percentage of population in formal education was 0.2%.

Conference on Education Policy and Practice in British Tropical Africa

In 1952, the Colonial Office and the Nuffield Foundation co-sponsored two Commissions, one for West Africa and the other for Central and East Africa. Perhaps the sponsoring authorities took their cue from the Phelps-Stokes Fund Education Commissions of 1920–1924 [113].

The Commissions were tasked to report on the state of education in the British colonies they visited. The Commission for Central and East Africa was led by A.L.

Binns and it visited Somaliland Protectorate for about two weeks in January 1952. The Conference was held at Cambridge University, UK, 8–20 September 1952. Mr Thompson, Director of the Department of Education, and Mohamoud Ahmed Ali, Inspector of Elementary Schools, represented Somaliland Protectorate at the conference.

The recommendations of conference for Somaliland Protectorate were reflected in the 1952 annual report on education and they are summarized below:

1. That the elementary course should continue to be of three years, having regard to the comparative excellence of the teaching and the foundation of the elementary course in the *Qur'aanic*/Arabic schools.
2. That elementary schools be provided as quickly as possible for all children living in the urban settled areas whose parents were willing to send them to school.
3. That the elementary course be followed by an intermediate course for all pupils living in settled urban areas, with the exception of the comparatively few pupils who prove incapable of proceeding to further education or wish to go to the trades school.
4. That in the trades school, the general education of the pupils be continued, since it is intended to recruit them from the elementary schools.
5. That the elementary and intermediate school buildings be provided in future by the urban communities of the area in which they are situated, acting through the school committees established by the Education Department.
6. That a small senior secondary boarding school, organized on tutorial lines, be provided as soon as possible, in association with one of the intermediate schools
7. That experimental pre-marriage courses should be started for girls in settled areas.
8. That the help of married women in girls' education should always be encouraged.
9. That an immediate beginning should be made with the education of nomadic peoples on lines discussed in the territory (ie Somaliland) with the Education Department.

Recommendation (2) put the onus on the urban parents willing to enrol their children in the elementary classes. Many parents were willing and tried to do so but could not secure places for their children, because of a severe shortage of places. Recommendation (3) is about the capable children who completed the elementary stage to go to the intermediate level. However, because of limited places in the intermediate schools, only a tiny fraction of the eligible children could be admitted into these schools.

It was a situation where demand vastly outstripped supply. The proof of this, if one was needed, is what I labelled as "wastage" after the Intermediate School Entrance and Intermediate School Leaving Examinations. The children included in the "wastage" were not classified as to whether they were failures or not. As far as the government was concerned, that did not make any difference.

The commission which came to Somaliland Protectorate in January 1952 and travelled up and down the country to assess the state of education in the country was well aware of the very limited educational facilities in the country. In its recommendations, it shied away from pointing out the government's neglect of education in the country and the resulting gross inadequacy of educational facilities. Yet, it made recommendations that it knew the protectorate government would not implement; it was nothing short of a bad joke!

In recommendation (7), education for girls was to be "experimental". It was not clear whether this meant to see whether the girls could learn or whether the girls' education was acceptable to the Somalis. Either way, this approach to girls' education was not only deplorable but was also inappropriate for an educational body to suggest it.

The education prescribed for the nomads will be dealt with later.

Parliamentary questions on education in Somaliland Protectorate [192]

In 1952, some Members of the British Parliament (MPs) took special interest in the education in Somaliland Protectorate. The following Parliamentary exchanges were taken from *Hansard* (12 November 1952). As was the practice, the answers of the Secretary State for the Colonies to questions raised by the British Parliamentarians were supplied by the Governor of Somaliland Protectorate.

> **Mr P. Freeman, MP**, *asked Mr Lyttelton, the Secretary of State for the Colonies: How far the children residing in the reserved area of Ethiopia, which has been occupied by Her Majesty's Government since the war, have freedom and facilities to attend Ethiopian schools at Jigjiga, Harar, Dire Dawa and Addis Ababa; and to what extent the Ethiopian Government has freedom to establish schools in the reserved area under British occupation and what schools exist there.*
>
> **Mr Lyttelton:** *The British Administration places no restrictions on children who wish to attend schools in Ethiopia. As far as is known there are no schools in the reserved area, and no application from the Ethiopian Government to establish such schools has been received.*

Mr Lyttelton was wrong in saying that there were no schools in the reserved area. There was an elementary school at Aw Bare, built by the Somaliland Protectorate

Government, as earlier stated. The Somali communities in the reserved area demanded that since the area was administered by the Somaliland Protectorate Government, they should receive educational facilities like the rest of the people of Somaliland Protectorate. The Somali communities in the Hawd made similar arguments. Thus, the protectorate government built the elementary schools at Aw Bare and at Aware.

There seemed to have been some communication breakdown between the governor and the Colonial Office, and the governor later admitted that that was the case. Mr Freeman, MP, (*Hansard*, 12 November 1952) questioned Mr Lyttelton further:

> **Mr Freeman:** *What provision is made for education in British Somaliland Protectorate; how many elementary, secondary and higher schools, respectively, are in operation there; and how many pupils, Somalis and other, attend each class of school.*
>
> **Mr Lyttelton:** *The financial provision during 1952–53 is for estimated expenditure of £ 48,511 from Protectorate funds and, in addition, for special expenditure of £17,000 from the Colonial Development and Welfare vote. There are 13 Government elementary schools with 815 pupils (765 Somalis and 50 others), three Government intermediate schools, including one trade training school with 315 pupils (303 Somalis and 12 others) and junior secondary school with 25 Somali pupils. In addition, there are 42 Koranic schools, grant-aided by Government, providing education of a pre-primary standard for approximately 1,300 pupils; one small Government-aided European primary school (14 pupils) and a small Indian school (37 pupils). Twenty-five Somalis are maintained by Government in technical and secondary education at schools abroad.*

Because of the financial year of Somaliland Protectorate, the estimate of £65,511, (£48,511 plus £17,000) was for 1952, but the actual annual expenditure on education in 1952 was £48,358. At the end of 1952, there were 12, not 13, government elementary schools, excluding the European and Indian Schools. According to the annual report on education for 1952, the enrolment at the 12 elementary schools was 942, not 815; there were, in the elementary schools, 65 Arabs and 21 other Somalis – a total of 86 others, not 50, as given by Mr Lyttelton.

Mr Lyttelton mentioned 42 *Qur'aanic* schools, catering for about 1,300 pupils. All Lyttelton's replies were provided by the governor of the protectorate. As usual, the governor made the most of the *Qur'aanic* schools and attempted to present, fraudulently, the meagre formal educational services in the country in good light! (*Hansard*, 12 November 1952):

> **Mr Mallaieu, MP,** *asking the Secretary of State for the Colonies, Mr Lyttelton: The number of Government Schools in British Somaliland; the size*

> of the population; and what proportion of it receives primary and secondary education?
>
> **Mr Lyttelton:** *The answer to the first part of the question is 17; to the second, approximately 640,000. There are 1,130 pupils at Government Primary and Intermediate Schools and 50 at Secondary Schools, of whom 25 are maintained by Government at Secondary Schools abroad. In addition, approximately 1,300 pupils receive education of a pre-primary standard at 42 Government-aided Qur'aanic Schools.*

As mentioned earlier, educational facilities beyond the intermediate level were considered to be equivalent to the secondary level. For example, the VTC was counted as a secondary school. The government had predetermined policy that the country would not have proper secondary education for a long time to come.

With regard to Mr Lyttelton's replies, at the end of 1952, there were 16, not 17 schools – in other words, 12 elementary and 3 intermediate schools and the VTC. There were 59 students, not 50, studying at secondary level. Out of the 59 students, 29 students, not 25, were studying at secondary level abroad, and 30 students were at the VTC. The combined enrolment at the 12 elementary and the 3 intermediate schools was 1,269, not 1,130. There were 10 young boys at the PWD, as apprentices, but I did not include them in the total enrolment at the schools at the end of 1952, as they could not fit into any of the normal education levels.

As already mentioned, two of the students studying abroad at secondary level were from Somalia and were sent by the Somaliland Protectorate Military Government in 1949 to Hantoub Secondary School, Sudan [199]. The Secretary of State quoted the figure of 1,300 pupils at *Qur'aanic*/Arabic private schools, to mask the insignificant number of students at government schools. The protectorate government made much of the private *Qur'aanic* and/or Arabic schools.

It was about this time that the Colonial Office questioned the way the protectorate government was misusing the aided *Qur'aanic*/Arabic schools to conceal the inadequacy of education in the country. The protectorate government was instructed not to include the aided *Qur'aanic*/Arabic schools in the tabulation of the annual reports of the Education Department, although those schools which received government grants could be mentioned in the narrative. The Somaliland Protectorate Government's manipulation of the *Qur'aanic*/Arabic schools was at last exposed and brought to an end (*Hansard*, 19 November 1952):

> **Mr Mallalieu, MP**, asked Mr Lyttelton: *How many Government Schools there are in that part of British Somaliland which lies to the west of the meridian passing immediately to east of Burao; how many to the east of that line; and what proportion of the population live east of Burao meridian?*

Mr Lyttelton: *Fifteen schools to the west of the line and two Schools to east of the line. Many boys from the east attend three central Schools situated in the west, where boarding facilities are available. About one-third of the population live east of Burao meridian.*

Mr Lyttelton's answer should have been 14 schools to the west – the two in the east were correct. Mr Mallaieu raised the questions for a particular purpose that he had in mind. He had a sneaking suspicion that, as a matter of policy, the protectorate government was deliberately restricting educational services east of Burao, to punish the Dhulbahante Clan for supporting Seyyid Mohamed Abdullah Hassan and his Dervishes. The protectorate government, which supplied the answers given by the Secretary of State for the Colonies, denied that there was any such policy. But of course, they would have denied such policy, wouldn't they? To see that Mr Mallaieu had a point, see Ref. 22.

It was true, and still is the case, that the eastern part of the country was sparsely populated and predominantly nomadic. The 1/3 and 2/3 proportions of the population were just guesstimates, since no proper census was never ever conducted in the protectorate. Nevertheless, it was true that the country was/is more populated west of Burao. But that did not justify severe limitation of educational facilities east of Burao. In fact, other social developments were also scarce in that part of the country.

There is no denying that the communities in the east of the country were educationally ill-served by the protectorate government. Two small day elementary schools (one in Erigavo and the other in Las Anod) for the whole eastern part of the country, predominantly populated by nomads, was neither sufficient nor appropriate provision. What was really needed was sufficient boarding educational facilities to suit the way of life of the nomadic communities. I have already mentioned that, in 1945, the government rejected making Erigavo Elementary School a boarding school.

The Egyptian Revolution and its influence in Somaliland Protectorate [193]

Some readers may consider this item out of place in Section 4. However, my excuse for keeping it in this section was because of the profound effect the Egyptian revolution had not only on education but also on the political situation in the country in the final stages of the protectorate. The Egyptian revolution was a significant event which had far-reaching implications for the Middle East, including Somaliland Protectorate.

On 23 July 1952, a group of military officers, led by General Mohamed Nagiub and calling themselves "The Free Officers" staged a coup d'état in Egypt and ended the reign of King Farouk and the monarchy in Egypt. They declared the country a republic. A young colonel among the officers, by the name of Colonel Gamal Abdul Nasser, became impatient with the slow pace of General Nagiub and eventually replaced him. Colonel Nasser emerged the undisputed leader of Egypt and the Arab world as well. He appealed to Arabism to rekindle Arab nationalism. He urged the Arabs to wake up from their slumber, sink their differences and unite. He alarmed the British by attacking their colonial policy in the Middle East, especially defence treaties which some Arab countries had with the British. Somaliland Protectorate was affected, educationally and politically, by the policies pursued by Gamal Abdul Nasser – more about this later.

Annual report on education for 1953 [194]

At the beginning of almost every year, it became customary for the protectorate government to make some sort of policy statement about the education in the country, and 1953 was no exception. Thinly disguising the grossly limited formal education in the country, the government disingenuously stated, in the 1953 report on education, that:

> *A choice lay between producing a limited number of really well-educated boys and girls or turning out a much larger number of half-educated persons.*

When the government made that statement, there was not even a single secondary school in the country, so how could they talk of "really well educated"? The scope of education in the country was already so restricted that it was pointless for the government to pretend that there was such a choice. If we considered the number of boys in the elementary and intermediate schools who were rejected for lack of places locally or scholarships overseas – what I labelled as "wastage" – it was obvious that the government was unwittingly producing a large number of boys who had only a rudimentary education, the very situation the government implied it wanted to avoid!

The first Government Elementary School for Girls [195]

At long last, in the history of formal education in Somaliland, a boarding elementary school for girls was built in Burao at the cost of £18,858, fully furnished and staffed. It was opened on 1 January 1953 with 30 girls, 12 of them boarders. The teaching staff was composed of two female British teachers, Miss Maclaran and Miss Naylor, two Somali assistant teachers, Amina Ma'alin Qasim Haji Mohamed and Edna Adan Ismail, and Sheikh Mohamed, a religious instructor. Unlike the boys' elementary course, the course for the girls was planned to last four years, instead of three. Although it was not said so, the course for the girls was lengthened because few girls at that time attended *Qur'aanic* or Arabic schools, at which the boys who were enrolled for the elementary schools learnt how to read and write the *Qur'aan* – an unfair advantage which the boys always had over their sisters in the country.

The first class of the first girls' elementary school opened on 1 January 1953 in Burao. The girls are entertaining themselves with traditional Somali dance. (Photo, courtesy of Amina-Weris Sh. Mohamed Jirde, who was one of the pupils).

I wish to insert in here, details from an account given by one of the girls who attended the school. In it, she reveals the attitude of some members of the Somaliland community towards female education. Asha Haji Deria Mohamoud was one of the girls who were enrolled into Burao Elementary School for Girls in 1954, just one year after the school had been opened. Asha wrote a piece about life in the school and her appreciation of the late Mohamoud Ahmed Ali in a book by his son Ibrahim entitled *Geel-Jire iyo Aqoon-Jire* [196]. The Somali title of the book translates as *Camel-herder and Educator*, capturing Mohamoud's nomadic background and continual link with the nomadic life, in spite of his serious mission in fostering the development of formal education in the country.

Asha gives insightful account of what life was like at the school. She skilfully describes female education in her appreciation of Mohamoud Ahmed's contribution to formal education for girls and boys alike in British Somaliland Protectorate. Asha's appreciation of Mohamoud Ahmed is profound. She says that whenever she performs religious or charitable act, she dedicates God's blessings for such acts to the memory of Mohamoud Ahmed Ali. She conjures up the picture that, had it not been the tireless struggle of Mohamoud Ahmed for the education of the Somali girls and boys, many of these children would have remained illiterate nomads or town children. For the girls, it would have been even worse, as they would have been illiterate women confined to their houses (*maxajabado*, in Somali). She gives a picture of the prevalent idea about female education at that time and how disparagingly many ill-informed Somalis used to talk about educating girls. Some thought that their education was unwarranted, since they would not contribute much to society (as was also implied in the justification for building the girls' school, mentioned earlier). She mentions how street boys used to make schoolgirls' lives uncomfortable by hurling insults at them. One particular insult, favourite with the street boys, was: *beware, the man who sends his daughter to school – if she becomes a girl of easy virtue, she will still remain your daughter!* Asha names some of her contemporaries at Burao Elementary School for Girls and they included the following:

Deka Olad Jama, Rakiya Haji Duale, Amina Sh. Mohamed Jirde, Kaltun Iman, Jawahir Abdulla Haji Fareh, Fadumo Ali Jawahir, Habiba Haji Mohamed Sirad, Amina Hussein Haji Hassan, Fadumo Haji Bandare, Nura Haji Miaten, Amina Haji Yahein, Ruun Maydhalalis, Fadumo Ahmed Mohamoud Nur, Khadija Mohamoud Ahmed Ali, Shuun Said, Shamis Osman, Kinsi Abdul-Kadir Fareh, Kaltuun Jibaahe Ese, Khdija Mohamed Jama, Halimo Ahmed Yei, Sakin Jirde Hussein, Amina Basbas, Asha Ibrahim Qalab-jaan.

It was the first time that I had come across a written account by one of the girls who attended Burao Elementary School for Girls, around the time it was opened. Asha's account is really worth reading. I should mention that I translated, with Asha's kind permission, the extract from her account from Somali, as the book, *Geel-Jire iyo Aqoon-Jire* about Mohamoud Ahmed Ali, is in Somali. I gratefully acknowledge the book, the copyright holder of which is deceased.

In this connection, ten years before Asha joined the elementary school for girls at Burao in 1954, I myself was a first-year pupil in the boarding elementary school for boys at Sheikh in 1944. Then some religious elements in Burao used to preach against formal education, making some outrageous statements; for example, that, "the father who sends his son to a government school runs the risk of his marriage being annulled; and that a person who sees a white Christian for 40 consecutive mornings will become one of them." So, the boys too did not escape the attention of those ill-informed about formal education.

I have already mentioned, elsewhere in the book, Sheikh Adan Hassan (aka Sheikh *Kulmiye*) who was a staff member of Sheikh School. Part of his job was to travel round the country, to counter misinformation about formal education, on religious grounds, in the country, and to enlighten those who misunderstood and/or misinterpreted the religion.

In 1953, in the routines of the juvenile prisoners, a daily school period was put aside for an elementary general course of education by a teacher from the Education Department. This was an enlightened policy; it was, perhaps, remembered what Governor Kittermaster had advocated in 1928 (see 4.3).

The demand for joining the trades school increased so dramatically that the intake was "rationed". But the way the rationing was presented was dubious. The department claimed that in order to give equal opportunity to every boy from elementary schools to compete for a place in the trades school, it was necessary to *select* the boys annually for *biennial intake*. That meant that half the boys who were selected for admission must wait for a year between the time of their selection and their actual entry into the school. This, in effect, meant that every year, half of the selected boys were deliberately denied a place at the school! Of course, the obvious solution to the problem would have been to increase the capacity of the school, in staffing and places, so that all the selected boys would join the school together. But the government had no intention of doing that! That was the manifestation, in its severest form, of the policy of running the country "on care and maintenance basis and no development" [23, 37]. It did not say what the selected-but-not-admitted boys would do in the year they had to wait! Perhaps some of the boys who had to wait for a year after their selection had lost interest in the whole thing and turned their attention to other gainful activities.

In 1953, five new elementary schools, including the girls' school, were built, and the number brought the total elementary schools in the country to 17. Also, as a matter of policy, the number in each class of all the elementary schools was limited thus: Class I: 40 boys, Class II: 35, and Class III: 28 boys. The headmasters of the elementary schools were instructed to observe that policy strictly. The demand for places in the elementary schools exceeded all expectations that the Education Department was compelled to introduce waiting lists for these schools. Attendance at *Qur'aanic* school was also made a condition for enrolling into the elementary schools.

In 1953, Mohamed Shire was sent on a two-year teacher training course to Bristol University, UK, and Abdisalam Hassan on two-year Headmaster course to Exeter University, UK – both on protectorate government scholarships.

The first Secondary School for Boys [197]

Because of the influence of the Egyptian Leader, Gamaal Abdul Nasser [193], many Arab countries became hostile to British presence in the Middle East. Sudan used to be the destination for secondary education for students on government scholarships from Somaliland Protectorate. However, Sudan was technically a Condominium, jointly governed by Britain and Egypt, although the British was the dominant partner. But the British Government panicked and considered the Arab countries inimical to British interests. The British imagined that if further boys were sent to Sudan for secondary education, their young impressionable minds would be affected by the *poisonous propaganda* (in the eyes of the British) emanating from Cairo. Thus, in 1953 the government stopped sending boys to Sudan for secondary education, without having readily available alternative secondary education facilities. It seemed that the protectorate government was instructed to open, by hook or by crook, some sort of secondary school in the country.

All along, the protectorate government of Somaliland was blindly following Mr Bell's advice of 1944, that there would be no need for a secondary school in the country for a long time to come. That time came in 1953, although it should have come much earlier.

At the end of the school year in June 1953, 159 boys sat the Intermediate School Entrance Examination:

- 90 boys were accepted into the 2 intermediate schools
- 17 boys were accepted in the trades school
- The wastage was 33%
- The enrolment at the 16 elementary schools for boys was 1,021 boys
- The enrolment at the only elementary school for girls was 29 girls

64 boys sat for the Intermediate School Leaving Examination:

- 16 boys were accepted in "as-of-yet unbuilt" secondary school (see later)
- 2 boys were sent on government scholarships to the Religious Institute, Omdurman, Sudan
- 2 boys were sent on government scholarships to Aden Technical College
- 1 boy was sent on government scholarships to the Secondary School, Aden
- 16 boys were accepted in the VTC
- The wastage was 42% – this included 17 boys who, for lack of places for further education, entered into government service; 4 boys who entered private businesses; and 6 boys who went to Egypt for further education

In addition, the enrolment at the three intermediate schools (including the trades school) was 394 boys. The annual expenditure on education in 1953 was given as £50,053, including £1,500 grant to 39 assisted *Qur'aanic*/Arabic Schools.

The school fees charged at the government schools in 1953, were as follows:

- Elementary and intermediate schools:

    - tuition only – Sh. 30/annum

    - boarding only – Sh. 225/annum

- Trades day school

    - tuition only – Sh. 150/annum

- Secondary school

    - inclusive boarding and tuition – Sh. 400/annum

According to the Education Department, the boarding fees entitled the pupils to food, clothing, medical attention, medicines and all tuition, and games equipment without extra charge. No meals or clothing were provided for day schoolboys, but medical attention and school materials were given free.

The government was at a loss as to what to do with the 16 boys to whom secondary education was promised in June 1953 and were admitted into a non-existent secondary school. As already mentioned, the boarding elementary school at Sheikh was due to close down by one class yearly from 1953, and to close down completely in 1955. The first class became available in August 1953 and it was converted to a makeshift one-class secondary school, thus creating the nucleus of the first secondary school for boys in Somaliland Protectorate.

In August 1953, the first class, composed of the 16 boys, was enrolled. It was the first time that boys in Somaliland Protectorate could have their secondary education in their own country. Here are the names of the 16 students (courtesy of my friend, Osman Hassan Omer (Osman-Badow):

Ahmed Mohamed Mohamoud (Silanyo)
Abdullahi Said Abby
Musa Ahmed Bore
Musa Haji Deria (Idaar)
Adan Amin
Yusuf Dirir
Ahmed Mohamoud Goonleh (Hurreh)
Abass Iman Dhooreh

Qalib Muse
Muhumed Abdullahi (Muhumed-Awr)
Hussein Bile
Said Bile
Hussein Hassan (Badag)
Ali Abdulqadir
Ismail Haibe
Ali Abdullah (Ali Baran-Baro)

A group from the very first secondary school class in Somaliland Protectorate. Left to right: standing – Ismail Haibe, Abbas Iman, Ahmed Mohamed (Silanyo), Abdullahi Said Abby; sitting – Muse Ahmed Bore, Musa Haji Deria (Idaar), Ali Abdulqadir, Said Bile. Abdullahi Said Abby (back row, far right) was killed in the December 1961 in an attempted coup by young Somali military officers. Silanyo (back row, third from the left) became the fourth President of the Republic of Somaliland (27 July 2010 to 13 November 2017). (Photo from the *Journal of the Anglo-Somali Society*, No. 49, 2011. Reproduced with permission.)

Since the school was opened hurriedly and without prior proper preparations, the conditions under which the students worked were far from ideal. It could be said that the boys lost a lot in the first year.

Classification of the teaching staff [194]

At the end of 1953, the total number, including their classification, of the teaching staff was as follows:

Teaching staff in Somaliland Protectorate, 1953

Graduates (European, male)	3
Non-graduates (European, male)	6
Non-graduates (European, female)	3
Temporary teachers (European)	4
Grade I teachers (Somali)	4
Grade II teachers (Somali)	7
Grade III teachers (Somali)	22
Grade IV teachers (Somali)	24
Ungraded teachers (Somali)	9
Technical instructors (Somali)	6
Total	**88 Teachers**

The European teachers included one for a class for European children in Hargeisa. A trained but non-graduate European teacher was recruited as an Education Officer. The Somali teachers' grading mirrored, more or less, that of the clerks in the administration and that situation remained until 1954, as will be seen later.

During the period 1950–1953, the following mature students (senior clerks) attended Gordon College, Sudan, to upgrade their knowledge of the different aspects of public administration: Osman Ahmed Hassan, Ahmed Sheikh, Ahmed Jama Jengele, Ismail Duale (all studying public administration); Mohamoud Abdi Arale (studying public finance); Mohamed Haji Hussein (taxation); Haji Adan Ahmed Naleye (Hudur) (dates plantation).

Central Educational Facilities

At the end of 1953, there were seven central educational facilities (all governmental) serving the whole country:

- One boarding elementary school for boys at Sheikh
- One boarding elementary school for girls in Burao

- Two boarding intermediate schools for boys, at Sheikh and at Amud, Borama
- One day trades school (for boys) in Hargeisa
- One vocational training centre (VTC) at Amud, Borama
- One-class boarding secondary school for boys at Sheikh

System of Educational set-up in the country, 1953

By the end of 1953, the system of education in the country assumed a definite pattern which could be described thus:

- Pre-elementary *Qur'aanic* and/or Arabic schools (non-governmental, grant-aided)
- 3-year elementary governmental schools for boys
- 4-year elementary governmental school for girls
- 4-year intermediate governmental schools for boys (Academic)
- 4-year governmental post-elementary trades school for boys (Technical)
- 2-year governmental post-intermediate VTC for boys (Vocational)
- 4-year governmental secondary school for boys (Academic)

A Brief History of Formal Education in British Somaliland Protectorate

The educational system in Somaliland Protectorate, 1953, depicted diagrammatically

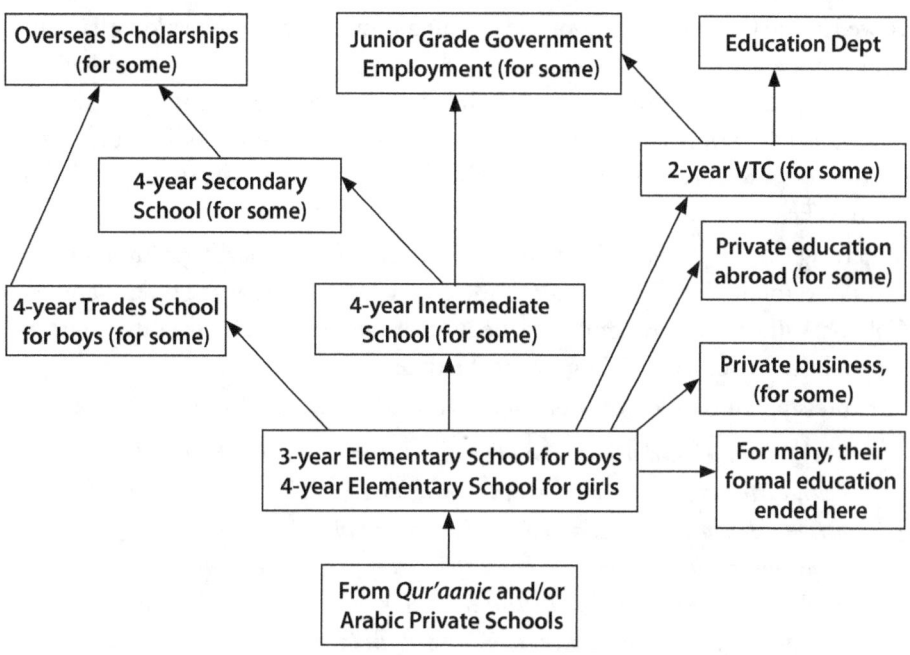

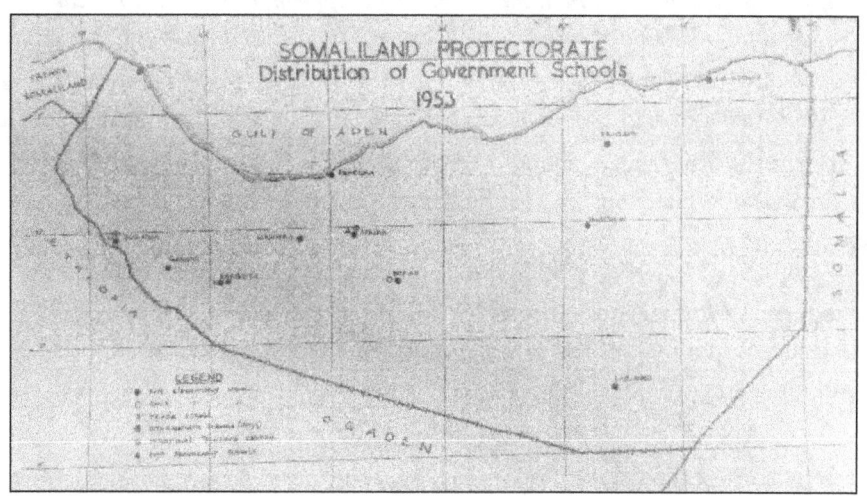

Map showing distribution of governmental schools in the country, issued by the Education Department in 1953.

Mr Whitehead [198] was transferred to Uganda in 1953 to join Mr Bell in the Ugandan Education Department. At the end of their careers, British officials who worked in the British African Colonies used to deposit, with particular British Universities, summaries of their experiences. Mr Whitehead summarized his experience as a teacher at Sheikh School, Somaliland Protectorate, 1948–1953, in a Memorandum which he deposited with Oxford University.

Reminiscing about his experience, he mentioned that when he was being interviewed at the Colonial Office for the teaching post, an official remarked that "the object of the work was just to train a few African clerks and that sort of thing." After all, "that sort of thing" was what the protectorate government planned for the country – in other words, the education of the vast majority of the students ending at elementary or intermediate schooling and training a few adult males for junior office work.

Having later observed how the British Government was dealing with Somaliland Protectorate, Mr Whitehead remarked that "perhaps what the official at the Colonial Office said was significant, because of the lack of interest in the country shown by many officials in London at the time."

Expressing his opinion of Mohamoud Ahmed, he wrote [198]:

> *Mohamoud Ahmed was a man of great integrity and dedication and a devout Muslim, and in a long and varied life I had never met a finer person. He played a vital and outstanding part in building up the education in the country. The public had great confidence in him and this made it much easier for the British education officers to gain the respect of the Somalis which was so vital to our work. In fact it was a common experience of one called in at any Somali encampment or settlement to hear the public enquiring of each other "who is this Infidel" and when it was discovered one was the man from the School, out would come the best china and tea produced.*

In this regard, I have already mentioned earlier that Sheikh School was apprehensive about any hostility to the school, because of the few British teachers there.

Mr Whitehead shows that Mohamoud Ahmed's positive influence helped the development of formal education in the country in more ways than one.

The table opposite gives the names of the students on government scholarships abroad for secondary education, 1947–1953 [199].

Year sent	Name	Educational Institution
Jan. 1947	Ahmed (Kaise) Haji Duale Abdirahman Ahmed Ali (Tur) Mohamed Ali Magan	Habtoub Secondary School, Sudan
	Mohamed Hashi Abdi Ahmed Mohamoud Qayir	Bakht el-Ruda, Sudan
Jan. 1948	Adan Omar Eleye Ali Sh. Ibrahim (Ali Qadi) Abdullahi Duale (Nile)	Hantoub Secondary School, Sudan
	Mohamed Mohamoud Garaad Mohamed Ismail Samater (Kebed)	Bakht el-Ruda, Sudan Agriculture Institute, Duwein, Sudan
Jan. 1949	Abdul-Aziz Haji Deria (from Somalia) Elmi Ahmed Duale (from Somalia)	Hantoub Secondary School, Sudan
Jan. 1950	Hassan Adan Gudaal Abdirahman Haji Adan Abdillahi Essa Jama (Dayah) Yusuf Ali (Shihari) Abdi	Hantoub Secondary School, Sudan
	Mohamoud Essa Jama Yusuf Hassan Adan (War Side)	Agriculture Institute, Duweim, Sudan
	Mohamed Mohamoud Garaad (from Bakht el-Ruda) Abdul-Karim Ali Yare	School of Commerce, Omdurman, Sudan
July 1951	Mohamoud Sh. Ahmed Musa Abdirahman Elmi Mohamed-Saleh Haji Hassan Seyyid Mohamoud Abdulla	Hantoub Secondary School, Sudan
	Mohamed Haji Abdi (Jiin) Ali Haibe	Mombasa Institute of Muslim Education (Technical), Kenya
July 1952	Saleh Haji Farah Dirir Abdirahman (Jeep) Sh. Ali Gaile Hassan (Kayd) Abdulle Walanwal Said (Sheef) Mohamed Ali Bulay Ahmed Botan Dhakkaar Abdullahi Deria Abdi (the author)	Hantoub Secondary School, Sudan *(The last group sent to Hantoub)*
	Jama (Gaile) Hassan Abdirazaq Ahmed Mohamed Ahmed Tafadal Daud Ali Yahye	Aden College (Secondary), Aden
	Mohamed Esa Abdi Yusuf (Qurab) Ibrahim Ali (Aar) Mohamed Hersi	Aden College (Technical), Aden
July 1953	Musa Rabile Goad Ahmed Sh. Adan Hassan	Religious Institute, Omdurman, Sudan
	Abdirahman Haji Deria Mohamed Musa Awale	Forestry study, Southern Sudan, Sudan
	Ibrahim Mohamoud Ahmed Ali	Aden College (Secondary), Aden

As far as I know, all the students listed above, from 1947 to 1953 (except the two students from Somalia), returned to Somaliland Protectorate after completing their various courses. Later, at different times, they were sent on government scholarships to the UK for higher education. The exception was Hassan Adan Gudaal who was first sent to Beirut University, Lebanon. After obtaining his University Degree in 1957, majoring in Arabic, and Diploma in Education, he returned to Somaliland Protectorate and joined the Education Department to teach Arabic in the secondary school at Amud, which later moved to Sheikh. Hassan was later sent to the UK for further specialization in education.

Annual report on education for 1954 [200]

The government repeated its ritual of talking despairingly about formal education in the country. In the 1954 report, it was stated that:

- The education could not be expanded because of lack of funds, lack of teachers and lack of opportunities in later life.

- The aim of the schools in the protectorate was to provide an adequate number of well-educated boys who are capable of filling posts in the government departments and to train artisans and technicians for employment in the protectorate and elsewhere.

- The elementary school course would be maintained at three years for the following reasons:

    - valuable pre-elementary work was being done in *Qur'aanic*/Arabic schools

    - high competitive entry from *Qur'aanic*/Arabic to elementary schools whereby only the best boys gain admittance

    - the limited extent of the education system permitting the high standard teaching being maintained by close supervision

- The Government would not take any more clerks below GCE standard, as the junior clerical establishment was almost full. As a result, the VTC, as such, would cease to exist after May 1956.

The government could not bring itself to admit that the education in the country was grossly inadequate in all respects and, worse of all, the government was not in the mood to remedy the situation. It was ludicrous to decree that the only opening for post-secondary education was to become a clerk. Because of lack of places for secondary education, many post-intermediate boys grounded in English and mathematics joined the government service and boys with two-year clerical training in the VTC also became available. Those boys could work their way up the clerical ladder to the top position – in other words, Grade I – which was a dead-end. The fact that the government decided to recruit clerks only from boys with secondary education was a clear indication that the government had no intention of providing educational facilities in the country beyond secondary level, and very inadequate at that.

The internal inconsistency of government policy was clear. Post-secondary boys had to be trained as clerks. But by the time these boys became available, the VTC would have been closed down! In practice, the government limited formal education in the country to producing mainly clerks. What a confused educational policy that was!

The public, through the Local Education Committees, was pressing the government to increase the educational facilities, both horizontally and vertically, as well as the intakes of boys and girls at all levels of education. The government thought otherwise and, in quick succession, cruelly closed down the elementary school in Zeila in April 1954, followed by the closure of the boarding elementary school at Sheikh before the scheduled date of 1955. The reason given for the closures was for lack of sufficient number of boys for the schools. A more plausible explanation was the government's obsession with cost-cutting! That was the government's response to the communities' appeal for more educational facilities!

Whenever the communities in Somaliland asked the government to expand the educational facilities in the country, scarcity of funds was the government's stock-in-trade answer.

It is important to recognize the role played by the indigenous *Qur'aanic*/Arabic schools in the education in the country – both formal and non-formal. However, the protectorate government used these institutions as a ploy to cover up the woefully inadequate government investment in formal education in the country.

The glass ceiling that was oppressively set for the Somali teachers' promotion was at last shattered in April 1954 when Mohamoud Ahmed Ali was promoted from Inspector of Elementary Schools to the position of Education Officer for Elementary Schools. Until then, the title "Officer" was reserved for the British teachers, graduate and non-graduate alike. As far as I could ascertain, Mohamoud Ahmed Ali was the first Somali to hold an Officer's position in the protectorate government. The salary of a Somali Officer would not, as a matter of government policy, exceed 60% of that of a European Officer. On the same date, Yusuf Haji Adan was also promoted from Assistant Master to the position of Inspector of Elementary Schools, and an Assistant to Mohamoud Ahmed. The supervision of the Elementary Schools and the grant-aided *Qur'aanic* and/or Arabic schools became too burdensome for one person alone. With this new arrangement, either Mohamoud Ahmed or Yusuf Haji Adan would, at most of the times, be in the field for supervisory activities.

The first ten boys who completed the two-year course for teachers' training for the elementary schools graduated from the VTC in 1954, and that eliminated the need to send any more boys to Bakht el-Ruda to be trained as elementary school teachers. However, there was still need for Bakht el-Ruda for training Arabic teachers in the intermediate schools and in the solitary secondary school.

The government, determined to dispense with the VTC earlier than planned, declared that the centre was not functioning as planned. It cited the excuse that, because of the fees to be paid, the boys preferred to join the government services direct after completing intermediate education, when they could draw salaries. The government's contradictory policy of not taking any more clerks below GCE standard, while deciding that the VTC should not exist beyond 1956, has already been mentioned. The government's education policy centred on production of no more than junior functionaries in government offices. It was making educational policy for the country on the hoof, without vision.

Belatedly, the government realized that the situation of the secondary school at Sheikh was indeed unsatisfactory. At the end of 1954, the Government closed the VTC and moved the secondary school boys, as second year class, to Amud to occupy the VTC buildings which became available.

A small teachers' training centre was built at Sheikh. Also, the government, reluctant to recruit Arabic teachers from the Arab countries, appointed a Palestinian (perhaps stateless) as Arabic teacher for the secondary school. One of the students he had taught told me that the teacher was later discovered to have used false qualification documents to get the teaching job. As a result, he was dismissed. Such chop and change educational policy bore the hallmarks of a government without a carefully thought through educational plan.

Since the government stopped sending boys to Sudan for secondary education (leading to Cambridge University GCE O-level), it was decided to drop the Sudan curriculum and, instead, to follow the Aden College curriculum – which was a four-year secondary course leading to London University GCE O-level. Later, Aden College changed to Cambridge University GCE O-level and also introduced GCE A-levels. However, Somaliland secondary school remained with London University.

The Education Department was concerned about the boys who obtained secondary education but none of them chose teaching as a profession. In an attempt to correct the situation and enhance teaching in the schools, the Education Department established a special scholarship known as the "Director's Scholarship". For that purpose, in 1954, four additional scholarships were offered for a four-year course in the protectorate secondary school to boys who had to sign a written statement acknowledging their obligation to take up teaching as a profession on completion of their course. It was an innovative step worthy of support. Four unnamed boys took up the offer.

In 1954, the Education Department took the progressive step of splitting the intermediate school at Sheikh into two schools. A European teacher would remain the Principal of both schools, with two unnamed Somali teachers under him, each one of them becoming the Vice Principal of one of the intermediate schools so created. I imagine this was meant to train the Somali teachers to gain experience in school management and to eventually become principals of the intermediate schools.

In 1954, public-spirited ex-Sheikh School boys, in government service or in private businesses in Hargeisa, formed an association named Sheikh Old Boys Association (SOBA). The late Abdullahi Omaar, a graduate from the adult courses held at Sheikh School, as well as being a successful businessman, was the driving force behind creating the association. Members of the association in Hargeisa used to conduct evening classes for adult males.

The initiative was well received in Hargeisa. The Education Department, in the furtherance of the cause of formal education in the country, donated Sh. 400 to the SOBA for the purchase of literature for its clubroom.

The Education Department published the number of students on internal or overseas scholarships (excluding UK) who were on secondary courses in 1954:

Students on internal/overseas scholarships (excl UK) following secondary courses, 1954

Institution	No. of students
Protectorate Secondary School at Amud, Borama	29
Hantoub Secondary School, Sudan	10
Aden College (Secondary), Aden	5
Aden College (Technical), Aden	7
Mombasa Muslim Education (Technical), Kenya	2
Religious Institute of Omdurman, Sudan	2
Forestry studies, Southern Sudan, Sudan	2
Total	57

The government set up a Standing Committee on Education in 1954 and its membership and terms of reference were as follows:

Standing Committee on Education, 1954

Chairperson	Director of Education
Members	Mohamoud Ahmed Ali, MBE, Education Officer The Commissioner of Somali Affairs (European) Six unnamed Somalis nominated by the governor
Terms of reference of the Committee: 1. To make recommendations concerning the priorities, financial and executive, to be allocated to the improvement of existing educational facilities and to the extension of the same. 2. To make recommendations for the broad lines of future education policy.	

In 1954 the Government requested funds, under the Colonial Development & Welfare Fund, for the following projects for the period 1956 to 1960:

- Expansion of the trades school, expatriate teaching staff and houses for them
- One education officer for the secondary school
- One female education officer for the girls' central elementary school at Burao
- One female education officer for the girls' district elementary schools
- Extension of accommodation at the secondary school
- Construction of a new intermediate boarding school for boys in the east of the protectorate
- Construction of an adult education centre

The requested post for a female European teacher for the as-yet-non-existent girls' district elementary schools would probably be a non-teaching one. If that was the case, it would have made sense if a senior Somali teacher had been recruited instead, and the money saved on salary used for quick expansion of girls' education in the country.

At the end of the school year in June 1954, at the 14 government elementary schools for boys, the enrolment was 934 boys. The reduction in the enrolment at the elementary schools in 1954 was explained by the Education Department as being due to (a) the restriction of the maximum class sizes and (b) closing down the boarding elementary school at Sheikh and the elementary school at Zeila in April 1954.

At the solitary government elementary school for girls, the enrolment was 47. The total enrolment at the two intermediate schools for boys was 325 boys. The enrolment at the trades school was not recorded by the Education Department.

At the end of the school year in June 1954, 215 boys sat the Intermediate School Entrance examination:

- 90 boys were accepted for the two Intermediate schools
- 18 boys were accepted for the trades school
- The wastage was 50%

Also, at the end of the School year in June 1954, 64 boys sat the Intermediate School Leaving Examination:

- 13 boys were accepted for the secondary school at Amud, Borama
- 9 boys were accepted for the VTC – but the VTC was closed down in 1954; perhaps the boys were to be trained as teachers at the teachers' training centre at Sheikh
- 2 boys were sent on government scholarships to Aden College (Technical), Aden
- The wastage was 62%

For the elementary and intermediate schools, the tuition fees were increased from Sh. 30 to Sh. 40/annum. The boarding fees were increased from Sh. 225 to Sh. 264/annum. In 1954, the annual expenditure on education was given as £49,865 including £1,895 grants to 39 assisted *Qur'aanic*/Arabic schools, six of them for girls. The revenue raised from the school fees amounted to Sh. 94,970 in 1954. The Education Department stated that the actual cost to the government of maintaining boarding pupils (exclusive of tuition) was about Sh. 620/year per pupil. The tuition cost only to the government was Sh. 350/year per pupil. The Department also stated that about 19% of the total boarding fees and 16% of the tuition fees were paid for from government bursaries for boys from poor families.

The Education Department rarely published the revenue raised from the school fees every year. But it would appear that the fees payable by the pupils in the boarding and day schools contributed considerably to the financing of formal education in the country.

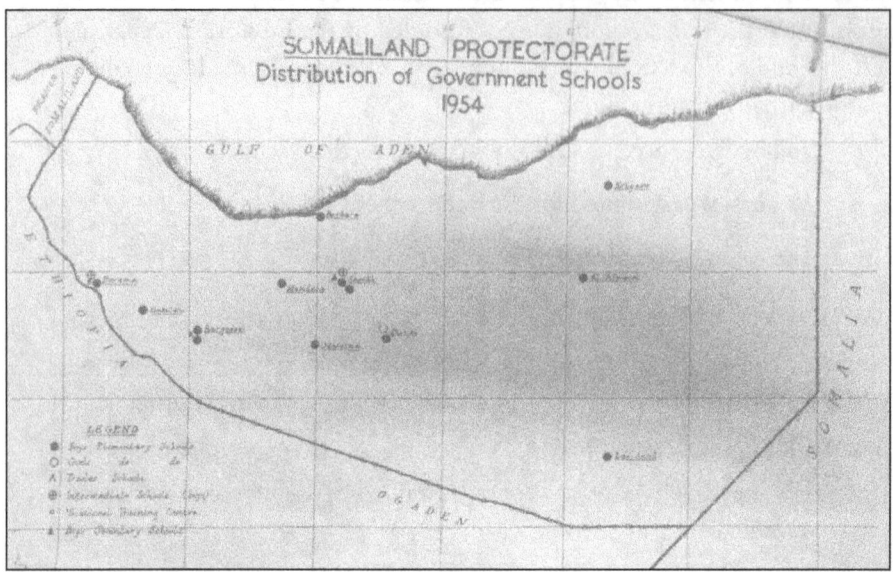

Map showing the distribution of governmental schools in the country, issued by the Education Department in 1954

Students from Somaliland Protectorate on Egyptian Government scholarships [201]

From its intelligence sources, the government was receiving secret information that some boys who completed intermediate education finished up in Egypt for higher education. There was also rumour making the rounds in the country that the Leader of Egypt, Gamal Abdul Nasser, declared that "any boy in Somaliland Protectorate who can write his name can come to Egypt for education". In response to the rumour, the government mounted a fierce campaign to denigrate the quality of the qualifications awarded by Egypt's educational institutions, and to discourage parents from sending their sons to Egypt. The response of the public to the government's campaign was "some education is better than none". The main socio-political organization then in the country, the Somali National League (SNL), was actively engaged with the Arab League (based in Cairo, Egypt) which sponsored some scholarships for Somali boys through the SNL. The government came to know "secretly" that there were already about 35 boys studying in Egypt on the Arab League scholarships, some of them receiving military training.

There is no denial that Nasser's policy in the Arab world gave the British Government and, by extension, the protectorate government the jitters, to put it mildly.

Visit of the Director of Education to Somalia [202]

Before leaving the educational activities in 1954, I would like to include here a brief write-up based on notes which the Director of Education, Mr Thompson, prepared about his visit to Somalia in 1954.

But before that, it might be of general interest to point out what the situation was like in both Somaliland and Somalia at that time. By 1954, the protectorate government in Somaliland was pretty well convinced that the independence of the country and union with Somalia was inevitable. At that time, Somalia was under the United Nations (UN) Trusteeship and the Italian Government was running the country on behalf of the UN, which was not happy with the pace of progress in the fields of education, economics and politics. In 1954, the UN introduced a seven-year development programme in Somalia.[9]

The UN Development Programme (UNDP) and the US Agency for International Cooperation (USAIC) – later US Agency for International Aid (USAID) – helped the Italian Administration in the planning of the programme.

The main thrust of the programme was on stimulating agriculture, improving the infrastructure in general and expanding the educational facilities. The UN told the Italians to get on with the job and quickly. The Somaliland Protectorate Government was keen to keep abreast of what was going on in Somalia. It was in that context that Mr Thompson made the visit to Somalia to compare notes with his opposite number in Somalia.

Mr Thompson had extensive discussions with the education authorities of Somalia and reviewed the educational system of the country. He jotted down the outcome of his discussions with the authorities in jumbled notes. What follows is what I could cull from the notes [202], with simple analysis and a few comments from which Mr Thompson shied away.

Some recorded data on the education of Somalia, based on official statistics for 1954 follow:

Enrolments in various types of school in 1954:

110 elementary schools: total enrolment of 7,556 boys and 1,642 girls = 9,198

1 intermediate school: with enrolment of 183

1 agricultural school: with enrolment of 28

1 marine and fishery school: with enrolment of 31

1 trades school: with enrolment of 36

1 domestic science school (for girls): with enrolment of 64

---

9 http://countrystudies.us/somalia/

1 school for political and administrative training: with enrolment of 83

1 secondary school: with enrolment of 18

1 teacher training centre: with of enrolment of 37

Unlike Somaliland Protectorate, the pupils in Somalia who failed to gain places in the intermediate school had the chance to go to one of other six schools in Mogadishu (see below). In the case of Somaliland Protectorate, any pupil who could not get into either of the two intermediate schools or into the trades school would have his education ended there, with only three years of elementary education. In Somalia, even if the pupil did not advance beyond elementary education, the pupil would still have had gained a six-year education which was much superior to the education the pupil in Somaliland Protectorate acquired at the elementary level.

It was clear that in Somalia in 1954, the places at the intermediate level were very restricted – where a single intermediate school catered for 110 elementary schools. In 1954 in Somaliland Protectorate, 215 students from 14 elementary schools competed for 108 places in the three intermediate schools (including the trades school) and 50% were accepted.

The UN was chivvying the Italian Government to operate more quickly as time was of the essence. The government had to work towards a fixed date – that of 1960, when the country was to become independent. However, one could surmise that, with such rapid pace, there was the risk that the quality of the education provided could have been somewhat compromised! Shortage of Somali teachers trained in the different fields of education in Somalia was a constant problem, just as it was in Somaliland Protectorate.

The Italians, responding to the lashes of the UN whip to expand the education in the country, imported a large number of Italian teachers:

The composition of teachers in 1954

	Somalia	Somaliland Protectorate
Somalis	194	87
Europeans	136	14
Libyans	11	0

It was not only on teaching staff that Italian staff were lavished. The administrative side was also strongly staffed with Italians. The Director of Education of Somalia came under the Department of Social Development.

The headquarters staff of the Education Department proper consisted of the following in 1954:

Education Department HQ staff, 1954

Somalia (all Europeans)	Somaliland Protectorate
Director of Education Assistant to Director of Education Two typists	Director of Education (European) Assistant to Director of Education (European)
	Education Officer (Somali, Mohamoud Ahmed Ali)
Director of Secondary Education One typist	Inspector of Elementary Schools (Somali, Yusuf Haji Adan) One typist
Director of Primary Education Assistant to Director of Primary Education	
Director of the School for Political & Administrative Training (No typists mentioned)	

The expenditure on education in 1954

	Somalia	Somaliland Protectorate
Capital expenditure	£63,795	£7,431
Personnel emoluments	£189,750	£37,142
Recurrent expenditure	£130,000	£22,346
Total	**£383,545**	**£66,919***

* The figure given in October 1954. The final audited expenditure on education at the end of 1954 was £49,865. Personnel emoluments in Somaliland (ie salaries) accounted for 74%. In Somalia, the figure was 49%. This implied that more development in education was taking place in Somalia.

The heavy expenditure on education in Somalia was due to the high proportion of Italians employed both as teachers and administrators, as well as the development activities taking place. The meagre expenditure on education in Somaliland Protectorate was a reflection of the government's policy never to expand education in the country.

In contrast to what was happening in Somalia, in Somaliland Protectorate, where the whip of the UN did not crack, education expansion was not in the calculation of the Somaliland Protectorate Government. The protectorate government talked a lot about quality (which of course is desirable) before quantity in education. But quality used as a means of cost-cutting tool was perverse!

There were certain features on which the educational systems in Somalia and Somaliland Protectorate, in 1954, could be compared and contrasted, as shown in the table overleaf:

Educational systems in Somalia and Somaliland, 1954

	Somalia	Somaliland Protectorate
A. Elementary Education		
1. Duration of Elementary Course	6 years	3 years
2. Number of Elementary Schools	110	17 [a]
3. Enrolment of pupils in Elementary Schools	9,198	1,017 [b]
B. Intermediate Education		
4. Duration of Intermediate Course	3 years	4 years
5. Number of Intermediate Schools	1	4 [c]
6. Enrolment in Intermediate Schools	183	390 [d]
C. Vocational Training		
7. Duration of Vocational Course	3 years	4 yrs + 3 yrs apprenticeship
8. Number of Vocational Courses	5	2
9. Enrolment in Vocational Courses	242	78
D. Secondary Education		
10. Duration of Secondary Course	4 years	4 years
11. Number of Secondary Schools	1	1
12. Enrolment in Secondary Schools	18	47
E. Departmental Staff		
13. European administrative staff, clerks, etc.	38	2
14. European teaching staff	136	12
15. Somali teaching staff	194	87
F. Education Expenditure		
16. Personnel Emoluments	£189,750	37,142
17. Recurrent Expenditure	130,000	22,346
18. Capital Expenditure	63,795	7,431
Total	£383,545	£66,919 [e]
G. Population		
19. Estimated Population	1,263,584	640,000
20. Estimated Population of school age	252,717	128,000
21. % of the above actually in school	4% approx.	1–2% approx.

a. The number should be 15, including the girls' elementary school at Burao. b. The figure at the end of 1954 was 934 boys and 47 girls, a total of 981. c. The number of intermediate schools (including the trades school) was 3. d. The figure was 325 at the end of 1954. e. The audited expenditure at end of 1954 was £49,865. [213]

It would appear that the long 6-year elementary course provided by the Italian Government was intended to be an adequate form of education in itself for the average Somali pupil. Only the very best would proceed to intermediate or secondary school. The "bottle neck", where 110 elementary schools were catered for by a single intermediate school, was much too narrow! In this respect, Somaliland Protectorate did not fare any better.

The teachers of all the schools in Somalia also ran evening classes for the adults, teaching them the 3Rs. The country attained an enrolment of 13,332 men and women for these classes, which was a considerable achievement.

I have shown the set-up of the educational system in Somalia for 1954 in the chart below:

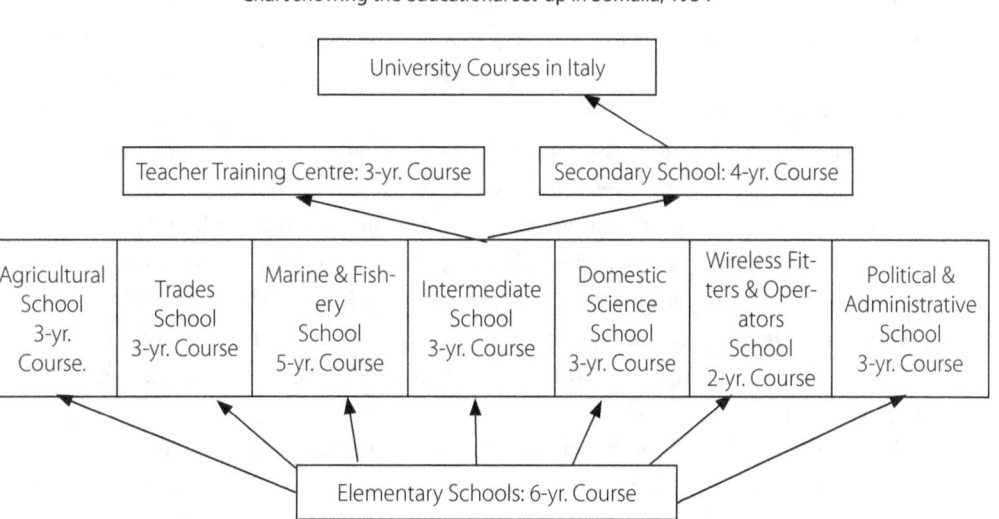

Chart showing the educational set-up in Somalia, 1954

Visit of the Director of Education of Somalia to Somaliland Protectorate [203]

Before leaving this intervening chapter on education in Somalia, I wish to link it to a return visit that the Director of Education of Somalia made to Somaliland Protectorate in 1955. The Director, Mr Puccioni, was accompanied by his Assistant, Ali Hussein Guray.

In 1954, the Assistant Director of Education of Somalia was a European. In my search, I did not find any report prepared by the two-man team from Somalia. I came across a brief mention of the visit in a Somaliland Government Newsletter called *War Somali Sidihi* (in English, *Somaliland News Carrier* or just *Somaliland News*) of November 1955. The newsletter was, incidentally, first issued by the Information Department of Somaliland Protectorate in 1953, ostensibly to publish objective news about the work of the protectorate government!

The visitors – accompanied by the Director of Education of Somaliland, Mr Thompson, and Mohamoud Ahmed, Education Officer – toured the country to observe the district schools. The visitors commented on the similarity of the contents of the syllabuses followed in the two countries, as well as the shared problem of shortage of the number of sufficiently trained national teachers.

However, the problem was very acute in Somalia, in the face of rapidly expanding education provision – hence the need to recruit many Italian teachers. The difference, they pointed out, lay in the length of the courses. In Somaliland Protectorate, Intermediate School Leaving Certificates were only issued to boys who completed both their elementary and intermediate education. That involved three years of elementary schooling followed by four years of intermediate schooling. In Somalia, on the other hand, the elementary school provided a complete six-year course of instruction followed, for some, by further three years in what was termed a "lower secondary school". At both schools, pupils were granted School Leaving Certificates.

The visitors also had discussions with the governor and the Secretary to the Somaliland Protectorate Government. They were keen on the writing of the Somali language – an issue that was not then encouraged in Somaliland Protectorate. After some discussions, it was agreed to establish a Permanent Joint Board for the Somali Language between the two territories. The visitors also presented to the protectorate government copies of a new Somali Grammar written by a Dr Martino M. Moreno, whom they described as a well-known Italian authority.

I would have liked to see the visitors' report – especially what they really thought of the state of education in Somaliland Protectorate. That report is probably gathering dust in a facility in Rome. But, for now, that ends our review of education in Somalia.

The protectorate government was approaching its final stages leading to the independence of the country. As early as 1955, the Colonial Office signalled the process of disengagement from Somaliland by instructing the Somaliland Protectorate Government to issue only summaries of the annual reports, highlighting only the salient events in the year. The Education Department followed suit and thus reduced its already brief annual reports to summaries. Accordingly, I tried to make some sense of what the Education Department put out, starting with the annual report on education for 1955.

Annual report on education for 1955 [204]

The Nomadic Betterment project was first proposed in 1952 [189] for the Education of the Nomads. It was later renamed, replacing "Education" with "Betterment". In 1955, the Education Department piloted the project. Four *Qur'aanic* teachers recommended by the DCs were brought to Sheikh for a six-month course. They were put on the following simple programme of work under, the supervision of Mohamoud Ahmed Ali:

- Observation of the methods of teaching the *Qur'aan* in government schools

- Observation of simple supplementary talks on the Muslim Religion as given to the government elementary schools
- Observation of methods of teaching very simple Arithmetic in Arabic
- Improvement of their own handwriting and figuring
- Instruction to improve their own knowledge of Arabic
- Instruction in local affairs as a background to Civics
- Soil erosion, preservation of trees
- Co-operation with government departments and its necessity: veterinary, medical, agriculture, police, education and district administration
- Short talks on protectorate history from 1884
- First Aid and hygiene

The project was experimental and was supposed to be under frequent review. Once they completed the course, the religious teachers would go back to their communities and teach them what they had learnt. After some months in the field, whatever success they achieved would be assessed. If the result was encouraging, the scheme would be repeated and enlarged, provided finances allowed. It was not mentioned whether the religious men were volunteers or were paid while in the field.

When a project with such an eye-catching title was read in the Colonial Office, it was usually hailed as a ground-breaking initiative for which the governor might deserve a pat on the back. However, the title could not conceal the inadequacy of the project. Every nomad knows that the priorities of the nomads are, first and foremost, water, pasture for their livestock, and security. Everything else is secondary to these essential components, which directly influence the life of the nomads. On this score, the project fell short of that. What could four religious teachers from different districts possibly achieve, in the face of widely scattered and perpetually mobile nomadic communities, where the teachers' reach would not extend beyond their immediate and perhaps extended families? I think the project was nothing more than a feeble attempt at "public relations exercise" and a substitute for a more substantial developmental programme.

The protectorate government misguidedly obsessed about the *Wadads*, a few of whom led the opposition to written Somali in the 1930s. The government did not know how to go about education for the nomads, just as, in 1938, the first Director of Education for the Protectorate, Mr Ellison, admitted that he did not know how to introduce education into a country where 95% of the population was nomadic (see 4.3).

Yes, the nomads would need education. However, before formal education, the nomads must be provided with practical information, meaningful to the nomads. Education for the nomads must be holistic and be based on the nomadic ecology.

The project that the government piloted could not have been a match for the Siad Barre's literacy project for the nomads in 1974–1975 [188]. All the same, the fact that the nomads' need for education was recognized was in itself an important development.

The project also reminded me that in all my school life at Sheikh School, 1944–1952, I cannot ever remember the class that I was in being taught the history of Somaliland from 1884. In this respect, the religious teachers were much luckier than my class! Instead, we were taught, *inter alia*, the industrial revolution in Britain and trading in the African people as *slaves*. Even then, we were not at a stage where we could grasp the significance of the two topics mentioned!

The picture below is similar to ones which the British history teacher of my class at Sheikh School in 1949–1950 used to show us in the history lessons. We heard about mentally ill people in chains, but we could not make much sense of people in chains, for sale, as in the photo below shows:

Africans rounded up and chained together; later to be exported to Britain and America to be auctioned in the slave trading markets! That was what the Scramble for Africa was about! The chained "human commodity" is guarded by two armed African "slave-herders".

There was some movement in 1955, in both Somaliland Protectorate and Somalia, to look into writing the Somali language. In order to try to obtain some agreement on an orthography which would be both practical and acceptable for the Somali language. A conference between representatives of Somaliland Protectorate and Somalia was held in June 1955 in Mogadishu. Musa Galaal and the Director of Education, Mr Thompson, represented Somaliland Protectorate. An agreement was reached on a practicable orthography in the Roman script, but it remained to be seen whether it would be acceptable to the Somali people. (For more on this, see 4.5). It is noteworthy that in Somalia, unlike Somaliland Protectorate, written Somali language and Christian missionary work in the country were never controversial issues.

In 1955, the Hargeisa community realized that the government was not ready to respond any time soon to the great need for more educational facilities in the district. To benefit from the cost-sharing policy introduced by the government in 1952, the community, led by the District Education Committee, collected sufficient money to build a one-class day intermediate school and the Education Department assumed responsibility for equipping and staffing the school. It was opened in July 1955. The government also opened an elementary school in Ainaba, bringing the total number of elementary schools in the country in 1955 to 16. The Girls' Boarding Elementary School at Burao was enlarged to accommodate 48 instead of 24 girls.

The fees at the Teacher Training Centre were waived, the post-intermediate boys preferred to enter the government services and draw salaries rather than volunteer to join the TTC as fee-paying students.

The fees at the trades school were reduced from Sh. 150 to Sh. 100/year per boy. Abdisalam Hassan and Mohamed Shire, who were sent to the UK in 1953, returned to Somaliland Protectorate in 1955 after successfully completing a two-year course. Abdisalam Hassan was appointed Principal of an unnamed boarding intermediate school and Mohamed Shire was put in-charge of the Teacher Training Centre. Ali Mire was sent to the UK in 1955 on two-year course on Scouting.

In 1955, a Trades Training Board was created to follow the progress of the boys in the trades school and in their apprenticeship at the Public Works Department, and also to advise the Director of Education on all matters relating to trades training. The Board membership was as follows:

- Director of Education – Chairperson
- Principal, Trades School – Secretary
- Director of Public Works – Member
- Ali Sh. Mohamed Jirde – Member
- Osman Ismail Samater – Member
- Nasir Nahar – Member

At the end of the school year in June 1955, a total of 74 boys sat for the Intermediate School Leaving Examination: 15 boys were accepted in the secondary School, 2 boys were accepted in the trades school, 8 boys were taken by the Education Department to be trained as teachers. The wastage – in other words, those boys for whom there was no further educational provision – was 66%.

The Intermediate Entrance examination was not mentioned in the annual report for 1955. The annual report on education for 1955, and subsequent annual reports will each be summarized in four tables (although there was little narrative to draw on) which will give a view of the status of formal education in the country each year at a glance:

Table a: Numbers/descriptions of schools, by enrolment and by educational level, 1955

Level of education			Government schools	Local authority schools	Total
Elementary	Enrolment	M	793	314	1107
		F	64	0	64
		Total	857	314	1171
	No. of schools		16	3	19
Intermediate	Enrolment	M	368	0	368
		F	0	0	0
		Total	368	0	368
	No. of schools		3*	0	3
Secondary	Enrolment	M	47	0	47
		F	0	0	0
		Total	47	0	47
	No. of schools		1	0	1
Teacher Training Centre	Enrolment	M	13	0	13
		F	0	0	0
		Total	13	0	13
	No. of schools		1	0	1
Trades School	Enrolment	M	87	0	87
		F	0	0	0
		Total	87	0	87
	No. of schools		1	0	1

*Including the day intermediate school at Hargeisa.

Table b: Teachers in Training, 1955

Description of course	Number of Institutions	Student admitted during 1955			Total students at end of 1955			Students passing final exams in 1955		
		M	F	Total	M	F	Total	M	F	Total
2-Year Local Teacher Training Course for Elementary School Teachers	1	13	0	13	13	0	13	-	-	No exams in 1955
2-Year Certificate Course in U.K. for Senior Teachers	Training in the UK	2	0	2	4	0	4	2	0	2

Table c: Teachers Classified by Qualification, 1955.

		Elementary schools		Intermediate schools		Secondary schools		Trades School		Teacher Training Centre		Totals	
		Government or LA**		Government		Government		Government		Government			
		M	F	M	F	M	F	M	F	M	F	M	F
Approved Graduates or Equivalent	Trained	0	0	2	0	2	0	0	0	0	0	4	0
	Untrained	0	0	0	0	1	0	0	0	0	0	1	0
Completed Secondary School Course	Trained	0	3*	2	0	0	0	1	0	0	0	3	3
	Untrained	0	0	2	0	0	0	2	0	0	0	4	0
Not completed Secondary Course	Trained	12	0	5	0	1	0	2	0	1	0	21	0
	Untrained	44	1	12	0	1	0	7	0	0	0	64	1

*Two of the British women teachers were at the Girls' Elementary School, Burao, the other was at the European Elementary School, Hargeisa, but who paid her salary was not mentioned. It would appear that Mohamed Shire was the only staff at the TTC. ** Local Authority

Table d: Expenditure on education, 1955

Recurrent expenditure	By Education Department	By Local Authority
Elementary Education	£13,388	£3,325
Intermediate Education	£17,850	-
Secondary Education	£5,582	-
Teacher Training	£1,502	-
Vocational Training	£4,133	-
Administration/unallocated	£5,853	-
Non-recurrent expenditure	£7,370	
Total	£55,678	£3,325
Grand total	£59,003	

Development funds for 1957–1960 [205]

It was on the basis of the final conclusion of the British Government deliberations on Somaliland [82] that, in 1956, the Colonial Office informed the Governor of Somaliland Protectorate to plan for development funding of £2.4 million for the period 1957 to 31 March 1960. Out of that fund, a sum of £619,707 was allocated to the Education Department for the same period (1957 to March 1960).

On top of that, up to 200 overseas scholarships were made available, subject to *there being sufficient suitably qualified candidates*. The scholarships would cover all branches of education – university and professional training of Somali students, technical training, apprenticeships overseas, provision for administrative and technical courses for serving Somali members in all branches of the civil service. Since the scholarship money was provided under the Colonial Development & Welfare Fund, it would supposedly be used for capital expenditure, not for recurrent expenditure.

In connection with the development funds mentioned above, the government once again expressed its ambivalent attitude towards the country by reminding itself:

> *…to ensure not to erect a system for which the natives were not ready, and which could never be sustained from internal revenues, especially as the position of ultimate abandonment of the country has not been excluded.*

The above was not something new, as there were already two occasions when the protectorate government abandoned the country partially or completely – in 1910 and 1940, respectively. On each occasion, the government was in two minds as to whether to return to the country or abandon it altogether. As already mentioned, the government mooted the idea of washing its hands of Somaliland on several occasions from the 1920s, as discussed under 3.6.

Annual report on education for 1956 [206]

It was in connection with the "windfall" of £619,707 for the Education Department that the Director of the Department, lamenting the past neglect of education in the country, made the following statement in the annual report:

> *The need for rapid expansion in education is urgent and cannot be disputed, and it is now clear that the very slow rate of progress between the years 1943 and 1956 has resulted in an acute shortage of boys and girls with the necessary basic educational qualifications required for admission to courses of technical and professional training overseas. This shortage has become all the more apparent since considerable Colonial Development & Welfare Funds have been made available for the award of scholarships for such courses with the intention of providing suitably qualified Somalis for appointments to posts in the Government service. It would be wrong, however, to suppose that the demand is from the Government alone for there is also a shortage of well-educated men in local commercial ventures.*

The situation described by the Director confirmed that the educational policy that the government had been following since 1944 was not only short-sighted but also damaging to the Somaliland people. Again, the likelihood that the overseas scholarships might not be effectively utilized for lack of eligible candidates would be an embarrassment for the government, but a disaster for the Somalis. As mentioned before, it was only in 1954 that the Government declared that "The education cannot be expanded for lack of funds".

Perhaps the British Government, by making £2.4 million available, knew the limited absorptive capacity of the protectorate government and that a good amount of the money would expire and remain with the British Treasury! The Education Department had to plan for the funds allocated to it – in other words, £619,707 – as well as for the 200 overseas scholarships. Accordingly, the Education Department formulated what was billed as a "programme for the expansion of education" in the country for the period 1957 to March 1960.

I summarize the main planned activities in a tabular form, to show what was planned for at a glance:

Planned educational facilities and training courses in different fields: 1957 to March 1960

Elementary Education	Boys	To build up to 20 elementary schools: 6 in 1957; 6 in 1958 and 8 in 1959. The location of the schools will be decided by the Standing Committee on Education
	Girls	To build 4 new elementary schools in 1957 – in Berbera, Hargeisa, Borama and Burao. The Burao School will have boarding accommodation for girls from Erigavo and Las Anod
Intermediate Education	Boys	To build 6 new intermediate schools to open thus: In 1957: Hargeisa (day, second stream); Erigavo (boarding, second stream, also to provide for Las Anod); Burao (day), In 1958: Odweine (boarding); Gabeilay (boarding); Borama (day)
	Girls	The first intermediate class will open in 1957 in the existing boarding elementary school in Burao which will gradually convert into intermediate school, with boarding accommodation for all pupils
Secondary Education	Boys	To build a completely new double-stream boarding secondary school (50 boys each year) in 1958 at Sheikh or elsewhere, depending on water supply
Technical Education		The existing trades school in Hargeisa is to be improved as follows: a) boarding accommodation will be provided for all pupils not resident in Hargeisa b) two education officers (technical) will be recruited and they will be responsible for appropriate training in the Public Works Department (PWD) c) more equipment will be provided for instruction for both the trades school pupils and the PWD apprentices
Adult Education		It will be provided as follows: a) residential course at Sheikh similar to the post-war courses (30 pupils per course of 9 months' duration b) evening classes in community centres at district headquarters; honoria will be paid to volunteer teachers until permanent staff are available c) Larger numbers of nomadic Wadads will be brought in for training
Teacher Training		a) the Teacher Training Centre will occupy Borama Secondary School buildings when the secondary school moves into its new buildings. Borama buildings will be extended to accommodate 100 teacher-trainees. b) overseas courses will be increased from 5 or 6 to 8 a year, as soon as possible c) female teachers will be trained at Burao Girls' Intermediate School
Administration		a) departmental headquarters will be moved to Hargeisa in 1957 b) educational stores and teachers' library will be built in Hargeisa c) additional departmental transport will be provided d) expatriate principals of intermediate schools will gradually be replaced by Somalis and post of Officer-in-Charge Intermediate Schools will be created e) Somali officer's post of Officer-in-Charge Adult Education will be created f) District Education Office will be opened in Burao

It was clear from the content of the planned activities that it was not envisaged to broaden the scope of the current educational system. Rather, it was just inadequate increase in the size of the system horizontally, without vertical expansion. In other words, a bit more of the same. No educational level above that of secondary level was planned for. Female education was kept at intermediate level, and very inadequate indeed at that. Since the education expansion initiative was up to March 1960, the government had a golden opportunity, if it were sincere about the education of the Somalis, to at least raise the level of the academic and technical educational facilities in the country above secondary and trades school levels. The government could have built a college where post-secondary boys and girls and post-trades school boys could study for Diplomas in academic and technical subjects. The government only went through the motions without planning for anything substantial that would greatly advance formal education in the country. The timid horizontal expansion betrayed a government wedded to a discredited policy of producing government civil servants and indirectly banning liberal education.

I wonder whether there was an ex-British colonial country that, at Independence, did not have at least a college for higher education! The government could not even provide for the secondary boys to take their GCE A-level course in the country, before being sent to the UK for higher education.

The expansion plan included a new secondary school that would be built in as-yet-unidentified place in the country. The buildings which would be vacated by the secondary school would be occupied by the Teachers Training Centre (TTC). It was only two years before, in 1954, that the VTC was closed and its buildings in Amud occupied by the secondary school. The new secondary school mentioned above was opened mid-May 1960, less than six weeks before the country became independent! The government's policy on education, if ever there was one, was so erratic that it verged on the ridiculous!

In 1956, Las Anod Elementary School was reduced to two classes. According to the Education Department, the nomadic parents found it difficult to maintain children in town. To overcome the problem and shame the protectorate government, the District Education Committee, with the help of the local community, built in 1956, a "hostel" for the nomadic children in the District and thus enabled the nomadic children to attend the government day elementary school. The Las Anod community realized what seemed to be beyond the grasp of the government and replaced the class that the government sacrificed. The government could not see nor care about the great need for boarding educational facility in the district which had, and still has, a predominantly nomadic population. The government opted for the iniquitous solution of curtailing the education of the nomadic children by partially closing the only elementary day school in the District, just because nomadic parents could not keep their nomadic children in Las Anod town!

Worse still, the District was left out in the planning for educational expansion in the country for the period 1957–1960. Rather than planning for a boarding intermediate school for the District, it was instead decided that Las Anod District would share with Erigavo District a second stream boarding intermediate school planned for Erigavo. I like the idea of children from different Districts studying and living together, as happened in Sheikh and Amud Boarding Schools. But I am sure that was not the way the government was thinking. The British Parliamentarian who, in 1952 [192], sought information about educational facilities east of Burao was onto something. He was alluding to the common knowledge that the Dervishes' activities were in the east of the country. The Parliamentarian was under the impression that the government was deliberately restricting educational services in the east, to make a point! The fact that the Dhulbahante Clan never had treaty with the British Government perhaps also influenced the protectorate government attitude towards this clan.

Since the bitter struggle with the Seyyid and his Dervishes, at the dawn of the twentieth century, the government had a blind spot about the development of the country as a whole. For the government, the east of the country, in particular, had become synonymous with Dervishes, and the government could not bring itself to live down the Dervish struggle, which it had found not only painful but also an embarrassing experience, bearing in mind how poorly-armed the Dervishes were, and yet how they pinned down the Imperial Forces for 20 years! Anyway, there is no denying that the protectorate government failed to develop the educational facilities in the east of the country.

In July 1956, the first class was enrolled for a new boarding intermediate school at Dayaha, about 15 km outside Erigavo. The first batch of 34 boys in the trades school completed the four-year course (1952–1956) in 1956. The government had some difficulty in placing the boys. There were practically no facilities for apprenticeships except the Public Works Department which could only handle very few boys at a time. The final placements of the boys are shown in the table opposite.

In 1956, there were 16 government elementary schools (one of which was for girls) in the country. The girls' elementary school had four full classes in 1956. However, the 15 elementary schools for boys did not all have the full complement of three classes – eight of them (53%) had only one or two classes, as shown in the second table opposite. :

The acute shortage of intermediate schools was further exposed when, at the end of the school year in June 1956, 325 pupils sat the Intermediate School Entrance Examination and only 120 were accepted for the three intermediate schools and the trades school. The wastage was 63%.

Final placements of boys, 1956

Agency	Position	Number
Agriculture & Veterinary Services	Forest Rangers	2
	Tractor Drivers	3
	Sawyers	1
Somaliland Scouts (Works Dept.)	Carpenters	2
	Masons	2
Somaliland Police Force	Armourer	1
Education Department	Technical Instructors	2
Messrs A. Besse & Co. Ltd.	Mechanic	1
Apprenticeship with PWD	Mechanics	4
	Carpenters	6
	Masons	2
Awarded Scholarships Overseas	Mason	1
	Mechanic	1
	Carpenter	1
	Total	**29***

*Five boys did not ask for employment.

Classes per elementary school, 1956

Town	Number of classes per elementary school
Borama	3 classes
Aware	1 class
Gabiley	3 classes
Hargeisa (Fisher)	3 classes
Hargeisa (Reece)	3 classes
Mandera	2 classes
Berbera	3 classes
Sheikh	2 classes
Burao	3 classes
Odweine	2 classes
Ainaba	1 class
Las Anod	2 classes
Eil Afwein	2 classes
Erigavo	3 classes
Las Qorey	2 classes

The Hargeisa Day Intermediate School, opened in July 1955, was one-class and there was no intake at that school in 1956. The number of assisted *Qur'aanic* and/or Arabic Schools was given as 90 in 1956. The secondary school intake was increased from 15 to 20 boys, although the total number of boys in the intermediate schools from which the 20 boys came was not given. For the first time, a special post-intermediate examination was introduced. The aspirants for admission to the secondary school must first qualify, for the secondary entrance examination, on their results in the Intermediate School Leaving Examination, and then take a special test to be enrolled into the secondary school.

The cynic would say that the intention of the government (though it did not spell it out) was that the extra hurdle in the way to secondary education would reduce the number of boys who could, in the end, qualify for places in the secondary school, as the number of places was grossly limited. This was a form of education rationing, just as was the case for the trades school entrance in 1953.

In July 1956, six boys, including the author, who completed the GCE O-level course (Cambridge University) at Hantoub Secondary School, Sudan, returned to the country. The minimum number of subjects to take for the GCE O-level examination at Hantoub Secondary School was seven and the maximum was nine subjects. Failure in English was a failure in the whole examination. When our examination results became available in late 1956, the Education Department of Somaliland Protectorate recorded our GCE O-level results thus:

> *As a group of 6, they sat for an average of 45 papers. They achieved Distinctions in nine papers, Credits in thirty-three papers and Passes in three papers.*

In short, we all passed the examination. Shortly thereafter, we were called for interviews at the Government Secretariat in Hargeisa. The interviewers were a Group composed of the Directors of the different Departments. Subjects suitable to study were suggested to us – for example, veterinary, agriculture, engineering, medicine, education, etc. Law and economics were "no go" areas. The Group considered these two subjects dangerous, fit only for political agitators and troublemakers in the British colonies! The Group feared that those who opted for the two subjects would go to the London School of Economics, London University, which the Group considered to be a hot bed of socialists and radicals!

Three of us selected law or economics but the Group rejected our selections out of hand. In the end, not to lose the scholarships, our selections before arriving in the UK were as follows:

- Hassan (Kyde) Abdulla Walanwal – Military (his main interest, no change)

- Ahmed Botan Dhakkaar, Public Administration (his main interest, no change)

- Abdirahman (Jeep) Sh. Ali Gaile – Architecture (changed to Law while in UK)
- Said (Sheef) Mohamed Ali Bulay – History (changed to Economics while in UK)
- Salah Haji Fareh Dirir, Medicine (changed to Chemistry while in UK)
- Abdullahi Deria (the author) – History (changed to Medicine before going to UK)

Some of us were given temporary jobs before all of us were sent to the UK in September 1957, to follow GCE A-level courses, prior to joining universities and other higher educational institutions.

Some statistical details on education at the end of 1956 follow:

Table a: Numbers/descriptions of schools, by enrolment and educational level, 1956

Level of education			Government schools	Local authority schools	Total
Elementary	Enrolment	M	766	330	1096
		F	95	0	95
		Total	861	330	1191
	No. of schools		16	3	19
Intermediate	Enrolment	M	431	0	431
		F	0	0	0
		Total	431	0	431
	No. of schools		4	0	4
Secondary	Enrolment	M	63	0	63
		F	0	0	0
		Total	63	0	63
	No. of schools		1	0	1
Teacher Training Centre	Enrolment	M	25	0	25
		F	0	0	0
		Total	25	0	25
	No. of schools		1	0	1
Trades School	Enrolment	M	73	0	73
		F	0	0	0
		Total	73	0	73
	No. of schools		1	0	1

Table b: Teachers in Training, 1956

Description of course	Number of Institutions	Students admitted during 1956			Total students at end of 1956			Students in final year		
		M	F	Total	M	F	Total	M	F	Total
2-Year Local Teacher Training Course for Elementary School Teachers	1	11	0	11	25	0	25	5	0	5
2-Year Teachers Certificate Course in U.K. or Sudan	Training Overseas	3	0	3	5	0	5	2	0	2

Table c: Teachers classified by qualification, 1956

		Elementary Schools		Intermediate Schools		Secondary Schools		Technical and Vocational		Teacher Training		Total	
		Government /Local Auth.		Government		Government		Government		Government			
		M	F	M	F	M	F	M	F	M	F	M	F
Approved Graduates or Equivalent	Trained	0	0	1	0	3	0	1	0	0	0	5	0
	Untrained	0	0	0	0	0	0	0	0	0	0	0	0
Completed Secondary School Course	Trained	1	4*	5	0	1	0	3	0	2	0	12	4
	Untrained	0	0	4	0	0	0	4	0	0	0	8	0
Not completed Secondary School Course	Trained	30	0	5	0	0	0	1	0	0	0	36	0
	Untrained	33	2	13	0	1	0	6	0	0	0	53	2

* Three of the European female teachers were at the girls school in Burao, the other was at the European children's school in Hargeisa.

Table d: Expenditure on education, 1956

Recurrent expenditure	By Education Department	By Local Authority
Elementary Education	£20,200	£5,267
Intermediate Education	£26,900	-
Secondary Education	£8,664	-
Teacher Training	£2,400	-
Vocational Training	£5,920	-
Administration/unallocated	£8,920	-
Non-recurrent expenditure	£4,874	
Total	£77,878	£5,267
Grand total	£83,145	

Promotions and Training Board [207]

In early 1957, the Colonial Office sent an expert to Somaliland Protectorate to work out, among other things, a fixed establishment for each department for the foreseeable future. Also, a study was made in order to estimate the length of time it would take for the various posts then held by expatriates to be taken over by Somalis.

There was a government board called the Promotions and Training Board. Incidentally, the Board might have been the group which interviewed the six boys who returned from Sudan in 1956, mentioned in Ref. 206. The Board, as the name implies, was to consider and recommend promotions for government employees, and to recommend people for training abroad. It was composed of senior officials of the Secretariat and the Directors of the various departments of the protectorate government. There was no Somali member on the Board. It was working on the assumption that, when the students on government scholarships completed their studies in the UK, they would return to join the protectorate government services and take over posts occupied by expatriates or fill new vacancies created by expansion in the various Departments. Thus, the Board decided that the students who were sent to UK should follow certain courses only – in other words, those that would qualify them to take over government posts later. The Board was not interested in liberal education, where students could study subjects of their choice, but was merely concerned with filling the vacancies that they estimated would occur in the various departments, or finding eventual replacements for expatriates sometime in the future. It seemed that the government equated liberal education with political subversion!

The Colonial Office appeared to be making up for lost time by speeding up the Somalization process and indicating that money was no object. The protectorate government was instructed to take a chance with ten students from the first intake in the secondary school at Amud and send them to the UK for GCE A-level courses, soon after taking the GCE O-level examination, without waiting for the results of that examination. Those who did not obtain the necessary number of passes would continue to obtain the GCE O-level passes needed while on the GCE A-level course in UK.

The Board asked the Headmaster of the secondary school, Mr Darlington, to submit individual reports on the 10 students whom he thought had good chance of passing the GCE O-level examination. He selected the following 10 students: Ahmed Mohamed Mohamoud (Silaanyo), Musa Ahmed Bore, Yusuf Dirir, Ali Abdulqadir Farah, Musa Haji Deria (Idaar), Hussein Hassan (Badag), Ismail Haibe, Ahmed Mohamoud (Hurreh), Hussein Bile and Adan Amin.

The students were interviewed by the Board, which put the students through the process described earlier for the six students from Sudan in 1956. Those who did not get the subjects of their choice accepted whatever other subjects were on offer and, once in the UK, set about changing to the subjects they really wanted to study.

Annual report on education for 1957 [208]

It was announced in the annual report on education for 1957 that the headquarters of the Education Department, which had been at Sheikh since 1944, had been moved to Hargeisa in early 1957. The staff of the headquarters of the Department consisted of the following:

- Mr Thompson, Director of Education
- Mr Badham, Deputy Director of Education
- Mr Lloyd, Education Officer for Intermediate Schools
- Mohamoud Ahmed Ali, Education Officer for Elementary Schools
- One assistant accountant
- Two clerks

It was indicated in the annual report on education for 1957 that the idea of moving the Education Department headquarters to Hargeisa was prompted by the need for the Director of the Education Department to liaise with the Government Secretariat and with the other government departments in Hargeisa, *vis-à-vis* the planned expansion of the activities of the Education Department [205].

First group to graduate from Amud Secondary School, 1957

In May 1957, the 16 students at Amud Secondary School, from whom the ten above-named students were selected, sat for the GCE O-level examination (London University). The group photo shows the students of the same group individually named in Ref. 197.

A Brief History of Formal Education in British Somaliland Protectorate

Group photo of the 16 boys who sat for GCE O-levels in 1957. I can recognize 12 faces. The group was the first cohort to have their secondary education in Somaliland Protectorate [222]

The Government's policy then was that if a student obtained five or more passes in the results of the GCE O-level examinations and was recommended by the Promotions & Training Board for further education, then they would proceed to institutions in the UK for tuition to obtain such passes at GCE A-level as the condition of university entrance might demand.

On grading alone, 14 students (out of a total of 16) qualified for UK scholarship, as shown below:

- 6 boys obtained 7 passes
- 6 boys obtained 6 passes
- 2 boys obtained 5 passes
- 1 boy obtained 4 passes
- 1 boy obtained 3 passes

The decision to send the 10 students to the UK immediately after taking the GCE O-level examinations was made so late in the year that it was not possible, in the time available, to arrange polytechnics and/or technical colleges for the 10 boys, and this meant that they were kept in Somaliland Protectorate until the next academic year, 1958. Some were given temporary jobs, as was done in 1956 for my group from Hantoub Secondary School, Sudan.

Since the policy for education expansion, announced in 1956, many Somalis, on different courses, were sent to the UK and the government published a list of them in training in 1957, as shown in the table below:

Studying on government scholarships, in the UK, 1957

Government department for which training was intended	Nature of the Course	Number of Students
Education	Degree Courses	4
	2-year Teacher Certificate	7
Health	Medical Degree Courses	4
	Dental Degree Course	1
	Nursing Training Courses	5
Agriculture & Veterinary	Degree Courses	2
	Diploma Courses	2
Public Works	Civil Engineering Degree Courses	2
	City & Guilds Courses	4
Judicial	Law Degrees	2
Posts & Telegraphs	Diploma Courses	1
Administration	Degree Courses	3
	Diploma Courses	2
Accountant General	Accountancy Courses	3
	Total	42

The government did not name the individual students listed above. There were also about a dozen senior drivers from the Public Works Department who were sent to the UK and attached to Motor Manufacturing Companies, for practical experiences.

The government had been awarding overseas scholarships only to those who were in government service or who, the government assumed, would join the services in the future. Anyway, since there were practically no opportunities for employment outside of what the government could offer, the vast majority of those who benefited from the overseas scholarships had no alternative but to become government employees. The private sector was not developed to any extent. Somali businesses were one-man businesses. The few relatively well-to-do businessmen in the country usually managed their business accounts in Arabic or used, on an ad-hoc basis, the services of young men who knew some basic Arabic and arithmetic. Those who engaged in simple businesses and who did not even have bases from which to operate, carried their business accounts in their "heads or pockets"! There were hardly any Somali companies.

As the country's independence approached, the process of Somalization in the civil services gathered momentum and this was quite obvious in the Education Department, as detailed in the annual report on education for 1957, as the table opposite shows:

Senior administrative, inspecting and teaching staff of the Department, end 1957

Position	Name	Appointment
HQ Office	C. Sykes Thompson P.H.C. Badham K.D. Lloyd Mohamoud Ahmed Ali	Director of Education Deputy Director Education Officer for Intermediate Schools Education Officer for Elementar Schools
Secondary School	R.R. Darlington W.A. McKinley Abdisalam Hassan	Education Officer, Principal Education Officer, Teacher Assistant Education Officer, Teacher
Vocational Training Centre	Tanner Mohamed Shire	Education Officer, Principal Assistant Education Officer, Teacher
Trades School, Hargeisa	J.F.V. Magner	Education Officer, Principal
Intermediate Boys Schools	Yusuf Haji Adan Yusuf Ismail Samater Hashi Abdulla Farah Ali Mire Adan Isaq	Education Officer, Principal, Sheikh Assistant Education Officer, Principal, Borama Grade I Teacher, Principal, Erigavo Grade I Teacher, Principal, Hargeisa Grade II Teacher, Principal, Burao
Girls Schools	Miss Darke Miss Robertson Miss Begg Miss Harding	Senior Education Officer, Burao Education Officer, Burao Education Officer, Burao Education Officer, Hargeisa

Mr F.J. Raine, Education Officer, was seconded to the Department of Natural Resources to run the Rural Training Centre. It was not explained what type of training was conducted at this Centre. One of the European female teachers was for adult Somali female education and another was for the elementary school for European children in Hargeisa.

The Education Department could not make up its mind about whether the VTC and the TTC were one and the same centre or different. In the table above, what would have been the TTC was given as the VTC! The VTC was closed in 1954. Anyway, both the VTC and the TTC were, in effect, vocational training centres.

In 1957, six new elementary schools for boys were built – one in each of Abdul-qaadir, Tog-wajaale, Burao, Harufadhi and two in Hargeisa; one girls' elementary school was built in Hargeisa. In addition, four new intermediate schools for boys were built in 1957, but it was not mentioned where in the country they were built. Also the first intermediate school for girls was created within the girls' elementary school at Burao, and the first Form IV was enrolled in 1957. In this respect, Burao Central Boarding School for Girls was modelled on Sheikh Central Boarding School for Boys. Burao Boarding School for Girls developed in the same way Sheikh Elementary Boarding School for Boys did. In each school, over the years, more classrooms and dormitories were added to the schools. There had been no secondary school for girls in the country during colonial rule.

Ali Mire, who was sent to the UK in 1955, returned to the country in 1957 after successfully completing his course on Scouting and other studies. Mr Clerk, Principal of the Trades School, was transferred to Uganda and the vacancy was filled by Yusuf Haji Adan, who was promoted to Education Officer.

At the end of the school year in June 1957, 73 boys sat for the Intermediate School Leaving examination:

- 21 boys were accepted for the secondary school at Amud
- 3 boys were given overseas scholarships, to the Institute for Religious Studies in Omdurman, Sudan, to study Muslim religion and Arabic,
- The wastage was 67%; of these, 35 boys entered the government services

Also, 298 boys sat for the Intermediate School Entrance examination:

- 255 boys were accepted for the intermediate schools
- The wastage was 14%

The number of aided *Qur'aanic*/Arabic Schools in 1957 was given as 120, six of them for girls. The Education Department intended that the six schools for girls would eventually become elementary schools, pending availability of female teachers.

The school fees payable at the government schools in December 1957 were given as follows:

- Elementary schools:
    - day schools – Sh. 40/annum per student
    - boarding schools – Sh. 264/annum per student
- Intermediate schools:
    - day schools – Sh. 80/annum per student
    - boarding schools – Sh. 264/annum per student
- Trades school:
    - day pupils only – remained at Sh. 100/annum per student
- Secondary school:
    - Boarding – remained at Sh. 400/annum per student

Further educational details for 1957 are given in the following tables:

A Brief History of Formal Education in British Somaliland Protectorate

Table a: Numbers/descriptions of school, by enrolment and by educational level, 1957

Level of education			Government schools	Local authority schools	Total
Elementary	Enrolment	M	507	767	1274
		F	97	0	97
		Total	604	767	1371
	No. of schools		23	10	33
Intermediate	Enrolment	M	595	0	595
		F	38	0	38
		Total	633	0	633
	No. of schools		9	0	9
Secondary	Enrolment	M	68	0	68
		F	0	0	0
		Total	68	0	68
	No. of schools		1	0	1
Teacher Training Centre	Enrolment	M	27	0	27
		F	0	0	0
		Total	27	0	27
	No. of schools		1	0	1
Trades School	Enrolment	M	86	0	86
		F	0	0	0
		Total	86	0	86
	No. of schools		1	0	1

Table b: Teachers in Training, 1957

Description of course	No. of Institutions	Students admitted during 1957			Total Students at end of 1957			Students in final year		
		M	F	Total	M	F	Total	M	F	Total
2-Year Local Teacher Training Course for Elementary School Teachers	1	13	0	13	27	0	27	11	0	11
2-Year Teachers Certificate Course in UK or Sudan	Training Overseas	5	0	5	7	0	7	2	0	2

Table c: Teachers classified by qualification, 1957

		Elementary Schools		Intermediate Schools		Secondary Schools		Technical and Vocational		Teacher Training		Grand Total	
		Government or Local Authority		Government		Government		Government		Government			
		M	F	M	F	M	F	M	F	M	F	M	F
Approved Graduates or Equivalent	Trained	0	0	4	0	5	0	0	0	0	0	9	0
	Untrained	0	0	0	0	0	0	0	0	0	0	0	0
Completed Secondary School Course	Trained	0	4*	1	2*	1	0	1	0	1	0	4	6
	Untrained	1	0	4	0	1	0	4	0	1	0	11	0
Not completed Secondary School Course	Trained	19	0	12	0	0	0	1	0	0	0	32	0
	Untrained	37	1	13	0	1	0	5	0	0	0	56	1

*One of the female European teachers was at the School for European children's school, Hargeisa, and the rest were at the girls' elementary/intermediate schools at Burao. NB. Within the year, the number of female European teachers increased from four to six, as a result of the newly created intermediate school for girls.

Table d: Expenditure on education, 1957

Recurrent expenditure	By Education Department	By Local Authority
Elementary Education	£11,770	£3,038
Intermediate Education	£12,073	-
Secondary Education	£3,265	-
Teacher Training	£2,468	-
Vocational Training	£3,797	-
Administration/unallocated	£3,702	-
Non-recurrent expenditure	£53,953	
Total	£91,028	£3,038
Grand total	£94,066	

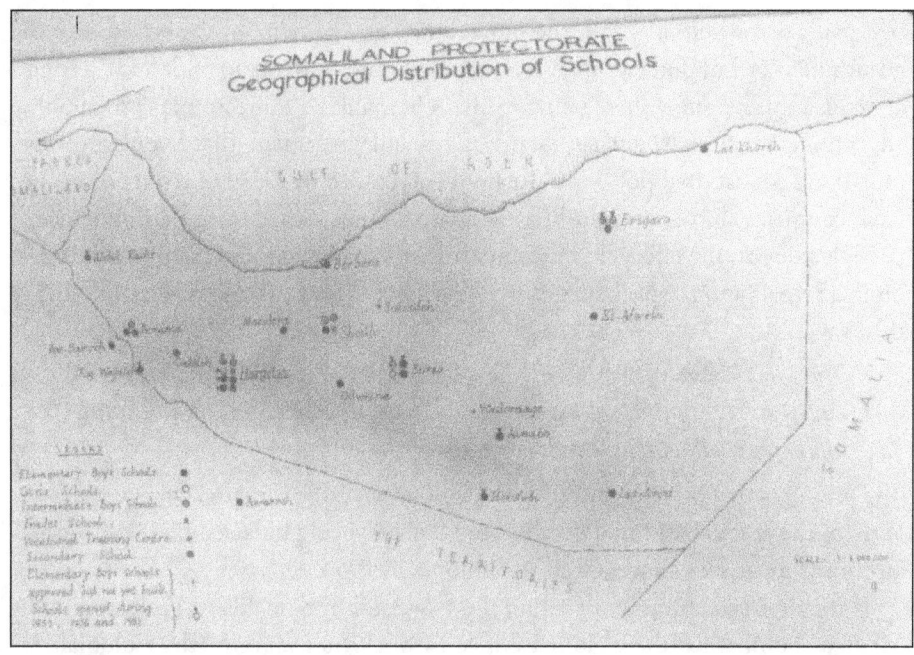

Map showing the distribution of the Governmental Schools in the country, issued by the Education Department, 1957.

Creation of the BBC Somali Service [209]

Before leaving 1957, I wish to insert here the above item. This radio service contributed to the general information and education of the Somaliland people – and, for its general educational value, I have therefore kept it in the education section. As already mentioned, the Leader of Egypt, Gamal Abdul Nasser, harassed the British in the Arab countries and he remained the bane of the British Government policy in the Middle East throughout the 1950s and 1960s. The British lording it over the Arab countries willy-nilly was no more! The fiery propaganda emanating from Cairo's *Sawt el-Arab* (Voice of the Arab), a voice that inspired or alarmed, depending on the audience concerned, put paid to Britain's cultural and political hegemony in the Arab world. The Arab counties, at least some of them, showed signs of defiance and refused to accept meekly whatever the British prescribed for them.

Meanwhile, parents in Somaliland Protectorate were, as mentioned earlier, sending their sons to educational facilities in that charged atmosphere in Egypt to soak up whatever came their way in the form of education, information or politics. On its part, the Government of Somaliland Protectorate was, to say the least, not happy about that, but was helpless to do anything about it.

However, the crunch came when Nasser included Somaliland Protectorate in *Sawt el-Arab's* target audience. Once again, the British Government panicked. The first panic was when, in 1953, the protectorate government, at the behest of the government in London, stopped sending any more students to Sudan for secondary education, without there being ready in Somaliland Protectorate comparable educational facilities to replace what was available in Sudan. That haphazard way of making educational policy on the hoof was caused by Nasser's influence in the Arab countries, and Somaliland Protectorate did not escape from that influence.

Reflecting on the effect that the anti-British broadcasts from Cairo might have on the Somaliland people, the protectorate government expressed its opinion in this way:

> *The Somalis were not inherently pro-Egyptians nor anti-British, but the circumstances in the protectorate were putting an almost unbearable strain on the goodwill of the Somali population.*

The protectorate government did not spell out what the "circumstances" were. Perhaps the government had in mind the Somalis being harassed by the Ethiopians in the territories handed over to Ethiopia in 1954.

Throughout the summer of 1956, the Governor of Somaliland Protectorate, Mr Pike, bombarded the Colonial Office with telegrams, urging the Colonial Office to establish BBC Somali Service to counter Nasser's propaganda. The National United Front (NUF) in Somaliland Protectorate also campaigned for such a service, but for a different reason. In the NUF case, the BBC Somali Service would combat the Ethiopian propaganda, which was calling on the Somalis in what used to be called "the Hawd and the Reserved Area" to take Ethiopian nationality.

Eventually, the British Colonial Office was sufficiently concerned about the Cairo broadcasts to Somaliland Protectorate and it turned to the BBC to explore ways and means of countering Nasser's propaganda. In October 1956, a senior official from the Colonial Office wrote to the Colonial Secretary saying, in part:

> *Any danger there was of Somalis falling under the influence of Egypt came not from anything we were doing, but from the Ethiopians' imperial ambitions and the way the Ethiopians were treating the Somalis, particularly in connection with Hawd Agreement.*

However, the British Government was convinced that Nasser was determined to stir popular discontent with the protectorate government. Be that as it may, a decision was finally made to create a service broadcasting in Somali within the BBC. However, within the BBC, a certain amount of politicizing arose. Up to then, it had not been the policy of the BBC to broadcast in the vernacular African languages. The Arabic language was not considered to be a vernacular. Some senior BBC employees raised the issue that, apart from Somali, other African languages should also be considered for broadcasting. After some horse-trading within the BBC, the Swahili and Hausa languages were also selected. That was how the trio languages – Somali, Swahili and Hausa – came to form the BBC African Service.

The BBC man in charge of the process of creating the Somali Service called for a meeting in London, attended by Mr Michael Mariano, Mr Andrzejewski and an unnamed Somali man employed by the British Museum. It was not said whether Michael Mariano was invited from Somaliland Protectorate for the meeting or that he happened to be in London at that time. The question for the meeting was whether there was adequate talent available in London to start up a Somali Service, in advance of the recruitment of full-time broadcasters from Somaliland Protectorate. The conclusion was that there was none. It was then that Radio Hargeisa was prevailed upon to release to the BBC their inimitable broadcaster, Abdi Duale. It was on 18 July 1957 that Abdi Duale broadcast the first transmission, in Somali, of the BBC Somali Service. For some time, the service relied on students from Somaliland Protectorate, who were mainly studying in London, for part-time broadcasting, and the pocket money earned was welcome. The rest is history.

Abdi Duale in the Studio of Radio Hargeisa, around 1956.

Regardless of the purpose for which the BBC Somali Service was created in the first place, there was no doubt that it proved useful. It offered opportunities for well-informed Somalis to discuss, on air, in their mother tongue, topics touching the Somali culture – as well as other subjects. In that respect, it could be said that the service played a role in the general education and information of the Somalis, not only within Somaliland Protectorate, but beyond. It also supplemented Radio Hargeisa Service. In later years, when the State of the Somali Democratic Republic collapsed and the Somalis were scattered in all the four corners of the world, relatives turned to the BBC Somali Service to trace relatives with whom they had lost contact. This relative-tracing social service in the 1990s became a common feature of the broadcasts of the BBC Somali Service.

The downside of the BBC Somali Service, from my perspective, is that it militated against any initiative to develop a credible indigenous broadcasting service which could replace – or at least compete with – the BBC Somali Service. The service is part and parcel of the BBC World Service, funded by the British Commonwealth & Foreign Office and which naturally projects British interests in the wider world. In this respect, the Somali Service also projects the global interests of the British Government.

The BBC World Service (of which the Somali Service is part) is an example of the soft power for influence which I have mentioned in the introduction to Section 3.

Perhaps I am making the BBC Somali Service the scapegoat for the failure of the Somali Governments to institute trustworthy governments which could provide reliable broadcasting services. Until such time as good governance is in place, we will remain stuck with the BBC Somali Service. When not satisfied with its output, some Somalis used to dub it *"Been Been Sideh"*, in English, "Lie Lie Carrier"!

I dwelt somewhat on this item – establishment of the BBC Somali Service – for the benefit of the Somali listeners who may not be aware of the circumstances which led to the creation of the service to which they are so used – or, dare I say, addicted!

Since the creation of the BBC Somali Service in 1957, the mass media, especially in the electronic field, have been advancing in leaps and bounds that the BBC Somali Service is no longer as dominant as it used to be. The service is already competing with Voice of America/Somali.

The irony was that petty politics trumped historical context when, of all locations, the fiftieth anniversary of the BBC Somali Service was celebrated in Nairobi, Kenya, in 2007. End of the BBC story – over and out.

The 1958 annual report on education – the final education annual report [210]

In 1958, imminent independence was the talk of the town and the general mood in the country was euphoric. The protectorate administrators saw this as the writing on the wall for their future in the country! They saw no point in clinging to the high positions they had occupied so far. One by one, they started to look for employment elsewhere. But posts in the colonial service were getting scarcer and scarcer. The march for independence in Africa as a whole was bringing down the curtain on the British Empire, which, in its heyday, boasted itself to be the Empire where the sun never set!

Inevitably, the process of Somalization of the civil service in the country started in earnest. As was apparent in the staffing of the Education Department in 1957, the substitution of Somali teachers for expatriate teachers continued in 1958. Although not named, two Somali teachers were promoted to the positions of Education Officers and two more to Assistant Education Officers.

For the first time, all the intermediate schools for boys in the country were staffed by Somali teachers, except for a few Indians who taught mathematics and science. Also, all the elementary schools had at least one teacher for each class. Because, historically, girls' education lagged far behind boys' education, there were as yet no female Somali teachers and that was why there were still several female European teachers at both the elementary and intermediate schools for girls.

The educational activities of the Department in 1958 were based on what was planned for the 1957–1960 expansion project, already explained.

Under the scheme for Nomadic Betterment, launched in 1955, by 1958 a total of 16 religious teachers were recruited. However, it did not say whether their previous work was evaluated, as planned, to decide whether or not to continue with the scheme.

Nine new elementary and five new intermediate schools for boys, and four new elementary schools for girls, were opened in 1958. The elementary schools for girls were opened in Borama, Hargeisa, Berbera and Burao – the latter was a boarding school and had to cater not only for Burao pupils but also for those from Erigavo and Las Anod. It was not mentioned where in the country the elementary and intermediate schools for boys were built. Two unnamed girls were sent to the UK to study domestic science. The aided *Qur'aanic*/Arabic schools totalled 100, catering for an estimated 1,500 boys and 150 girls.

The Local Government Council of Hargeisa opened the first public library in the country in 1958.

The Director of Education, Mr Thompson, was transferred back to Kenya where he had been before coming to Somaliland Protectorate. Instead of promoting a Somali to the vacancy, C.J.O. Cooper was brought from Tanganyika to fill the post of Director of Education. It could not have been that Mr Cooper chose to go to Somaliland Protectorate to further his colonial career, given the political situation then in the country. More likely, he was approaching the retirement age and was pushed to make room for a younger employee.

Second cohort who graduated from Amud Secondary School, 1958

The class was composed of twelve boys. Their names, courtesy of my friend, Osman (Badow) Hassan, who was a member of the class, and their group photo are below:

Left to right: back row, standing – Ismail Ali Abokor, Mohamoud Ahmed (Alone), Mohamed Abdullahi (Fode-Ade), Suleiman Mohamoud Adan, Said Abdul-Qadir, Osman (Badow) Hassan; front row, sitting – Mohamed Abdullahi (Hah'i), Jama Saleh, Mohamed Ali Shire, Fareh Warsame, Abdullahi Haji Duale (Shakur). Abdi (Tuuhe) Ahmed Osman is missing from the photo [222].

The Class sat for the GCE O-level examinations (London University) in 1958. On grading alone, 11 students qualified for further education in the UK, according to the conditions set for the first cohort in 1957:

- 4 students obtained 8 passes
- 4 students obtained 7 passes
- 2 students obtained 6 passes
- 1 student obtained 5 passes
- 1 student obtained 4 passes
- Total of 12 boys

Those who passed the examination were put through the process to which their predecessors were subjected by the Promotions and Training Board.

The following seven students were selected for further education in the UK: Osman Hassan (Osman-Badow), Suleiman Mohamoud Adan, Mohamoud Abdullahi (Food-Ade), Abdi (Tuuhe) Ahmed Osman, Farah Warsame, Abdillahi Haji Duale (Shakuur) and Said Abdulqadir. Shortly after the seven students left school, they, together with the ten students whose departure to UK was delayed in 1957, were sent to UK in August 1958.

The 1958 annual report on education, dated 1 January 1959, was the final one the protectorate government published on education. However, the expenditure on the protectorate, including that on education for 1959, was published on 1 January 1960. The results of the Intermediate School entrance and the Intermediate School leaving examinations were not published in 1958.

Mr Darlington, who joined the Education Department of the Somaliland Protectorate in August 1949 was still with the department at Independence in June 1960, and he stayed on much longer.

Some statistical details on education in the country at the end of 1958 follow:

Table a: Numbers/descriptions of school, by enrolment and by educational level, 1958

Level of education			Government schools	Local authority schools	Total
Elementary	Enrolment	M	671	1006	1677
		F	221	0	221
		Total	892	1006	1898
	No. of schools		36	13	49
Intermediate	Enrolment	M	856	0	856
		F	58	0	58
		Total	914	0	914
	No. of schools		14	0	14
Secondary	Enrolment	M	81	0	81
		F	0	0	0
		Total	81	0	81
	No. of schools		1	0	1
Teacher Training Centre	Enrolment	M	22	0	22
		F	0	0	0
		Total	22	0	22
	No. of schools		1	0	1
Trades School	Enrolment	M	71	0	71
		F	0	0	0
		Total	71	0	71
	No. of schools		1	0	1

A Brief History of Formal Education in British Somaliland Protectorate

Table b: Teachers in Training, 1958

Description of course	Number of Institutions	Students admitted during 1958			Total students at end of 1958			Students passed final exam.		
		M	F	Total	M	F	Total	M	F	Total
2-Year Local Teacher Training Centre	1	15	0	15	22	0	22	14	0	14
2-Year Certificate Course in U.K.	Training in U.K.	5	0	5	10	0	10	1	0	1
Intermediate Teacher Training in Sudan	1	2	0	2	2	0	2	1	0	1

Table c: Teachers Classified by Qualification, 1958

		Elementary Schools		Intermediate Schools		Secondary Schools		Technical and Vocational		Teacher Training		Total	
		Government or Local Auth		Government		Government		Government		Government			
		M	F	M	F	M	F	M	F	M	F	M	F
Approved Graduates or Equivalent	Trained	0	0	5	0	5	0	1	0	1	0	12**	0
	Untrained	0	0	0	0	0	0	0	0	0	0	0	0
Completed Secondary Course	Trained	1	5*	6	2*	0	0	3	0	2	0	12	7
	Untrained	0	0	1	0	1	0	1	0	1	0	4	0
Not completed Secondary Course	Trained	20	0	20	0	0	0	0	0	0	0	40	0
	Untrained	44	0	20	0	0	0	1	0	0	0	65	0

* One of the female European teachers was at the European children elementary school, Hargeisa, and the rest were at the girls elementary/intermediate schools. ** Includes a Somali university graduate educator (Hassan Adan Gudaal). The Department did not differentiate, by number, the Somali and non-Somali teachers. However, going by qualifications, the number of Somali teachers would be 110. The non-Somali teachers would be 30.

Table d: Expenditure on Education, 1958.

Recurrent expenditure	By Education Department	By Local Authority
Elementary Education	£12,776	£5,276
Intermediate Education	£18,478	-
Secondary Education	£3,878	-
Teacher Training	£3,148	-
Vocational Training	£5,799	-
Administration/unallocated	£8,624	-
Non-recurrent expenditure	£58,242	
Total	£110,945	£5,276
Grand total	£116,221	

It is important to bear in mind that the new elementary schools, especially in the last four years (1955–1958), were opened in a hurry and many of them did not contain more than one or two classes. So, the impressive numbers of the educational facilities could be misleading, particularly when classes per elementary school and numbers per class are considered. The performance of the elementary schools under the Local Authorities was an unknown quantity.

From 1955, the local communities paid for at least 50% and up to 100% of the capital cost of the elementary and intermediate schools built, but the Education Department equipped and ran these schools.

It is doubtful whether the Education Department could, in 1958, fully staff nine new elementary schools for boys; four new elementary schools for girls; five new intermediate schools for boys, even if all these new 18 schools were one class each! The teaching staff must have been hard pressed to cope! Quality in education in the country had been, ostensibly, an article of faith with the protectorate government. It would appear that the government realized that it would not remain long in the country and found that lofty idea was no longer tenable! Quantity became the order of the day. That was what happened when the Government tried to make up for decades of neglect at one fell swoop!

The rushed, haphazard and incomplete implementation of what was planned for 1957–1960 distorted the figures, and I think the expenditure on both the protectorate, as a whole, and on education in particular, were either much less than what the government reported or there must have been a lot of waste!

Since the educational programme began in 1944, the annual expenditure on education had been inflated by the relatively few British teachers who had been drawing relatively large salaries. That situation could not have been avoided, given the severe shortage of adequate number of sufficiently qualified Somali teachers during colonial rule. In 1959, the government published summary of the number of students following higher courses abroad, as shown in the table below:

Students following higher courses abroad, 1959

Course	In the UK	In Aden	In Uganda	In Beirut	In Sudan	In Kenya
Public Administration	27	1	-	-	-	-
Accountancy	6	-	-	-	-	-
Audit	1	-	-	-	-	-
Education	22	-	-	3	6	-
Medical and nursing	17	2	-	-	-	-
Natural resources, eg agriculture, etc	12	-	-	-	-	-
Posts & telecommunications	1	-	-	-	-	2
Public works	11	3	6	-	-	9
Judicial and legal	4	-	-	-	-	-
Total	101	6	6	3	6	11

In 1959, Somalization was being implemented at a fast rate. The limiting factor was the availability of suitably qualified Somalis to fill the posts held by expatriates. The progress of the students listed in the table above, on different courses in different countries, was keenly followed and their return home eagerly awaited. In the Somalization plan, it was envisaged that by 1968 all the students would have completed their courses.

The government educational programme introduced into Somaliland Protectorate in 1944 ended at Independence in 1960. Other financial arrangements were made for the students who were still studying under that programme inside or outside the country. The details of the annual expenditure on the protectorate in the last decade of the protectorate follows:

Table 6: The annual expenditure (in sterling £) on Somaliland Protectorate: 1950 to 1959 [10]

	1950	1951	1952	1953	1954	1955	1956	1957	1958	1959
Local revenues	436,068	518,257	580,296	582,123	701,417	801,440	793,955	996,302	1,165,247	1,300,054
	-32.10%	-32.60%	-37.30%	-41.10%	-48%	(47.9.9%)	-40.50%	-39.30%	-41.20%	-48%
Government subsidies	922,729	1,073,042	975,703	834,943	760,586	872,269	1,164,984	1,541,455	1,661,966	1,408,596
	-67.90%	-67.40%	-62.70%	-58.90%	-52%	-52.10%	-59.50%	-60.70%	-58.80%	52(%)
Annual expenditure	1,358,797	1,591,299	1,555,999	1,417,066	1,462,003	1,673,709	1,958,939	2,537,757	2,827,213	2,708,650
Expenditure on education	31,078	38,215	48,385	50,053	49,865	59,003	83,145	94,066	116,221	127,025
	-2.30%	-2.40%	-3.10%	-3.50%	-3.40%	-3.50%	-4.20%	-3.70%	-4.10%	-4.70%

NB. The annual expenditure of £265,000 on the Somaliland Scouts is added to the annual government subsidies [68].

The state of formal educational facilities, as of 1st January 1959 [217]

I have summarized, in the table opposite, the achievement of British Colonial rule in the field of formal educational facilities and human resource for formal education in Somaliland Protectorate, from 1944 to 1958:

---

10 For expenditure data, see the following references: 1950 [211], 1951–1952 [212], 1953–1954 [213], 1955 [214], 1956–1958 [215], 1959 [216].

A Brief History of Formal Education in British Somaliland Protectorate

Table showing the educational facilities as of 1 January 1959 in Somaliland Protectorate

---

Total number of **teachers**: 140
Somalis = 110
Expatriate = 30

Total number of **elementary schools**: 49
Total enrolment of boys at these schools = 1,677
Total enrolment of girls at these schools = 221
Total = 1,898 boys and girls

Total number of **intermediate schools**: 14
Total enrolment of boys at these schools = 856
Total enrolment of girls at these schools = 58
Total = 914 boys and girls

Total number of **trades schools**: 1
Total enrolment of boys at these schools = 71
Total enrolment of girls at these schools = 0
Total = 71 boys

Total number of **secondary schools**: 1
Total enrolment of boys at these schools = 81
Total enrolment of girls at these schools = 0
Total = 81 boys

Total number of **teacher training centres**: 1
Total enrolment of male trainees at this centre = 22
Total enrolment of female trainees at this centre = 0
Total = 22 male trainees

Grand total enrolment at the above educational facilities = 2,986
- Male = 2,707 or 90.7%
- Female = 279 or 9.3%

There were no Somali female teachers.

Out of the 110 Somali teachers: one was University Degree holder (0.9%); four (3.6%) had secondary education but not teacher training; 40 (36.4%) had teacher training but not secondary education; 65 (59%) had neither teacher training nor secondary education.

The Somali teachers formed 78.6%, the expatriate teachers 21.4%, of the total number of teachers.

Development of formal education in Somaliland Protectorate

The Protectorate Government developed formal education in the country in the shape of a pyramid, with wide base and pointed apex, as I depict in the following figure:

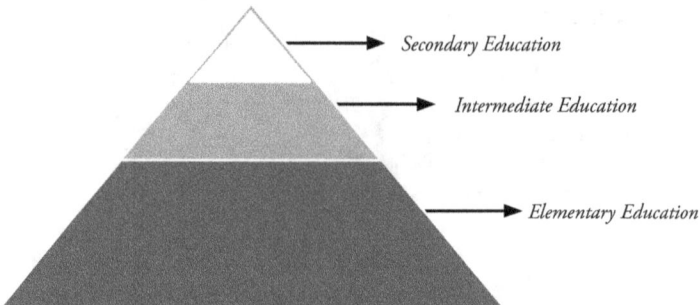

This was deliberately done for economic reasons, so that the service could be run cheaply. The protectorate government specialized in how *not* to develop meaningful facilities for social services in the country. The solitary secondary school was the highest level of educational facility in the country at Independence!

Parliamentary questions on education in Somaliland Protectorate [218]

I insert here exchanges which took place in the British Parliament in March 1959, just after Mr Lennox-Boyd, Secretary of State for the Colonies, returned from his visit to Somaliland Protectorate in February 1959 (see section 3.14). There was a Member of the British Parliament, who was concerned about Somaliland Protectorate, as the independence of the country approached. The following Parliamentary exchanges are quoted from *Hansard* (3 March 1959):

> **Mr Sorenson, MP,** *asked* **Mr Lennox-Boyd,** *the Secretary of State for the Colonies: How many students of British Somaliland are receiving secondary school and university education, respectively, in the United Kingdom, Somaliland, or elsewhere; and what proportion of Somalis are now filling Government administrative posts in British Somaliland?*
>
> **Mr Lennox-Boyd:** *Students receiving secondary education in the United Kingdom, the Somaliland Protectorate and elsewhere number 39, 81 and 26 respectively. There are 12 students at universities in the United Kingdom and 4 elsewhere. A further 42 students are undertaking various courses of higher education and practical training in the United Kingdom. Higher education is not available in the protectorate. All these students are Government sponsored. Eight Somalis hold Government administrative appointments out of a total of 33.*

> **Mr Sorenson, MP** *asked* **Mr Lennox-Boyd**: *Does not the Right Hon. Gentleman feel that the number of students receiving secondary and university education is quite inadequate in view of the very great responsibilities which Somalis will have to exercise next year when they have responsibility for their own Government"?*
>
> **Mr Lennox-Boyd**: *It is certainly not enough, but it is a very great improvement on what it was before.*

The British Government's past neglect of education in the country was laid bare. It was not a glorious day for Mr Lennox-Boyd. It was an embarrassing encounter which Mr Lennox-Boyd could well have done without. No wonder he advanced the date of the country's independence, to bring to an abrupt end to a shameful situation!

When Mr Lennox-Boyd replied "but it is a very great improvement on what it was before," perhaps he meant before the British occupied the country! The answers of Mr Lennox-Boyd were, as usual, supplied by the Governor of Somaliland Protectorate. The governor was careful not to include, in the number of secondary students, those at the Teacher Training Centre. This centre was counted as a secondary school, for local consumption! Perhaps Mr Lennox-Boyd was unaware of this deception.

I also wish, in this connection, to mention that the last Governor of Somaliland Protectorate, D. Hall, did not fare any better in another less demanding situation, quite distinct from parliamentarians raising fiery questions. On 1 December 1960, Mr Hall delivered a lecture entitled, "Somaliland's Last Year as a Protectorate" to a joint meeting of the Royal African and the Royal Commonwealth Societies. The meeting was chaired by his predecessor as Governor of Somaliland Protectorate, Mr Pike.

The following question from the floor was put to the lecturer:

> *What was the percentage literacy in British Somaliland at the time of Independence, and in Somalia at the same time?*

Mr Hall's reply [219] was as follows:

> *I am afraid I must confess myself defeated. I can only say it was a lower percentage than it should have been – we would have liked to have seen it much higher. There is of course a growing number who are literate in Arabic as a result of the religious schools which cover the whole country.*

Because Mr Hall had nothing worthwhile to say about government-funded formal education in the country he, in desperation, cited the private *Qur'aanic/*Arabic schools, as if the British Government introduced them into the country! Perhaps he was ashamed to mention the only secondary school in the country, which he himself officially opened on 15 May 1960, barely 40 days before the country was to become independent!

I earlier commented on how the protectorate governments used the *Qur'aanic* and/or Arabic private schools as a prop for the inadequate government-funded formal education in the country. Since he had practically nothing to say about Somaliland, he wisely thought better of it and did not reply to the part of the question related to Somalia! The chairman of the meeting, Mr Pike, must have been uncomfortably wriggling in his chair in embarrassment, as he himself governed, for over five years, the country which landed his successor in such a humiliating situation!

The new secondary school at Sheikh [220]

I wish to explore a little further how the new secondary school at Sheikh fared. The British Government bequeathed to Somaliland one secondary school. I have earlier described the political circumstances which led to the shambolic way the protectorate government started secondary education in the country.

In 1954, the government closed down the VTC at Amud. The one-class secondary school at Sheikh, in its second year, moved to Amud to occupy the buildings vacated by the VTC. Mr Darlington, who was running the VTC, remained at Amud and became the principal of the secondary school. It was soon realized that the buildings were inadequate for a secondary school. Also, since the school had to cater for the whole Somaliland Protectorate, it was essential that it was a boarding school and centrally located.

In 1956, the Adviser of the Colonial Office on education, Mr C. Cox, visited Somaliland Protectorate. During his visit it was decided to build a new purpose-built secondary school. That was why a new secondary school was included in the education expansion plan (1957 to March 1960), which has already been described. The question then was where to build it. There were two candidate sites to choose from: Sheikh or Mandera. Each site had its own proponents. In the minds of many people in Somaliland Protectorate, Sheikh was associated with knowledge and enlightenment. In the end, Sheikh was chosen. I don't know whether the fact that the main jail for long-term convicted criminals was, and still is, situated in Mandera counted against that site!

Just as the construction of the school started, the Duke of Gloucester arrived in the country. Perhaps it was the turn of a member of the British Royal Family to find out what was being done in the protectorate, in the name of the monarch. The Duke visited the protectorate in the twilight of its existence in November 1958. Among other activities, the Duke unveiled a plague on one of the incomplete walls of the school.

Early in March 1960, the school was ready for use and the students in Amud Secondary School were brought to the new secondary school at Sheikh. The school cost £142,760 [221] to build and equip. The last governor of the protectorate, Mr Hall, officially opened it on 15 May 1960, in the presence of the Prime Minister-elect, Mohamed Haji Ibrahim Egal, and the Minister of Education, Ali Garaad Jama. That was just about six weeks before the country became independent on 26 June 1960.

Sheikh Secondary School in 1960, showing mosque with curved roof

A recent view of Sheikh Secondary School since it was reopened in 2003

Top: The original secondary school, officially opened on 15 May 1960. Bottom: After it was rebuilt by the Agency "SOS" in 2003 [222].

The routine of the school was a continuation of what had been followed in Amud. The practice of the students to sit for the GCE O-level, London University, continued even after Independence. Before Independence, the late Qalib Musa was among the first Class with which the secondary school was started at Sheikh in 1953. He was among the successful students in the 1957 GCE O-level examination. While some of the successful students were sent on government scholarships to the UK, Qalib Musa was sent on government scholarships to Beirut University, Lebanon, where he obtained a degree (majoring in Arabic) and returned to the country to teach Arabic in the Sheikh Secondary School, as did Hassan Adan Gudaal before him, as already described.

As the number of students increased, Mr Darlington wanted to concentrate more on the teaching side and, in September 1963, Qalib Musa assumed more administrative responsibilities and, appropriately, became the Principal of the School. Apart from Qalib Musa and Mr Darlington, the other senior teachers included Mr Fieller who taught English, Mr McKinley who taught History and Geography, Mr Daniel (Indian) who taught Biology, Mr Elias (Indian) who taught Science and an unnamed Indian who taught Mathematics.

After the Military coup d'état of 21 October 1969 in the country, the local Commander at Sheikh became interested in what was going on and what was being said in the school. As the late Mr Darlington put it, "it became clear that the emphasis in education was to be on what to think rather than how to think."

The teaching services of Mr McKinley were crucial in preparing the students for the GCE examinations. In May 1971, the Military Government declined to renew the contract of Mr McKinley. Mr Darlington felt that time was up for him too and resigned in sympathy with his colleague, Mr McKinley. Mr Fieller who used to teach English also left.

The Government abandoned the GCE O-level examinations (London University) at the end of 1971. At Amud Secondary School in 1957, of the 16 students who sat for seven subjects in the GCE O-level examination (London University), 14 (88%) passed in five subjects or more. In 1971, the final year for taking the GCE O-level (London University), this time at Sheikh Secondary School, 53 students sat for an average of eight subjects and 37 (70%) passed in five subjects or more. Perhaps the number of the teaching staff did not keep pace with the increase in the number of students, which might explain the drop in the percentage passes. Other factors might also have accounted for the drop.

R.R. Darlington described how it came about for him to become a teacher in Somaliland Protectorate. He first came into contact with the people of Somaliland when he joined the 1st Somali Battalion of the King's African Rifles, who were taken to Burma in 1943 to fight the Japanese in World War II. In 1945, he returned with the Somali Battalion to Berbera where it was disbanded. He was transferred to the British Military Administration in Somaliland Protectorate and, as Civil Affairs Officer, was stationed in Gigjiga. It was not long before he was demobbed. He returned to Cambridge University to complete his degree course, which was interrupted by the war. Instead of his previous subject (Classics), he read Geography. Perhaps his exposure to Africa and Asia influenced his choice of subject. He then joined the Colonial Service and joined the Education Department of Somaliland Protectorate in August 1949. After 22 years of his working life spent in the service of educating the Somalis, Mr Darlington left Sheikh Secondary School and Somalia in May 1971, thus becoming the longest-serving British educator in Somaliland Protectorate and later in Somalia. Mr Darlington (*Ga'ma-dheere,* to his students) was a dedicated educator. I think his students, myself included, will agree with me that he had the educational interests of the people of Somaliland at heart.

The following details (with some remarks of mine) are based on an unpublished document by Mr Darlington [222]:

British scholarships to Somali students from Amud and Sheikh Secondary Schools, 1957–1970:

Year	Number of scholarships
1957	10
1958	7
1959	10
1960	10
1968	10
1969	10
1970	12

At Independence in June 1960, Somaliland joined Somalia and ceased to be a member of the Commonwealth, and British scholarships for Somaliland stopped. In March 1963, the Somali Republic broke diplomatic relations with the UK. The relations were restored in October 1967. British scholarships to Somali students from the secondary schools were reinstated (see table above).

In 1971, the Government of Siyad Barre abandoned the GCE O-level examination of London University. By terminating the contract of the British teacher, Mr McKinley, and precipitating the resignation of the Principal of the Secondary School, Mr Darlington, badly-needed scholarships were unnecessarily lost. The ideology-driven regime of Siyad Barre cut off its nose to spite its face! However, since the GCE O-level examinations from London University were stopped in 1971, perhaps the departure of the British educators was inevitable.

The following information about Darlington's legacy was kindly given to me by Eid Ali Ahmed, Member of the Trustee Board of the R.R. Darlington (*Gacma-dheere*) Foundation:

Darlington's legacy

Mr Darlington's commitment to the educational development in Somaliland was expressed in a practical way. The trustees who administer Darlington's estate have established two different scholarships, under the R.R. Darlington (*Gacma-dheere*) Foundation:

- **Local scholarships**: Somalilander students who complete their intermediate education in the intermediate schools in Somaliland compete, each year, for about eight places (scholarships) in the secondary schools in Somaliland.
- **Scholarship abroad**: Somalilander students who have completed their university education in the universities in Somaliland compete, each year, for

one postgraduate place (scholarship) in Cambridge University, UK, to follow a postgraduate course of his/her choice.

Photo of the late Mr R.R. Darlington, Principal of Sheikh Secondary School, with his usual pipe. I couldn't find a photo of the late Qalib Musa who succeeded Mr Darlington as Principal. (Photo from *Journal of the Anglo-Somali Society*, No. 42, 2007. Reproduced with permission.)

Darlington retired to Wales. He died, aged 88 years, on 7 April 2007. His obituary written by Mr Richard Sills is in the *Journal of the Anglo-Somali Society*, No. 42, 2007.

4.10 The published annual expenditure on the protectorate: 1900–1960

I have summarized the annual expenditure on Somaliland Protectorate for the period 1900–1959 (where annual expenditure data was available) in the Tables 1–6, on pages 145–318. As far as I could ascertain, no annual expenditure on Somaliland Protectorate was published before 1900. However, the British Government started to raise local revenues from 1884, when the government occupied the Somaliland Coast [6]. It would appear that, before 1900, they used the collected revenues for the expenditure on their offices in Zeila, Bulahar and Berbera. The expenditure on Somaliland Protectorate was mainly on maintaining law and order, the salaries of the British administrators and the Indian civil servants of the government.

It was not easy to compile the annual expenditure on the protectorate. The government used different methods of reporting the annual expenditure at different periods from 1900. For example, at different stages, it reported the expenditure quarterly, six-monthly or yearly. Again, in certain cases the same annual expenditure was recorded in different documents with some slight discrepancies. Bookkeeping was rather sloppy, especially when the documents were hand-written. Anyway, despite my brief remarks, I tried to document the information available to me as objectively and carefully as I could.

As already pointed out, British colonial policy was that the colonies would raise sufficient local revenue to cover the expenditure on the administration of the colony or the protectorate concerned. In this and other aspects, British colonialism represented a dark phase in the human history.

In Table 7 below, I further consolidated the contents of tables 1–6, on 10-yearly basis.

I also added the expenditure on the protectorate for the last nine months of April-December 1960. For further details of this expenditure, see 3.14.

Table 7: Available expenditure (in sterling £) on Somaliland Protectorate: 1900–1960

	1900-1909	1910-1919	1920-1929	1930-1939	1940-1949	1950-1959	April-Dec.1960	Grand Total	% of total Exp.
Local Revenues	319,458	395,511	966,986	1,450,552	2,775,145	7,875,159	652,663	14,435,474	39.3%
Govt. Subsidies	3,094,888	771,773	990,072	473,354	5,077,478	11,216,273	640,000	22,263,838	60.7%
Total Expenditure.	3,414,346†	1,167,284	1,957,058	1,923,906	7,852,623	19,091,432	1,292,663*	36,699,312	100%
Expenditure on Education	788	1,369	2,393	9,099	109,186	697,056	70,983^ + 142,760** = 213,743	819,891 +213,743 = 1,033,634	2.8%

† Includes £2,450,100 on the campaigns against the Dervishes (1901–1904) [see 3.4].
*Includes £265,000: annual expenditure on Somaliland Scouts, as do the annual expenditure for 1940–1960, explained earlier. ^Expenditure on education for the period April–Dec 1960. **Cost of building the new secondary school at Sheikh, published on 25 June 1960 [221].

The final cost of the new secondary school at Sheikh was communicated to the Somaliland Protectorate Government by the Colonial Office on 25 June 1960, just one day before Independence Day. The cost included teachers' quarters and science equipment. The cost was a big one-off expenditure on education, accounting for 13.8% of the total expenditure (£1,033,634) on education from 1900 to 1960. It is what the statistician calls an "outlier", and the law of averages will take care of it. Sure, this costly item grossly distorted the expenditure on education for the period April to December 1960. The building of a secondary school for the country was first recommended in 1952. It was in gestation all that time. Its final cost became available in the *dying day* of the protectorate! Since government policy was not to develop the country, whenever the local revenue increased, the government subsidy was proportionately decreased [75].

I was in two minds about including some already mentioned expenditure items which, in the end, I have reluctantly left in. The expenditures, shown below, did not confer any benefits whatsoever on the people of Somaliland:

- Expenditure of £2,450,100 on the campaigns against the Dervishes, 1901–1904
- Expenditure of £84,000 on air/land campaigns against the Dervishes in 1920
- Expenditure of £500 on burning down Burao in March 1922 (for Gibb's murder in Burao)

These expenditures included locally raised revenues, without any form of social service to the people of Somaliland. Instead, harm was done to the people in incurring these expenditures. Before the military protectorate government (1941–1948), the protectorate government hardly provided any social services in the country.

With reference to Table 7, the protectorate government used to say that the country was run on British taxpayers' money. It was true that the grand total of government subsidies compared with the grand total of the local revenues was in the ratio of about three to two. But the government usually failed to mention the local revenues. The Somaliland public, predominantly nomadic and not privy to the financial policies of the country, believed that the British Government alone was wholly financing the country. However, the expenditure published by the protectorate government and summarized in Table 7 did not bear out the impression created by the protectorate government.

In this regard, because of the protectorate government's mantra that the country was run and maintained at the expense of the British taxpayers' money, a Somali member of the Local Authority was quoted as telling the government that:

> *If a coffee shop doesn't pay its way, we close it. If the Government is running Somaliland at a loss, why shouldn't the Government leave the country?*

I do not know whether the protectorate government ever responded to that unexpected question! The important thing was: what was done with the money? The greater part of the expenditure was on law and order maintenance and administration. The salaries of the British administrators and the Indian civil servants absorbed a good percentage of the annual expenditure. What was termed as "law and order maintenance" was represented by the Somaliland Camel Corps (later the Somaliland Scouts), the Somaliland Police Force and the *Ilaalo*. Together, these forces accounted for the greater share of the annual expenditure – sometimes up to 60–65%. These forces functioned, more or less, as the "private army" of the governor and they were mainly used for swooping down on recalcitrant clans and looting their stock, which had to be auctioned. These forces were tools for executing the unjust collective punishment, based on the abhorrent *Xeer*.

One hardly saw a policeman on the beat in the streets of the towns. The style of training the police dated back to the beginnings of the struggle of the Dervishes and was not dissimilar to that of the army training.

The expenditure was practically devoid of meaningful developmental schemes, except the limited educational programme which was introduced in 1944 and lasted 16 years. Medical care at the headquarters of the districts was slightly improved – but no water resources, roads, or other infrastructure were developed.

The limited formal education of the country was geared to the needs of the limited administration of the country. Employment opportunities outside the government services were rare. At Independence, formal education in the country was at a rudimentary stage.

4.11 Epilogue

I wish to conclude my brief survey of formal education in British Somaliland Protectorate with a few general observations about what, on the whole, is presented in the book. The summary in Ref. 217 encapsulates the sum total of the types of the educational facilities and enrolment at each type of establishment, as of 1 January 1959, just 18 months before the British rule in Somaliland was to come to an end.

The situation of educational facilities was not much different on 26 June 1960, when the country became independent. At Independence, there were only two Somalis in the country who held university degrees – namely the late Ahmed (Kaise) Haji Duale and Hassan Adan Gudaal. There were no qualified nurses or doctors in the country.

At Independence, there were many fields for which no suitably qualified Somali replacements were available – for example, Female Education, Health Department, Finance Department, Audit Department, Attorney General's Department, Judicial Department, and Posts & Telegraphs Department. There may well have been other fields in a similar situation.

At Independence on 26 June 1960, the highest level of educational institution in the country was a single secondary school for boys which had opened seven years before, in 1953, and was for the whole country. From 1953 to 1957, for which figures are available, the yearly intake, respectively, was as follows: 16, 13, 15, 20 and 21. This was a damning testament to the formal educational legacy left by the British Government for Somaliland. And it took the British Government 76 years of occupation to achieve that dismal level of formal education in the country. Not a legacy to look back on with pride, as evidenced by the replies of the Secretary of State for the Colonies, Mr Lennox-Boyd, and the last governor of Somaliland Protectorate, Sir Douglas Hall, both quoted earlier [218, 219].

Overview of formal education in Somaliland Protectorate

I would like now to recapitulate briefly the underwhelming short history of formal education in Somaliland Protectorate.

The protectorate government mistook the people of Somaliland for pagan savages without religion and misguidedly allowed a Christian Catholic mission to open a small school in Berbera in 1894 (although negotiations for establishing the mission school started in 1891). The mission wrote the Somali language in Roman script, so that the children converted into Christianity could read the Bible in Somali. The mission extended its missionary work to the interior in the Dhaymole area, about 30 miles south of Berbera.

Later, trading Arabs in the coastal towns of Zeila, Bulahar and Berbera opened small private elementary schools in each of these towns. The *Qur'aan*, a little Arabic and arithmetic (in Arabic) were taught in these schools. The protectorate government subsidized these private schools.

The mission school was closed down in 1910 – but not before triggering off the struggle of Seyyid Mohamed Abdullah Hassan and his Dervishes, as well as being prejudicial to the future development of formal education in the country. The protectorate government was severely criticized for allowing the Christian mission into the country by the two-man fact-finding team, sent by the Colonial Office in 1909, to advise on the future of the country (see 3.4). By 1920, only the Berbera School remained open. Six boys, including Mohamoud Ahmed Ali, who studied in Berbera, were sent to Sudan for education in December 1919 (see 4.1).

In 1920, the protectorate government engaged Mr Hussey from Sudan, to advise on education for Somaliland. He recommended limited elementary education to be started in the country, and the medium of instruction was to be in English. He also proposed direct taxation on the livestock to pay for the education.

Governor Archer tried to introduce the proposed taxation in 1922, but the Somalis, who were the nomads to be taxed, objected to it as the concept of direct taxation was alien to the Somalis. The governor's attempt at taxation resulted in the murder of the District Commissioner of Burao, Mr Gibb. Collective punishment of 3,000 camels was imposed on the clan accused of the murder and Burao was burnt to the ground (see 3.5). With regard to education, the protectorate government adopted a position tantamount to "no education without taxation", and indeed no other development, for that matter.

In 1937, the idea of elementary education in the country was revived and a new government elementary school was built in Berbera. Then the search for a British Superintendent of Education started. R.E. Ellison, who was in the educational services of Nigeria, was appointed as Director of Education in April 1938, with his Christianity baggage and supporter of writing the Somali language in Latin script.

As already explained under 4.2, British Colonial policy for Colonial Tropical Africa was predicated on the following three cardinal tenets:

- Admission of Christian missions into a British colony or protectorate
- Writing the local vernacular (local language)
- Raising sufficient local revenue, through direct taxation and other means, to cover the expenditure on running the country

The people of Somaliland rejected Christian missions, the Somali language to be written in Latin script, and direct taxation. It must be restated that it was the written Somali, as distinct from formal education, that the Somalis objected to. It was largely the insensitive way the protectorate government introduced formal education into the country that muddied the waters (*vide* the mission school in

Berbera). The Somalis were under the strong impression that written Somali would lead to the Bible being translated into Somali and Christianity being imposed on the people, as happened in some African countries.

The old Berbera elementary school was closed in June 1938. With difficulty, the new elementary school built in 1937 was opened with the pupils of the old school and a few additional boys in December 1938. The school functioned for two terms only and was closed in May 1940, because of World War II. The staff of the school was composed of: R.E. Ellison, Director of the Education Department; Mohamoud Ahmed Ali, Headmaster; and the teachers, Hassan Dhoore Fareh and Haji Hussein Haji Duale.

The protectorate government evacuated the country in August 1940, following the Italian occupation of the country in August 1940. The British Government reoccupied the country from Italy in March 1941 and established a military protectorate government in the country.

In 1942, five Somali teachers, trained in Sudan and led by Mohamoud Ahmed Ali, opened three elementary schools, one in each of the three towns of Hargeisa, Berber and Burao. The other teachers were Yusuf Haji Adan, Mohamed Shidre, Abdi-Salam Hassan Mursal and Yusuf Ismail Samater. They were, in effect, running a mini Education Department, in all but name. The military government (1941–1948) recruited C.R.V. Bell as Director of Education in December 1943 and the government introduced an educational programme in 1944. The government built a few elementary schools in the Districts and boarding elementary and primary schools at Sheikh. Teachers' training and adult courses were also conducted at Sheikh. A few boys, who completed intermediate schooling, were sent to Sudan for either secondary education or for teacher training course for elementary school Arabic teachers. Very few trained Somali teachers were then available.

However, it was to the credit of the few dedicated Somali teachers who, despite academic limitations and material scarcities, effectively turned the limited educational programme, introduced in 1944, into a credible educational service for the very few who benefited from it. The effective contribution of the few British and Sudanese teachers must also be acknowledged. These expatriate educators brought with them expertise in education and thus helped in building up, from scratch, the educational system in the country and not only trained but also professionally guided the young Somali teachers.

Little did we then realize how amazing it was for a young Somali teacher, with intermediate education and perhaps a two-year teacher training course locally, confidently running, as a Headmaster, a three-class elementary school far away from the headquarters of the Education Department at Sheikh! The secret that enabled young Somali teachers to assume such onerous responsibilities was that the Education Department built into the educational system three important elements which were conducive to self-improvement and which kept up the morale and interest of the young Somali teachers and maintained the standard of their teaching skills. The three elements were regular supervision, annual refresher courses and planned promotion through departmental examinations. There was thus a clearly structured career for the young Somali would-be teacher. The supervision was mainly carried out by the senior staff of the Education Department, especially the Inspector of Elementary Schools (Mohamoud Ahmed Ali, later Yusuf Haji Adan), the Director of the Education Department (Mr Bell) and the Principal of Sheikh School (Mr Badham). Mohamoud Ahmed, more than any other, shouldered the greater part of the supervisory activities.

The supervision was not just an inspection, but an educational component of ongoing in-service training for the young Somali teachers. It was, to a large extent, that type of supervisory support that sustained the spirit of the young teachers who manned the far-flung network (from Las Qorey to Zeila) of the few educational facilities in the protectorate. The Somali teachers, knowing that they had to pass departmental examinations to improve their lot, tried hard to study, although reading material was not particularly plentiful in the country at that time. They had no access to libraries or bookshops.

The civil protectorate government (1949–1960), which succeeded the military protectorate government, rather than further develop and expand the educational programme horizontally as well as vertically, used spurious excuses of lack of funds and dragged its feet on formulating clear policy for substantially advancing formal education in the country. The government made too much of the grant-aided private *Qur'aanic* and/or Arabic schools, to draw attention away from the severe shortage of government-funded educational services.

The government introduced girls' education and built more elementary and intermediate schools. A vocational/teacher training centre, trades school and a secondary school for boys were also built. A few boys were sent to Sudan for training as Arabic teachers. Senior Somali clerks were also sent to Sudan to study public administration. In the late 1950s, more students, young and old, on different courses – some of them destined for university education – were sent to the UK.

However, it cannot be said that the government did anything like enough, and the dismal results of this tardy progress in educational development in the country are summarized in Ref. 217. The last full annual report on education was published in 1958. The annual expenditure on education for 1959 formed part of the annual expenditure on the protectorate for 1959 (Table 6), but no annual report on education for 1959 was published.

The 1944 educational programme, limited though it was in scope and despite my criticism of it, was nevertheless not without merit. Those who completed intermediate education were well-grounded in basic education. The small number of boys who had their secondary education in the protectorate, under the 1944 educational programme, did very well, as shown by their results quoted in this book. Also, some of those who attended the male adult courses became very good educators. In short, the educational programme fulfilled, more or less, what it set out to achieve, which was not all that ambitious. The protectorate government itself summed up the dire situation in which the education in the country was when, in 1945, Governor Fisher made the following statement: "The first step in developing education in the country is aimed at raising the schools to a level comparable with a nominal African territory about 1930s" [178]. If that was the assessment of the government on formal education in the country, what more could be said about it?

However, and at least from my perspective, there was a socially positive by-product, perhaps not fully appreciated, which resulted from the educational programme of 1944. Children of different circumstances were brought together in the schools and they interacted with each other. This was especially so at the boarding schools in which children representing all the districts in the country were brought together. Impressionable young boys and girls in their formative years, who before had no prospect of meeting each other, were brought together in one place to learn and live together. This gave the boys as well as the girls the opportunity to get to know each other and make friends among themselves. This also weakened clan sensitivities to a large extent and fostered *esprit de corps* among the young boys as well as among the young girls.

It ought to be pointed out that there was at that time no co-education in the formal education in the country. These boarding and non-boarding schools in the country produced cohorts of ex-schoolboys and girls who, in some cases, maintained long-lasting friendships. The civic spirit of some ex-schoolboys was displayed in 1954 when a few of them joined forces and ran evening classes in Hargeisa for male adult literacy in English.

I leave formal education here, and move on to make a few general remarks about the colonial government's lack of interest in the country.

Overall picture of colonial experience in Somaliland

It was not only in education that the country lacked development, it was the whole gamut of the socio-economic sectors of the country. Rather than develop the country, the British Government looked for ways and means of getting rid of it altogether. Various proposals were mooted, at different stages in the history of the protectorate, to effect the abandonment of the country. It was during the great depression in the 1930s that the government seriously put into concrete form possible methods of the disposal of the country. These ways were spelt out in 1931, as described under 3.6 and they are repeated here:

- For the government to remain in the coastal strip, ie Zeila, Bulahar, Berbera and Las Qorey, and not bother with the rest of the country

- To amalgamate the country with Aden, to effect some economy, by running one instead of two countries
- To cede the country to Ethiopia or Italy
- To put the country under the mandate of the League of Nations
- To dispose of the country in the most profitable market
- To introduce a forward development policy and possibly annex the country at some future date
- To administer the country at minimum cost and without meaningful development – called the "Stagnation Policy"

Out of the above list of options, the government implemented the last one and stuck with it right up to when the country became independent. In the eyes of the British Government, Somaliland was an albatross around its neck! In World War II, the government concluded that Somaliland was not worth defending and abandoned the country, allowing Fascist Italy to walk in.

Having read and/or heard some of what the people of Somaliland Protectorate used to ask the government to do for the country and the government responses, one would be forgiven for gaining the distinct impression that the Somalis and the protectorate government were all along talking at cross purposes! The Somalis expected, understandably, that the protectorate government, having occupied the country by force and by stealth (*vide* the fraudulent treaties), would make something of the country, invest in it and develop the socio-economic life of the people – but not a bit of it!

What the people of Somaliland, as a whole, did not realize was why the British government occupied the country in the first place. It had some ulterior motives in occupying the country. My views of these ulterior motives of why the British government colonized different countries are mentioned in the introduction to Section 3 and are repeated below:

- To find in the colonized country natural resources for their own exploitation
- To ascertain the suitability of a country for British settlers
- To find the possibility of profitable investment and trade in a country
- To find markets for British manufactured goods
- To spread Christianity
- To spread its culture, especially the English language as "soft power" for influence, as fronted by the British Council. (The BBC World Service, funded by the Foreign and Commonwealth Department, can be considered as part and parcel of that "soft power")

- To enhance its global presence/power, and for strategic considerations
- Other…

If the objectives of the colonial government were as stated above, then one would not have expected the government to develop the country for the Somalis; and that was what had happened. But why was that? When all is said and done, the answer, in my view, mainly boils down to a combination of the following factors already mentioned, in one form or another, in the body of the book but brought together and repeated below:

1. From the start, the British Government was only interested in the occupation of the coastal strip of the country for strategic reasons. The government later extended its presence into the hinterland to suppress the Dervishes and also to search for resources for exploitation.
2. The government conducted several surveys for minerals and other natural resources that could be exploited, but failed to find any. It is a matter of conjecture whether the government did not then possess the material and technical know-how for what they were looking for, or whether such resources were not there in the first place, or whether they kept quiet about their findings for strategic reasons. Anyway, the protectorate government was disappointed when its hopes for its searches and expectations regarding natural resources were dashed.
3. The poor and the small population size of the country would not provide sufficient market for British manufactured goods nor for profitable British investment. With such apparent lack of natural resources, coupled with the harsh conditions in the country, and without the requisite social amenities for Europeans, the protectorate government concluded that the country was not fit for British settlers. Lord Delamere reached similar conclusion in 1896 and he moved from Hargeisa to Kenya, where he exploited the virgin land there. Some of his family still have holdings in Kenya (see 3.3). For Somaliland, lack of creature comforts for European settlers was, perhaps, a blessing in disguise!
4. The Somalis rejected Christian missions, written Somali and direct taxation on their stock – not only that, but they also became suspicious of any government measures. It would appear that the government took the Somali rejection of the pillars of British colonial policy as a signal for the government not to venture on development in the country, and thus the government practically abandoned any idea of development in the country. On at least two occasions in the 1940s and 1950s, the protectorate government recruited taxation experts to advise on direct taxation in the country. On both occasions, the recommendations of the experts were that direct taxation was not appropriate in the situation pertaining in Somaliland Protectorate. Of course, to run a

country, it is normal to raise local revenue through taxation and other legitimate means. However, colonialism was an abnormal phenomenon, based on humans subjugating fellow humans. The subjugated Somalis rejected direct taxation which would otherwise have been a normal practice. But, perhaps, what the Somalis were rejecting, subconsciously, was the colonial system itself, using taxation as a proxy for colonial rule – a system which they were subjected to and which controlled their lives, without they having a say in the system! The history of colonialism was one on dehumanization.

5. Also the Somalis realized how the British Government dishonoured the treaties with the Somali clans, by giving away, secretly, to Ethiopia a vast swathe of the pasture and the agricultural land of Somaliland, which the British Government promised to protect. This further added to the Somalis' mistrust of the government.

6. The British Government concluded early on that Somaliland was a huge drain on the British Treasury, bringing in nothing in return. In line with this negative attitude, the protectorate government of the country was provided by a small number of colonial administrators, acting without vision and according to a "no development default policy" – which was a peculiar situation in the British Empire. Somaliland remained in the British Empire, while it lasted, on sufferance! It was mainly due to the factors outlined above that the British Government neglected the development of the country. As if to endorse needlessly the lack of development in the country, the British Government dubbed Somaliland the Cinderella of the British Empire!

Appendix
Keeping clanism at bay

This item is outside the scope of what the book is about. However, while I have this opportunity, I wish to express some personal views on certain social issues which pertain to our Somalilander society, and to share my views on it. The issues I have in mind are clanism, *Xaq* (compensation for injury or murder, as we practise it), *Xeer* (our Customary Law) – and their socially undesirable ramifications, especially how clanism, which is the "mother" of so many evils, poisoned our social interactions and national politics. I consider the words "clan" and "tribe" to be interchangeable, but I prefer to use the word "clan".

In this connection, it may be of interest to mention here how, in 1958, nine students from British Somaliland Protectorate, including myself, who were at that time studying in the UK, saw *Xaq* and *Xeer* as practised in our society. We were aware of why our forefathers adopted *Xaq* and *Xeer* in the first place, well before the British Government occupied the country. There was then no central authority of any kind in the country that could unite the people and provide security for them. It can be said that the law of the jungle prevailed in the country at that time. The way I see it is that the people of Somaliland realized, out of necessity, that there was safety in numbers and they formed themselves into closely related groupings (clan affiliations) for collective security. They adopted *Xaq* and *Xeer* for the regulation of their affiliations. *Xeer* was not, as far as I know, imposed on the Somalis from outside. It was a Somalis' invention in a unique period in the history of the country.

But that period is long gone. The situation since changed. A colonial government imposed control over the country and, by treaties with the clans, promised to "protect" the people and the land of Somaliland. Hence the name: "British Somaliland Protectorate". It was in that context that we, the students mentioned above, came to the conclusion that we could not in good conscience support *Xaq* and *Xeer* which had been helping to bolster destructive clanism in our society. We took the view that *Xaq* and *Xeer* were inimical to social progress in our society. We had the courage of our conviction by dissociating ourselves from our erstwhile clans. We conveyed our collective decision to the protectorate government and to the relevant Clan Chiefs in a letter dated 12 August 1958, signed by all the nine of us. Our position was that the Somalis should be individually responsible for their actions. I have my copy of that letter and a scan of it is shown overleaf.

> BRITISH COUNCIL RESIDENCE?
> 1, Hans Crescent, Knightsbridge,
> London, S.W.1
> 12th August, 1958.
>
> The Hon'ble Chief Secretary to the Govt.,
> Hargeisa, Somaliland Protectorate.
>
> Sir,
>
> Whereas the Haq and Heer as practised in Somaliland are inconsistent with the spirit of the Islamic religion, and contrary to the conscience of any good moslem and repugnant to natural justice;
> Whereas the Haq and Heer are the fundamental cause of all the ill-feelings and communal hatred so widely spread amongst the Somali nation
> Whereas the Haq and Heer are the main obstacle to any progress in the Protectorate;
> And whereas they work to the detriment of establishing any democratic Government or introducing any democratic principles;
> We, the undersigned persons hereby declare that, with effect from the 12th August, 1958, we disassociate ourselves from our previous individual tribes and shall no longer belong to any others and hence from the aforesaid date we are no longer bound by the Heer and we, therefore, shall neither receive nor pay any Haq contrary to the spirit of the Islamic religion.
> We individually hold ourselves responsible for any offence we may commit, while we look to the Government, as ordinary citizens of the Somaliland Protectorate, for the protection of life and property to which any law-abiding citizen is entitled.
> We are giving copies to our previous Akils just for notification and their possible disapproval will in no way affect our decision.
>
> We are, Sir,
> Your most obedient servants,

Letter to the Government of the British Somaliland Protectorate, signed by nine students (incl. the author) disassociating themselves from their previous clans or tribes, 12 August 1958.

This meant that, for a start, we would neither contribute to nor receive a share of *mag* (*dia* or compensation) for injury or murder. I have never divulged to any person the names of the other students or the Clan Chiefs concerned. Also, in deference to the other signatories – some of them sadly no longer alive – I withheld their names from the scanned letter, as well as the list of the Clan Chiefs to whom the letter was copied. It would have been improper for me to disclose the names of the other signatories or the identities of the Clan Chiefs concerned, without their prior consent. I doubt whether any of the Clan Chiefs are alive today. I am using "Clan Chiefs" for the collective name of *Aqils, Suldaans, Garaads, Boqors, Ugaas* and their ilk.

In this regard, it is worth pointing out how, as far as I am aware, the word *Aqil* came to be used in Somaliland. When the Khedive of Egypt (on behalf of the Ottoman Empire) occupied the Somaliland Coast (Zeila, Bulahar and Berbera) in 1874, the occupying Egyptians appointed a few Somalis who would act as intermediaries between them and the Somalis in the Coastal areas. They called these appointees *Aqils,* and the word is Arabic in origin [223] and roughly means "wise man". The *Aqils* were appointed on clan basis. I do not know if there had ever been a Somali word equivalent to *Aqil* before the Egyptian occupation. The Protectorate Government of Somaliland further expanded the *Aqil* system and used the *Aqils* for the implementation of government measures related to the clans – sort of primitive imitation of *indirect rule!* The protectorate government maintained that the introduction of the *Aqils,* who became government agents, diminished the influence of the traditional Clan Chiefs, namely the *Suldaan, Boqor, Graad* and *Ugaas.*

As for me, whatever clanism baggage I carried with me was lost when I was enrolled into Sheikh Boarding Elementary School in 1944. This was especially so when I was first made monitor of the Class I was in, and later Head Prefect of Sheikh School in 1951. I had to try my best to deal with the students fairly and without prejudice. These responsibilities, early in my life, taught me something about impartiality.

Collaborating with my fellow students in 1958 on anti-clanism and anti-*Xaq/Xeer*, further reinforced my determination to live by the convictions expressed in the letter reproduced here. When this book comes out, those who read this Appendix and happen to be among those who appended their names to the letter will, after serious soul-searching, determine to what extent they have been conducting themselves according to what they themselves had committed to. It is a matter of great regret that, 64 years after the above letter was written, clanism still plagues our society. The pernicious influence of clanism is still with us.

The protectorate government created districts in the country in 1927 – the five Districts of Zeila, Hargeisa, Berbera, Burao and Erigavo [35]. Las Anod District was created in 1944 from part of Burao District [70]. All the districts so created were clan-based. As described below, the Somaliland governments since 1991 should not have been aping the defunct protectorate government, by adopting the policy of creating clan-based regions and districts. This clan-based, short-sighted and ill-defined divisions helps to further perpetuate the socially and culturally damaging phenomenon, which clanism is. Clan-based administrative divisions will have negative unintended consequences. It is bound to sow the seeds of friction between communities which hitherto have been living together in peace and harmony. Some clans may even claim *de facto* ownership of certain districts and/or regions!

This policy of dividing the country in that manner is in direct contrast to the position that the Somali members of the first Somaliland Protectorate Advisory Council took in 1946 when the protectorate government had proposed to divide the county on clan basis, so that each clan would look after a particular grazing area in the country. The Somali members of the Advisory Council rejected the proposal outright [73]. As discussed in the body of the book, some Somalilander

Councillors proposed to abolish *Xeer* in 1953 [76], and in 1957 [78]. In 1956 the protectorate government set up a commission (not including Somalis) to look into the *Ilaalo* (clan-based police) position. This commission not only recommended abolishing the *Ilaalo* but also the *Xeer* as well [77]. The Somalilander councillors were not as educated as our present-day politicians, but they were not ignorant and they grasped the injustices *Xeer* represented. Our educated politicians dismally failed to emulate our wise councillors.

The Somaliland governments (since secession from Somalia in 1991) have been wasting their energy on clan balancing, not talent selection, in ministerial and government civil servants distribution, where merit counts for little or nothing. Numerous ministerial and civil service posts have been created, simply to satisfy the whims of the clans, when the economy of the country can ill-afford such wasteful expenditure. All this indulgence in accommodating every wish of every clan is at the expense of the higher national interests and good governance.

It has become a practice for a clan to complain of inadequate representation in the government and/or civil service; or to call a *Shir* (gathering) for the clan faithful to deliberate on the clans' future (in Somali, *aaayo ka tashi*). If the clans succeed in manipulating the workings of the government or take upon themselves to look after their own future independently of the government, is not that an indication that we are heading – if something is not done about it – for a future when the clans, rather than the government, will be calling the shots? No sooner were these lines written down than the predicted future of when the clans would call the shots arrived! For the elections of May 2021, the clans first selected the candidates who would represent them in the local governments and in the National Council of Representatives. It was only then that the political parties selected some of the candidates recommended by clans to participate in the elections. So, in effect, we will have a "Representative Council of Clans", not of political parties. But there is already a Council, in the form of the *Guurti* (the Upper House of the Parliament) which represents the clans. It is a confusing situation, to put it mildly!

The country took a lamentable retrograde step from which it will take a long time to recover. The question is: cannot we think of any other system than clanism on which to build our political and governmental system?

We are regrettably sleep-walking into a system where clanism will dominate our social and political life. We must not allow ourselves to be governed by clanism. Our national politicians who colluded with the clans to frame our national elections in 2021 betrayed the higher national interests at the altar of short-term self-interests.

The existence of the Clan Chiefs was born of clanism; and without them clanism will have no legs to stand on. The main function of these Clan Chiefs is to oversee the implementation of *Xaq* and *Xeer* and to promote only the interests of the clans they belong to. Their outlook is not orientated to think and act in terms of the overall national interests. By definition, they are merely concerned with the affairs of their clans. These Clan Chiefs, *Xaq* and *Xeer* are all inextricably linked. Likewise, the *Guurti* does not only represent entrenched clanism but also has become ineffectual and has outlived its usefulness. Sadly, the National Council of Representatives has also now become Clan Representatives!

It is obvious that, on the whole, clanism is the major determinant of our social and political life! Clanism remains a serious impediment to our socio-political progress. However, I cannot stress strongly enough that I am not blaming the Clan Chiefs. What I object to is the obsolete system, ie clanism, which spawns the Clan Chiefs.

It is unlikely that democracy and good governance will take root in a country where clanism dominates. I think a governmental system based on clanism is neither democratic nor stable. Clanism and democracy are incompatible and together they form a toxic mix, resulting in dysfunctional government. The general impression is that the twin evils of clanism and nepotism have insinuated themselves into the fabric of our political institutions. In the resulting murky and polluted environment, corruption is bound to find fertile soil to breed in.

The political parties failed the people of Somaliland. Rather than rising above clanism, they degenerated into what can only be called clanish outfits. They spout democracy but pay only lip-service to it. It is naïve to assume that one can become democratic by talking about it, without practising it. It is a gross mistake to equate democracy with merely holding elections. Worse still, and to our shame, our elections are partially paid for by external donors. This foreign funding itself corrupts the very essence of democracy. We are being bribed to conduct elections that could be considered as democratic. Instead of holding such elections, cannot we plan elections within our means?

Calculations of all our political parties are in clan terms, which are devoid of principled and enlightened long-term vision for the country. Our political leaders waste their time bickering with each other over petty things and tit-for-tat point-scoring in the media. Our political leaders do not pause for a moment to reflect on where Somaliland fits in the community of nations or why they themselves are conspicuous for their absence from the international corridors of power!

Be that as it may, there is no denying that, so far, no Somaliland government has even attempted at formulating a credible strategy for tackling the disruptive and divisive influence of clanism. In fact the reverse is true, as already pointed out.

From the start we adopted a system of government the members of which are selected by an Executive President. As such, the government members are beholden not to the public, but to the Executive President, who can hire and fire them at will. They will be constrained to speak their minds. They will toe the line and observe the first law of nature – self-preservation. To be frank, that form of government is not to my liking. I see it as a one-man show, where a president heads a government selected by him, not elected by the public.

I understand why we initially adopted a government headed by an Executive President. It was because of the difficult situation the country was in in 1991; elections could not have been organized. It was an expedient step. Since then we should have been learning something about political and governmental systems!

I prefer a prime ministerial form of government, with clearly defined checks and balances built into it, and where all the members of the government are elected by the public. Such government is subjected to daily questioning, by the opposition parties, about its actions and the public has the opportunity to follow such grilling! Any system of government designed by human beings can never be one hundred percent perfect. A government is as good as the values it represents and the integrity of the people who run it.

The Somaliland Protectorate Government introduced capital punishment in 1928 [36] and we still maintain it. When it was introduced, there was practically no legal system or justice in the country [47]. It is generally accepted that capital punishment has no deterrent effect. It is fraught with miscarriage of justice. The government also introduced collective punishment in 1933 [43], because of *Xeer* [42].

Being where we are now, what is the way forward? Readers of this Appendix will no doubt give different answers. There is no point in raising issues without suggesting their possible solutions.

My answer, which will remain my legacy, follows.

I see in my mind's eye the society I wish we would be and the political and governmental system we should have!

The solution of diminishing the influence of clanism (with eradicating it as a long-term aspiration) lies in having a like-minded critical mass willing to debunk and expose clanism for what it is. To create such critical mass, we have to educate the young at homes and in the schools about the harmful effects of clanism. Children learn more by example than by precept. It follows that parents and those who educate the young should themselves have no truck with clanism, so that the young will look up to and emulate them. Improved economic circumstances of the citizen and good governance will also go a long way towards lessening reliance on clan support. Well-informed public opinion about the negative aspects of clanism will play a crucial role in combating clanish tendencies.

Above all, we desperately need a daring Somalilander leader who will put his/her head above the parapet to seek election on a platform of a Prime Ministerial Government, free from clanism, for the country. The government will do the right thing and steel itself against the inevitable clamour for clan balance which, so far, has been the default setting of our successive governments. The government will be run by people of high calibre and integrity and who are qualified for the posts which they will hold, and they will do more with little. Quality over quantity will remain the watchword of the government. The process of reformation will not be for the faint-hearted. It will be long-drawn-out. When the going gets tough, the government will have to persevere in its efforts.

I have a *manifesto* for that daring leader. The manifesto will embrace certain principles and policies which will form the basis upon which to build up a government that will introduce, among other reforms, good governance. The government will carry out root and branch reforms, which will include, but by no means limited to, the reforms listed hereunder:

Constitution

The interim Constitution of the country, which was for three years only, was approved in a national referendum held on 31 May 2001 and came into effect on 13 June 2001. Since then no Somaliland Government bothered to revise and update the Constitution! The country has no permanent Constitution. I do not know why this is so. Perhaps our leaders have been waiting for the country to be recognized internationally.

The interim Constitution will be thoroughly revised and updated. All ambiguities in it, which might give rise to different interpretations, will be removed. Explanatory notes (*Xeer-nidaamiyaal*, in Somali) will be prepared for the Articles which need further explanation for their interpretation and implementation. Under the Constitution, the country will have a Prime Ministerial form of Government, elected by the public and accountable to the public for its actions. The Constitution will guarantee the rights of the citizens, who will be equally treated before the law, regardless of social status or wealth. Under the Constitution, every citizen will be responsible for his/her action and he/she will never be held responsible for the wrongdoing of another citizen. Under the Constitution, it will be the responsibility of the government to ensure the security of the citizens and their properties. It will outlaw detention of a citizen without valid written warrant. The legal authority which issues the warrant must have been presented with reliable evidence that an offence might have been committed. The Constitution will guarantee the freedom of the media and free associations *not* based on clanism. The Constitution will guarantee the right of the workers to strike peacefully. The public will have the right to demonstrate peacefully. It will define the rare conditions under which such freedoms may be curtailed and for how long. A citizen of Somaliland will lose his/her Somali nationality if he/she voluntarily acquires a foreign nationality and renounces his/her Somali nationality. No Somalilander who holds a foreign nationality will hold a public office in Somaliland. (This is to discourage the Somalilander who holds dual nationality and when he/she loses a governmental or political post moves to his/her second country. Otherwise, ordinary Somalilanders can hold dual nationality).

The Constitution will outlaw capital punishment. It will outlaw the use of funds or any other form of support from external sources in elections for public office in the country. The functions of the Legislature, Executive and the Judiciary will be precisely delineated in the Constitution and it will be ensured that they do not overlap. The freedom and independence of the Judiciary in its deliberations and judgements will be strictly observed and will be free from any form of political or any other interferences and influences.

The Constitution will recognize that the land is a national *asset* and it will be protected from over-grazing, soil erosion, degradation and deforestation. The Constitution will outlaw any claim made by a clan that it owns any part of the country. As a large part of our society leads a pastoralist life, the land use will be spelt out in the Constitution, so that built-up and agricultural areas will not encroach upon the pastureland, and no person or group of persons will misuse the land. The Constitution will outlaw government misuse or abuse its authority. It will ban mention of clans and titles of Clan Chiefs by the government and political parties in their official documents and/or communications. It will also ban the government and the political parties from associating or dealing or holding meetings with clans and/or their Chiefs, overtly or covertly. It will ban the government and the political parties from appealing, in writing or by word of mouth, to the clans and/or their Chiefs for political or any other support.

The Constitution will not recognize clanism or clans or Clan Chiefs of any category and it will not recognize *Xeer*. In this context, "not recognizing" does not mean banning clanism and *Xeer* by law. It means "officially and strictly ignoring their existence and not dealing with them in any form or shape". The expectation is that if the "ignoring policy" is rigidly adhered to, clanism and *Xeer* will gradually peter out for lack of support. The government will not officially or unofficially associate the individual citizens with clans.

Under the Constitution, the following standing and independent regulatory bodies, with defined terms of reference, will be established:

- Commission for Elections
- Commission for the Legal Profession
- Commission for the Health Professions
- Commission for Further Education
- Commission for the Pharmaceutical Products and Medical Appliances
- Commission for the Development of the Somali Language and Culture

The Commission for Elections will be under the National Council of Representatives (NCR). The other five Commissions will be under the Office of the Prime Minister.

The Constitution will be carefully drafted to make it a model for a modern and liberal Constitution, fit for the twenty-first century. In revising the Constitution, external independent expert advice may be sought, if deemed desirable.

Head of State (non-Executive President)

Strict criteria will be set for the person and the position. These will include age, integrity, academic qualifications and experience of the person. In a Presidential election, any Somalilander who:

1. Has been resident in Somaliland for the past twenty consecutive years (except on being abroad for education for not more than three years, and not been outside the country for more than six months within the last five years)
2. Declares that he/she does not belong to any political party or clan
3. Does not have foreign nationality
4. Has never been convicted in a Court of Law inside or outside the country
5. Is not in debt to anybody
6. Is in good health
7. Fulfils all the criteria set for the person and the position

will be eligible to stand in an election for the post. He/she will not belong to any political parties or claim to belong to any clan and will politically remain neutral. He/she will be elected by the public. If more than two candidates stand for the election, the Commission for Elections will devise further conditions under which candidates will be eliminated until in the end only two candidates are short-listed for the election. The elected President will declare his/her *total* wealth and that of his/her immediate family (in other words, his/her spouse and children) *in* the country and *outside* the country, and this wealth will be registered. The President's tenure of office will be limited to two terms, each term lasting five years. Election of a President will not be postponed, *except* in the event of the country being at war.

A President who fails in re-election for a second term or completes two consecutive terms will never be elected as President in the future. Apart from ceremonial functions, the President will have very limited powers, strictly defined in the Constitution. The President will essentially remain as a *Figure Head*. The President will not have the authority to appoint or dismiss a Prime Minister or national government or declare war. The President will never give audience to a person or a group representing clan(s). As the President will not be running the government, he/she will have a small staff of about a dozen, excluding his/her bodyguard, and the staff and the bodyguard will be paid for by the State. The staff will be managed by a Director General. The staff will include one Political Adviser and one Legal Adviser. The salary of the President will be commensurate with the dignity of the office he/she holds. The President will lose office by resignation or by being convicted in a Court of Law or by being proved to have dealings with individuals or groups on clan basis or by death. If he/she is incapacitated to the extent that he/she can no longer discharge his/her functions, as determined by a duly constituted Medical Board, a new President will be elected. He/she will have the usual two terms and the conditions described above will apply. When the President is abroad on a matter approved by the government, the Speaker of the National Council of Representatives will tend to the limited routine functions of the President, except receiving foreign Ambassadors or Heads of States or endorsing appointments of Ambassadors. There will be *no post* for a Deputy President.

The above paragraph and any further details thereon will be enshrined in the Constitution.

Regions and districts

The internal boundaries in the country will be completely redrawn and the administrative divisions inherited from the colonial rule will be eliminated. The boundaries of the new Regions and Districts will be drawn in such a manner that the clan-based boundaries will disappear. This will entail bringing together, in the new Regions and Districts, the citizens who hitherto have been separated by clan-based internal boundaries. The new boundaries will cut across the areas wherein the nomads roam about with their herds and flocks. The present set-up will be replaced with eight *new* Regions and twenty-five *new* Districts. Each District will contain a fixed number of *Sectors* for electoral purposes. The number of sectors in the individual Districts will depend on the population size of the particular District. The total number of the electoral sectors in the Districts will equal to sixty-five sectors. The Regional and District Headquarters will be located away from international border areas.

The new set-up will be the first step in breaking down the clan separations and bringing together the Somalilanders in communities living together as citizens with common interests and outlook.

National Council of Representatives (NCR)

The number of the Political Parties in the country will not exceed *four* and will not be fewer than *two* Political Parties. There will be no limit on how long a Political Party may exist. A Political Party may join another Political Party or may dissolve itself. The number of the National Council of Representatives (NCR) members will be limited to sixty-five members. Strict criteria will be set for who will be eligible to stand in elections for members of NCR. These criteria will include age, integrity, academic qualifications, etc. In an election for NCR, any Somalilander who:

1. Has been resident in Somaliland for the last fifteen consecutive years (except on being abroad for education for not more than three years, and not been outside the country for more than three months within the last five years
2. Declares that he/she does not belong to any clan
3. Does not have foreign nationality
4. Has never been convicted in a Court of Law inside or outside the country
5. Is not in debt to anybody
6. Is in good health
7. Fulfils all the criteria set for the person

will be eligible to stand in an election for NCR.

The NCR members will be elected on a five-yearly basis. The election will be based on the newly restructured Regions and Districts and on the first-past-the-post system, ie only the person who gets most of the votes in an *Electoral Sector* in a District will be elected. The elected NCR members will declare their *total* wealth and that of their immediate families (in other words, their individual spouses and children) *in* the country and *outside* the country. This wealth will be registered. The Political Party which gains the majority of the elected members in NCR will form the government. The Party with the second largest number of elected members in NCR will become the main Official Opposition Party to the government and will closely shadow the government and act and behave as a *Government-in-waiting*. In legislating for the country, NCR will, after serious debate on any draft law, pass it or reject it with a two-third majority of NCR members present and voting. An NCR member who is proved to have dealings with individuals or group of persons on clan basis will be expelled from NCR. It is hoped that the opposition parties will be effective enough to hold the government to account for its policies and decision-making. The Guurti Council will be abolished.

Right from the days of the British colonial rule, formal education for girls has badly lagged behind the provision for their brothers. That is why female politicians in our national politics are rare. The female forms about 50% of our population. The Political Parties will be well advised to put forward sufficient number of female candidates in the elections for Local Governments and for NCR. *At least* one female must be elected from each District in the elections for the NCR.

The above paragraphs and any further details thereon will be enshrined in the Constitution.

Prime Ministerial Government

As a matter of formality, the President will invite (*not* appoint) the Leader of the Political Party with the majority of the elected members in NCR, to form a Government, of which the leader will become the Prime Minister. The Prime Minister will appoint Deputy Prime Minister. The Government term of office will be five years. It will be the Prime Minister who will have the authority to call for a general election for a new NCR. The Prime Minister will select his/her Ministers and Deputy Ministers from the elected members in NCR on merit, with proper regard to Regional representation, *not clan balance*. Reasons for the Prime Minister to lose office will include: losing a vote of "no confidence" by two-thirds of the NRC members present and voting, resignation, being convicted in a Court of Law, proved to have dealings with individuals or groups of persons on clan basis, or death. If the Prime Minister is incapacitated to the extent that he/she can no longer perform his/her duties, as confirmed by a duly constituted Medical Board, the Deputy Prime Minister will become the new Prime Minister, and he/she will appoint a new Deputy Prime Minister. The five-year term and the other conditions will apply.

When the Prime Minister calls for a general election for NCR, the President will dissolve the current NCR. The government will remain in office, but will function as a *caretaker* government and its work will be confined to dealing with the routine day-to-day services before a new government is formed; and will keep law and order in the country.

While a caretaker, the Government will not:

- make any changes in the composition of the government
- propose new legislation or change or abolish existing legislation
- initiate new projects or cancel existing projects
- appoint new staff or dismiss serving staff in the civil (including Ambassadors) and military services
- introduce a new budget
- introduce new policies
- embark upon any new initiatives
- enter into new international agreements or modify or cancel existing agreements
- declare war

The campaign for NCR elections will last for fifteen days only, from the date the election is announced to the day previous to Election Day. There will be no election campaigns of any form on Election Day. Outside that period, it will be illegal for the political parties to carry out election campaign activities, including meetings or distribution of literature about the elections. It will also be illegal for civil and military personnel, at Central, Regional and District levels, to participate in political activities, such as political campaigns, fund-raising, distributing literature; it will also be illegal to use government property for electioneering.

If the Prime Minister postpones NCR elections, except in the event of the country being at war, the government will remain a caretaker, as described above, for as long as the postponement continues. If the postponement lasts for more than one month, the individual salaries of the members of NCR will be cut by five percent for each month the postponement lasts. The monthly cut in the salaries of the individual Ministers/Deputy Ministers will be seven percent and the cut in the salaries of the Prime Minister and his/her Deputy will be nine percent as long as the postponement remains in place.

The number of the Ministries will not exceed eighteen and that of the Deputy Ministers seven. The new Ministries will be as follows:

Suggested Government Ministries in Somaliland

Ministries	Portfolios
1. Ministry of Development	National Planning & Finance
2. Ministry of Education	Education up to Secondary Level
3. Ministry of Further Education	Further Education above Secondary Level, Science & Technology
4. Ministry of Health	Health Services, both curative and preventive
5. Ministry of Justice	Courts, the Legal and Constitutional applications and taking necessary remedial actions therein
6. Ministry of Natural Resources	Water & Mineral Resources, Wind & Solar Energy
7. Ministry of Veterinary	Livestock health, Grazing-Land Management & Rural Advancement
8. Ministry of Production	Agriculture & Fisheries
9. Ministry of Trade	Commerce & Investment Promotion
10. Ministry of Interior	The Police, Local Governments, Population Data, Resettlement & Rehabilitation
11. Ministry of Public Works	Town Planning, Housing, Sanitation, Roads & Road Transportation
12. Ministry of Environment	Environment, Industries, Pollution Control
13. Ministry of Social Affairs	Employment & Pensions
14. Ministry of Communication	Civil Aviation & Telecommunication
15. Ministry of Foreign Affairs	Dealings with Foreign Countries, United Nations & Non-Governmental International Agencies
16. Ministry of Defence	The Army, Navy and Air Force and the welfare of the personnel and their dependents
17. Ministry of Moral Guidance	Endowment & Religious Matters
18. Ministry of Information	Media, Sports & Tourism

The idea is to have a small-sized, efficient and effective national government. There will no longer be a bloated government, inefficiently staffed and run by under-employed and under-achieving people. Each Ministry will have a Director General and the requisite number of Directors, depending on the magnitude of services for which each Ministry is responsible. The Deputy Ministers will also be assigned to the Ministries as described for the Directors. The Governmental Agencies will, as far as practicable, be merged into the Ministries to which they are related. Such Agencies will not be created for the sake of job creation.

The Government will not adopt any form of policy in which consideration of clans plays a part, nor will the Government receive or accept any communications in the name of clan(s). *Xaq* (*mag* or *dia*) will be dealt with in accordance with the enacted laws of the country. The government will not make payments to clans or to their Chiefs. The government will identify the root causes of why clanism, rather than decrease with increased urbanization and education in our society, it has further intensified. Specific effective measures will be developed for dealing with the causes identified. The government will appoint the civil and military personnel based on merit and in their capacity as individuals rather than representing clans or political parties, but regional balance will be maintained. Those who will serve the country abroad, as Ambassadors, will represent the *country*, not a political party. Ambassadors, like other government civil servants, will not participate in the activities of the political parties, while they remain in government employment. The government will prepare a Code of Conduct for the government civil servants.

The days of fossil fuels for all purposes are numbered. The global trend is to decarbonize economies. The sooner this is done the healthier will be the environment for the living, including plants. The government will no longer support prospecting for fossil fuels in the country. Instead, the national policy on energy will focus on developing *wind* and *solar* energy for the country. We have both wind and sun rays in abundance. The government may look for international support for harnessing this form of energy. There is a global movement afoot to wean the developing countries off the use of fossil fuel. Major donors are beginning to be receptive to requests for support in the development of solar and wind energies (clean energies). Some donors have already declared that they would not support fossil fuel development abroad. Within a few years' time, electricity will replace petrol and diesel for running the car. The discarded plastic items – which are not only real eyesore in the towns but also hazardous to children, animals and marine life – will disappear from the scene. The message is clear that the fossil fuels should be left to remain underground.

The government will introduce proper town planning, so that towns will not continue to grow haphazardly, making it difficult to plan for the provision of public utilities, such as piped public water supply, sanitation/sewerage, electricity, etc. Industrial plants will be located at safe distances away from the towns, and the effluent they discharge, as well as the sewer, will be managed in ways that will not pose health hazard to the public, other living creatures or to the environment.

Without valid information about the population, planning for the country will depend on guesswork. The government will conduct a national census, which will at least provide information about the total population, the population by Region and by District, and the demographic structure of the population. The information so gained will permit to formulate a developmental masterplan, which will encompass, among other things, resource distribution, social services distribution and political representation in the country. Under the masterplan, supplementary and detailed developmental Regional and District plans will be prepared. The national census will be held every ten years. The Local Governments will, among other things, register births, deaths, marriages and divorces. The birth certificates will contain the names of both the mother and the father of the newborn. In carrying out the census, the government may seek support from the United Nations.

Chewing *Qaad* (its technical name is *Catha edulis*) is harmful to human health and social life; it undermines the work ethic and it is a time waster. It is also a huge drain on the country's foreign currency. The government will consider *Qaad* as *narcotic* and will deal with it as a prohibited substance and will control it accordingly.

It will be illegal in the country to advertise tobacco and tobacco products in the public and private media. The following warning: "SIGAARKU WAA DILAA – CIGARETTES KILL" will be printed on the cigarette packs. It will be illegal to bring into the country cigarettes without the above-mentioned warning. To discourage smoking, cigarettes will be heavily taxed.

Conclusion

We need a radical rethink of our system of government. We have to move on from an outmoded mindset rooted in clanism. We have to adopt a new way of electing our national politicians who will govern the country. If we do not try out new ways, we will not know what will work for us best. As the maxim goes: *nothing ventured, nothing gained*. I realize that the proposed reforms will not happen overnight. The manifesto outlined herein envisages a process through which a credible political system and truly democratic prime ministerial government will eventually emerge. The role that the clans play in our social and political life will be something of the past. The government which this manifesto foreshadows will be elected or voted out of office by the public. It will not be appointed or dismissed by one individual, in other words, an executive Head of State. The essential elements of good governance will permeate through the government that I have in mind. The concept of good governance is intrinsic to democracy. The government will foster the ideas expressed in the manifesto, with the long-term aim of building a Somaliland society liberated from clanish groupings and clanish strife. It will not be beyond the wit of a brave and committed Somalilander to present to the people of Somaliland a manifesto similar to the one outlined herein. Who will be that Somalilander hero?

In the meantime, I sincerely hope that the Somalilanders will start, voluntarily and individually, to opt out of clans till we reach a stage when clanism in Somaliland will have died out. A direct way of going about this is to renounce *Xeer* for good and not to associate yourself with any particular affiliations or support or defend them on clan basis. The "Motto" (*Himilo* in Somali) of the manifesto will be "clan-less nation" (*Qaran Qabiil La'*, in Somali).

Lastly, I need not apologize for writing, at length, on clanism and *Xeer* and other related issues, because of the serious problems they pose to our society. They undermine the cohesion of our society and render good governance in our country well-nigh impossible! Writing this book afforded me this rare opportunity to express my views on these issues. Also, I wanted to share my ideas with the rest of the Somalilanders.

I expect that some readers of this Appendix may not agree with, or even criticize, the views I have expressed in it. That is the beauty of it. They will put forward their arguments against my ideas, and still others may join the discussion. Opposing views will give rise to a chain reaction and these different views will be pitted against each other. This is one way that public opinion is stimulated and informed. I will be more than happy if my views provoke a public debate on the issues I have raised. I think the public debate will lead to the realization of how socially and politically damaging clanism and *Xeer* are, and how they militate against social harmony and good governance. If that happens to be the case, the next step will be to do something about them. Informed public opinion can positively influence the policies of the political parties and the government of the day.

The content of the Appendix is my contribution to the hoped-for public debate. The reader might think that I am an idealist in my views, having his head in the clouds! Not at all. I have both feet firmly on the ground. It is only that I have taken the *perfect* as a departure point for my discussions. If you aim for the perfect, you may get something good; but if you aim for the good you may finish up with something mediocre. Therein lies the choice.

To finish, I wish to make it abundantly clear that, in putting forward my views for public debate, I have no axe to grind and I am doing this only for the common good.

References

[Consulted archival documents held at the National Archives (NA) at Kew, London, UK, and prefixed with 'NA Box ...' contain public sector information licensed under the Open Government Licence v3.0].

1. Burton, R.F., *First Footsteps in East Africa* Vol. 1, London, 1894, Preface to 1st edition, pp. xxi–xxii, out of print.
2. Burton, R.F., *First Footsteps in East Africa* Vol. 2, London, 1894, pp. 99–106, out of print.
3. The Berlin Conference (1884/85).
4. Omar, M.O., *The Scramble for the Horn of Africa: History of Somalia, 1827–1977*, India: Somali Pub. Co. Ltd., 2009, pp. 50–64, publisher no longer exists.
5. Walsh, L.P., *Under the Flag and Somali Coast Stories,* London: Andrew Melrose Ltd., 1932, pp. 199–206, out of print.
6. NA Box CO 535/131 contains file on: Zeila Synopsis, collection of Customs, 1884.
7. NA Box CO 535/59 contains file on: Government assertion that, before October 1889, no records about the protectorate government existed, 1920.
8. NA Box FO 844/3 contains file on: Lack of Treaty between the British Government and the Dhulbahante Clan, 1892.
9. Fitzgibbon, L., *The Betrayal of the Somalis*, London: Rex Collings Ltd., 1982, pp. 22–33, publisher no longer exists.
10. NA Box CO 535/98 contains file on: Anglo-Italian Agreement about their spheres of influence in the Horn of Africa, 1894.
11. Drake-Brockman, R.E., *British Somaliland*, London, 1917, p. 67, out of print.
12. Walsh, L.P., *Under the Flag and Somali Coast Stories*, 1932, Andrew Melrose Ltd., London, pp. 361–362, (out of print).
13. Omar, M.O., *The Scramble for the Horn of Africa (History of Somalia 1827–1977)*, Somali Pub. Co. Ltd., India, 2009, pp. 122–141.
14. Omar, M.O., *The Scramble for the Horn of Africa (History of Somalia 1827–1977)*, Somali Pub. Co. Ltd., India, 2009, pp. 182–206.
15. Gleichen, Count Edward, *With the Mission to Menelik (1897)*, London, 1898, out of print. (The whole book is about the Mission and contains the Anglo-Ethiopian Treaty of 1897, related to Somaliland Protectorate/ Ethiopia boundary.)

16. Rodd, J.R., *Social and Diplomatic Memories (1884–1893)*, London, 1922, pp. 71–72, out of print.

17. Swayne, H.G.C., *Seventeen Trips through Somaliland and a Visit to Ethiopia*, 2rd Edition, London, 1900, out of print.

18. Jardine, D.J., *The Mad Mullah of Somaliland*, London: Herbert Jenkins, 1923, out of print. (The whole book is about the Seyyid, aka (wrongly) "The Mad Mullah of Somaliland").

19. Omar, M.O., *The Scramble for the Horn of Africa (History of Somalia 1827–1977)*, India: Somali Pub. Co. Ltd., 2009, pp. 309–478.

20. NA Box CO 353/2 contains files on: Clan-based militia men trained for fighting the Dervishes, 1905.

21. NA Box FO 844/6 contains file on: Mr Sadler's Dispatch about Haji Musa of Hahi, 16 June 1899.

22. Official history of the 1901–1904 operations in Somaliland, Vol.1, pp. 54–62, London, UK, 1907, www.iwm.org.uk.

23. NA Box CO 535/3 contains file on: Government taking stock of the situation vis-à-vis the Dervishes, 1905.

24. NA Box CO 535/1 contains file on: Letter in Arabic sent by the Sayyid to Commissioner Swayne, 1905.

25. NA Box CO 879/97 contains file on: Churchill's minutes, dated 28 October 1907, about his visit to Berbera, 1907.

26. NA Box FO 881/9507 contains file on: Confidential report of Wingate's special mission to Somaliland Protectorate, 1909.

27. RAF operations in Somaliland Protectorate: 2nd Supplement to *The London Gazette*, 8 November 1920, https://www.thegazette.co.uk/london/issue/32116/supplement/10829.

28. Jardine, D.J., *The Mad Mullah of Somaliland*, London: Herbert Jenkins, 1923, pp. 289–308, out of print.

29. Beachey, R., *The Warrior Mullah: The Horn Aflame (1892–1920)*, London: Bellew Publishing Company Ltd, 1990, pp. 146–154, the publisher was dissolved in 2010.

30. Archer, R.F., Commissioner, later Governor, of Somaliland Protectorate (1913–1922), *Personal and Historical Memoirs of East African Administrator*, London, 1963, pp. 122–130, out of print.

31. NA Box T 161/538 contains file on: Governor Archer advocating the country to be occupied, not to be administered, 1922.

32. Archer, R.F., *Personal and Historical Memoirs of East African Administrator*, London, 1963, pp. 134–137, out of print.

33. NA Box CO 535/69 contains file on: Revenge for the Murder of Mr Gibb, Burao, 1922.
34. NA Box CO 535/80 contains file on: Contradictions between the Anglo-Ethiopian Agreement of 1897 and Treaties with Somali Clans (1884–1886), 1927.
35. NA Box CO 535/83 contains file on: Creation of Districts in the protectorate, under Order-in-Council of 1926, 1927.
36. NA Box CO 535/85 contains file on: Ordinance No. 4 of 1928 about Capital Punishment, 1928.
37. NA Box CO 535/94 contains file on: Deliberations on what to do with the protectorate, 1931.
38. NA Box CO 535/91 contains file on: Governor Kittermaster's austerity budget, 1931.
39. The British Section final report of the Joint Anglo-Ethiopian Boundary Commission on Somaliland Protectorate/Ethiopia boundary demarcation, in *Geographical Journal*, Vol. 87, No. 4, April 1936, pp. 289–307, courtesy of the Royal Geographical Society, London, UK.
40. NA Box CO 535/98 contains file on: Proposal to extend southern border of Somaliland Protectorate to *Wal-waal* and *War-dheer* and, in return, Zeila be given to Ethiopia, 1933.
41. NA Box CO 535/94 contains file on: Retroactive Ordinance No. 10 of 1931 about the boundary pillars, 1931.
42. NA Box CO 535/92 contains file on: Justification, based on *Xaq* and *Xeer*, for introducing Collective Punishment in the protectorate, 1928.
43. NA Box CO 535/119 contains file on: Ordinance No. 4 of 1933 about collective punishment.
44. NA Box CO 535/120 contains file on: Retroactive Ordinance against a Somali, 1935.
45. NA Box PC 2/379 contains file on: The first Order-in-Council of 7 October 1899, for administering the country.
46. Somaliland Protectorate Ordinances, CSC. 180, Vol. II, 1906, 1906/07, British Library, London, UK.
47. NA Box CO 1015/801 contains file on: Order-in-Council of 1929, 1930.
48. NA Box CO 535/120 contains file on: Lay British Administrator passing death sentences on Somalis, 1936.
49. NA Box CO 535/127 contains file on: Legal Adviser of the Colonial Office intrigued by justice administration in Somaliland Protectorate, 1938.
50. NA Box CO 535/102 contains file on: Government "agent" spying on Haji Fareh Omaar in Dire Dawa, 1934.

51. Questions raised in the British Parliament about the judicial practice in Somaliland Protectorate, *Hansard*, 1938.

52. NA Box CO 535/127 contains file on: Ethiopian refugees in Somaliland Protectorate, 1938.

53. NA Box CO 535/132 contains file on: Conquered Ethiopian Empire reduced to an Italian Colony, 1936.

54. NA Box WO 32/11421 contains file on: Britain's capture of Somalia and Ethiopia from Italy in 1941.

55. NA Box CO 535/131 contains file on: Government decision to disarm the Somali nomads, 1938.

56. NA Box CO 535/138 (part 1) contains file on: Office established in Aden in 1938 for Somaliland Protectorate affairs, 1941.

57. NA Box CAB 106/548 contains file on: War Office document giving details about the military operations in Somaliland Protectorate, 1939–1940, May 1946.

58. NA Box CO 535/142 contains file on: The expenditure on Governor's Office, 1939.

59. Waterfield, G., *Morning Will Come*, London: Butler & Tanner Ltd., 1944, pp. 27–32, out of print.

60. NA Box WO 230/5A contains file on: Setting up Military Government Protectorate, 1941.

61. NA Box 32/12658 contains file on: Creation of Somali Guard Battalion, 1943.

62. NA Box CO 535/137 contains file on: Somalis' Financial support for the War effort, 1942.

63. NA Box CO 535/137 contains file on: Governor Glenday's response to the Colonial Secretary, 1940.

64. Turton, E. R., "Somali Resistance to Colonial Rule and the Development of Somali Political Activity in Kenya, 1893–1960", in *The Journal of African History*, Vol. 13, No. 1, 1972, pp. 119–143, by permission of the Editor.

65. NA Box CO 820/27/1 contains file on: Somaliland Camel Corps mutiny, 1936.

66. NA Box WO 32/10863 contains file on: Somaliland Camel Corps mutiny, 1944.

67. NA Box CO 537/5844 contains file on: The creation of the Somaliland Scouts (the National Army).

68. NA Box CO 968/590 contains file on: The annual expenditure on the Somaliland Scouts (1940–1960).

69. NA Box FO 371/46052 contains file on: The Anglo-Ethiopian Agreement of 1944.

70. NA Box CO 535/141 contains files on: Colonial Development and Welfare Fund; Hargeisa as Capital of the protectorate (1945); Las Anod as new District (from July 1944), 1945.

71. NA Box CO 535/141 contains file on: Incident in Burao involving Sheikh Bashir Yusuf, 1945.

72. NA Box CO 535/146 contains file on: Commission for War Claims Settlement, 1945.

73. NA Box WO 32/13261 contains file on: First Session of the protectorate Advisory Council, 1946.

74. NA Box WO 32/9606 contains file on: Civil Government replaced the Military Government, 1948.

75. NA Box CO 535/151 contains file on: Instructions for how the protectorate government had to budget, 1950.

76. NA Box CO 1015/801 contains copy of: *War Somali Sidihi* (ie "Somaliland News") of 25 September 1953, containing proposal to abolish *Xeer*, 1953.

77. NA Box CO 1015/1225 contains file on: Proposal to abolish *Xeer*, 1956.

78. NA Box CO 1015/1374 contains file on: Proposal to abolish *Xeer*, 1957.

79. NA Box CAB 21/4567 contains file on: Proposal for land swap with Ethiopia, 1953.

80. NA Box CO 1015/1354 contains file on: Anglo–Ethiopian Agreement of November 1954.

81. NA B0x FO 371/113458 contains the record on: The activities of the Somaliland Delegation in Britain, Egypt and UN, 1955.

82. NA Box CAB 130/121 contains file on: British Government deliberations on Somaliland Protectorate, 1957.

83. NA Box CO 1015/1769 contains file on: Seyyid Ahmed Sheikh Musa, 1958.

84. NA Box CO 1015/1949 contains file on: Visit of Secretary of State for the Colonies to Somaliland Protectorate, February 1959.

85. Ismail, A. I., *Governance: The Scourge and Hope of Somalia*, Trafford Publishing, 2010, pp. 75–83, by permission of the copyright holder.

86. NA Box CO 1015/2517 contains file on: Colonial Secretary's Statement on Radio Hargeisa, 9 February 1959.

87. NA Box CO 2303 contains file on: Setting up the Executive Council, 26 February 1960.

88. Minutes of proceedings of the Legislative Council, CSC.179, Issued as *Supplement to the Official Gazette*, Vol. XX, No. 21, 14 May 1960, London: British Library.

88. NA Box CO 1015/2518 contains file on: Governor Hall's letter of 13 April 1960.

90. NA Box CO 830/24 contains file on: The Executive Council minutes of 13 April 1960.

91. NA Box CO 830/26 contains file on: The expenditure on the "Northern Region" for the period April to December 1960.

92. NA Box CO 830/24 contains file on: Clarification on Somaliland union with Somalia before becoming Independent on 26 April 1960.

93. Tripodi, P., "Back to the Horn: Italian Administration and Somalia's Troubled Independence", *The International Journal of African Historical Studies*, Vol. 32, No. 2/3, 1999, p. 378, by permission of the Journal's Editor.

94. NA Box CO 1015/2368 contains file on: Conference on Somaliland Independence, London, May 1960.

95. Hall, D., "Somaliland Protectorate's Last Year as a Protectorate", *African Affairs*, Vol. 60, no. 238, January 1961, pp. 26–37, Oxford Journals, British Library, London, by permission of the Journal's Editor.

96. NA Box CO 1015/2519 contains file on: The ceremonial proceedings at the union of the State of Somaliland and Somalia on 1 July 1960.

97. NA FO 881/9507 contains file on: The confidential report of Mr Wingate's special mission to Somaliland Protectorate, including detailed information about the Roman Catholic Mission in the country, 1909.

98 NA CO 879/103 contains file on: The diary of the government during coastal concentration, 1911.

99. NA Box CO 535/11 contains file on: The enrolment of three schools in the coastal towns, 1907.

100. NA Box CO 535/61 contains file on: Non-Somali census taken Zeila, Bulahar and Berbera, 1911.

101. NA Box CO 535/2 contains files on: Annual expenditure on the protectorate for 1900, 1901, 1902, 1903, 1904, 1905.

102. NA Box CO 535/8 contains files on: Annual expenditure on the protectorate for 1906, 1907, 1908.

103. NA Box CO 535/20 contains file on: Annual expenditure on the protectorate for 1909.

104. NA Box CO 535/15 contains file on: Annual expenditure on the protectorate 1910.

105. NA Box CO 535/20 contains file on: Annual expenditure on the protectorate for 1911.

106. NA Box CO 535/24 contains file on: Annual expenditure on the protectorate for 1912.

107. NA Box CO 535/28 contains file on: Annual expenditure on the protectorate for 1913.

108. NA Box CO 535/34 contains file on: Annual expenditure on the protectorate for 1914.

109. NA Box CO 535/61 contains files on: Annual expenditure on the protectorate for 1915, 1916, 1917, 1918, 1919.

110. NA Box CO 535/61 contains file on: Six boys sent to Sudan for education, December 1919.

111. NA Box CO 535/60 contains file on: Progress report on the six boys studying in Sudan, March 1920.

112. Brown, G.N., "British Educational Policy in West Central Africa", *The Journal of Modern African Studies*, Vol. 2, No. 3, 1964, pp. 365–377, article purchased from Cambridge University.

113. The Phelps-Stokes Fund Education Commission's reports on Africa, 1922 & 1924; in the public domain.

114. Education Policy in British Tropical Africa, H.M. Stationery Office, London, 1925.

115. Graham, S.F., *Government and Mission Education in Northern Nigeria, 1900–1919, with special reference to the work of Hanns Vischer*, Ibadan University Press, Appendix A, 1966, British Library. The publisher stopped this book's publication.

116. British Government Educational Policy for British Tropical Africa, H.M. Stationery Office, London, 1925.

117. Graham, S.F., *Government and Mission Education in Northern Nigeria, 1900–1919, with special reference to the work of Hanns Vischer*, Ibadan University Press (1966), pp. 9–22, British Library, London.

118. Newman, P. *The Etymology of Hausa "boko"*. Mega-Chad Miscellaneous Publications, 2013, pp. 1–13 (Under the Creative Commons Attribution 4.0 International license CCBY 4.0).

119. Umar, M.S., *Islam and Colonialism: Intellectual Responses of Muslims of Northern Nigeria to British Colonial Rule, 1903–1945*, Brill, 2005, pp. 22–23, British Library, London, by permission of the publishers.

120. NA Box Co 535/60 contains file on: The Catholic Mission request to reopen Berbera School, 1920.

121. Archer, R.F., *Personal and Historical Memoirs of East African Administrator*, London, 1963, pp. 133–134.

122. NA Box Co 535/119 contains file on: Mr Hussey report on education and Governor Archer's covering letter, 1920.

123. NA Box Co 535/85 contains file on: Governor Kittermaster's proposal for Reformatory School, 1928.

124. NA Box Co 535/119 contains file on: Introduction of Government grants to *Qur'aanic*/Arabic Schools, 1930.

125. NA Box T 161/78 contains file on: Annual expenditure on the protectorate for 1920, 1921.
126. NA Box T 161/149 contains file on: Annual expenditure on the protectorate for 1922.
127. NA Box CO 535/75 contains file on: Annual expenditure on the protectorate for 1923, 1924.
128. NA Box CO 535/81 contains file on: Annual expenditure on the protectorate for 1925.
129. NA Box CO 535/29 contains file on: Annual expenditure on the protectorate for 1926, 1927.
130. NA Box CO 535/93 contains file on: Annual expenditure on the protectorate for 1928.
131. NA Box CO 535/86 contains file on: Annual expenditure on the protectorate for 1929.
132. NA Box CO 535/119 contains file on: Governor Lawrance's policy on elementary education, 1935.
133. NA Box Co 535/119 contains file on: Governor Lawrance's Commission on the proposed school in Berbera, 1936.
134. NA Box CO 535/119 contains file on: Building the Berbera School, 1937.
135. Olden, A., "Somali Opposition to Government Education: R.E. Ellison and the Berbera School Affair (1938–1940)" in *History of Education*, Vol. 37, No. 1, January 2008, pp. 71–90, British Library, London, by permission of the Journal's Editor.
136. Olden, A., "Somali Opposition to Government Education: R.E. Ellison and the Berbera School Affair (1938–1940)" in *History of Education*, Vol. 37, No. 1, January 2008, pp. 71–90, British Library, London.
137. NA Box CO 830/3 contains file on: Mr Ellison's opinion of elementary education in Somaliland Protectorate – in the annual report on education for 1938.
138. NA Box CO 535/129 contains file on: Opinion of Sudan Education Department about written Somali, 1938.
139. Olden, A., "Somali Opposition to Government Education: R.E. Ellison and the Berbera School Affair (1938–1940)" in *History of Education*, Vol. 37, No. 1, January 2008, pp. 71–90, British Library, London.
140. NA Box CO 535/128 contains file on: Petition by Borama elders for education, 1938.
141. NA Box CO 535/129 contains file on: Governor Lawrance's proposal of an elementary school for Borama, 1938.
142. NA Box CO 830/3 contains file on: Urban Somalis asking for formal education; in annual report on education for 1938.

143. NA Box CO 535/129 contains file on: Minutes of a meeting between Burao elders DC of Burao, 1938.
144. NA Box CO 535/127 contains file on: Dr Gurney's missionary activities, 1938.
145. NA Box CO 535/129 contains file on: Governor Lawrance's change of mind about written Somali, 1938.
146. NA Box CO 535/129 contains file on: Berbera elders' petition against Mr Ellison, 1938.
147. Olden, A., "Somali Opposition to Government Education: R.E. Ellison and the Berbera School Affair (1938–1940)" in *History of Education*, Vol. 37, No. 1, January 2008, pp. 71–90, British Library, London
148. NA Box CO 535/129 contains file on: Report of DC of Hargeisa on *Wadads* at Aw Barkhadle, 1938.
149. NA Box CO 830/3 contains file on: The Annual Report on Education for 1938.
150. Olden, A., "Somali Opposition to Government Education: R.E. Ellison and the Berbera School Affair (1938–1940)" in *History of Education*, Vol. 37, No. 1, January 2008, pp. 71–90, British Library, London.
151. Olden, A., "Somali Opposition to Government Education: R.E. Ellison and the Berbera School Affair (1938–1940)" in *History of Education*, Vol. 37, No. 1, January 2008, pp. 71–90, British Library, London.
152. NA Box WO 32/11421 Contains file on: Anglo-French Conference, in Aden, on the defence and Berbera and Djibouti, May 1939
153. NA Box CO 535/132 contains file on: Board of Enquiry into the Burao School Incident, 1939.
154. NA Box CO 535/132 contains file on: Governor Glenday's covering letter of 7 October 1939.
155. NA Box CO 535/136 contains file on: Governor Glenday on leave in Nairobi, 1940.
156. NA Box CO 535/133 contains file on: Mr Ellison's meeting with the Sub-Committee on Colonial Education for Africa, London, 1939.
157. Olden, A., "Somali Opposition to Government Education: R.E. Ellison and the Berbera School Affair (1938–1940)" in *History of Education*, Vol. 37, No. 1, January 2008, pp. 71–90, British Library, London.
158. NA Box CO 830/3 contains file on: The annual reports on education for 1938 and 1939.
159. NA Box CO 535/91 contains file on: Annual expenditure on the protectorate for 1930.
160. NA Box CO 535/99 contains file on: Annual expenditure on the protectorate for 1931.

161. NA Box CO 535/102 contains files on: Annual expenditure on the protectorate for 1932, 1933, 1934.
162. NA Box CO 535/119 contains files on: Annual expenditure on the protectorate for 1935, 1936.
163. NA Box CO 535/130 contains file on: Annual expenditure on the protectorate for 1937.
164. NA Box CO 535/142 contains file on: Annual expenditure on the protectorate for 1938.
165. NA Box CO 535/133 contains file on: Annual expenditure on the protectorate for 1939.
166. NA Box CO 535/124 contain file on: The Bible Churchmen's Missionary Society, 1937.
167. NA Box CO 535/124 contains file on: Colonial Office's view on banning Christian missions from Somaliland Protectorate, 1937.
168. Omar, M.O., *The Scramble for the Horn of Africa: History of Somalia, 1827–1977*, India: Somali Pub. Co. Ltd., 2009, pp. 9–10.
169. NA Box CO 535/120 contains file on: British Soldiers/Administrators to learn the Somali language, 1936.
170. NA Box WO/5A contains file on: Setting up Military Protectorate Government, 1941.
171. NA Box WO/5B contains file on: Education considered not a priority, 1941.
172. NA Box CO 535/137 contains file on: Proposed educational plan, 1942.
173. Adan, F.Y., *Geedi Nololeedkii Yusuf X. Adan*, London, 2007, pp. 46–58, in Somali, by permission of the copyright holder.
174. NA Box WO 32/10862 contains file on: Governor Fisher on lack of development in the country, 1943.
175. Lacey's report of 1943 in Appendix I of T.R. Holland, *Education in British Somaliland*, Reading University Library, 1949, by permission of the copyright holder.
176. NA Box CO 535/140 contains file on: Mr Bell's report on introducing the 1944 educational programme.
177. Holland, T.R., *Education in British Somaliland*, Reading University Library, 1949 pp. 61–157.
178. NA Box CO 535//141 contains the annual Government report for 1945.
179. Ordinance on Education (1948), Supplement No.2 to the *Somaliland Protectorate Gazette*, Vol. viii, British Library, London.
180. NA Box CO 535/152 contains file on: Visit of Lord Lloyd, Permanent Under-Secretary of State for the Colonies, to Somaliland Protectorate, 1949.

181. NA Box CO 535/137 contains files on: Annual expenditure on the protectorate for 1940, 1941.
182. NA Box WO 32/10862 contains files on: Annual expenditure on the protectorate for 1942, 1943, 1944.
183. NA Box CO 535/139 contains file on: Annual expenditure on the protectorate for 1945.
184. NA Box CO 535/142 contains files on: Annual expenditure on the protectorate for 1946, 1947, 1948.
185. NA Box CO 535/143 contains file on: Annual expenditure on the protectorate for 1949.
186. NA Box CO 535/151 contains the annual report on education for 1950.
187. *Corona*, November 1950, SOAS, London University, UK.
188. NA Box CO 830/6 contains the annual report on education for 1951.
189. NA Box CO 1015/546 contains the annual report on education for 1952.
190. NA Box CO 535/151 contains file on: The Vocational Training Centre (VTC) at Borama, 1952.
191. NA Box CO 1015/659 contains file on: The Trades School at Hargeisa, 1952.
192. Parliamentary questions on education in Somaliland Protectorate, 1952.
193. The Egyptian Revolution, 1952.
194. NA Box CO 1015/1149 contains the annual report on education for 1953.
195. NA Box CO 535/151 contains file on: The first Elementary School for Girls, 1953.
196. Ahmed, I.M., *Geel-Jire iyo Aqoon-Jire*, Sagaljet, Hargeisa, pp. 229–235, 2015, the copyright holder who alone could have given permission is deceased.
197. The first secondary school for boys, 1953.
198. Whitehead, J.B., *Memorandum* on his career in the Colonial Education Service, 1948–1953 in Somaliland Protectorate, courtesy of Bodleian Library, University of Oxford, UK.
199. Students sent abroad on government scholarships for secondary education: 1947–1953.
200. NA Box CO 1015/1149 contains file on: The annual report on education for 1954.
201. NA Box CO 1015/1145 contains file on: Students from Somaliland Protectorate on Egyptian Government Scholarships, Egypt, 1954.
202. NA Box CO 1015/1149 contains file on: The visit of the Director of Education to Somalia, 1954.

203. NA Box CO 1015/1153 contains: *Somali War Sidihi* of 22 November 1955, containing information about the visit of the Director of Education of Somalia to Somaliland Protectorate, 1955.
204. NA Box CO 1015/1149 contains file on: The annual report on education for 1955.
205. NA Box CO 1015/1374 contains file on: Development Fund for 1957–1960.
206. NA Box CO 830/8 contains file on: The annual report on education for 1956.
207. Darlington, R.R., "Somali Students: Higher Education in UK", unpublished document, courtesy of Dr Susan and Richard Sills, Executors of the Darlington Estate.
208. NA Box CO 830/9 contains file on: The annual report on education for 1957.
209. Dodd, M., "Creation of the BBC Somali Service", *Anglo-Somali Society Newsletter*, London, 1988.
210. NA Box CO 830/9 contains file on: The annual report on education for 1958 (last one).
211. NA Box CO 830/5 contains file on: Annual expenditure on the protectorate for 1950.
212. NA Box CO 830/6 contains files on: Annual expenditure on the protectorate for 1951, 1952.
213. NA Box CO 830/7 contains files on: Annual expenditure on the protectorate for 1953, 1954.
214. NA Box CO 830/8 contains file on: Annual expenditure on the protectorate for 1955.
215. NA Box CO 830/9 contains files on: Annual expenditure on the protectorate for 1956, 1957, 1958.
216. NA Box CO 830/10 contains file on: Annual expenditure on the protectorate for the year 1959.
217. State of formal educational facilities, as of 1 January 1959.
218. Parliamentary questions on education in Somaliland Protectorate, 1959, *Hansard.*
219. Hall, D., "Somaliland Protectorate's Last Year as a Protectorate", *African Affairs*, Vol. 60, no. 238, January 1961, pp. 26–37, Oxford Journals, British Library, London, by permission of the Journal's Editor.
220. Darlington, R.R., "The School At Sheikh", *Anglo-Somali Society Newsletter*, London, 1989.
221. NA Box CO 1015/2487 contains file on: Final cost of the new secondary school at Sheikh, 1960.

222. Darlington, R.R., "Somali Students: Higher Education in UK", unpublished document, courtesy of Dr Susan and Richard Sills, Executors of the Darlington Estate.

223. NA Box CO 535/92 contains file on: *Aqils*, 1931.

How long will it take before Somali nomadism gives way to a settled way of life?

Map of Somaliland

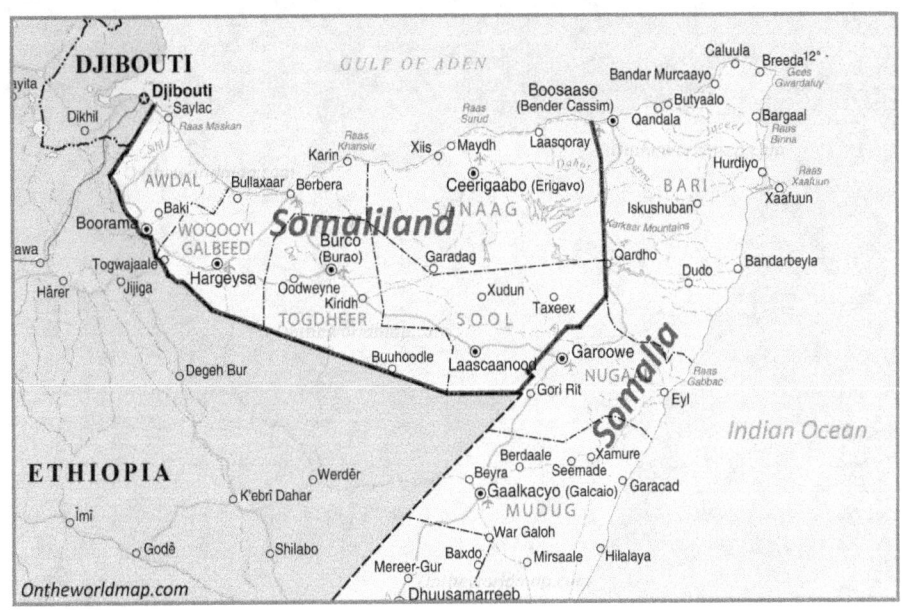

Source: Ontheworldmap.com

www.ingramcontent.com/pod-product-compliance
Lightning Source LLC
Chambersburg PA
CBHW061423300426
44114CB00014B/1510